LOGICS OF HISTORY

CHICAGO STUDIES IN PRACTICES OF MEANING
Edited by Jean Comaroff, Andreas Glaeser, William H. Sewell Jr., and Lisa Wedeen

Also in the series:
Producing India: From Colonial Economy to National Space
by Manu Goswami

WILLIAM H. SEWELL JR.

LOGICS OF HISTORY

SOCIAL THEORY AND SOCIAL TRANSFORMATION

THE UNIVERSITY OF CHICAGO PRESS Ｏ CHICAGO AND LONDON

The University of Chicago Press, Chicago 60637
The University of Chicago Press, Ltd., London
© 2005 by The University of Chicago
All rights reserved. Published 2005
Printed in the United States of America
18 17 16 15 14 13 12 11 10 09   4 5 6 7 8
ISBN-13: 978-0-226-74917-4 (cloth)
ISBN-13: 978-0-226-74918-1 (paper)
ISBN-10: 0-226-74917-7 (cloth)
ISBN-10: 0-226-74918-5 (paper)

Library of Congress Cataloging-in-Publication Data

Sewell, William Hamilton, 1940–
     Logics of history : social theory and social transformation /
William H. Sewell, Jr.
          p.   cm.—(Chicago studies in practices of meaning)
          Includes bibliographical references and index.
          ISBN 0-226-74917-7 (cloth : alk. paper)—
          ISBN 0-226-74918-5 (pbk. : alk. paper)
          1. Social sciences and history.   2. History—Philosophy.
     I. Title.   II. Series.
     D16.166.S48   2005
     901—dc22   2004024683

To my colleagues in

the SOCIAL HISTORY WORKSHOP,

the IAS SOCIAL SCIENCE SEMINAR,

the SEMINAR ON SYMBOLIC ANTHROPOLOGY,

the SEMINAR ON SYMBOLISM AND SOCIAL CHANGE,

the DAVIS CENTER SEMINAR,

the NEH SUMMER SEMINAR ON LABOR HISTORY,

the ARIZONA SOCIOLOGY BROWNBAG,

the MSG-TUCSON,

the MSG-ANN ARBOR,

    CRSO,

    CSST,

the SEMINAR ON SOCIAL MOVEMENTS AND STATE BUILDING,

the CASBS SEMINAR,

    CCP,

the WORKSHOP ON COMPARATIVE POLITICS AND HISTORICAL SOCIOLOGY,

the WORKSHOP ON SOCIAL THEORY,

the MODERN FRANCE WORKSHOP,

the SOCIAL THEORY GROUP,

the MELLON SEMINAR ON CONTENTIOUS POLITICS,

the WILDER HOUSE FACULTY SEMINAR,

the CIAR SUCCESSFUL SOCIETIES PROGRAM,

and CCCT,

whose friendship, conversation, and boundless capacity for critical thought have made this book possible.

CONTENTS

PREFACE

The origins of this book go back to the late 1980s, when I was serving as the first director of the Center for the Study of Social Transformations (CSST) at the University of Michigan. CSST was a university-funded experiment in interdisciplinarity, a collection of historians, anthropologists, and sociologists — as brilliant as they were argumentative — who met regularly to thrash out questions of theory and method. Our discussions were intense and absorbing; they spilled over into lunches, parties, and countless ad hoc seminars in the corridors. The discussions certainly vindicated the founding group's assumption that scholars in these three disciplines had plenty of interests in common and much to learn from each other. They also made it clear that disciplinary divides were very real: disagreements between those hailing from different fields were often sharp and sometimes heated.

It was in the midst of these rather dramatic interdisciplinary debates that the idea of writing this book took shape. At the time, I had a joint appointment in history and sociology and had been reading anthropology and hanging out with anthropologists for years. I was convinced then, and remain convinced today, that a social science combining historians' nuanced sense of social temporalities, anthropologists' recognition of the power and complexity of culture, and sociologists' commitment to explanatory rigor is both possible and necessary. My own particular obsession in our debates was to insist that we recognize the fundamental historicity of all social forms. Understanding the operations of social temporality was no less important, I was convinced, for anthropologists or sociologists studying "the present" than for historians studying "the past." I argued that central theoretical categories—like "culture" and "structure"—needed to be reconceptualized to make them capable of confronting the unavoidable fact of historical change. This book, which has taken many years to write, is dedicated to building the problematics of historical transformation into the conceptual vocabulary of social theory.

In 1991, I took up a position in political science and history at the University of Chicago, thus extending my experience as a participant observer to a fourth social science discipline. By then, I had written three of the essays that were to find their way into this book and had several others in mind. But in the helter-skelter of contemporary academic life, I never found the time to sit down and write the book through end-to-end. Instead, I took advantage of invitations to give a paper here or attend a conference there and composed them one at a time. The essays have, therefore, gradually been scattered about in various journals and edited collections. But in spite of their varied histories, all the essays in this book—with the exception of chapter 9, which I have revised extensively to make it fit the book's themes—were written with this volume in mind. I hope readers who know previous versions of these essays will find that they gain in depth from each others' company.

Scholarship, which may seem a lonely occupation to those who do not pursue it, is in fact profoundly social. Our ideas are produced within the socially constructed network of puzzles, problems, and obsessions that are the stuff of intellectual communities, and they are advanced by endless discussion and argument. This general observation is particularly pertinent for a book like this, which attempts to bridge the conversations of several more or less distinct academic specialties. My ability to formulate the questions asked in this book and my confidence that the answers I propose may prove useful to others depends utterly on a long string of overlapping interdisciplinary conversations I have carried on with other scholars in several different cities over the past four decades. These conversations have been sustained above all in a succession of more-or-less organized discussion groups. These have varied enormously in form, focus, and institutional location, but they have had one thing in common. They have made it possible to explore a range of topics and ideas that would have been far beyond my ken as an individual scholar—and to do so in a framework of unfettered discussion, critical probing, and mutual respect. It is in these discussion groups that my thinking about history and the social sciences has been stimulated, tried out, criticized, reformulated, and, I hope, improved. I feel that the arguments I have made in this book are a joint product, co-authored with the many friends and colleagues who have collaborated in my reflections over the years. It is to them, and to the discussion groups that sustained our conversations, that I dedicate this book.

Scholarship also requires material support. During the years I worked on this book I was awarded a fellowship from the John Simon Guggenheim Foundation and spent glorious year-long research leaves at the Center for Advanced Study in the Behavioral Sciences in Stanford, California and at the Institute for Advanced Study in Princeton, New Jersey—the first supported by the National Science Foundation (grant number BNS-870064) and the second by the National Endowment for the Humanities. I also received generous support from the Universities of Michigan and Chicago and from the Successful Societies Program of the Canadian Institute for Advanced Research.

I would like to thank David Brent, my editor at the University of Chicago Press, for skillfully guiding this book to publication. I received valuable and generous readings of the entire manuscript from the Press's two referees, Michèle Lamont and Keith Baker. During the final two years of writing and rewriting this text, I benefited from the loving companionship, the constant intellectual stimulation, and the fine critical eye of Jan Goldstein, who was always willing to take time out from the book she was finishing to hear my latest thoughts or to read a chapter. I hope we'll finish many more books in each other's company.

1

THEORY, HISTORY, AND SOCIAL SCIENCE

The goal of this book is to initiate a serious dialogue about social theory between history and the social sciences. The groundwork for such a theoretical discussion already exists. Social scientists and historians have been talking to each other and reading each other's work for a long time, and both groups of scholars discuss social theory and make use of it in their research. Yet, for reasons I sketch out below, an adequate dialogue about social theory has not developed. In particular, historians' complex and many-sided understanding of the temporalities of social life has scarcely found its way into social theoretical debate. Having spent the better part of my career as a simultaneous participant in the everyday academic life of history and various social science disciplines, I am convinced that a deeper theoretical engagement between historians and social scientists could be mutually enlightening. In this book I indicate what shape such an engagement might take, some of the topics it could illuminate, and how it might affect thinking on both sides of the disciplinary divide. If my arguments are not found convincing, I hope they will provoke counter-arguments. I firmly believe that social theory, history, and the social sciences—and more importantly, our common project of gaining knowledge about the social world—can advance only by means of free, open, and spirited intellectual exchange.

HISTORY AND THE SOCIAL SCIENCES

It is hardly novel, at the beginning of the twenty-first century, to call for dialogue between historians and social scientists. Such a dialogue was, for example, one of the stated ideals of Marc Bloch and Lucien Febvre as long

ago as 1929, when they founded the famous and influential French historical journal *Annales*. In the decades following World War II, and particularly in the 1960s and 1970s, the discipline of history all over the world was
profoundly affected by methods and theoretical perspectives borrowed
from the social sciences. Since the 1970s, this borrowing has increasingly
been reciprocated by social scientists: sociologists and anthropologists, in
particular, have become increasingly interested in questions of historical
change. Moreover, at least in the abstract, social scientists and historians
have always been interested in the same fundamental problems: the functioning, reproduction, and transformation of social relations. Finally, history and the social sciences crystalized out of a single field of discourse.
It was only between the 1880s and World War I that sociology, history,
political science, anthropology, geography, and economics emerged as the
distinct and professionalized academic disciplines we know today. Prior to
that time, intellectual discussion flowed easily across the indistinct boundaries between different genres of scholarship. It is difficult to assign major
thinkers of this era to a single field, as we understand these fields today.
Was Adam Smith or John Stuart Mill a philosopher, an economist, or a
political scientist? Was Marx an economist, a sociologist, a philosopher, or
a historian? Tocqueville a historian, a sociologist, an ethnographer, or a
political scientist? It was only in the early twentieth century that the academic disciplines, replete with their distinct departments, chairs, curric-
ula, and doctoral programs, became genuinely—if artificially—distinct
intellectual universes (Abbot 1999; Clark 1973; Keylor 1975; Lepenies 1988;
Novick 1988; Ross 1991). Only then were history and the various social sciences sufficiently clearly bounded that one could think about the necessity
of initiating a dialogue. The cross-disciplinary poaching that currently
prevails in history and the social sciences might therefore be seen as beto-
kening a return to the golden age of our predisciplinary past.

The academic disciplines, however, have utterly transformed the Edenic
intellectual landscape of the late eighteenth or early nineteenth centuries.
The disciplines, true to their name, wield powerful disciplinary mechanisms of control and constraint. With their monopoly on certification and
their control over curriculum, hiring, tenure, and allocation of research
funding, the disciplines have entrenched themselves within clearly drawn
borders. The untiring efforts of several generations of academic social scientists and historians have succeeded in forming distinct communities of
discourse, with distinct methods, vocabularies, and standards of evaluation. It is because the disciplines have so successfully divided up the intel-

lectual terrain—not of course, without smuggling and recurrent boundary disputes—that conversation between historians and social scientists must take the form of dialogues between disciplines.

It is certainly true that in the past forty years or so the borders have become ever more porous. It has become de rigueur in academic circles to praise interdisciplinarity in scholarship and in graduate training—although it should be said that the actual practice of interdisciplinarity often falls short of articulated ideals, especially when it comes to hiring decisions. It is common for current work in historical studies to transcend disciplinary boundaries in multiple ways, with historical research being carried out by scholars with various formal disciplinary affiliations, using methods and theories of the most assorted provenance. In this sense, dialogues between history and the social sciences are carried on every day. Both historians and social scientists have also widened this discourse to include theoretical borrowing from the humanities. The "linguistic turn" or "cultural turn" that has swept over the social sciences and history alike in the past quarter century has brought theories about meaning and representation, many developed by literary critics and philosophers, into the interdisciplinary mix. Nevertheless, the nature of these dialogues has been strongly shaped by the disciplinary cultures of the fields from which the scholars come. It is for this reason that I feel comfortable speaking of the need to initiate a dialogue about social theory between historians and social scientists, even in the current landscape of widespread interdisciplinarity.

Theory has a strikingly less central place in history than in the social science disciplines. From the beginnings of the systematic differentiation of disciplines in the late nineteenth century, historians and social scientists alike have contrasted the "ideographic" or "descriptive" research of historians—which attempts to capture the uniqueness and particularity of its object—with the "nomothetic" or "explanatory" research of social scientists—which aims to establish general laws or at least valid generalizations. Social science fields might be said to be defined by their theories and formal methodologies; history is more informally (but no less effectively) defined by its careful use of archival or "primary" sources, its insistence on meticulously accurate chronology, and its mastery of narrative. This difference is clearly marked in the fields' graduate programs. Graduate students in the social sciences are usually required to take courses in the discipline's theory and/or methods at the beginning of their careers. By contrast, courses in historical theory or methods usually are purely elective, if they are offered at all. The most important site of disciplinary training in history graduate programs is not the required theory or methods course, but the research seminar, where students learn to be historians by doing research in primary sources and writing historical narratives, rather than by mastering the theories and explicit methodologies of their fields. At the point when they have finished their formal coursework, historians typically are already quite sophisticated researchers and writers but lack systematic theoretical training. Social scientists, at this moment in their careers, often have little sense of how to carry out a research project, but can argue about fine points of theory indefinitely.

This difference in the place of theory in the disciplines remains true at all stages and in all aspects of the career. Articles in social science journals nearly always begin with a discussion of the relevant theory, whereas articles in historical journals are more likely to begin with something that evokes the particularity of their subject matter — for example, an anecdote or a salient quotation from contemporary sources — than with discussions of theory or historical interpretation.[1] The same difference shows up in definitions of jobs: it is common for positions to be advertised as sociological theory, economic theory, or political theory, but I have never seen a job advertised in historical theory. Countless famous social scientists have made their reputations on the basis of work in theory, but it is hard to think of more than a handful of historians whose eminence arose from theoretical writing, and the few cases that come to mind generally do not have exclusively history appointments. Hayden White, the only historian I can think of whose fame rests almost entirely on theoretical works, spent most of his career teaching in the interdisciplinary History of Consciousness humanities program at the University of California, Santa Cruz (1973, 1978, 1987, 1999). Others — such as Joan Scott, a historian who is an eminent feminist theorist, or Dominick LaCapra, an intellectual historian who is also an important figure in literary theory, or William Reddy, who has done path-breaking theoretical work on the social and historical significance of emotions; or Dipesh Chakarabarty, who is a major "post-colonial" theorist — initially rose to prominence on the basis of more em-

1. I have checked this perception by looking at the opening paragraphs of articles in a handful of recent history and social science journals and coding them as either theoretical or descriptive. In both the *American Journal of Sociology* in 2002 and the *American Journal of Political Science* in 2002, articles that begin by invoking theoretical issues vastly outnumbered those that begin by invoking some temporally and spatially delimited trend, situation, or event (27 out of 30 and 51 out of 56, respectively). In both the *American Historical Review* in 2001 and 2002 and the *Journal of Modern History* in 2002, articles were about twice as likely to begin with invocations of trends or events as with theoretical or interpretive issues (21 out of 31 and 8 out of 12, respectively).

pirical works and continue to publish in the empirical genre. Moreover, it is surely not coincidental that they all have some kind of extra-history-department appointment.[2] That there are a handful of historians whose theoretical writings have received considerable attention even outside the history profession certainly indicates that theory is no longer off-limits to historians, but the fact that their numbers are so few and that their institutional location is commonly at once inside and outside of history shows that theory remains peripheral to the historical enterprise.

At present, it is common for historians to read social theory and to cite theorists in their written work. Indeed, such figures as Clifford Geertz, Antonio Gramsci, Michel Foucault, and Pierre Bourdieu—not to mention Karl Marx, Max Weber, and Emile Durkheim—have become something like household names in contemporary historical discourse. Yet even this growing use of theory does not constitute a genuine *dialogue*. There is no dialogue because the historians rarely speak back. They use social theory to orient their thinking, or borrow its vocabulary in their interrogation of historical sources or in formulating their arguments. What remains exceptional is for historians to intervene actively in social-theoretical debates. When historians borrow social-theoretical concepts we often find that the concepts don't quite fit, that they need to be adjusted, nuanced, or combined with concepts from other, apparently incompatible, theoretical discourses in order to be useful in historical research. In this sense, our use of theory is, practically speaking, critical. But we almost never reflect in print about these critical adjustments, nuancings, or recombinations. We tend not to ask whether something is systematically amiss in the theories we are borrowing that makes them ungainly for use in historical research, or to propose new vocabularies or conceptual schemas that might improve upon or supersede the existing concepts.[3] As a consequence, our use of social theory, while often implicitly critical in practice, has little impact on

2. Scott is a professor in the interdisciplinary School of Social Science at the Institute for Advanced Study, LaCapra holds a professorship in Humanistic Studies at Cornell; Reddy holds a joint appointment in History and Anthropology at Duke, and Chakrabarty has appointments in both History and South Asian Languages and Civilizations at Chicago. (For what it is worth, my own appointment is joint in Political Science and History at Chicago.) These historians' best-known theoretical works are Scott (1988), LaCapra (1983, 1985, 1989, 1991), Reddy (2001), Chakrabarty (2000). But see also Scott (1974, 1996), LaCapra (1972, 1982), Reddy (1984, 1997), and Chakrabarty (1989).

3. An instructive exception to this rule is Jan Goldstein's "Afterword," in the reedition of her *Console and Classify* (2001). Published fourteen years after the appearance of the original edition, Goldstein's afterword is precisely a reflection back upon the categories of social theory, in this case sociological theories about professionalization and Michel Foucault's opposition between disciplines and the law.

the store of social theory available to historians or to other scholars. Thanks to our training and to the prevailing culture of professional history, we have lacked the confidence to become active participants in theoretical debates.

In this book, I hope to show that this lack of confidence is mistaken: that historians have important and illuminating things to say about central issues in social theory. As I see it, social theory badly needs a serious infusion of historical habits of mind. But we can't expect sociologists, geographers, political scientists, and anthropologists to do the job for us. Only if historians enter the fray and develop systematic critiques and reformulations of the theories we borrow from social scientists can we expect to build social theories adequate for grasping the ever-changing world that is our common object.

WHAT HISTORIANS KNOW

What historians generally think of themselves as knowing about are their topics of research—the Russian Revolution, the Italian city-state, the Indian Ocean trade, the New Deal, the Ming Dynasty bureaucracy, the Boer War, Brazilian popular culture. This includes, of course, knowledge about how to use and interpret the relevant published and archival sources. But historians, whatever their particular topic, also know something else: how to think about the temporalities of social life. The common topic of historians is the unfolding of human action through time. Our thinking about time tends to be implicit rather than explicit, to be embodied in specific narrative accounts of particular series of events or particular transformations of communities, states, or fields of discourse. We don't think of ourselves as having a *theory* of social temporality. Yet I am convinced that most historians actually share a set of assumptions about how time is implicated in the organization and transformation of social relations and that these assumptions can be stated abstractly. In other words, historians have implicit or working theories about social temporality. Moreover, these theories are of considerable subtlety and sophistication, far superior, in my opinion, to the rather clumsy temporal assumptions that plague most theorizing in the social sciences. It is precisely as theoreticians of temporality that historians can most usefully participate in social theoretical debates.

How, then, do historians think about social temporality? First, and most fundamentally, I think we believe that time is *fateful*. Time is irreversible, in the sense that an action, once taken, or an event, once experienced, cannot be obliterated. It is lodged in the memory of those whom it affects and therefore irrevocably alters the situation in which it occurs. Although I might make a promise and then retract it, the fact of my having made the promise is not obliterated by the retraction. I become, both to myself and to others who know about the incident, a different person, one who has made and retracted a promise. Most of our actions, of course, do not transform the situation in which they are undertaken. By nodding to my co-worker when we pass in the hall, I merely reaffirm our common employment status. Yet this simple gesture is itself significant for the ongoing history of social relations in my work unit (in my case, a department of political science). That this is so becomes immediately obvious if I fail to produce the acknowledging nod. If I simply walk by with no acknowledgement, this might be read as an ominous act, as a sign that I have entered a hostile faction of the department or that I have decided to vote no on his upcoming promotion. Especially if repeated, failing to give the expected nod will result in a chilling of social relations between me and the snubbed colleague. Either act, the nod or the lack of a nod, leaves a historical residue; it inflects the social relations between me and my colleague and potentially those of my department as a whole. And it goes without saying that more dramatic actions — denouncing a colleague at a faculty meeting, arguing vociferously against making new hires in one of the department's rival subfields, or inviting a previously nodding acquaintance to co-teach a course or collaborate on a paper — will generally have considerably more powerful effects on the course of social relations in the department.

Although individual actions can be shown to have fateful social effects, it is also true that every act is part of a *sequence* of actions and that its effects are profoundly dependent upon its place in the sequence. My relations with my nodding-acquaintance colleague will be more profoundly ruptured by my non-nod if I have failed to nod to her the past three times we've passed in the hall, or if she has recently been snubbed by one of my known friends and allies, or if I have recently said disparaging things in a department meeting about the kind of research she does. By contrast, the effects of my non-nod will be decreased if we have recently been on the same side in a struggle to reform the department's voting procedures or if she has just gotten an article accepted in one of the field's leading journals. Historians believe that we cannot understand why things happened as they did without figuring out the sequence in which things happened. As this implies, historians assume that the outcome of any action, event, or trend is likely to be *contingent*, that its effects will depend upon the particular complex temporal sequence of which it is a part. The effects of a given happening may be nullified, magnified, deflected, compounded, channeled, or broadcast by previous, subsequent, or simultaneous happenings. The fact that the outcome will be contingent upon not only a wide range of other actions, trends, or events, but also upon the precise temporal sequence in which these occur, means that historical happenings are extremely unpredictable.

It is of course true that social scientists also recognize the fatefulness of time in their personal lives. Sociologists or economists are just as aware as historians that having a baby, deciding to take a new job, being left by one's spouse, making friends with a colleague whose ideas transform one's own, or learning that one's child has a life-threatening disease have major and unpredictable consequences for one's life. The difference, as I see it, is that while social scientists recognize temporal fatefulness as a truth of everyday existence, most of them bracket this truth out of their scientific consciousness. Although they see these everyday or personal experiences as fateful and existentially wrenching, they view them as essentially random, as noise, from the point of view of the whole. As social scientists, they see their task as rising above the contingency and messiness of everyday life to find the lawful regularities that actually govern the whole. Historians' practices imply a rejection of this partitioning of everyday life from the social totality and claim instead that temporal fatefulness we experience in our personal lives is replicated at every level of social life.

The conceptual vehicle by means of which historians construct or analyze the contingency and temporal fatefulness of social life is the *event*. Historians see the flow of social life as being punctuated by significant happenings, by complexes of social action that somehow change the course of history. Historians constantly talk about "turning points" or "watersheds" in history and spend much of their conceptual energy dividing the flow of history into distinct eras that events — the establishment of the Han Dynasty, the Crusades, the rise of printing, the Reformation, the Industrial Revolution, the Russo-Japanese War, the Nazi seizure of power, the Cuban Missile Crisis, the rise of electronic media, the fall of the Berlin Wall — mark off from each other. Historians see events like these, which transform the histories of entire human collectivities, as having the same sort of fatefulness and contingency as the smaller events — divorces, new jobs, angry breaches in department meetings — that inflect the course of our personal lives. As usual, historians haven't engaged in much abstract theoretical reflection about how events have such dramatic, historically transformative effects. They have, rather, given countless narrative accounts of how particular sequences of happenings have indeed changed the course of history of some collectivity or other—Oxford dons, Shanghai workers, New Yorkers, Russians, Roman Catholics, or the world as a whole. As against the implicit assumption of most social scientists, that social change takes place according to smooth, gradual, predictable, and linear processes, historians assume that historical temporality is lumpy, uneven, unpredictable, and discontinuous.

Thinking about historical events makes clear another fundamental assumption about temporality that is probably less obvious (although no less true) at the level of personal experience: that social temporality is extremely *complex*. One significant characteristic of historical events is that they always combine social processes with very different temporalities— relatively gradual or long-run social trends, more volatile swings of public opinion, punctual accidental happenings, medium-run political strategies, sudden individual decisions, oscillating economic or climatic rhythms— which are brought together in specific ways, at specific places and times, in a particular sequence. That there are a diversity of temporalities operating in any present raises difficult analytical challenges. How do we handle the problem of sequence when we are dealing not with a chain of discrete and precisely timeable decisions, but the intertwining of long-term with punctual processes? Which social processes, with which temporalities, will emerge as dominant in an event that mixes them together? How, and when, do short-term processes override, deflect, or transform long-term processes? How do long-term trends reassert themselves in situations where they seem to have been eclipsed by more pressing political processes? Writing convincing historical narratives often hinges on the ability to resolve such complex temporal conundrums.

The historians' "eventful" conception of temporality certainly posits that different historical times have, effectively, different rates of change— that history may be "accelerated" by events. But it also posits that events transform or reconfigure social relations. The consequence is that they see distinct historical eras as having varying forms of life and different social dynamics. Historians, to put it differently, assume that time is *heterogeneous*. We assume that what entities exist in the social world, how they operate, and what they mean change fundamentally over time. This is not to say that the world is in constant flux and chaos; the social temporality posited by historians is always a mix of continuity and change. But our working assumption is that every important form of social relations is potentially subject to change: not only ideas, institutions, and identities, but tools, forms of shelter, sex, gods, climate, diseases, cultivated plants, and languages. Another way of putting this is to say that historians implicitly assume that social life is fundamentally constituted by culture, but by culture in the widest possible sense—that is, by humanly constructed practices, conventions, and beliefs that shape all aspects of social life, from agriculture and procreation to poetry and religion. We assume that because these practices are humanly constructed, humans are also capable of destroying, altering, neglecting, forgetting, or radically reconstructing them, either purposely or unintentionally.

Temporal heterogeneity implies *causal heterogeneity*. It implies that the consequences of a given act are not intrinsic in the act but rather will depend on the nature of the social world within which it takes place. This assumption is quite contrary to the practices of mainstream social scientists, whose entire mode of operation is to discover and apply *general* causal laws, laws implicitly or explicitly assumed to be independent of time and place. The model case would be economists, who assume that all social actors everywhere are utility maximizers and that the laws of supply and demand are universal. Historians of course admit the existence of causal regularities of considerable duration. But rather than assuming that the world of the past must have been governed by the same logics as the world of the present, historians assume that the social logics governing past social worlds varied fundamentally, and therefore that their logics must be discovered and puzzled out by the researcher.

Temporal heterogeneity also implies that understanding or explaining social practices requires *historical contextualization*. We cannot know what an act or an utterance means and what its consequences might be without knowing the semantics, the technologies, the conventions—in brief, the logics—that characterize the world in which the action takes place. Historians tend to explain things not by subsuming them under a general or "covering" law, but by relating them to their context.

Finally, if the world in which actions take place is temporally heterogeneous, it makes sense for historians to insist on the importance of *chronology*. Indeed, chronology—the precise placement of a happening or a fact in time—is important for two reasons. First, as I have already pointed out, historians insist that we cannot know why something happens or what its significance might be with-out knowing where it fits in a sequence of happenings. Meticulous attention to chronology is the only way to be sure that we have the sequence straight. But chronology is also important because the meaning of an action or an event depends on the temporal context in which it occurs. In order to understand the relation of one social fact to another, one needs to know whether the temporal boundaries of the social facts placed them within the same "historical era"—that is to say, within a period during which some particular historical logic obtained. Chronology is crucial because it tells us within what historical context we must place the actions, texts, or material artifacts we are attempting to interpret or explain.

The historian's implicit theorization of social temporality—as fateful, contingent, complex, eventful, and heterogeneous—is, I hope to have indicated, reasonably coherent. And its methodological corollaries—a concern with chronology, sequence, and contextualization—seem to me logically consistent with the theory. I think that the vast majority of working historians would concur with at least the general outlines of what I have claimed on their behalf, although I am sure many would contest one or more of my specific formulations. This theorization is intentionally very abstract, and even historians who accept my abstract outline might disagree violently over how its various points might be specified: What counts as an adequate contextualization? What social causalities vary from one period to another? What is it about events that enables them to "change the course of history"? What is contingent and what is necessary in a given course of change?

Historians, at least implicitly, conceptualize social temporality with considerable care and finesse. But with rare exceptions, they do so only implicitly. They don't regard their understanding of the temporality of social life as being a matter of theory at all, but simply as how the world works, as the mere factuality of things. They learn their conception of temporality by a kind of scholarly osmosis, by reading other historians and internalizing the ways they narrate accounts of historical change and continuity. They know a lot about social temporality, but they know it as a kind of professional common sense, all the more so because it is roughly consistent, as I have tried to indicate above, with a more everyday common sense about the temporality of our personal experience. Moreover, historians, in my experience, suffer from a kind of narrative overconfidence. When they reach tight spots in their arguments, they tend to try to narrate their way out of trouble, going back to the sources for yet more detail, laying on more and more examples, instances, and anecdotes. This often means that important conceptual questions—about temporal dynamics, about causation, about the nature of the relations between events or entities—get lost in a welter of narrative detail, rather than being addressed at the appropriate conceptual level. Historians may be virtuosos of social temporality, but their theoretical consciousness is often so underdeveloped that they are not conceptually aware of what they know.

It also must be said that there are plenty of sociologists, political scientists, anthropologists, or geographers whose working assumptions about temporality more closely resemble the historians' model I have sketched above than the assumptions of mainstream social science. Indeed, most of the examples of adequately historical conceptualizations of temporality that I discuss in this book were assembled by sociologists or anthropologists, not historians.[4] I have chosen these examples in part because it is important to show that sophistication about temporality is not fated to be a unique possession of professional historians and in part because sociologists and anthropologists tend to be more self-consciously aware than historians of the theoretical problems posed by their historical arguments. Yet it is symptomatic of the primitive state of theoretical dialogue between history and the social sciences that even these social scientists, whose general theoretical and methodological instincts are finely honed, are often insufficiently explicit themselves about their temporal assumptions. This is another reason to believe that a more robust theoretical dialogue between social scientists and historians would be beneficial to both.

WHAT SOCIAL SCIENTISTS KNOW

Social scientists tend to be much more self-conscious about theory than historians. That is why it makes sense for historians to enter into theoretical dialogue with them. But in initiating a dialogue, it is important to note the internal diversity of the social sciences, both within and between disciplines. The same professionalization of the academic fields that divided history from the social sciences also made each of the social science disciplines distinct from the others. The predominant epistemological culture of most social science fields in the United States is positivist, but anthropology has developed in a very different and much more interpretivist direction. The theoretical assumptions of most social or cultural anthropologists are probably closer to those of historians than to those of other social scientists. Indeed, many anthropologists pay more attention to the work of humanities scholars than to that of sociologists, political scientists, economists or—for that matter—historians. Economics, by contrast, is the most fully mathematical and quantitative of the social sciences, while

4. See, especially, chapters 3 and 7, below.

sociology, political science, and geography are deeply rent by theoretical and methodological disputes. There is, for example, almost no epistemological overlap between the views of symbolic interactionists and demographers within sociology. This diversity in theoretical outlook among social scientists means that the notion of a dialogue between history and social science is something of an oversimplification. In fact, a dialogue with anthropologists will be different in form and content from one with sociologists or economists, and one with symbolic interactionists different from one with demographers. Nor are all social scientists likely to be equally good or willing interlocutors for historians. Indeed, most of the social scientists who practice "mainstream" quantitative social science begin with theoretical premises so incompatible with the working assumptions of historians that we might expect conversation with them to be largely a dialogue of the deaf.[5]

Practically speaking, the most valuable dialogic partners for history are social scientists who are interested in historical and cultural questions, and who either use or are at least willing to countenance what are called "interpretive" or "qualitative" methods. Nearly all social scientists who write what would normally be called "social theory" fit into this category, as would most social or cultural anthropologists. But in predominantly positivistic and quantitative fields like sociology, economics, political science, and geography, such scholars are a dissident minority. If my experience is any guide, one reason that interpretively inclined social scientists might be interested in theoretical exchanges with historians is their sense of embattlement within their own fields. What I am actually advocating and attempting to carry out in this book is not and cannot be a general and diffuse dialogue between "history" and "social science," but a more specific theoretical dialogue with those social scientists who might be ready to join in a common enterprise. At the same time, it is important to realize that historians' theoretical insights of are valuable not only to social scientists who work on specifically historical topics. Because the social world is in fact ever-changing, because it is structured by complex and contingent temporalities, it is as crucial for someone who studies the contemporary

---

5. See Andrew Abbott's (1988) classic critique of the standard assumptions of quantitative sociology. I hasten to add that I certainly do not oppose quantitative research and have indeed done a fair share of it myself. In the final chapter of this book I make a specific argument for the value, even the necessity, of quantitative methods—but from a theoretical perspective very different from that which currently dominates the social-scientific mainstream in the United States.

social world to understand the logics of history as it is for someone who studies the past.

What, then, do social scientists know that they can bring to a dialogue with historians—other than their generally higher level of theoretical consciousness? Social scientists' most theoretically valuable habit of mind, in my opinion, is their strong penchant for *structural* thinking, a penchant that interpretivists generally share to a greater or lesser degree with positivists. By contrast with historians, who tend to opt for multiple causality and detailed circumstantial narrative, social scientists tend to look for explanations in terms of a relatively limited set of enduring, entrenched, and causally powerful features of the social world—such features as class relations, dominant ideologies, enduring occupational or demographic patterns, powerful economic interests, stubborn cultural beliefs, or built-in characteristics of organizations. Where historians tend to be satisfied with multi-stranded but ultimately causally diffuse accounts, social scientists tend to single out what they take to be the most causally important features of the world and to elaborate their dynamics systematically. This insistence on explaining phenomena by means of well-defined structural features tends to push researchers to greater theoretical and methodological clarity. In my opinion, structural thinking is a social-scientific virtue that historians could profitably emulate. Indeed, I think one reason for historians' widespread borrowing of concepts from social theory in the past few decades has been precisely an attempt to introduce more structural forms of thought into historical research.

However, social scientists' structural thinking is commonly flawed by inadequate temporal assumptions. "Structure," in most social-scientific usage, is at least implicitly conceived of as *given*, as the solid social facts or underlying and fundamentally invariable logics that determine the phenomenal shapes of social action. Social conduct, the specific features of institutions, or particular beliefs and opinions may vary widely, but these variations are seen as effectively shaped or regulated by underlying structures. In the rhetoric of social-scientific discourse, the buck tends to stop at structure. Once social or cultural variations have been attributed to structures—to institutional design, occupational distributions, gender stereotypes, binary systems of classification, consumer preferences, and so on—the explanation is regarded as complete. The problem, of course, is that the underlying causal structures themselves undergo mutations or transformations over the course of historical time. They, too, have histories. Many social scientists are aware of the ultimately historical character of structures, but they often don't know quite how to think about the problem. This seems to me one of the most obvious places where deeper theoretical dialogue between social scientists and historians could yield substantial benefits. What both social scientists and historians need is forms of structural thinking that are compatible with historical conceptions of temporality.

A second valuable habit of mind that historians might pick up from social scientists—this time from historical sociologists, themselves only a minority subfield within sociology—is a willingness to confront the biggest historical questions. Historians, with their emphasis on archival research, exact chronology, and detailed narration, tend to be very diffident about questions that take them beyond the limits of their scholarly mastery. Historical sociologists, by contrast, have traditionally been willing to address the biggest questions: the rise of capitalism, the nation-state, or modernity; the dynamics of revolutions; the governance of empires; the rise and fall of civilizations.[6] According to the scholarly standards of the history profession, scholars should possess a full command of the relevant historical literature and must have the ability to read documents in the original language; sociologists, by contrast, lack these admirable but also crippling scruples. This has freed historical sociologists to look for larger historical patterns that professional historians care about in principle but feel paralyzed about pursuing in practice. By reminding historians of the big questions and challenging us to examine, confirm, or refute their arguments about them, historical sociologists consistently enlarge historians' horizons.[7]

The social sciences, thus, have important virtues that historians should emulate. But they have their vices as well. Most fundamentally, mainstream social scientists are hampered by an uncritical, or at least insufficiently critical, embrace of a certain natural science model—by what in-

6. Examples include Eisenstadt (1963), Moore (1966), Wallerstein (1974a), Bendix (1978), Skocpol (1979), Mann (1986, 1993), Tilly (1990), and Arrighi (1994).

7. It is by no means the case, it should be said, that social scientists are in general more wide-ranging than historians. It is, for example, rare for even the most mundane historical works to approach the empiricist triviality that threatens to become the norm in the political science subfield of American politics, where article after article contributes to our knowing more and more about less and less—detailed statistical estimations of the effect of ballot initiatives on voter turnout, or of the effect of party influence or campaign contributions on congressional roll-call votes; or mathematically elaborate game-theoretic models of signaling in legislative-judicial interaction, of tactical maneuvering on omnibus bills in congress, or of the effects of separation of powers on congressional decision-making.

terpretivist wags have aptly dubbed "physics envy." The ideal of social
science, at least since Auguste Comte announced the foundation of "sociology" in the early nineteenth century, has been to attain the degree of ex-
actness that had already been achieved by physics at the time of Isaac
Newton. Comte's schema has been repeated ever since: physical science,
which deals with the simplest phenomena, was the first to reach the scientific stage; biology, which deals with more complex phenomena, attained scientific status later; and sociology (or, as we would say, social science), which deals with the most complex phenomena, will be the last to
become fully scientific. The social sciences, so the litany goes, are still
young sciences, and to become mature they must emulate their elders,
adopting strict "scientific methods" and using mathematics and quantitative data whenever possible. This program has been carried out most fully
in economics, which in recent decades has attained a status second only to
physics among advocates of the natural science model.

One might regard it as strange that a science could still remain "immature" some century and a half after its foundation, or that it could still
be under the thrall of a long-surpassed Newtonian form of physics. The
repeated failures to make the social sciences more efficacious by making
them mathematical should have long since rendered the neo-Comtean
schema implausible, but they have not. We are faced here with an extremely powerful historical structure indeed, a stubborn intellectual
founding myth whose abandonment seems equivalent, in the eyes of most
American social scientists, to giving up the project of seeking exact social
knowledge altogether. Indeed, as I argue in chapter 3 below, a version of
this myth is powerful even among historical sociologists, who might seem
the obvious allies of historians within the social sciences. The prestige of
the natural sciences, the wish to emulate their "scientific methods," to seek
legitimation in quasi-experimental rigor—this continues to haunt even
the most historically inclined social science fields. One of the most difficult
obstacles facing a dialogue between history and the social sciences is this
entrenched belief that some form of natural science model is the royal road
to truth in the study of social life.

This overvaluation of the natural science model reinforces a deep resistance among social scientists to the notion that society is culturally constructed—which, as we have seen, is central to contemporary historical
thinking. If societies are indeed culturally distinct at some deep level, this
implies that any putative "social laws" can only be valid locally, that truly
general social laws are an impossibility. This means that social physics, in-

cluding the form of social physics already invented by the economists and widely copied by quantitative political scientists and sociologists, must be illusory. Admitting that social relations are culturally constituted would imply that the Newtonian grid of uniform space and time posited by the quantitative social sciences is in fact crumpled and rent—that the world is too messy a place to be understood by a Newtonian social science. And so it is. This book is based on the premise that our messy and mutable world needs the conceptual tools that only a collaboration between interpretive social scientists and historians is likely to provide.

Social and cultural anthropology, which has for the most part eschewed the natural science model, is in many ways a natural ally for theoretically minded historians. Anthropologists generally assume that the social world is culturally constructed all the way down. In the 1970s, when historians initially became enamored of the works of anthropologists, anthropological conceptions of culture tended to be entirely synchronic. They could explain how seemingly strange or exotic forms of life were coherently structured by cultural systems, but they were at a loss when it came to explaining historical change in cultural patterns. Over the past twenty-five years or so, historical questions have become much more central to anthropology, and anthropologists have developed much more sophisticated conceptions of historical temporality. But it is the encounter with poststructuralist philosophy and literary criticism that has had the biggest theoretical impact on anthropology since the mid-1980s. Critical anthropologists have effectively deconstructed the older conception according to which culture was a coherent system of meanings that could account for the orderliness of social life. This philosophical critique has been mixed with much soul-searching about the moral standing of the field. Anthropology, as the critics properly point out, has from the beginning been associated with European and American colonialism. Its attempts to speak for the people whom it studies is consequently fraught with moral and political ambiguities. Such moral and political critiques are certainly well taken. And the development of a more fragmented and contradictory concept of cultural forms is certainly laudable, as is the attempt to introduce multiple voices into ethnographies.

However, I believe that the hypercritical thrust of much contemporary anthropological thinking has resulted in an effective abandonment of some of the field's most powerful insights and useful conceptual tools. I think that the more classical or structural conception of culture remains extremely valuable—indeed, indispensable—for constructing a properly historical form of social theory. Anthropology's classical notions of culture, no less than sociology's classical notions of social structure, need to be infused with historical temporalities. We need to develop conceptions of culture that make change as normal as reproduction and that build in continuing practical struggles over cultural meanings. But in doing so, I think we must begin from the strong conceptions of culture developed before anthropology's deconstructive turn. A more systematic focus on logics of historical change might help to restore a certain rigor to a field that sometimes seems more intent on critique of past errors than on constructing a viable way forward.

HOW THE ARGUMENT PROCEEDS

The essays that make up this book were written over the course of fifteen years, for a variety of occasions, and many of them have been published previously. But most were written with this book in mind. My intention is to carry out and exemplify in the following chapters the sort of theoretical dialogue between history and the social sciences that I have called for above. The chapters do this in different ways.

Chapter 2 is a partly autobiographical reflection on the history of historical scholarship during the four decades since I began graduate studies. The outstanding developments of this period were the rise of social history in the 1960s and 1970s and its surprisingly rapid displacement by cultural history in the ensuing years. I was an enthusiastic participant in both phases of this historiographical development, but I have recently come to feel that something important has been lost in the turn from social to cultural history. In particular, I worry that the currently dominant forms of cultural history are not capable of grasping the historical transformation of world capitalism that is powerfully altering social relations in our own era. I attempt, in this chapter, both a critical diagnosis and a historical explanation of the current state of historical thought, pointing out the political as well as intellectual stakes of the encounters between history and social theory.

Chapter 3 is a critical evaluation of sociology's encounter with history. It argues that the potentially radicalizing effects of historical sociology on the discipline's epistemological assumptions has been blunted by the historical sociologists' own conventional and limiting conceptualizations of temporality. On the basis of critical readings of representative texts, I distinguish three different conceptions of social temporality employed by historical sociologists: the conventional teleological and experimental conceptions and a more historical (and more interesting) eventful conception. I try to show that certain classic works employing teleological and experimental temporalities owe much of their intellectual success to untheorized but nevertheless crucial eventful historical analyses. Historical sociology, and sociology as a whole, I argue, needs to recognize, and to integrate into its theoretical arsenal, the complex social temporalities that historians take for granted.

Chapter 4, like chapter 3, is an effort to introduce a more historical temporality into sociological thinking. Chapter 4 takes on the key sociological concept of structure. I attempt to develop a theory of structure that bridges the very different sociological and anthropological implications of the term; that internalizes a concept of agency; and that can account for the transformation of structures over historical time. The argument is developed largely by means of a critique and appreciation of the works of the British sociologist Anthony Giddens and the French sociologist Pierre Bourdieu.

If chapters 3 and 4 attempt historical critiques and reformulations of sociological theory, the following three chapters are primarily confrontations between history and anthropology. Chapter 5 examines the notion of culture, long anthropology's central concept. Over the past two or three decades, the concept has escaped from anthropology and has been taken up enthusiastically by scholars in many other disciplines — for example, history, sociology, political science, geography, and literary studies. At the same time, anthropologists have become increasingly ambivalent about the culture concept, which they increasingly see as tainted by imperialism and orientalism. I argue that culture is, as anthropologists have traditionally claimed, the inescapable ground of the human sciences, and that it needs to be conceptualized more carefully rather than abandoned or avoided.

In chapter 6, I look at the work of Clifford Geertz, the anthropologist whose work has done more than any other's to spread an interest in culture beyond the discipline of anthropology. Historians, in particular, have been profoundly influenced by Geertz. The adoption of Geertz by historians is paradoxical, on the face of it, because his work is insistently synchronic and therefore seemingly antihistorical. I argue, however, that it is precisely his brilliant deployment of synchronic argument that makes his work so interesting to historians, whose conceptions of temporality in fact combine both synchronic and diachronic elements. Finally, I show that Geertz's famous definition of culture as at once a model of and a model for social life, which underwrites his synchronic cultural analyses, can actually be mobilized diachronically, as a way of explaining cultural and historical change.

Chapter 7 examines the work of another anthropologist, Marshall Sahlins, who has developed a particularly sophisticated anthropological theorization of historical change, via the category of the event. Sahlins, whose anthropological theory is strongly influenced by that of the famous French "structuralist" Claude Lévi-Strauss, uses a striking historical event—the first arrival of Europeans in Hawaii—as a means of developing a potentially general theory of cultural transformation. Sahlins argues that the Hawaiians took Captain Cook to be an incarnation of one of their deities, whose seasonal arrival was being celebrated just as Cook's ships came ashore. Sahlins shows how the Hawaiians' actions, which began with Cook's veneration and ended with his murder, simultaneously reproduced Hawaiian culture (by assimilating things European to Hawaiian cultural categories) and transformed it (because the assignment of such novel beings to conventional categories changed the meanings of the categories and therefore altered the entire categorical system). I argue that Sahlins's theorization is of very general value, in spite of the unique and seemingly exotic character of his exemplary case. But I also argue that his theory of historical change requires certain modifications—largely the building of a more variegated conception of historical duration into the argument.

Chapter 8 continues the theme of the event, but moves from the historical anthropology of Oceania to what is generally acknowledged as one of the central events of European history, the taking of the Bastille on July 14, 1789. The chapter attempts to work on two levels. First, it elaborates a historical argument, claiming that the initial formulation of the modern conception of revolution arose from this particular event. But it also uses the example of the taking of the Bastille as a kind of analytical template for developing a more general theorization of the event. In this chapter, I attempt to take historians' conventional assumptions about the nature of social temporality, raise them to the level of explicit theory, and use this theory to illuminate an important historical case.

Chapter 9, like chapters 7 and 8, is a theoretically informed case study. It examines what might be thought of as the opposite of a transformative event: a case of the endurance, against what would seem to have been insuperable odds, of a highly anomalous institution. It looks at the history of the dockworkers of nineteenth-century Marseille, whose trade society maintained extraordinary privileges for its members during a period when such societies were officially outlawed. I also use the case as a means of thinking through the relationship between a large-scale global process—capitalist development—and the strikingly variable economic and political experiences of different categories of workers. Using a combination of quantitative and interpretive methods, the chapter stresses the unevenness of the social temporalities operating in nineteenth-century Marseille and shows how human agency, contingency, and inexorable social processes were twisted together in a surprising and dramatic historical sequence.

Chapter 10, the final essay in this book, attempts to cover the whole territory laid out in the previous nine, but from a different and more philosophical angle of vision. It attempts to set forth the ontological assumptions that underlie the historically inflected social theory laid out in the previous chapters. It does so by attempting to define the "social" in social science. "Social," I note, is an exceptionally vague but also extremely capacious term—one that signifies the complex totality of human interrelatedness. I suggest that the social, in this sense, is constituted by overlapping and interconnected streams of semiotic practices. To flesh out this notion, I start with an assumption shared either explicitly or implicitly by most cultural historians and cultural anthropologists: that social life should be understood as constituted by language, that is to say as a kind of complex and open-ended text. Beginning from this point, I attempt to complicate and broaden this linguistic conception of the social: by including forms of semiotic practice that are not strictly speaking linguistic; by investigating the problem of articulations between different kinds of semiotic practices; by showing how such varied semiotic practices can generate patterns of human actions whose deciphering may require recourse to quantitative or mechanistic forms of reasoning. Thus, I recreate what is in some ways a familiar picture of social science: one that includes both cultural/semiotic and quantitative/mechanical methods. But there is an important difference. Whereas semiotic and quantitative research in the existing social sciences are based on completely incompatible ontological assumptions, I try to found both on a single ontological basis, and one in harmony with interpretive methods. This common ontology, I argue, can generate the entire complex gamut of historical logics explored in this book.

⊰ 2 ⊱

THE POLITICAL UNCONSCIOUS OF SOCIAL AND CULTURAL HISTORY, OR, CONFESSIONS OF A FORMER QUANTITATIVE HISTORIAN

This chapter straddles the boundaries between scholarly essay, personal reflection, and political critique. My topic is the history of social history over the past forty years or so, that is, since I began graduate school, at Berkeley, in 1962. In the American context, these four decades correspond rather neatly to an entire developmental parabola of the research program that was commonly called the "new social history"—from its meteoric rise in the 1960s and 1970s to its surprisingly rapid displacement by a "new cultural history" in the 1980s and 1990s. In this essay, I shall focus above all on the American case, which I know from the inside as a participant, but I shall also glance repeatedly at both Britain and France, where developments were roughly parallel but by no means identical, in intellectual substance, politics, or temporality. I shall not attempt to survey the research accomplishments of social or cultural history but will concentrate instead on the epistemological and methodological presuppositions that underlie these two types of historical research. I shall pay especially close attention to the relationship between epistemology and politics, a relationship that, in the case of social and cultural history, has been complicated,

This is a considerably extended version of an essay by the same title that appeared in *The Politics of Method in the Human Sciences: Positivism and Its Epistemological Others*, ed. George Steinmetz. Copyright © 2005 Duke University Press; reprinted with the permission of Duke University Press. Chapter 2 also incorporates some passages from "Whatever Happened to the 'Social' in Social History," which appeared in *Schools of Thought: Twenty-five Years of Interpretive Social Science*, ed. Joan W. Scott and Deborah Keates. Copyright © 2001 by Princeton University Press; reprinted with the permission of Princeton University Press. I would like to thank Laura Downs, Geoff Eley, Jan Goldstein, Dagmar Herzog, Lynn Hunt, Jacques Revel, Joan Scott, and George Steinmetz for comments on earlier versions of this chapter.

paradoxical, and at times even perverse. This chapter is at once a somewhat disillusioned reflection on what I and my fellow cultural historians have wrought over the past quarter century and an argument that we need to revive some of the lost virtues of social history without abandoning the tremendous intellectual gains attendant upon history's linguistic turn. I wish to make it clear from the outset that I write as a fully engaged participant in the history I am chronicling and that my critiques should be read, at least in the first instance, as a form of self-criticism. My mode of political interpretation will be a form of Marxist criticism. I shall try to indicate how changes in the social and political forms of world capitalist development have—for the most part unconsciously—affected the politics of social and cultural history. Although my title invokes Fredric Jameson (1981), my approach to the recent intellectual history of social and cultural history actually has more in common with the work of Raymond Williams (1973, 1977). Like Williams, I am attempting to trace the emergence and expression in discourse—but in historical writing rather than in literature—of "structures of feeling" that arise from the writers' experiences of fundamental transformations in the social relations of capitalism.

My reflections are inevitably influenced by the peculiarities of my own experience. Three of these should probably be noted immediately. The first is that I work in French history. American historians of France have naturally been influenced by the example of the powerful and prestigious "Annales school," which led the way internationally both in social history from the 1930s through the 1960s, and in the turn to cultural history in the 1970s. This tended to give us the sense of being in the historiographical avant garde and meant that the gravitational pull of political history, which outside France often remained the specialty of the vast numerical majority of historians, was particularly weak. The history of the past forty years might look quite different to an American historian of Germany or the United States. The second peculiarity is that I was actually raised a positivist. My father was an eminent sociologist whose life-project was to make his discipline more fully "scientific." He was instrumental in building the University of Wisconsin's powerful and notoriously positivist sociology department and in obtaining a place for sociology at the federal feeding trough, especially at the National Institutes of Mental Health and the National Science Foundation (Sewell 1988). I began my career as a historian fully equipped with a positivist vision of science that I had learned at my father's knee. My first published paper, which dates from my graduate student days, was an attempt to explicate Marc Bloch's use of comparative history according to a positivist notion of hypothesis testing (Sewell 1967), and I undertook a dissertation that involved a massive effort of quantitative research (Sewell 1971). It seems clear that I was more deeply imbued with positivist views than were most of my social historian contemporaries.

A third peculiarity of my experience is that it has been far less bounded by history departments than is the norm. Even in graduate school, my training was cross-disciplinary: my major concentration was in the inter-disciplinary field of economic history, and I completed significant course work in economics and did a minor field in sociological theory. Moreover, in only ten of the thirty-five years since I gained my first academic post has my appointment been exclusively in a history department. In addition to unalloyed history department appointments (at the University of Chicago from 1968 to 1975 and the University of Arizona from 1980 to 1983) I had a five-year interdisciplinary social science appointment (in the School of Social Science at the Institute for Advanced Study from 1975 to 1980), and have had joint appointments in sociology and history for seven years (the University of Arizona from 1983 to 1985 and the University of Michigan from 1985 to 1990) and in political science and history for fourteen (at the University of Chicago, from 1990 to the present). This unusually interdisciplinary professional experience means that I have, in effect, engaged in a good deal of participant observation of the theoretical, methodological, and rhetorical practices of several social science fields.[1] This has certainly made me far more aware than most historians of the wide range and the "culturally constructed" character of disciplinary epistemic practices; and it surely is at least partly responsible for the emergence in my work of a much stronger interest in theory than is generally characteristic of historians. (Of course, this last point could also be read the other way around; surely it was in part my penchant for theory that led to my unusually inter-disciplinary career.)

Despite these idiosyncrasies, I do not think that my methodological views or my styles of historical research have been radically different from those of the mainstream of my generation of social historians. I began as a committed new social historian and made considerable use of quantitative data in my early work; subsequently I moved increasingly toward work with a cultural bent. This trajectory, as I will argue later, was actually quite

---

1. Another important disciplinary influence that does not show up in this enumeration of academic appointments is anthropology, which—as will become apparent later in this essay—affected me profoundly in the course of the 1970s.

common in my age cohort and has by no means been limited to historians
working in the United States. Meanwhile, my political views and experiences have been almost embarrassingly typical of historians of my generation. Like many of my contemporaries, I was involved in a whole range of
1960s political and cultural movements: the Civil Rights movement, the
movement against the Vietnam War, the university revolts (in my case, the
Berkeley Free Speech Movement), and the counterculture. My active participation in politics slackened in the 1970s, as a result of both the declining vitality of the various movements[2] and changes in my personal and
professional life — the demands of increased family responsibilities, of
holding down a teaching job, and of producing publications so as to attain
tenure. But I remained politically on the left and eventually became one of
the "tenured radicals" who were so vehemently bemoaned by right-wing
commentators during the Reagan and George H. W. Bush presidencies
(Kimball 1990) and who are, indeed, currently very plentiful on the faculties of major American universities, in history departments as elsewhere.

SOCIAL HISTORY

In the years following World War II, social history was very much an international project. Its leading early centers were France, where the school of
historical studies associated with the journal *Annales* gained intellectual
and institutional ascendancy under the leadership of Lucien Febvre and
Fernand Braudel; Britain, where the lead was taken by an extraordinary cohort of Marxist historians; and the United States, where a school commonly known as "the new social history" rose to prominence in the 1960s.[3]
I was a member of the younger generation of "new social historians," those
who completed dissertations in the late 1960s and early 1970s.

Eric Hobsbawm, writing about social history in 1971, noted "the remarkably flourishing state of the field," concluding "it is a good moment to
be a social historian" (Hobsbawm 1971, 43). It certainly was a good moment
for the large cohort of historians who, like me, had entered graduate school
in the 1960s, chosen to write dissertations on social historical topics, and

2. Of course, the great exception to the decline of such movements was the feminist movement, which became more prominent and more militant in the 1970s than it had been in the
1960s. But in this case I could be only a supporter and sympathizer, not a direct participant.

3. As far as I know, there is no proper history of "the new social history" in the United States,
although there are pertinent sections in Novick (1988). On the Annales school, see Burke (1990)
and Dosse (1994). On the British Marxists, see Kaye (1984, 1988) and Kaye and McClelland
(1990).

secured good academic jobs in the rapidly expanding American university
system with an ease that now seems almost obscene. Most of this rising
generation of social historians were largely self-taught. We sought out dissertation advisors who were sympathetic to the kind of work we wanted to
do, but found few who could give us detailed methodological guidance. We
educated ourselves in method and theory largely by taking courses in sociology, political science, or economics. There were a handful of older scholars, in American universities and abroad, whose work served as crucial
models for our research, but most of us knew them by their books rather
than as teachers. I was most influenced by three books published in 1963
and 1964, precisely when I was developing a dissertation topic—E. P.
Thompson's *The Making of the English Working Class* (1963), Charles Tilly's
The Vendée (1964), and Stephan Thernstrom's *Poverty and Progress* (1964).
But even most of the "elder statesmen" of the new social history were still
quite early in their careers when the 1960s ended. It was the entry into the
profession of my cohort of social historians, and the outpouring of our articles and monographs over the course of the 1970s, that secured the ascent
of social history in the United States. By the mid-1970s, the new social history had achieved a strong institutional presence and was quickly moving
toward hegemony in the profession. One clear sign of the rise of social history was the proliferation of social historical journals. *Comparative Studies
in Society and History,* founded in 1958, was the only American journal devoted to social history before 1960. *The Journal of Social History* and *Historical Methods Newsletter* (later *Historical Methods*) appeared in 1967, and in the
early 1970s there was a new social history journal virtually every year.
These included *The Journal of Interdisciplinary History* in 1970, *International
Labor and Working Class History* in 1971, *Peasant Studies* in 1972, *The Journal
of Urban History* in 1974, *Social Science History* in 1976, and *The Journal of Family History* in 1976. Moreover, articles on social history also became common in such general journals as the *American Historical Review* and the *Journal of Modern History,* dozens of social history monographs were flowing
from the university presses,[4] and social historians were getting tenure and
moving rapidly up the ranks in all the major departments.

   The rise of social history in the United States not only represented the
arrival of a new generation of historians; it also effected a profound and

---

   4. The flood of works in social history can be illustrated by my own field of nineteenth-
century French history, which was transformed by the appearance of such books as Bezucha
(1974), Johnson (1974), Scott (1974), Moss (1976), Margadant (1979), Judt (1979), Hanagan (1980),
Lehning (1980), Smith (1980), Sewell (1980), Aminzade (1981), Moch (1983), and Reddy (1984).

lasting intellectual transformation—something like a paradigm shift—in the field of history. Social history represented a change in subject matter, in methods, and in intellectual style. One of its most significant and lasting achievements was a vast enlargement of the scope of historical study. This enlargement was twofold. First, social history studied categories of people who had previously been ignored by historical scholarship. Rather than political leaders and great thinkers, who had previously been the prime subjects of history, social historians tended to work on the obscure and downtrodden: servants, workers, criminals, women, slaves, shopkeepers, peasants, or children. This interest in the forgotten millions of ordinary people was, clearly, consonant with the populist tendencies of 1960s political activism. Second, rather than concentrating on politics narrowly defined, social history attempted to capture the whole range of ordinary people's life experiences: work, child-rearing, disease, recreation, deviant behavior, kinship, popular religion, sociability, procreation, consumption. Social history thus not only studied new categories of people but asked new questions about them. And in order to answer new questions about new categories of people, it used new forms of evidence. All sorts of records previously not thought to contain information relevant to historical research suddenly became gold mines of documentation. Old census manuscripts, tax registers, wills, advice books, inventories of estates, popular songs, city directories, statutes of mutual aid societies, building permits, records of marriages, baptisms, and deaths: all these and many other kinds of documents yielded evidence about the social structures, institutions, and life experiences of millions of ordinary people.

These new forms of documentation were also subjected to new methods of analysis. A characteristic mark of the new social history was the systematic use of quantitative methods. The kinds of people social historians studied were often illiterate, and even those who could read and write rarely left papers that revealed much about their lives. But such people came into contact with public authorities when they paid taxes or tithes; when they were drafted; when they had contracts notarized; when they registered births, marriages, and deaths; when they got counted by the census or were arrested by the police. It was largely by aggregating the rather thin and stereotypic information contained in the records of such encounters between ordinary people and public authorities that social historians were able to reconstruct the patterns of these otherwise anonymous lives. Quantification as a method of analysis was thus intimately linked to social history's radical expansion in subject matter.

It was from the social sciences that historians borrowed the quantitative methods they applied to these novel data sources. But the borrowing
involved far more than a simple transportation of a set of methods: along
with the methods came a distinctive theoretical and epistemological outlook. The borrowing of methods was but one aspect of a self-conscious
modeling of ourselves and our work on the social sciences. Because we
tended to regard what we called "traditional narrative history" as atheoret-
ical and intellectually bankrupt, the neighboring social science fields of sociology, political science, economics, demography, and geography looked
very attractive. In the course of the 1950s and 1960s, these fields had become overwhelmingly positivist and quantitative, encouraged by massive
federal spending on social science research (Kleinman 1995; Ross 1991;
Steinmetz forthcoming; Turner and Turner 1990). By the 1960s, these
quantitatively inclined social sciences had high prestige within the academy and seemed far more methodologically rigorous and theoretically sophisticated than history. Not surprisingly, their positivist and objectivist
stance was carried over into the new social history.

The various changes introduced by social history were mutually reinforcing—they made up a fairly coherent package, constructing a distinct
epistemic object for social history. The new social historians' "social" was
above all of what we (following our social scientist friends) called "social
structure." Social structures were objective and transpersonal patterns or
forces of which actors were at best incompletely aware and that tightly
constrained their actions and thoughts. These social structures—occupational distributions, business cycles, demographic patterns, inheritance
systems, hierarchies of wealth, urban settlement patterns, systems of land
tenure, and the like—left palpable traces in historical records, especially in
the quantifiable records that supplied what we called "hard data." We
thought of social structures as essentially autonomous from political or intellectual history. Indeed, we often argued that they formed the underlying
conditions for, even the determinants of, the political or intellectual developments that historians had previously taken as primary. The distinction
between the "hard data" of quantitative history and the "soft" or "impres-
sionistic" data of political and intellectual history subtly implied an underlying ontological distinction between a determining social structure and a
determined politics and culture. In short, the rise of social history entailed
a redefinition of the primary object of historical knowledge—from politics and ideas to anonymous social structures—as well as the discovery of
new means of gaining knowledge about this object.

The new social history paradigm I have just outlined is of course an ideal type. Not every social historian adhered equally to all aspects of this epistemic package. Those strongly influenced by demography or economics, for instance, tended to be particularly enthusiastic about quantitative methods and "hard" data, while those who worked on rebellions and social movements tended to combine quantitative data with verbal accounts culled from archives, memoirs, or newspapers. But for all the internal differences among social historians, we tended to adopt a common front in our struggles for recognition within the field, arguing for the necessity of interdisciplinary borrowing, for the recognition of quantitative methods as part of the historian's toolkit, for the expansion of history's subject matter beyond politics and great ideas, and for recognizing the historical importance of ordinary people's experiences. These arguments were, it seems to me, largely successful; social history did succeed in significantly redefining the object of historical knowledge. Social history, I would even say, briefly became hegemonic in the field in the United States. Although social historians never accounted for a numerical majority, they were hegemonic in the sense that they managed to define the terms of historiographical debate—so that, for example, political and intellectual historians themselves began to ask more social-historical questions and to experiment with the new methods.[5] By the mid-1970s, social history was generally recognized, even by those skeptical of its claims or methods, as the "cutting edge" of historical research.

The relationship of this research program to the political commitments and sentiments of the rising generation of American social historians was complicated, in part because the social historians' political commitments were themselves far from simple. As I have already intimated, quantitative techniques were quite consonant with the strong populist impulses of 1960s radicalism—because they made it possible to carry out detailed studies of classes or categories of the population who were poorly represented in the sources used by more traditional historians. Quantification, in other words, was one important way of pursuing the populist goal of "history from the bottom up." But social historians' politics could also make their embrace of positivist social science significantly ambivalent. It is important to remember that the politics of the 1960s was by no means limited to an upsurge of populism. Sixties politics also featured a powerful

5. For two influential early articles about what was often called "the social history of ideas," see Darnton (1971a, 1971b).

revulsion against the bureaucratic conformity that student radicals saw as characteristic of contemporary American society. Sixties radicalism, especially its "countercultural" moment, must be seen as a rejection of the corporate political and cultural synthesis of "big government, big business, big labor" that became dominant in the 1950s and 1960s—what has since come to be called "Fordism."[6] The term Fordism designates the mode of macrosocial and macroeconomic regulation that underwrote the long postwar economic boom, which stretched from the late 1940s to the early 1970s. The Fordist package combined mass production technologies, relatively high wage levels, stable systems of collective bargaining, Keynsian management of aggregate demand, full employment strategies, welfare state institutions, and highly bureaucratized forms of both public and private management (Aglietta 1979; Amin 1994; Gramsci 1971b; Harvey 1989; Jessop 1992; Lepietz 1987).

From the perspective of the hypercompetitive, predatory, and extraordinarily inegalitarian American capitalism of the early twenty-first century, the Fordist mode of regulation may seem remarkably humane, a kind of quasi social-democratic "world we have lost." But from the point of view of young critics of the system in the 1960s, its benefits (for example, economic stability and steady productivity gains) were hardly noticed. They seemed givens of modernity itself, permanent and unproblematic acquisitions of an irreversible social progress. Meanwhile the defects of Fordist capitalism— especially corporate conformity, bureaucratic monotony, repressive morality, and stultifying forms of mass culture—were highly visible and repugnant, at least to the youthful political intelligentsia who made up the student movement. The countercultural style of the 1960s movements— psychedelic music, consciousness-altering drugs, infatuation with "Eastern" meditative practices, outlandish clothing styles, sexual experimentation—was largely a revolt against the standardization associated with the Fordist mode of socio-economic regulation. And while the leftist political movements and the counterculture were by no means one and the same, it was difficult to participate in the political movements of the era without also exploring and embracing some of the new possibilities offered by the counterculture.

I am convinced that this anti-Fordist strain in the politics of the 1960s endowed many social historians with at least a latent ambivalence about

6. For similar arguments dealing primarily with European social movements of this era, see Hirsch (1983) and Steinmetz (1994).

quantitative methods and the positivist philosophical assumptions that came in their baggage. It certainly did so in my case. It seemed undeniable to me that quantitative methods were useful, indeed essential, for overcoming the "elitism" of "traditional" history—for expanding the social range and subject matter of history so as to encompass the lives of the poor, the oppressed, and the marginalized. Yet we social historians were to some degree aware that in adopting quantitative methodology we were participating in the bureaucratic and reductive logic of big science, which was part and parcel of the system we wished to criticize. At least in my case, this awareness arose in part from contacts with leftist students in disciplines like political science and sociology who in the 1960s were themselves criticizing the blind-spots in their fields' positivist methodologies. As George Steinmetz has pointed out, these critiques were based on an implicitly anti-Fordist political project (Steinmetz forthcoming, 2004; Steinmetz and Chae 2002). In retrospect, I would say that we new social historians found ourselves in the objectively contradictory situation of using big-science Fordist methods in pursuit of an at least partly anti-Fordist political agenda.

One sign of my own ambivalence, and, I believe, that of many of my contemporaries, was the extraordinary role played by the work of E. P. Thompson as an inspiration even for American new social historians who, like me, had enthusiastically embraced the possibilities of quantitative history. Many of us admired Thompson's work greatly, even though Thompson was profoundly hostile, almost allergic, to quantification, which he regarded as a violent abstraction from the textures of lived experience. His own work probed the thoughts, feelings, and experiences of the English poor, attempting, as Thompson put it, to rescue them from "the enormous condescension of posterity" (Thompson 1963, 13). In retrospect, I think that Thompson was so appealing in part because he made the victory of laissez-faire capitalism in early nineteenth-century England seem contingent rather than necessary and set forth the alternatives championed by working-class communities in such vivid detail. The sheer richness of Thompson's history of working class experience—his convincing reconstructions of manifold distinct, vibrant, and rebellious forms of life in late eighteenth and early nineteenth century England—struck a responsive chord among young women and men who were attempting to find radical alternatives to the rather different Fordist capitalist culture that formed our own social world. Hence it was common for new social historians to mix a little E. P. Thompson with their quantitative sociology—to add to their quantitative analyses whatever they could glean about the lived experiences of the poor.[7] Although our epistemological stances may ultimately have been incoherent, it seemed clear in practice that both quantitative and Thompsonian qualitative methods helped us toward the ultimate goal, which was to understand the lives of ordinary people in the past. In my own case, at least, the qualitative material on lived experience served as a kind of supplement to the quantitative core of my research. This was reflected in an epistemic metaphor I used in the introduction to my dissertation, where I described quantitative methods as providing a hard skeleton to which the flesh and blood of available qualitative data might be attached (Sewell 1971, 17–18).[8] In short, although quantitative history seemed both exciting and politically compelling in the late 1960s, the moral ambivalence of our embrace of quantification and the incoherency of our epistemological stances probably rendered us vulnerable to the cultural turn once it got under way.

Social history in France and in Britain had somewhat different temporal rhythms, preoccupations, and political affinities than in the United States, but the redefinition of the object of historical knowledge described above was a common product of social historians in all three countries. The development of social history in postwar Britain was indelibly marked by a group of self-consciously Marxist historians, especially E. J. Hobsbawm, E. P. Thompson, George Rudé, Christopher Hill, and Rodney Hilton. All were members of the British Communist Party and participated in the Communist Party Historians' Group until 1956, when most of them resigned from the party (Kaye 1984; Hobsbawm 2002). It was particularly in the late 1950s and the 1960s that the works of these historians achieved sufficient density to be regarded as a "school" of history. Their version of social history differed in a number of ways from the American new social history. First, although some of the British Marxists made significant use of quantification in their research, and most certainly did not share Thompson's outright hostility to counting, they certainly had none of the new social historians' programmatic enthusiasm for quantitative meth-

7. For three examples from my own field of nineteenth-century French labor history, see Bezucha (1974), Scott (1974), and Sewell (1974b). Ronald Suny (2002) also stresses the importance of Thompson's project, and of the humanist "Western Marxist" currents out of which it arose, in predisposing social historians to participate in the "cultural turn" once it got underway.
8. Upon rereading Lawrence Stone's *Crisis of the Aristocracy* shortly after completing my dissertation, I found that he had used a version of the same metaphor in his introduction (Stone 1965, 3).

ods.[9] Second, it took a particular interest in what has been called "history from below" or "history from the bottom up." This, in practice, meant not simply an attempt to reconstruct the social-structural and economic determinants of the lives of ordinary people. It was, in addition, an attempt to write history from something like poor people's point of view. The British Marxists attempted to portray sympathetically both the beliefs and the political, economic, and social struggles of the poor. Ordinary people, in their work, are never mere categories or numbers in a table, but agents in their own history. It was Thompson's *Making of the English Working Class* (1963) that carried out this effort most brilliantly, but it was an important element in the work of all the British Marxist historians (Hill 1964a, 1964b, 1972; Hilton 1973; Hobsbawm 1959, 1964; Rudé 1959, 1962, 1964). Fourth, the British Marxists were Marxists, and as such had a more self-conscious theoretical orientation than most of their more eclectic American and French counterparts. Their Marxism was open and nondogmatic, but it centered the problematic of history squarely on the rise and development of capitalism, and it assumed that the appropriate way to explain social and cultural developments was to relate them to the class dynamics that arose from the mode of production and its transformations.[10]

Finally, the British Marxist historians, largely because they were Marxists, remained institutionally marginalized. In this respect their experience was very different from that of the American new social historians, who rapidly rose to a position of prominence within academic history, and—as we shall see—even more strikingly unlike that of French historians of the Annales school, who not only captured the commanding heights of the historical profession but made themselves the dominant partners in French social science more generally. The British Marxists did play a central role in founding and managing the most internationally prestigious British historical journal, *Past and Present*. But, in spite of their brilliant and prolific scholarly output, only Hill, who taught at Oxford, had an Oxbridge appointment. Hilton taught at Birmingham and Hobsbawm at Birkbeck College in London; Rudé spent most of his career in Australia and Canada;

9. Some of Hobsbawm's early writings on labor history and on the standard of living in Britain during the industrial revolution relied significantly on quantitative argument. Many of these essays are collected in Hobsbawm (1964). Additionally, both Rudé (1959, 1962, 1964) and Hobsbawm and Rudé (1968) made use of quantitative methods to determine the social characteristics of attackers and victims in episodes of collective violence.

10. For an argument that this was true even for E. P. Thompson, in spite of his denunciations of the base/superstructure model, see Sewell (1990b).

and Thompson taught from the mid-1960s to the mid-1970s at Warwick University, retiring on his private income around the age of fifty to write and engage in political activism.[11] There were, of course, important non-Marxist social historians of a similar generation in Britain—for example Asa Briggs, Peter Laslett, Keith Thomas, and E. A. Wrigley—who were rather better-placed than their Marxist brethren. But the British historical establishment, right into the 1980s, remained rather skeptical of social history, hostile to Marxism, and strongly attached to political, institutional, and narrative history. Younger generations of British social historians, most of whom were admirers of the work of this extraordinary pioneering generation rather than actually their doctoral students, have tended to retain an intense political leftism and a sense of embattlement up to this day. Nevertheless, the younger generation of British social historians gained a solid foothold in the British academy, although more often in the "red brick" universities than in Oxbridge. Their coming of age might be marked by the appearance of two new and excellent social historical journals in 1976: *Social History* and *History Workshop Journal*.

It was in France that the triumph of social history over other forms of historical scholarship was earliest and most complete. The story of the rise of social history in France is conventionally dated back to 1929, when Marc Bloch and Lucien Febvre founded a new historical journal, the *Annales d'Histoire Économique et Sociale*.[12] From the beginning, the *Annales* was dedicated not only to the development of social history but to fostering contact and cooperation between historians and other social scientists—principally economists, geographers, and sociologists. In the 1930s, historians of the Annales group were a dissident minority in French academic history. After World War II, Febvre formed and presided over the sixth section of the École Pratique des Hautes Études (later the École des Hautes Études en Sciences Sociales or EHESS), which soon surpassed the Sorbonne as the most prestigious center of historical studies in France. When Febvre died in 1956, he was succeeded as president of the École by his student Fernand Braudel, who was not only a great historian but an extraordinary academic entrepreneur. Under Braudel's leadership the "sixième section" (later the EHESS) not only consolidated its position as the leading center of historical studies in France but became the preeminent cen-

11. Hobsbawm relates in his recent autobiography that he was "turned down for several posts in economic history in Cambridge" (2002, 182).

12. Its name has been altered periodically, to *Annales d'Histoire Social* in 1939, *Annales: Économies, Sociétés, Civilisations* in 1946, and *Annales: Histoire, Sciences Sociales* in 1992.

ter of research in the social sciences as well. In sharp contrast to the situation in the United States, however, history was definitely the senior partner in this collaboration (Burke 1990; Dosse 1994; Revel 1995). It was not until 1985 that a social scientist (the anthropologist Marc Augé) served as president of the École, and he was succeeded in 1995 by another historian, Jacques Revel (Dosse 1994, 143). Meanwhile, social history's dominant position within historical studies was consolidated above all by a veritable flood of vast and impressive *thèses d'État* by the "third generation" of Annales historians between 1960 and the mid-1970s.[13] So thorough was the victory of the Annales school that by the 1980s all the major chairs of modern history at the Sorbonne were themselves staffed by Annales historians.[14]

The Annales school had no strict or monolithic definition of social history. The history advocated—and practiced—by Bloch, Febvre, and Braudel was broadly and self-consciously inclusive, ranging from economic history and historical geography, through the history of social structures, to what would today be called cultural history. It was also painted on a rather vast canvas—Bloch was a master of comparative history and Braudel's history began with all the states and civilizations inhabiting the shores and waters of the sixteenth-century Mediterranean and then moved on to the history of the world. But with few exceptions, the *thèses* of the third generation of Annales historians had a much narrower geographical scope and generally shared a quite specific procedure of research. First, most of the great *thèses* of the 1960s and 1970s were studies of a clearly delimited French region, either an entire province (Languedoc, Limousin, Auvergne, Provence) or a city (Amiens, Lyon, Paris, Caen), and they had some pretension to portraying that local society as a whole—the French term was *l'histoire totale* (total history). Second, they shared an implicit model of the social totality. Their *thèses* began with an analysis of the geographical, economic, demographic, and occupational structures that were assumed to

13. On the "third generation," see Burke (1990, 65–93). French *thèses d'Etat* during this period were heroic undertakings that normally amounted to between six hundred and a thousand printed pages. A number of them required two volumes, and Maurice Agulhon's (1970a, 1970b, 1970c) was printed as three, not counting his superb 252 page *thèse complementaire* (1968). Among the great *thèses* of this era were Baehrel (1961), Bois (1960), Corbin (1975), Daumard (1963), Deyon (1967), Flandrin (1976), Garden (1970), Gascon (1971), Goubert (1960), Lebrun (1971), Lequin (1977), Le Roy Ladurie (1966), Meyer (1966), J.-C. Perrot (1975), M. Perrot (1974), Poitrineau (1965), Roche (1978), and Vovelle (1973).

14. Maurice Agulhon and then Alain Corbin in "contemporary history," Michelle Vovelle in the French Revolution, and Daniel Roche in "modern history" (what in the United States would be called "early modern history").

constitute the bedrock of society. It was typically only after some hundreds of pages of such solidly materialist history that they proceeded, if at all, to questions of popular mentalities, politics, and social life. The Annales historians had, in short, a kind of implicit (although not particularly Marxist) base/superstructure model of the social. Finally, most third-generation Annales historians made massive use of quantitative techniques. It was hardly rare for a *thèse* to contain a hundred pages or more of graphs, tables, and charts summarizing the results of the quantitative research; sometimes the graphs and tables were published as a separate volume. Thus, despite many differences of emphasis or style, French social historians' working model of social history in this period was not far from that already described for the United States.

The politics of the founders of the *Annales* were not particularly leftist, although they were certainly pronounced republicans.[15] But most of the historians in the Annales' "third generation"—those who began their Lycée studies after the war—commenced their political lives on the far left, many in the Communist party.[16] The young Marxists almost invariably chose the economic historian C.-E. Labrousse as their thesis director. Labrousse, a specialist on the history of prices in eighteenth-century France and a major exponent of quantitative history, held the chair of economic history at the Sorbonne. A disciple of the sociologist François Simiand, he was sympathetic to Marxism but never identified himself as a Marxist. He was also a friend of Fernand Braudel and agreed with the general outlines of the Annales project. Studying with Labrousse, who was an exceptionally charismatic lecturer and generous thesis director, the young leftists could be Marxists and adherents to the Annales school simultaneously.[17]

One might speculate that the easy acceptance of these young Marxists by the Annales school also made it relatively easy for them to gradually abandon strictly Marxist intellectual positions over time—as most of

15. Marc Bloch may be said to have died for the republic when he was captured and shot as a member of the French Resistance during World War II. On Bloch, see Fink (1989).

16. Among those who were Communist party members were Maurice Agulhon, André Besançon, Pierre Deyon, François Furet, Emmanuel le Roy Ladurie, Mona and Jacques Ozouf, Michelle and Jean-Claude Perrot, Denis Richet, and Michel Vovelle. For an informative memoir of a young Communist who became a famous historian, see Le Roy Ladurie (1982). On the politics of young historians in this era, see also Agulhon (1987) and Perrot (1987).

17. On Labrousse, see Le Roi Ladurie (1982, 220–22), Agulhon (1987, 25–27), Perrot (1987, 275–78), Goubert (1996, 134–42), Burke (1990, 53–56, 86), Dosse (1994, 51–53, 71–73), and Revel (1995, 17–20).

them did. This intellectual *glissement vers le centre* might have been more difficult to achieve had they been forced by their initial political leanings to organize themselves as an insurgent group, as had been the case of Marxist historians in Britain. In any case, the Annales school maintained its opening to the left. A number of young historians who were on the left during "les événements" in 1968 got absorbed into leadership positions at the *Annales* and the École des Hautes Études in the following years. And once again, their loyalty to the school tended to overshadow their particular political leanings. Thus, in sharp contrast to the situation in Britain, the French history profession has proved remarkably open to the left but this very openness has tended to inhibit the development of a specifically Marxist historiography. Even the work of Annales scholars who maintained their Marxist political convictions—for example, Michel Vovelle— normally lacked an explicit Marxist intellectual apparatus. It is surely paradoxical that in a country whose intellectual life was broadly open, indeed favorably inclined, to Marxism, there was virtually no attempt to develop a specifically Marxist form of historical reflection. The main exception to this statement may prove the rule: an increasingly explicit Marxism dominated the history of the French Revolution, where the school of Lefebvre and Soboul—both social historians, but social historians who kept a certain distance from the Annales school—held sway through the 1960s.[18] The Marxist interpretation of the French Revolution was, however, devastated in the 1970s, above all by the critiques of François Furet, an ex-Communist student of Labrousse who eventually became the *juste milieu* president of the EHESS in the late 1970s (Furet 1971, 1978).

Neither the successes of social history nor its elective affinity with the political left were confined to France, Britain, and the United States. In the course of the 1970s, social history caught on in nearly all the Western European countries. Social history in Spain and Italy owed much to the French model and to visiting appointments at the École des Hautes Études; in the Scandinavian and Germany countries the favored model was American, although with a strongly Weberian inflection among the Germans. When social history emerged in India, it was modeled above all on the work of the British Marxists. Yet social history everywhere was recogniz-

18. Another exception was Pierre Vilar, a social and economic historian of modern Catalonia (1962), who actually published a book on Marxism and historical method (1982). He seems, however, to have had very little influence on other Annales historians.

able as part of a single varied but interconnected international discourse, and this international flavor was sustained by a continual flow of scholars from one country to another—a flow that accelerated notably in the course of the 1970s.

Although social history in all its variants was easily recognizable as such, it is not easy to define precisely what historians meant by *social* history. Explicit definitions were rare in this period, and most attempts were either uninformative ("the essence of social history is the description and explanation of styles of life" [Stearns 1967, 5]) or tautological ("social history means the history of society or, more precisely, of social structures, processes and trends" [Conze 1967, 7]). Perhaps the most interesting effort to articulate what historians meant by social history is E. J. Hobsbawm's stock-taking essay of 1971 entitled "From Social History to the History of Society." There Hobsbawm points out that the term "social history" is different from such seemingly parallel terms as "economic history" or "intellectual history" or "political history" because the adjectives "economic" or "intellectual" or "political" designate a distinct sphere of human activities, whereas the term "social" is applicable to human activities of all kinds. As he put it, "social history can never be another specialization like economic or other hyphenated histories because its subject matter cannot be isolated" (Hobsbawm 1971, 24). Social history, in other words, made an implicit claim to be a history of the whole of society. It is for this reason that Hobsbawm employed the term "history of society" rather than "social history" for most of the rest of the essay. Yet the term "history of society" simply displaces the definitional problem, because "society" is nearly as vague and capacious a term as "social." Hobsbawm explicitly declined to take on the definitional task: "It is not possible for me to produce a definition or model of what we mean by society here, or even a checklist of what we want to know about its history. Even if I could, I do not know how profitable this would be" (29).

Nevertheless, a few pages further on, Hobsbawm provides a definition of sorts. He asserted, accurately in my opinion, that "a tacit consensus among historians seems to have established a fairly common working model" of how societies are structured. This model is rarely explicitly worked out but is, rather, "an approximate order of research priorities and a working assumption about what constitutes the central nexus or complex of connections of our subject." Here is his characterization of the "working model":

One starts with the material and historical environment, goes on to the forces and techniques of production (demography coming somewhere in between), the structure of the consequent economy—divisions of labor, exchange, accumulation, distribution of the surplus and so forth—and the social relations arising from these. These might be followed by the institutions and the image of society and its functioning which underlie them. . . . The practice is thus to work outwards and upwards from the process of social production in its specific setting. (Hobsbawm 1971, 31)

This might be characterized as a restatement of the Annales paradigm with a slight Marxist twist. I think it quite accurately captures the working model of most social historians in the 1960s and 1970s. Whether in France, Britain, or the United States, social history's coherence as a program was built upon a usually tacit assumption that economic structures were primary and that they constituted the privileged standpoint from which the structure and functioning of society as a whole could be grasped.

Furthermore, the rise, development, and impact of capitalism actually provided the central problematic of most social historical research undertaken in this period. This was of course explicit among the British Marxists. But it was hardly less true of the French and the Americans. I have pointed out that many of the third-generation Annales historians began as Marxists and that a number of them were members of the Communist Party up to 1956. André Burguière points out that although most of the third generation worked on the seventeenth and eighteenth century, they, like their mentor Labrousse, were generally concerned with the problem of the economic, demographic, social, and cultural preconditions for the "takeoff" of capitalism in France—a problematic that, by the 1960s, owed at least as much to W. W. Rostow as to Marx (Rostow 1960). According to Burguière, the problem of "modernization" or, alternatively, of the failure to modernize, pervaded the work of the Annales' third generation (Burguière 1995, 257–61). In the case of the United States, where the "modernization" paradigm underwrote the postwar boom in the social sciences, the problematic of the rise of "industrialization," its causes, preconditions, and consequences, was at the core of the new social history. American social historians, whether they worked on the United States or Europe, most commonly worked on nineteenth-century urban topics, where the impact of the industrial revolution was central and unavoidable, rather than on the Early Modern rural topics favored by the French. Although relatively few American social historians were Marxists, and although many (myself included) failed even to use the term "capitalism," the problem of capitalist development broadly understood was as constitutive of the new social history as it was of the social history practiced by the British Marxists or by the Annales school.

THE CULTURAL TURN

In the course of the 1970s, however, this consensus "working model" came increasingly under challenge from a new form of history focused on culture. The challenge was as international as was social history itself. My account of it, however, will begin with an extended consideration of the American case. Only after I have set forth an interpretation of my own experiences in the United States context will I attempt comparative assessments of developments in Britain and France.

As early as 1971, the year I completed my doctoral dissertation, I was beginning to feel frustrated by the limits of positivist quantitative history and by the "working model's" implicit materialist determinism. It seemed to me that although quantitative methodology had enabled us to understand more and more about the structural constraints and social forces that shaped people's lives, it offered no guidance for understanding how people actually made sense of and grappled with these forces and constraints — that is, for how they actually made history. The persistent objectivism of the new social history's practicing epistemology — the mode of thinking that C. Wright Mills brilliantly dubbed "abstracted empiricism" (Mills 1959) — virtually ruled out some of the most interesting questions about the past — the questions about agency, culture, and the textures of experience that had been at the heart of E. P. Thompson's work. I do not know at what point such doubts began to haunt other American new social historians, but it is clear that my case was not unique. It is remarkable that the turn to what in the course of the 1980s came to be called cultural history was actually pioneered by some of the same historians who had initially adhered to the new social history. In my own field of French history, for example, I would cite Joan Scott and Lynn Hunt as historians who, like me, moved from early work in a quantitative mode to later work in cultural history.[19] Unlike the rise of the new social history,

19. Scott (1974) and Tilly and Scott (1978) were in the quantitative mode, but the essays collected in Scott (1988), all written in the course of the 1980s, focused on the history of the linguistic construction of gender difference. Although Scott does not actually identify herself as a cultural historian (personal communication), I believe that most historians would see these essays as fitting within the genre of cultural history, broadly construed. Hunt (1978) was a fairly

which was effected above all by a generational succession, the rise of the new cultural history was at least in part a transformation of historical practices within the 1960s generation. In retrospect, I see my switch from social to cultural history as a belated working out of the anti-Fordist dimension of my 1960s radicalism. And I strongly suspect that many others were affected by the same underlying political motivations. But before discussing the politico-cultural dynamics of history's cultural turn, let me say more about when and how the turn took place.

My own path out of the new social history's abstracted empiricism — one that was followed by a number of others as well — was inspired by cultural anthropology. What anthropology offered was a way of getting at meaningful human action. Of course, questions about the history of meaning already had a significant place in the field of intellectual history. The beauty of cultural anthropology was that it made possible the pursuit of such questions not only in the texts of great thinkers, but in the rituals, conventions, language, and everyday conduct of ordinary people. It made possible, one might say, a kind of intellectual history of precisely the poor, marginalized, oppressed, illiterate, or semiliterate groups whose study was the bread and butter of social history. In this respect, then, social history's turn to anthropology was perfectly consistent with the field's frankly expansive ethos. Just as the use of quantitative methods enabled social historians to grasp the social, economic, or geographical structures that shaped the lives of the poor, the marginalized, and the oppressed, so the use of anthropological methods could enable us to grasp such people's cultural systems. Adopting anthropological methods was therefore a means of expanding or supplementing our conception of the social by adding cultural structures to the familiar social structures. Anthropology implied that cultural structures, rather than being reflections or products of underlying social structures, were in fact equal to them in ontological standing.

Thus, although the search for cultural structures was consonant with social history's expansive ethos, the turn to anthropology had some un-

---

typical work of the new social history. Hunt (1984) was a particularly clear example of the shift from social to cultural history, in that half of the book was quantitative social history and the other (far more influential) half cultural history. Unlike Scott, Hunt embraced, indeed promoted, the "cultural history" label; by the end of the decade, she had edited and written the introduction to the book that declared the triumph of "the new cultural history" (Hunt 1989). It should be pointed out that the real pioneer in cultural history among American historians of France was Natalie Davis, whose *Society and Culture in Early Modern France*, published in 1975, included several articles that had appeared during the previous decade.

settling epistemological and ontological implications. This was because anthropology—or at least the kind of Geertzian "symbolic anthropology" that historians tended to pick up (Geertz 1973a)—was fundamentally incompatible with the new social history's basically positivist epistemology and objectivist ontology. Unlike the new social history's presumption that social structures were analytically prior to social action, cultural anthropology implied that the social world was constituted by the interpretive practices of the actors who made it up. Hence, rather than scientists whose analysis of "hard data" revealed the structures of an objective social world, social historians who made the anthropological turn had to recast themselves as interpreters of the inevitably interpretive practices that produced intersubjective cultural patterns. Cultural anthropology seemed to imply that even social and economic structures, which appeared to be the concrete foundations or bony skeletons of social life, were themselves products of the interpretive work of human actors.

Making the cultural turn was therefore an exciting but also profoundly troubling step for an adept of the new social history. In my case, and I think in others as well, taking this step amounted to a sort of conversion experience—a sudden and exhilarating reshaping of one's intellectual and moral world. In my case, the initial "conversion" took place at the University of Chicago between 1972 and 1974, largely under the influence of Bernard Cohn and Ronald Inden.[20] My anthropological turn was powerfully confirmed and deepened during the academic year of 1975–76 at the Institute for Advanced Study, when I took part in an extraordinary seminar on symbolic anthropology. This seminar, led by Clifford Geertz, included the anthropologists Victor Turner, Hildred Geertz, James Fernandez, David Sapir, Michelle and Renato Rosaldo, and Ellen and Keith Basso, the sociologist Orlando Patterson, and five historians: Robert Darnton, Thomas Kuhn, William Reddy, Ralph Giesey, and myself. The seminar gave rise to an intense discussion of the relationship between anthropology and history, one that spilled over into lunch-table conversations and the seminar of the Shelby Collum Davis Center at Princeton University. This interaction between anthropologists and historians gave me a strong sense that my own interest in cultural anthropology was part of a larger convergence between the two disciplines. Anthropologists, it appeared, were as inter-

20. Cohn was a pioneer in historical anthropology; Inden, a historian, had been a student of Cohn's and was also, at that time, something of a disciple of the anthropologist David Schneider. See Cohn (1987), Inden (1976), and Schneider (1968). The published evidence of my initial conversion is Sewell (1974a).

ested in historicizing their traditionally synchronic discipline as historians were interested in applying to history the anthropological notion of culture.[21] Nevertheless, I can also testify that going over to anthropological methods and theories could attract considerable hostility from one's erstwhile new social history colleagues—especially in my subfield of labor history, where anything smacking of "idealism" was taken as evidence of political as well as intellectual apostasy.[22] But the anthropologists' vivid and persuasive ethnographies contained a double promise: first, that interpretive methods could uncover structures or systems of meaning no less real or far-reaching in their implications than the social structures uncovered by quantitative research and, second, that by doing so they could restore to history the dimension of meaningful human action that had been marginalized in the new social history. Anthropological history, in short, seemed a risky but also an irresistible intellectual adventure.

While it was by no means impossible to combine quantitative with interpretive methods, it did require something of a balancing act. Moreover, the intoxication and sense of discovery involved in these pioneering searches for past cultural systems made it hard for social historians to sustain in practice an integrated sociological-cum-anthropological research strategy. Instead, most of us threw ourselves wholeheartedly into the study of culture, leaving our data-sets, graphs, and statistical tables behind. My own experience indicates how difficult it could be in practice to combine cultural and social history approaches. I initially discovered the possibilities of cultural anthropology at a time when I was attempting to turn my dissertation on the workers of Marseille into a book. But before I could complete the task, an anthropologically inspired essay that I initially presented to the Symbolic Anthropology Seminar at the Institute for Advanced Study in 1976 burgeoned into a very different book (Sewell 1980), interrupting my work on Marseille for several years. When I returned to the Marseille project, I managed to publish only a highly statistical and utterly sociological first volume of what I had actually planned as a two-volume work (Sewell 1985b). The second volume, which was, precisely, projected to combine cultural and statistical methods, never got written. The question of the relationship between changing social structures and the emergence of working-class radicalism, which had seemed so com-

21. For astute accounts of relations between history and anthropology at this time, see Cohn (1980, 1981).

22. For a concise account of a hostile interchange that involved the anthropological turn, see Eley (1996, 197–78).

pelling in the 1960s and 1970s, had lost much of its interest for me by the mid-1980s.[23] I had, by then, effectively ceased to be a social historian.

Not all social historians found their way into cultural history by way of anthropology. Another, probably more common, route was via literary studies—which had themselves been transformed in the 1970s by the various post-structuralisms associated with the names of Derrida, Lacan, and Foucault. Precisely how social historians negotiated the cultural turn surely depended on local ecologies of knowledge. My appointments at Chicago and then at the Institute for Advanced Study in Princeton put me at two of the major crossroads between history and anthropology in the 1970s. Lynn Hunt and Joan Scott, two other social historians of France of my vintage who also made the cultural turn, did so primarily through local connections with literary scholars—although in quite different ways. Hunt explained in the preface to her transitional book *Politics, Culture, and Class in the French Revolution* that she had begun her research with "a different project in mind," but that her "original social history of Revolutionary politics turned increasingly into a cultural analysis." She attributed this in part to "the impact of my friends at Berkeley," but did not mention who these friends were (Hunt 1984, xi). I think, however, that we can get some insight into her social circles by noting that she served on the editorial board of the celebrated interdisciplinary journal *Representations* when it was launched in 1983, the year before she published *Politics, Culture, and Class*. A quick check of the disciplinary affiliations of the editorial board indicates seven English professors, two professors of French, three historians, one anthropologist, and one (very maverick) political scientist. This affiliation with the humanities is also reflected in the theoretical references in part 1 of Hunt's book (entitled "Poetics as Power"), which include citations to Jean Starobinski, Kenneth Burke, Susan Suleiman, Northrup Frye, Hayden White, Michel Foucault, Jacques Derrida, and E. H. Gombrich, along with the historians J. G. A. Pocock, Ernst Kantorowicz, Mona Ozouf, and François Furet. The only social scientists mentioned are Emile Durkheim and the ubiquitous Clifford Geertz.

Joan Scott made the cultural turn during a period when she was teach-

---

23. I did manage to publish one article on Marseille that, I believe, combined quantitative sociological and interpretive anthropological perspectives more or less seamlessly, thus carrying out more or less the sort of analysis I had intended to apply on a larger scale (Sewell 1988). A reformulated version of this article is included as chapter 9 in this book. For a long-term project that has successfully combined quantitative social history with anthropological history, see Sabean (1990, 1998).

ing at Brown University and serving as director of the Pembroke Center for Research on Women. In her introduction to *Gender and the Politics of History*, the book that contains her writings from this period, Scott notes that the essays grew out of conversations in the center's seminar. There, surrounded by feminist "literary scholars," she tells us that she "was forced to take post-structuralist theory seriously and wrestle with its implications for a social historian" (Scott 1988, 1). The theoretical citations in Scott's volume bear out this provenance: the post-structuralist humanities scholars Michel Foucault, Theresa de Lauretis, Barbara Johnson, Jacques Derrida, Michel de Certeau, Donna Haraway, Martha Minow, Gayatri Chakravorty Spivak, Michael Ryan, Denise Riley, and Luce Irigaray, together with the Marxist art historian T. J. Clark, are joined by four anthropologists (Clifford Geertz, Michelle Zimbalist Rosaldo, Gayle Rubin, and Maurice Godelier), two historians (Natalie Davis and Caroline Bynum), and one sociologist (Pierre Bourdieu). While Scott's theoretical references, like Hunt's, are largely to scholars in the humanities, hers are overwhelmingly to post-structuralists, whereas Hunt's include such classical humanities authors as Burke, Frye, and Gombrich. Moreover, feminist theorists are very prominent among Scott's references, making up fully half of the total, by my count. By contrast, only one feminist (Susan Suleiman) appears among Hunt's references. These striking differences mirror a fundamental divergence within the humanities in the late 1970s and early 1980s, when both feminists and post-structuralists were engaged in intense epistemological challenges to traditional humanistic scholarship. As these references imply, Scott's work includes a post-structuralist epistemological critique of historical thought, one that Hunt and her co-authors disagreed with emphatically in their epistemologically middle-of-the-road *Telling the Truth about History* (Appleby, Hunt, and Jacobs 1994, 226–28). Clearly, very different kinds of literary theory could be imported into history, with very different results.

It is instructive that both Scott's and Hunt's theoretical references were quite different from those in the introduction to my transitional book, *Work and Revolution in France* (Sewell 1980). My cited theoretical sources were five anthropologists (Clifford Geertz, David Schneider, Victor Turner, Max Gluckman, and Marshall Sahlins), two philosophers (Michel Foucault and Jacques Rancière), and four historians (E. P. Thompson, Ronald Inden, and Eugene and Elizabeth Genovese). The difference in profiles between these citations and those of Hunt and Scott are clear: a much higher proportion of anthropologists, no literary critics or feminists, and (to my

surprise) a higher proportion, across all disciplinary categories, of Marxist scholars (by my count five of eleven, as opposed to three of nineteen for
Scott and none among Hunt's fourteen).[24] This quick and dirty exercise in
citation analysis indicates that seemingly parallel and roughly simultaneous paths through the cultural turn could vary significantly in their fine
structures.

But at the same time, all three of these cases illustrate a major shift in the
epistemological frontiers of history. If the new social history was largely
defined by its borrowing of method and epistemology from the quantitatively inclined social sciences, the new cultural history that took shape in
the 1980s was defined instead by a large-scale transplantation of method
and epistemology from the humanities. Even the theoretical references of
someone like me, who followed a relatively "social scientific" route through
the cultural turn, included anthropologists and philosophers, but no sociologists—let alone economists. Indeed, the only works by sociologists
cited by Scott, Hunt, or myself were Emile Durkheim's *The Elementary
Forms of Religious Life* ([1912] 1965), a book claimed as a founding text by
anthropologists as much as by sociologists, and *Le sens pratique* (1980) by
Pierre Bourdieu, who spent his early career as an anthropologist before
turning to a highly interpretive form of sociology later in life. Moreover,
even historians who made the cultural turn primarily through borrowings
from the officially social-science discipline of anthropology found themselves in an intellectual world increasingly defined by literary studies. Clifford Geertz's essay on the Balinese cockfight (Geertz 1973b), which was the
anthropological work that influenced historians most widely (see Walters
1980), was famous for introducing into anthropology the notion of culture
as a text. Geertz's models of text interpretation, to be sure, were primarily
drawn from hermeneutics or new criticism. But many in the generation of
anthropologists who came of age in the 1970s and 1980s (including some of
Geertz's own students) were increasingly attracted to the post-structuralist
forms of theory that had gained dominance in literature departments. The
manifesto of anthropological post-structuralism, a collection significantly
entitled *Writing Culture: The Poetics and Politics of Ethnography*, was published
in 1986 (Clifford and Marcus 1986). From that time forward, anthropology

---

24. This latter categorization is admittedly slippery. Among my citations, I did not count
Sahlins, who had left his Marxism behind when he wrote the book cited, but did count Rancière,
whose cited work was Marxist but who later distanced himself from Marxism. I say that the
prominence of Marxist references in my footnotes surprises me because I certainly did not regard myself as a Marxist at the time I was writing *Work and Revolution*.

itself was less an exporter of theory to other disciplines than an importer of theory from literary studies.[25]

When the boundary with the humanities was breached in the early 1980s, much of the theory that flowed into history was post-structuralist. As the connections with literary studies multiplied, Foucault, Derrida, and Lacan became names to conjure with in historical circles. The influence of Michel Foucault on historians has been particularly notable (see Goldstein 1994). I believe that this prominence stemmed in part from the obvious fact that, unlike Derrida, Lacan, and their literary epigones, Foucault consistently worked on historical topics. Moreover, Foucault focused on marginalized groups and on the links between discourse, power, and inequality—interests that fitted with, but also challenged, social historians' preoccupation with history from the bottom up (see esp. Foucault 1977).[26] If the hermeneutical approach of Geertzian anthropology introduced at least a potential epistemological break between social and cultural history, the influx of post-structuralist theory did much to radicalize that break, making any attempt to develop a combined socio-cultural history ever more difficult.

Both the rapidity of the rise of cultural history in the 1980s and the widening of the epistemological fissure dividing it from social history were disproportionately fueled by developments in women's history—or gender history, to use the term that many would now prefer. Women's history was easily the most politically intense and intellectually creative field in historical studies during the 1980s.[27] Thanks largely to the organized efforts of feminist historians during the 1970s, there was a remarkable influx of women into history departments in the 1980s (remarkable, that is, by comparison with previous decades). Women's history was, therefore, also the most rapidly growing field in the discipline. Through the 1970s, women's history looked much like other subfields of social history, focusing on the familiar tasks of documenting the experiences of a previously ignored category of the population and specifying the structural sources of women's particular social and economic burdens. But during the 1980s, women's his-

25. To be fair, it should be noted that new imports of anthropology by literary scholars associated with "the new historicism" went some way toward righting the intellectual balance of payments between the disciplines (Veeser 1989).

26. It is surely no accident that Foucault was the only theorist other than Geertz to appear in the theoretical references of Hunt, Scott, and Sewell alike.

27. For a lucid brief account of the politics and epistemology of women's history from the 1960s through the 1980s, see Scott (1991).

torians—increasingly influenced by feminist philosophers and literary scholars (as in the bellwether case of Joan Scott discussed above) began to explore the intrinsically radical epistemological implications of the modern feminist movement. Feminism had, after all, challenged one of the supposedly most natural of social distinctions, the difference between male and female, arguing that its meaning was contingent and susceptible to fundamental redefinition. Hence the problem for historians, stated most influentially by Scott, became not to document the distinct historical experiences of women but to decipher the processes by which gender difference—indeed sexual difference itself—has been established, maintained, and transformed (Scott 1988). In this effort the resources provided by literary theory have proved tremendously valuable. This critical and deconstructive historical analysis of central cultural categories—sex and gender—has unquestionably helped to radicalize and energize cultural history as a whole. Over the past decade or so the question of how supposedly natural or settled identities have in fact been discursively established, maintained, and transformed has arguably become the central problematic of cultural history as practiced in America. The influence is particularly clear in histories of race, sexuality, and colonialism. Work in these areas has sustained both the political radicalism and the conceptual innovation that has characterized gender history since the 1980s.[28]

Social history, even quantitative social history, has certainly not disappeared. But its decline from hegemony in the history profession in the late 1970s to a position of intellectual marginality by the late 1980s was almost breathtakingly rapid. In part because many of the most prominent social historians themselves took the cultural turn, the no longer "new" social history failed to put up much of a struggle against the rise of cultural history. Abetted by the burgeoning of a culturally inflected gender history and the influx of women into graduate programs and faculty positions, cultural history quickly became the major growth area in the profession, attracting the best students in the major centers of graduate training. The publication in 1989 of an influential collection entitled *The New Cultural History* (edited by Lynn Hunt) might be said to mark cultural history's claim to have usurped definitively the hegemonic position achieved by social history only a decade earlier.

Because I was a pioneer in the field of cultural history, one might expect

---

28. Some examples are Bederman (1995), Briggs (2002), Chauncy (1994), Holt (1995), Roediger (1991), and Stoler (1995, 2002).

me to be thrilled by its rise to intellectual hegemony. The speed and thoroughness of the triumph, after all, has been quite exhilarating. As recently as 1985, I was convinced that the remainder of my academic career would be dedicated to a long and exhausting fight for the recognition of culture's role in social life. That the positions I had to argue for tooth and nail in the early 1980s had become the accepted wisdom by 1990 was a delightful surprise. Nevertheless, I have increasingly come to worry that the triumph of cultural history over social history has perhaps been too easy—that social-historical methodologies of considerable power have been given up without much resistance and that important concepts, especially the fundamental social-historical notion of social structure, have been abandoned almost without argument. Cultural history, it seems to me, has been largely spared the potentially bracing task of working out its relationship to the fundamental problems and techniques of social history; it has, instead, been able to dismiss them more or less out of hand.[29] The result, I fear, is a form of history that, for all its impressive achievements and in spite of its continuing vitality and political relevance, nevertheless finds itself disarmed in the face of certain important questions posed to us by the history of our own era. Here, indeed, is a vexing paradox: during the very period when historians have gleefully cast aside the notion of structural determination, the shape of our own social world has been fundamentally transformed by changes in the structures of world capitalism—in ways I shall attempt to spell out below. Given the political and intellectual challenges facing us at the beginning of the twenty-first century, I think that history can jettison the conceptual and methodological heritage of social history only at its peril.[30]

29. There were, to be sure, some quite fierce polemics in historical journals in the 1980s, but these were often debates among cultural historians over post-structuralism or postmodernism rather than between social and cultural historians. Joan Scott was at the center of a number of these polemics. Scott (1987a) was a response to Gareth Stedman Jones (1983). It was published with three critical comments (Stansell 1987; Rabinbach 1987; Palmer 1987); Scott (1987b) then replied to the comments. Scott (1992) was largely a criticism of John Toews (1987). Laura Lee Downs's (1993a) critique of Scott was followed by a reply from Scott (1993) and a rejoinder from Downs (1993b). There was also a prominent polemic between Robert Finlay (1988) and Natalie Zemon Davis (1988). Perhaps the most blistering denunciation of discursive history, this one from a distinctly social-historical point of view, was by Bryan D. Palmer (1990).

30. For a very different (and very stimulating) assessment of current historiographical conundrums, see Cabrera (2004). Cabrera characterizes the "new cultural history" as an attempt to work out the relationship between culture and social structures, with the latter still understood as objectively given. He argues that the "new cultural history" is now being replaced by a "postsocial history," which understands all of social reality as being constituted in discourse.

But how and why have the achievements of social history been so quickly abandoned? I have noted that the cultural turn involved a rejection of the naive objectivism of social history—the notion that social structures were ontologically prior to thought and action and that various forms of "hard data" afforded privileged access to these structures. One of the key arguments against these objectivist prejudices was to demonstrate that the documents containing so-called "hard data" were themselves cultural products that required interpretation and critique. Once again Joan Scott's work is emblematic of a mode of thinking that I believe was widespread during history's cultural turn. In an essay originally written in 1984[31] and eventually incorporated into *Gender and the Politics of History*, Scott subjected a statistical inquiry into work in mid-nineteenth-century Paris to a brilliant political and cultural reading, treating statistical categories themselves as discourse rather than taking the numbers they produced as objective data about social life (Scott 1988, 113–38). Her astute deconstruction of the categories employed in the inquiry demonstrated that this statistical text was structured throughout by a particular politics of gender. Her critique of normal positivist research procedures was devastating. She pointed out that "historians searching for unimpeachable data" have taken the report "at face value, incorporating its documentation without questioning its categories and interpretations." Such a procedure is doubly faulty, she argues, because it both "perpetuates a certain vision of the economy and of statistical science as an essentially objective enterprise" and "makes the historian an unwitting party to the politics of another age" (Scott 1988, 137). This does not mean that Scott disputed the utility of statistical reports as historical sources. "Rather," she asserted, "I want to argue against a simple positivist use of them and for a fuller and more complicated conceptualization of the 'reality' they represent; for a reading of statistical reports that problematizes and contextualizes their categories and conclusions; for an end, in other words, to the separation of statistical reports from other kinds of historical texts" (115).

But there is another question that Scott did not pose: once the inquiry's categories had been subjected to criticism and reinterpretation, could the

---

Because I figure in this book (and at some length) both as a heroic pioneer of "postsocial history" and as an unreconstructed new cultural historian, it will probably come as no surprise that I find the posited distinction between these supposedly utterly different forms of historiographical practice somewhat exaggerated.

31. "A Statistical Representation of Work: *La Statistique de l'industrie à Paris, 1847–1848.*" Scott indicates in a footnote (1988, 113) that the paper was initially delivered as a public lecture in 1984.

data it reports be used in a *statistically* critical fashion—perhaps revealing patterns that are present in the data but obscured by the inquiry's procedures of classification and interpretation? Scott successfully read the inquiry culturally to get at the mental categories and political strategies of its authors. But it is possible that the information gathered in the text could also be "read against the grain" statistically so as to reveal other characteristics of the world of work that the report was ostensibly about. It is possible that the data in this inquiry are presented in such utterly ideological categories that there is no way to use them to probe the lifeworld that they purportedly represent. But I think the fact that the question was not posed by Scott, who in her earlier work had carried out extremely sophisticated and critical quantitative analyses (esp. Scott 1974), speaks volumes about the epistemic assumptions of history's cultural turn. If social history tended to privilege quantifiable data as uniquely objective, cultural history, at least in its post-structuralist modality, seemed to deny the possibility of access to any realities beyond the discursive structures present in the text.[32]

It was above all post-structuralism, especially in its Derridean form, that made the unreflective realism underlying social history's evidentiary practices seem utterly naive. It has taught us that all of the texts and text analogues we use as evidence—like Scott's statistical inquiry—must be subjected to an acute critical reading and that much of what once passed for direct evidence of past "realities" might better be thought of as a textual reference to yet another level of textuality. The "undecidability" of texts and the potentially endless play of intertextuality has made cultural historians extremely reticent about referring to social structures, social forces, modes of production, or class relations as facts standing outside of textual logics. The pasts that cultural historians feel comfortable making claims about therefore tend to be the pasts of discourse, and above all of those forms of discourse readily available in textual form. This reticence about naming an "extratextual" social puts many of the questions and problematics that were central to the new social history beyond the pale of the new cultural history: questions, for example, about the distribution of wealth, the dynamics of economic development, changing patterns of landholding or employment, demographic structures, or patterns of geographical concentration and dispersion.

32. I hope it is clear that far from singling out Joan Scott as an epistemological offender, I mean to commend her for stating outright what others were thinking but lacked either the forthrightness or the clarity to say in published form.

Meanwhile, I think that the understandable preference of cultural historians for symbolically rich artifacts—usually texts—has also tended
over time to displace our gaze from the poor and powerless, who were the
favorite subject of the new social history, to those more favored categories
who were likely to commit their thoughts to paper and whose papers were
more likely to be conserved. This drift away from the socially marginal has
been compounded by post-structuralist epistemological doubts about the
possibility of knowing or representing the thoughts of the poor. Thus
Jacques Rancière (1981) showed that nineteenth-century French worker
poets and intellectuals, who had been taken (by himself and by me, among
others, see Faure and Rancière 1976, Sewell 1980) as expressing the
worker's point of view, were themselves in flight from the labor they glori-
fied in print, leaving the meanings of their writings open to fundamental
doubt. More radically, Gayatri Chakravorty Spivak (1988) intimated that
try as we might we cannot induce the subalterns to speak. In European history, at least, there has been a clear trend from studies of workers and peasants in the 1960s and 1970s to studies of the bourgeoisie since the 1980s.
Lest it seem that I am chiding others for abandoning the poor and downtrodden, let me cite my own trajectory, which began with a study of the
working class of Marseille (Sewell 1971, 1974b, 1974c), then moved to what
might be characterized as a study of literate artisans and their political
and intellectual relations with the radical intelligentsia (Sewell 1980), and
most recently to a highly textual study of the Abbé Sieyès, one of the leading constitutional theorists of the French Revolution (Sewell 1994).

But in spite of my own trajectory (or perhaps because of it) I worry that
the emergence of the current form of purely cultural history is extremely
inopportune, coming as it does in a period of fundamental transformation
of capitalism on a world scale—of decreasing ability of states to control
their own destinies, of growing income disparities in the United States
and in many other areas of the world, of ubiquitous declines in state welfare provision, and of sharp demobilizations of labor and the left—all
pushed forward powerfully by the ascendant discourses of economic neoliberalism. Somehow, at the very time when particularly powerful changes
in social and economic structures are manifested ever more insistently in
our daily lives, we cultural historians have ceased not only to grapple with
such structures but even to admit their ontological reality. In the next section of this essay, I shall attempt to sharpen the problem facing historians
by suggesting that history's cultural turn was itself causally intertwined
with these very socioeconomic transformations over the past three decades.

If we historians hope to participate in what I see as the great political and intellectual battle of the coming years—attempting to reclaim effective political and social agency from the juggernaut of world capitalism and the hegemony of so-called "free market" economics—I think we need to understand our own epistemological and political entanglements in world capitalism's recent social history.

POST-FORDISM AND THE CULTURAL TURN

Surely anyone who has made the turn from social to cultural history, myself included, could devise an essentially "internalist" (and "whiggish") story about how the intellectual and philosophical advantages of cultural history led to its inevitable triumph over an intellectually inadequate social history. Indeed, I have actually sketched out the rudiments of one such account from my point of view above. But I think there are reasons to be wary of the adequacy of any purely internalist account. First, such accounts tend to imply that the social history paradigm was more or less intellectually exhausted. I do not think that this was really the case.[33] Plenty of significant problems from within the social history research program still remained to be solved in the 1980s—or, for that matter, remain to be solved today. Data-sources certainly were not beginning to peter out. At the very time when historians were turning away from quantitative analysis, the development of personal computers was making such research far easier to do. By the 1990s, a single graduate student with an up-to-date laptop had vastly more computational resources at her or his disposal than I had in the 1970s with two or three research assistants and a sizable grant from the National Science Foundation. Moreover, excellent work in the new social history mode has continued to be done, but increasingly by historical sociologists rather than historians. In the years since historians essentially went out of the business of quantitative history, three brilliant quantitatively based studies in the new social history mode have been published in my own field of French revolutionary studies: Mark Traugott's work on the Parisian Revolution of 1848 (1985), Roger Gould's on the Paris Commune (1995), and John Markoff's on peasants in the French Revolution (1996). These books indicate that pathbreaking historical discoveries can still be made by means of quantitative analysis. Historians did not exhaust the possibilities of the new social history. Rather, they have shunned it for reasons of a quite different order.

---

33. For a different opinion on this matter, see Bonnell and Hunt (1999, 7).

Second, any purely internalist explanation of the cultural turn in history ignores the fact that in the 1980s, at precisely the time of history's cultural turn, a widespread rise of interest in culture—almost a culture mania—swept across a broad range of fields in the human sciences. In literary studies, the key move was to use the now dominant post-structuralist theoretical categories to analyze texts and text analogues previously regarded as outside the canon of literature: popular fiction, science writing, film, journalism, television, museums, advertising, hip-hop—in short, culture in general. The dynamic new transdisciplinary field of cultural studies has grown explosively in English, American, and Australian universities over the past twenty years.[34] Even fields like sociology, political science, and psychology, whose dominant scientism long made them highly resistant to taking culture seriously, now have important subfields devoted to the study of culture. Indeed, culture has become a buzzword of American popular discourse as well. It is hard to turn on television news or National Public Radio without hearing some commentator pontificate about the "business culture of Silicon Valley" or the "culture of the Senate." And political claims about the value of cultural particularity, especially with respect to issues of race and ethnicity, are ubiquitous. As much as we historians might like to think that we adopt new questions and methods because they are intrinsically intellectually superior, there is good reason to believe that in taking the cultural turn we were actually being swept along by much larger social forces of some kind.

The Marxist commentators Fredric Jameson and David Harvey have developed arguments that I find extremely useful for getting at the nature of these social forces. During the 1980s, they argued that the artistic and intellectual mutations that had come to be known as "postmodernism" should be understood as responses to an immense and systemic shift in the form of world capitalism (Jameson 1991, 1998; Harvey 1989). Writing in 1984, Jameson identified a postmodernist sensibility—characterized by depthlessness, spatial disorientation, the collapse of the boundary between high and popular culture, a loss of the sense of historicity, a waning of affect, and the rise of pastiche—which he discerned in painting, sculpture, literature, cinema, and architecture alike (Jameson 1984).[35] He argued that the postmodernists had rather precociously found ways of expressing in their art the "structures of feeling" generated by the emergent

---

34. For a particularly stimulating discussion of cultural studies, see Readings (1996, 89–118).
35. This essay was incorporated as the first chapter of Jameson (1991).

logic of "late capitalism," the origins of which he traced back into the 1960s.[36] Jameson's argument relied largely on parallels between the formal features of contemporary capitalism and postmodern art. David Harvey, writing a few years later, attempted to specify more concrete changes in political-economic structures—above all the myriad effects of capitalism's current round of "annihilation of space through time"—that made a post-modernist aesthetic and philosophical outlook plausible (Harvey 1989). Although both Jameson and Harvey were concerned specifically to explain the emergence of the postmodernist sensibility, I believe that their argu-ments are also highly relevant to the broad "cultural turn" undertaken by historians and other scholars in the 1980s.

In the course of the 1970s, many observers would agree, the Fordist regime of macroeconomic regulation unraveled and was gradually replaced by a very different regime. Harvey identifies the new regime as "flexible accumulation" (Harvey 1989, 141–88), but this is only one of a number of terms that have been suggested; indeed, many writers have simply desig-nated the new economic regime with the uninformative moniker "Post-Fordism." The transition between regimes can most conveniently be dated to 1973, the year of the "oil shock," the final collapse of the postwar Bretton Woods monetary regime, and the onset of "stagflation"—a combination of inflation and economic stagnation that proved impossible to remedy with the standard Keynesian tools. The contours of the new regime have taken some time to emerge, and it is a matter of some dispute whether the current form of macroeconomic governance of world capitalism has jelled into a regime with anything like the coherence of the Fordist regime it replaced (Amin 1994). Nevertheless, the broad differences between the emerging form of capitalism and its Fordist prececessor are clear and not very con-troversial. During the forty years I am covering in this essay, we have lived through an epochal transformation in the nature of the capitalist world economy.[37] I believe that this great transformation must be taken into ac-count in explaining the history of historical thought in these years.

Harvey (1989) calls the form of capitalism that had emerged by the 1980s "flexible" to indicate its contrasts with some of the key features of the regime prevailing in the 1950s and 1960s—features that had become dys-functional "rigidities" by the early 1970s. As against the highly bureaucra-tized and vertically integrated firms that dominated the economy during

---

36. Jameson borrowed the term "structures of feeling" from Raymond Williams (1977).
37. An acute history of this transformation is Brenner (1998); see also Brenner (2002).

the postwar boom, firms turned in the long economic crisis of the 1970s to "downsizing," "outsourcing," subcontracting, and the increasing use of temporary employees and business consultants, moves that made them able to reply more nimbly to changes in demand, supply, and technology. The introduction of numerically programmed tools and computer-based design enabled firms to move from mass production to smaller batch, more niche-oriented production. Consequently, the turnaround time of capital has been significantly shortened. In the consumer sector, design and advertising have become increasingly central to the production of goods, speeding up the "fashion cycle" that Fordist capitalism had already spread far beyond its original home in the garment industry. In the post-Fordist period, advertising and design have worked to diversify consumer tastes by creating and commercially exploiting a multitude of consumer "lifestyles." This effective merging of design, advertising, and production has made any distinction between culture and the economy ever more difficult to sustain. Meanwhile entertainment — film, cinema, sport, spectacle, and tourism — has become one of the dominant sectors of the economy.

Improvements in transportation and communications technologies — especially containerization, cheap air travel, telecommunications, computers, and the Internet — have enabled corporations to become increasingly transnational in character. Transnational corporations have adopted radically new forms of spatial division of labor, increasingly locating production facilities in low-wage countries while design, management, and financial functions are scattered through rich countries like the United States, Western Europe, and Japan. Increased internationalization of markets for labor, capital, and commodities, along with the end of the Bretton Woods system of strictly pegged currencies, has also tremendously increased the opportunities for worldwide investment and financial speculation. Meanwhile, new information technologies that make possible so-called "real time" worldwide trading, together with the invention of new financial products, especially derivatives, have led to the explosion of financial markets and the subjection of producers everywhere to increasing domination by the short-term logic of futures markets. This hypertrophic financial industry has also become increasingly "offshore" — that is, beyond the possibility of effective control or regulation by the governments of even the richest and most powerful countries. Increasingly, it is the whims of the "world market" (that is, the offshore worldwide financial industry) that determine the fates of firms, industries, classes, regions, and the populations of entire countries — without much hope of effective intervention

from the governments of individual nation-states. This entire transformation has of course been pushed forward by an immense discursive shift in
dominant political ideologies, with economic neoliberalism, whether of
the Thatcherite-Reaganite or Clintonite-Blairite variety, either sweeping
social democratic discourses from the field or, as in Germany or France,
turning social democracy into a defensive holding operation. Unlike the
expansive Keynesian welfare state of the Fordist era, consequently, post-
Fordist states have increasingly been either unwilling or unable to regulate
economic activities for the benefit of disadvantaged sectors of society.
Contemporary states tend to limit themselves to positioning national or
local capital for effective competition in the global market—for example,
by means of selective deregulation, tax breaks, cutbacks on expensive welfare provisions, and limiting the power of labor movements.

These systemic changes in the mode of economic regulation have had
profound effects on peoples' daily social experiences. Here I shall mention
only a few illustrative examples:

1. The sharply increased geographical mobility of capital and information has been accompanied over the past thirty years by a huge surge of migration on a world scale, especially from poor countries in Asia, Africa, the
Middle East, and Latin America to Western Europe and the United States.
This migration has occurred at both the bottom and the top of the social
scale—involving, for example, both poor Mexicans and North Africans
who find work in factories and in menial service occupations and highly
educated Indian programmers and engineers. This has resulted in the
emergence both of strikingly cosmopolitan urban textures in Western
cities and of what Arjun Appadurai (1996) has dubbed "global ethnoscapes" in which the boundaries of states and national communities no
longer coincide—so that, for example, Hindu fundamentalist movements
that rise to prominence in India rely for much of their financing on prosperous expatriate Indian communities in the United States.

2. "Global cities," those great urban agglomerations that have emerged
as particularly dense nodes of communication and control in the footloose
world economy, have largely left manufacturing behind and increasingly
compete among themselves on the basis of their cultural lifestyles for the
most lucrative financial and business service firms and the most talented
managers and "information" specialists. Urban beautification, the development of arts districts and their associated bohemias, and such "high
culture" institutions as opera companies, symphony orchestras, theater
districts, galleries, and museums have become marks of and means of pro-

ducing and sustaining top-flight nodes in the contemporary world economy. It is, moreover, precisely these global cities that tend to have the highest levels—and greatest complexities—of transnational ethnic diversity.

3. Organized labor, which had been an essential component of the
Fordist regime, has lost power everywhere. In the United States, where it
was attacked frontally by Reaganite Republicans in the 1980s, it has suffered a devastating collapse in membership. Real wages of workers have essentially stagnated for the past thirty years, while incomes of the very
wealthy have ballooned. At all levels of the occupational hierarchy, people's
sense of job security has evaporated, and the well-defined career ladder,
which was characteristic of the Fordist corporation both for managers and
for production workers, has been increasingly replaced by a kind of occupational picaresque. Frequent lateral movement between firms, bouts of
temporary work, episodes of self-employment, frequent retraining, and
career changes are becoming the norm, even for middle-class employees.[38]

4. These experiential shifts have been intertwined with and enhanced
by discursive shifts. Especially since the mid-1980s, commentators, pun-
dits, editorialists, and scholars constantly inform us that we are living in a
new world, that old economic paradigms have been superceded, that ours
is an entrepreneurial age, that contemporary global flows of populations
and ideas are unprecedented, and so forth. The bursting of the late-1990s
"dot com" bubble quieted the endless babble about the "new economy,"
which was supposedly capable of creating wealth without generating
actual revenues. Nevertheless, hyperbolic claims about the novelty of our
current condition remain common. (It is a sobering thought that this
chapter might itself be cited as an example.) In any case, the experiential
effects of changes in economic and social relations have been magnified in
the past two decades by discourses telling us that the new footloose relations are particularly significant—just as the discourse of the Fordist era
previously magnified our sense of the solidity and standardization of socioeconomic relations. Hence, while it is surely true that careers have actually
become increasingly unstable and entrepreneurial over the past few
decades, careers during the Fordist era were less stable than we imagined
and those in the current era are probably more stable than we imagine. The

38. These changes have also affected the academic humanists and social scientists, who frequently spend several years in postdoctoral fellowships, adjunct positions, or replacement jobs
before finally landing a tenure-track position—indeed, a rising portion remain in adjunct jobs
indefinitely. For those who attain tenure, however, the involuntary form of the occupational
picaresque ceases.

changes in what we experience are products both of changes in social relations and of changes in the cultural categories through which we understand them.

I think Jameson and Harvey are right to argue that this epochal increase in the experienced volatility of social and economic forms since the 1970s has been a fundamental source of the postmodernist sensibility. But the rise of postmodernism was just one of a range of possible intellectual responses to this subtle yet pervasive transformation of our social world. It is certainly plausible that the shift from Fordism to flexible accumulation lies behind the great wave of academic cultural turns in the 1980s and 1990s. The experienced decline in the regularity and predictability of life has surely made "social structures" seem far less solid and determining, and the progressive relativization of "majority" cultures and the ever-increasing role of information and aesthetics in economic production have surely made it plausible that our world might profitably be understood as culturally constituted.[39] Thus, the turn from social to cultural history would seem to be, at least in part, a response to the changing structure and textures of our life experience in the contemporary world. The volatilization of social relations over the past thirty years certainly did not determine in a rigid sense any specific changes in social thought. But it does seem to have made strong structural determinisms less plausible across the board and to have induced thinkers in a number of different intellectual locations and with a whole range of political and epistemological proclivities to turn toward more micro-level or actor-based forms of explanation. Thus, the widespread concern in social theory with the problem of agency or action, the development of social network methodology in sociology, the immense influence of Michel Foucault's claims about the predominance of the "micro-physics" of power over the formal trappings of state authority, the victory by the 1980s of microeconomics over macroeconomics, and the rise of rational choice theory in political science and philosophy — all of these extremely diverse movements of thought, no less than postmodernism and the various academic "cultural turns," can be read as alternative responses to the experienced volatilization of social relations that has accompanied recent transformations of world capitalism. It is noteworthy that some of

39. My argument here has been influenced by George Steinmetz's work on the epistemic effects of the transition from Fordism to post-Fordism, effects discernable in the targets and discourses of social movements as well as in academic discourses (1994, 2004, forthcoming; Steinmetz and Chae 2002). On this approach to social movements, see also Hirsch (1983) and Mayer and Roth (1995).

these intellectual movements—microeconomics, rational choice, and
social network methodology—are highly mathematical and positivistic in
character and lack any elective affinity with the political left. Recent transformations in social and economic relations have had major effects on both
sides of the positivist/antipositivist epistemological divide.[40]

In any case, I am convinced that I and my fellow social historians were,
when making our various cultural turns, significantly influenced in our
thinking by the subtle yet pervasive changes that were wrought in our lives
by the emergence of new forms of capitalist social relations. I believe that
our conscious model of the social order during the time that we undertook
our cultural turns was the collapsing Fordist order, not the newly emerging order of globalized flexible accumulation. As 1960s rebels, we had
thought of ourselves as rising up against the interlocking and claustro-
phobic system of social determinations that dominated contemporary
corporate America–a vision that was embodied most famously in Herbert
Marcuse's *One Dimensional Man* (1964). Most of us would probably have
agreed with Jürgen Habermas that in contemporary society the possibility of human freedom was progressively threatened by an "escalating scale
of continually expanded technical control over nature and a continually
refined administration of human beings and their relations to each other
by means of social organization" (Habermas 1973, 254). During the 1960s,
both as political radicals and as participants in the counterculture, we enthusiastically attempted to deny, by our own willful actions, some of the
oppressive determinisms of the corporate social order. And when, a few
years or a decade later, we revolted against the positivist research strategies
of social history and undertook studies of the cultural construction of the
social world, I think we obscurely felt ourselves to be freeing historical
scholarship (and, vicariously, freeing ourselves) from a mute social and
economic determinism that was incapable of recognizing human creativity. I can testify that it certainly felt liberating.

But in retrospect our efforts seem to have been politically out of phase
with socioeconomic realities. Our attack on the latent Fordism of social
history was launched only at the time when the Fordist system of social
regulation was itself entering into a deep and fatal crisis. The intensity and
radicalism of this attack was heightened by a cresting wave of academic
feminism, based on a political movement that remained vital long after the
other 1960s movements had subsided, and that had its own epistemic

40. I owe this point to the comments of Moishe Postone on an earlier version of this chapter.

scores to settle with determinist thinking. Thus, cultural historians were kicking down the door of Fordist social determinisms at the moment when such determinisms—Habermas's systematic "administration of human beings and their relations to each other by means of social organization"—were collapsing. In the far more anarchic social world that was emerging, relations between human beings were increasingly determined by market forces rather than by systematic administration; social organization of the Fordist sort was being restructured into networks of entrepreneurial actors; and economic production—given the growing significance of design, advertising, and the entertainment industry—itself was increasingly becoming a play of signifiers (although decidedly not a free play). Thus the explicit or latent oppositional politico-cultural project of the former 1960s intellectuals who undertook the cultural turn was not entirely appropriate to the context in which it was occurring.

There is, I think, nothing shameful about this admission. It was, after all, not until the late 1970s and the 1980s that even scholars who studied political economy began to argue that the economic troubles since 1973 betokened a major reshaping of capitalism rather than simply another iteration of the business cycle.[41] Such global economic restructurings take place piecemeal and are difficult to grasp until the pieces have begun to articulate into a system of some sort. It is only to be expected that those of us who were not experts on contemporary political economy would continue to carry the old models around in our heads for some time. I believe I first began to realize that the very structure of the world economy might be undergoing radical transformations when I participated in discussions with John Urry and Bob Jessop in Ann Arbor in the late 1980s. Nor were the old models a bar to serious and politically responsible intellectual work. The late 1970s and the 1980s was the era of feminism's most intellectually far-reaching breakthroughs and of the widespread reception of Foucault's thought among historians. And Jürgen Habermas erected an entire—and justly influential—philosophical project during these same years based precisely on the Fordist assumption that the "lifeworld" was increasingly being colonized by the "system" (Habermas 1984). Besides, Fordist social science was still alive and well in the 1970s and the early 1980s even if the Fordist system of economic regulation was collapsing.[42]

41. See Aglietta (1979), Boyer (1986), Gordon, Edwards, and Reich (1982), Jessop et al. (1988), Lash and Urry (1987), Lepietz (1987), Piore and Sabel (1984).
42. George Steinmetz (forthcoming) has argued that Fordist sociology is still alive and well, if less dominating and self-confident than it once was.

The critique of abstracted empiricism and the development of interpretive methods were intellectually and politically necessary and remain so today.

I want to make it absolutely clear that I remain a determined advocate of the cultural turn. But at the same time, I think it is essential to recognize that the cultural turn was also fueled, in ways we were essentially unaware of, by a secret affinity with an emergent logic of capitalist development. Cultural history's tendency to celebrate the plasticity of all social forms made good political sense as a critique of Fordist social determinisms, but its critical force in the context of a capitalist regime of flexible accumulation is far less evident. Indeed, such a celebration indicates an unacknowledged and troubling complicity between the cultural turn and the emergence of contemporary flexible forms of capitalism. Cultural history's lack of interest in, indeed effective denial of, socioeconomic determinations seems to me potentially disabling in an era when such determinations are so evidently at work in the world, including, it would appear, in our own conceptualizations of historical process. Critical awareness of the potential complicities between contemporary forms of capitalism and a purely cultural history seems to me an essential condition of clearheaded and efficacious epistemological, methodological, and practical work in historical studies today.

THE BRITISH AND FRENCH CASES

Although I have remarked that both social history and the cultural history that has grown up to challenge it have been international phenomena, I have thus far focused my discussion of the political unconscious of cultural history entirely on the American case. But developments I have proposed as a crucial context of the cultural turn in American historical studies—the replacement of Fordist forms of macroeconomic and macrosocial regulation by a new regime of "flexible accumulation"—are global rather than strictly American phenomena. This might be taken to imply that there should be important similarities between historiographical developments in the United States and elsewhere in the past thirty years. I shall attempt to show that there were indeed significant parallels in the British and French cases, in spite of important national differences in the timing, politics, and particular emphases of the cultural turns.

The parallels between Britain and the United States have been strong, in historical thinking, politics, and political economy alike. The similarities in their recent political and political-economic histories are particularly obvious. Margaret Thatcher and Ronald Reagan came to power only a year apart—Thatcher in 1979 and Reagan in 1980. Both were jingoistic nationalists and economic neoliberals. They attacked labor unions and the welfare state, undertook privatization of previously public functions, and engaged in a massive campaign of economic "deregulation." They blithely ignored the plight of the traditional industrial heartlands of their countries: the American "rust belt" and the English industrial North, areas that were, not coincidentally, strongholds of the American Democratic and English Labour parties. Instead, their economic policies tilted toward the American "sun belt" and the English South-East, regions already more receptive to the political right. Their "deregulation" policies encouraged the dominance of finance over industrial production. In both Britain and the United States, labor unions' power and membership declined precipitously, and welfare benefits, which had previously tended to expand under Conservatives and Republicans almost as much as under Labor and Democrats, were systematically whittled away. In both countries, the regimes tirelessly repeated the pieties of neoliberalism—the importance of entrepreneurship, risk-taking, self-reliance, and free trade; the necessity of cutting costs to increase international competitiveness; the moral and economic dangers of welfare; the need for strong "financial incentives" to encourage capitalists to invest and innovate; the economic imperative of cutting taxes, especially of those in the top income brackets.

Reagan and Thatcher, in other words, did everything they could to open up their countries to globalization and flexible accumulation. The cumulative effects—economic, social-structural, and ideological—were powerful and enduring. In the course of the 1980s, London's City and New York's Wall Street became the twin command posts of globalized finance, and employment in the service sector grew rapidly while employment in manufacturing plummeted. The political consensus moved sharply to the right. Even after both Reagan and Thatcher passed from office, in 1988 and 1990, the opposition parties were unable to gain power until they had accepted much of the Reagan-Thatcher neoliberal package. In this sense, the election of Clinton in 1992 and Blair in 1997 can be seen as marking the consolidation of many of the right's gains, as a recognition of the neoliberal order as essentially unchallengeable. It is significant that it was Clinton, not Reagan, who finally ended "welfare as we know it" in the United States, while his Treasury Secretary Robert Rubin presided benignly over the breakneck globalization and speculative financial bubble of the late 1990s. The remarkable similarities in the economies and politics of Britain and the United States in the 1980s and 1990s meant that their left-leaning social historians were certainly beset by similar challenges and pressures. It should not be surprising that they responded in roughly similar ways.

The generation of British social historians who came of age intellectually and politically in the 1960s were at least as leftist as American social historians of the same vintage, but their affinities tended to be much more explicitly Marxist and they were massively identified with the left wing of the Labour Party. Although they were much indebted to their British Marxist predecessors, members of this second generation of British social historians also established a certain distance from their elders. This can be seen, for example, in the foundation, in 1976, of *History Workshop Journal* and *Social History*, both managed by members of the 1960s generation. It was these journals, rather than *Past and Present*, that served as the second generation's major periodical outlets. Many members of this generation were deeply influenced as well by the influx of Althusserian and neo-Althusserian "structural" Marxism in the later 1970s, a theoretical enthusiasm certainly not shared by the founding generation of British Marxist historians, whose consistently humanist Marxism eschewed all forms of theoretical rigorism. This difference spawned a sharp polemic between the structural Marxists and Thompson, whose ferocious *The Poverty of Theory* (1978) was aimed precisely at this tendency.[43] From the perspective of the 1970s, British social history seemed both more theoretically combative and more solidly leftist than its American counterparts.

Yet by the early 1980s, the historiographical and theoretical winds in Britain seem to have shifted toward cultural history, just as they were doing in the United States. A useful marker of the shift is the publication in 1983 of Gareth Stedman Jones's long essay "Rethinking Chartism" in a volume significantly entitled *Languages of Class*. In this essay Stedman Jones, whose earlier work had been impeccably Marxist and materialist, argued with considerable polemical fire that the political consciousness of the Chartists was determined far more by the linguistic tropes of preexisting oppositional discourse than by any supposed imperatives of class. The vector of change toward cultural history was nicely registered in the pages of *History Workshop Journal*, as was the growing importance of feminism, which had a definite affinity with cultural history in Britain as in the United States. As early as 1980 (no. 10) there was an editorial urging attention to the issue of "Language and History." In 1982 (no. 13) the journal's subtitle was changed from "A Journal of Socialist Historians" to "A Journal of So-

43. For polemical critiques of Thompson, see Johnson (1978) and Anderson (1980).

cialist and Feminist Historians." In the following issue Jeffrey Weeks, a pioneer in gay history, published an essay entitled "Foucault for Historians"
(1982). This was followed in 1983 (no. 15) by an editorial on "Culture and
Gender." Ever since the early 1980s, *History Workshop Journal* has been a
major forum for studies in cultural and feminist history, and for debates
about the relationships of these new historical trends to social history.

Although the journal has also retained a strong commitment to social
history, the overall drift of topics and opinions in its pages has been strongly
in the direction of cultural history. One might cite an editorial on "Sex and
Gender" in 1996 (no. 41) which stated that "sex is at once both an imaginary
object and a material reality," but that its "disparate contents—composed of
desires and fears, sources of status and reward, and of identity and meaning—have no necessary or essential unity. Their outline and apparent coherence are, rather, the products of culture" (v). During the 1990s, two
prominent members of the journal's editorial collective published articles
assessing cultural history and giving their opinions about the correct ways
forward—Raphael Samuel in his two-part article "Reading the Signs" in
1991–92 (Samuel 1991, 1992) and Gareth Stedman Jones in "The Determinist Fix: Some Obstacles to the Further Development of the Linguistic
Approach to History in the 1990s" (Stedman Jones 1996). There were also
"features"—the journal's term for a set of related articles on a special
theme—on "Language and History" in 1989 (no. 27); on "Women's History" (no. 35) and "Colonial and Post-Colonial History" (no. 36) in 1993; on
"Culture and Politics of Postwar Consumption" in 1994 (no. 38); on "Spatial History: Rethinking the Idea of Place" in 1995 (no. 39); on "Colonial Encounters" in 1996 (no. 42); on "Identities" and on "Histories" in 1997 (no. 43);
on "Psychoanalysis and History" in 1998 (no. 45); on "Narratives, Memo-
ries" in 1999 (no. 47); on "Dreams" in 1999 and 2000 (nos. 48 and 49); and
on "Public Faces and Public Spaces" in 2001 (no. 51). Meanwhile, the editorial collective decided in 1995 (no. 39) to drop the subtitle "A Journal of
Socialist and Feminist Historians," explaining that "the political conditions
in which we work have changed almost out of recognition in the fourteen
years since we last amended our mast-head." There were now writers and
editors, the editorial explained, "who—whatever their feelings of attachment to the ideas of socialism and feminism—prefer to define themselves
by something else. . . . It would possible to extend our subtitle to include
some of the newer radicalisms on which we are drawing—gay and lesbian
history, for instance, postcolonial history or the politics of the environment.
We think it better for us to sail under our own colors, dispensing with any

attempt to find a shorthand expression for what we stand for" (iii). This multiplication of historians' radical identities recapitulates almost perfectly developments on the other side of the Atlantic.

Social History, the chief competitor of *History Workshop Journal*, was about a decade later and somewhat more hesitant in its embrace of cultural history. Its first entry into debates about the linguistic turn was a brief note in 1989 by Thomas Patterson entitled "Post-structuralism, Post-modernism: Implications for Historians" (1989). In 1991 there was a review essay by David Mayfield on "Language and Social History" and in 1992 Mayfield and Susan Thorne published a polemic against Gareth Stedman Jones's *Languages of Class*. This essay led to a veritable donnybrook, featuring Patrick Joyce, repeatedly (1993, 1995, 1996), Mayfield and Thorne (1993), Jon Lawrence and Miles Taylor (1993), James Vernon (1994), Neville Kirk (1994), and Geoff Eley and Keith Nield (1995). But meanwhile, *Social History* also began to publish programmatic articles on cultural history that were not involved in the mutual bloodletting set off by Mayfield and Thorne: Anthony Easthope's "Romancing the Stone: History Writing and Rhetoric" (1993); Carolyn Steedman's "Bimbos from Hell" (1994); Miguel Cabrera's "Linguistic Approach or Return to Subjectivism? In Search of an Alternative to Social History" (1999); James Epstein's "Spatial Practices/ Democratic Vistas" (1999); and Antoinette Burton's "Thinking Beyond Boundaries: Empire, Feminism and the Domains of History" (2001). *Social History*, true to its title, registered a certain resistance to the rise of cultural history, but as the new millennium dawned, it seemed to have made its peace with the new trends.[44] Indeed, Raphael Samuel's remark about *History Workshop Journal* in 1991 would have been equally apt as a description of *Social History* in the late 1990s: "The labour process, a dominating con-

44. My guess is that *HWJ* registered the trend toward cultural history more quickly than *Social History* because it was edited by a sizeable collective that from the outset included a number of women (four of ten in 1976, seven of seventeen in 1986, seven of nineteen in 1996, and nine of twenty-one in 2002), whereas *Social History* has had the same two editors, Janet Blackman and Keith Nield, from the beginning. The *HWJ* editorial collective clearly engaged in regular discussions and arguments about the contents and intellectual directions of the journal, which meant that new topics and perspectives were aired frequently. And the presence of a substantial number of women in the collective—quite a remarkable fact in 1976—meant that feminism, which articulated the most radical challenges to social history's orthodoxy in the 1980s, was amply represented. Editorial decisions at *Social History*, edited by only two people, were not subject to the same kind of freewheeling, ever-renewed debate. And although one of *Social History*'s editors was a woman, its editorial board had a proportionally smaller female contingent than did *HWJ*'s collective, and one that did not rise over time—four of fifteen in 1976, three of eighteen in 1986, three of fourteen in 1996, and three of fifteen in 2003.

cern in early issues of *HWJ* . . . has all but disappeared from our pages, while issues of representation and the politics of identity—body politics in particular—have increasingly come to the fore" (Samuel 1991, 97).

Historiographical developments in Britain were not identical to those in the United States. The turn to cultural history seems to have begun about a half-decade later and the resistance put up by social historians was more intense. It is my sense that "social history" remains a stronger identity among historians in the Britain than in the United States, even among those working on questions of culture and identity formation. Class, which has virtually ceased to be a major theme in American historical studies, remains much more prominent in Britain. It has long seemed to me that class has the same sort of enduring cultural prominence in daily life and politics in Britain that race has in the United States; even eighteen years of Thatcherism and the collapse of the power of the British trade unions have not managed to take problems of class off the agendas of politicians or historians. But in spite of these differences, it is the parallels that are most striking. Political, economic, and social changes strikingly similar to those in the United States have accompanied strikingly similar changes in historiographies. This makes it at least strongly plausible that the story I have told about the American case might have some validity for Britain as well.

Developments in France—historiographical, political, and economic—have differed substantially from those in the United States and Britain. Ever since the immediate postwar period, French intellectuals and academics had been predominantly on the left; Marxist sympathies were common, and the French Communist Party made up a solid if always minority block in the French electorate. The leftist uprisings of May and June 1968 were probably the most dramatic political upheaval of the 1960s in any of the Western democratic countries, and agitation by a swarm of leftist *groupuscules* (grouplets)—most of them Trotskyist, anarchist, or Maoist—continued sporadically for the next few years. But by the later 1970s, the left was in retreat. The revolutionary fervor of 1968 burned itself out, leaving little institutional trace behind. The Communists, who had been only reluctant participants in the movements of 1968, were further tarnished by their lingering Stalinism in an era when reformist "Eurocommunism" seemed to be on the agenda elsewhere in Europe. Moreover, the publication of Aleksandr Solzhenitsyn's *The Gulag Archipelago* touched off a wave of revulsion against both Communism and Marxism among French intellectuals that was unmatched elsewhere in Europe.

This collapse of the moral fortunes of Marxism in France provided an important context for the widespread reception of Jean-François Lyotard's announcement of the crisis of "grand narrative" or "metanarrative" in philosophy ([1979] 1984).

But electoral politics took a very different turn than they did in the United States and Britain. In 1981 François Mitterand, a Socialist, was elected president of France and there was a brief efflorescence of leftist hopes. However, it became clear within a few years that the French Socialists were heavily constrained by world economic forces and would be unable to accomplish much of their program. In the late 1970s and the 1980s, France experienced significant de-industrialization and a sharp fall in union membership; it could not help being subject to economic globalization and to the financialization of its economy. Nevertheless, Mitterand's possession of the presidency until 1995 meant that neoliberalism advanced far more hesitantly in France than in the United States and Britain, and that it never attained the ideological high ground it achieved under Reagan and Thatcher. The French welfare state, for example, remained more or less intact, and has remained so even under Jacques Chirac, Mitterand's Gaullist successor. Moreover, the most striking economic reforms in France were increased integration into the European Union; although there was a significant amount of deregulation and freeing of restraints on trade, these were carried out as much by initiatives coming from "Brussels" as by the French state. Full-scale Fordism disappeared in France, as it did elsewhere during the 1970s; indeed, it was the French "regulationist" school of economists who initially introduced the notion of Fordism and its supercession (Aglietta 1979; Boyer 1986; Lepietz 1987). But the continued influence of center-left politics in France and its full-scale participation in the European Union meant that the impact of Fordism's decline was both moderated in fact and made less ideologically prominent than in the United States and Britain.

Against this political and economic background, historiographical development in France had different contents and different rhythms than in the United States and Britain. The French were actually pioneers in the development of cultural history, in part because cultural history overlapped considerably with the "history of mentalities" that had been part of the Annales' repertoire ever since the time of Marc Bloch and Lucien Febvre (Burguière 1983). The history of *mentalités* was a form of cultural history, but *mentalités* implied attitudes and customs that were essentially unconscious, that tended to be highly resistant to change, and that were regarded as intimately attached to highly durable social structures. "Mentalité" therefore had a different set of connotations than "culture" came to have in the course of the 1970s. Cultural history has been an area of growth in France since the publication, in 1975, of Emmanuel Le Roy Ladurie's *Montaillou*, an "ethnographic" study of a Cathar village in the Pyrenees in the Middle Ages that became a runaway bestseller. That Le Roy Ladurie had previously been an advocate and practitioner of quantitative history and was widely regarded as the intellectual leader of the Annales' third generation made his cultural turn particularly influential. But other important works of cultural history were already well into gestation by the time *Montaillou* was published (Ozouf 1976; Furet 1978, 1981; Agulhon 1979) and the momentum of cultural history has been sustained right through the 1980s and into the 1990s.[45]

The turn to cultural history, however, far from provoking criticism from social historians of the Annales school, seems to have been accepted more or less without incident. This may in part have been because cultural history in France seems to have lacked altogether the political charge it had in the United States and Britain. Its pioneers were not the 1960s generation, but historians like Le Roy Ladurie, Agulhon, Furet, and Ozouf, who came of age politically in the 1940s and 1950s under the influence of the Communist Party. Indeed, one might speculate that historical works devoting such loving attention to what they would once have disdained as the "superstructure" marked a completion of their break from Communism. Moreover, cultural history in France lacked the familiar radicalizing link with feminism; indeed, feminism has failed to establish much of a foothold at all in the French historical profession — or, indeed, in French intellectual life in general. Nor has post-structuralism — in spite of its French origins — garnered many followers among historians in France. Even Roger Chartier, one of the most innovative and theoretically wide-ranging of the French cultural historians, is extremely critical of what he calls "the American linguistic turn" (1997, 4).[46] In any case, the link between political radicalism and cultural history that was so palpable among American and British historians seems to have been entirely absent in the French case. Probably the most celebrated products of French cultural history in the 1980s were those consolidating François Furet's conservative interpreta-

45. Among the most notable developments of the 1980s and 1990s have been Alain Corbin's work on the cultural history of the human sensorium (1982, 1994, 1995) and Roger Chartier's studies of reading practices in Early Modern France (1987, 1988, 1995).

46. For an explication and critique of Chartier's position see Sewell (1998).

tion of the political culture of the French Revolution (e.g., Furet and Ozouf 1988; Furet 1988) and Pierre Nora's *Les lieux de mémoire*, a gigantic and rather incoherent yet bestselling three-volume, seven-part collaborative project on French collective memory, whose only discernible valence, political or otherwise, is one of generalized nostalgia (Nora 1984–92, 1996–98).

The sense of nostalgia captured by Nora and his collaborators is worth pausing over. Nora claims in his introduction that the French have recently lost what was once a palpable identification with their history. "A world that once contained our ancestors has become a world in which our relation to what made us is merely contingent. Totemic history has become critical history. . . . We no longer celebrate the nation, but we study the nation's celebrations" (Nora 1996, 1:7). This loss of identification with the past is a consequence, Nora intimated, of a lack of confidence in the future. "Just as the future—once a visible, predictable, manipulable, well-marked extension of the present—has come to seem invisible, so have we gone from the idea of a visible past to one of an invisible past. . . . Given to us as radically other, the past is a world from which we are fundamentally cut off." Yet, paradoxically, "distance requires rapprochement to counteract its effects and give it emotional resonance. Never have we longed more for the feel of mud on our boots, for the terror that the devil inspired in the year 1000, or for the stench of an eighteenth-century city" (12). It was precisely this nostalgic sense of connection with an irretrievably lost past that Nora and his dozens of collaborators in *Les lieux de mémoire* offered to their apparently insatiable French readers. Nor is this the only instance of cultural history in France catering to a palpable sense of nostalgia. From Emmanuel Le Roy Ladurie's romantic identification with the free life of Pyrenean shepherds in *Montaillou* (1975) to Alain Corbin's evocation of nineteenth-century village church bells in *Les cloches de la terre* (1995), French readers have had plenty of opportunities to imagine the feel of French mud clinging to their boots.

Nostalgia is never a politically neutral emotion. Neither Nora, Le Roy Ladurie, nor Corbin are nostalgic conservatives in the usual sense; my guess would be that all three vote Socialist rather than Gaullist. Indeed, the nostalgia in *Les lieux de mémoire* is above all for the nineteenth- and twentieth-century nationalist republican project, one that believed in progress, sacralized the French Revolution, and trusted the rationality and progressive thrust of the centralized French state. Even though the long presidency of François Mitterrand helped to shelter France from some of the most wrenching effects of globalization, neoliberalism, and flexible accumulation, the worldwide political and economic restructuring that began in 1973 has had important effects in France too. Indeed, in some respects the effects there have been particularly psychologically devastating. In America the personal pain of economic restructuring is compensated for by global economic and political dominance. The "new world order" may impose all sorts of discomforts on Americans, but its economic, political, and military affairs are coordinated above all from Wall Street and Washington, and Americans, whether on the left or on the right, have the sense that they are living at the center of contemporary history. And the British, although clearly subordinated to the Americans, have managed to use their command of the world's leading language of business and politics, the residue of international connections that remained from their own period of imperial glory, and the financial power and knowhow of London's City to play a role almost equal to the Americans in the management of the world's financial system.

For the French, psychological compensations are harder to find. They speak the previous international language, and can be excused for feeling resentful about the switch to English. The French Republic, which still seemed potentially in danger as late as 1968, now seems utterly secure, and struggles on its behalf, which had defined the French left ever since 1792, have now been firmly consigned to history. In this sense, François Furet was right to pronounce, in 1978, that "the French Revolution is over" (1978, 1981, esp. 1–17). Moreover, it has been as much the remote European bureaucracy in Brussels as the French state that determines French responses to the challenges of economic globalization and flexible accumulation. The state—long regarded as the prime mover of French social life—has increasingly been reduced to the role of carrying out the local management of decisions taken by the European Union.[47] In short, in this most insistently and consistently political of all Western countries, politics, since the 1970s, has gradually been drained of drama and content. It is not hard to see why the French, including French historians, are increasingly reduced to nostalgia—for the good old days of intense political struggle and for the feel of mud on the boots. As Jacques Revel has pointed out, what the French public now wants from history is "no longer lessons, precedents, or ways of understanding the present but, rather, a refuge against the uncer-

47. Germany, the other former European great power, had its defining historical trauma in World War II. I think it is fair to say that simply achieving a "normal" quiet democratic regime, in which the biggest issues are settled in Washington or Brussels, feels much more satisfactory to Germans than it does to the French.

tainties of the moment." History, he says, has become "an exotic realm, a retrospective utopia" (1995, 34). Only a renewed political project, with a renewed source of political critique, is likely to change this situation. But the *Annales*, which from the beginning has maintained the strictest political neutrality, may not be the obvious venue for the development of a politically relevant historical project.

This is not to say that French historians have been entirely spared the intellectual redefinitions and struggles that have characterized recent American and British historical discourse. Although the *Annales* has lacked the polemics between social and cultural history that have taken place in English-language journals, French historians have also found themselves in an epistemological and historiographical crisis. The key provocation seems to have come from François Dosse's *L'histoire en miettes*, a book published in 1987 that was highly critical of the Annales school, especially for ignoring politics and political history. The title, which means "history in crumbs" or "the crumbling of history," implied that the Annales school has lost all cohesion and sense of direction.[48] In 1988, the editors of the *Annales* responded (in typical French academic fashion, without naming Dosse or his book) that it was true that the current social science paradigms—they mention Marxism, structuralism, and quantification—"are losing their structuring capacity" and that "multiform developments in research . . . render unacceptable the implicit consensus which assumed the unity of the social by identifying it with the real" (Les Annales 1989, 291). While denying that history was in crisis, and characterizing the recent denunciation of the *Annales* as "lazy," the editors admitted that history was in the midst of what they delicately termed a "critical turn," and announced that a special issue of the journal would soon be published to begin an assessment of the state of things (192–93).

When the special issue appeared the next year, the editors, under the title "History and Social Sciences: Let Us Attempt the Experiment," called for a thorough rethinking of the assumptions and categories of historical research. They argued strenuously that work in the Annales tradition had been seriously marred by the reification of social categories. "Social objects," they insisted, "are not things endowed with properties, but ensembles of changing interrelations, within configurations in constant adaptation" (Les Annales 1989, 1319). Rather than writing the history of pre-given

48. The English translation, however, was misleadingly entitled *New History in France: The Triumph of the Annales*, leaving out any hint of the book's critical agenda (Dosse 1994).

social categories, they argued that historians should be writing the history of the emergence and change of the categories: "The processes by which actors redefine continually the organization of the social, by means of both what they think they are doing and what they are unaware they are doing—it is these processes that form the very object of history" (1320).

Such was also the main theme of *Les formes de l'expérience: Une autre histoire sociale.* (Forms of Experience: A Different Social History). This collection of methodological essays, most of them written by study directors at the École des Hautes Études, was edited by Bernard Lepetit, the editor-in-chief *(sécretaire de la rédaction)* of the *Annales* (Lepetit 1995a). It was clearly intended as a critique of the Annales heritage and an elaboration of a new collective historiographical position.[49] Although Lepetit and his collaborators embraced the designation "social history," he insisted that "society" must be seen not as an ontological reality but merely as "a category of social practice." "Social identities or social bonds," as he puts it, "have no nature, only usages" (Lepetit 1995b, 13). Lepetit proposed that a "new coherence" of the proposed Annales program be built around the notion of "accord" (16). This concept was borrowed from the work of the French sociologists Luc Boltanski and Laurent Thévenot, whose action-centered sociology assumes that individuals are competent participants in "multiple worlds" with varying and sometimes contradictory normative orders. They see social order as being produced by actors, who, drawing on their multiple competences, establish "accords" in the course of their interactions with other actors. What sociologists have typically thought of as "social structures" or "institutions" are redefined by Boltanski and Thévenot as "accords" or, alternatively "conventions"—that is, as contingent outcomes of ongoing strategic interactions (1987, 1990). History, under this new sociological dispensation, should become the history of the formation, mutation, and disappearance of such accords or conventions.

In addition to embracing the action sociology of Boltanski and Thévenot, the Annales historians who are attempting to rethink their discipline have shown a keen interest in microhistory. Microhistory as a self-conscious historiographical movement is an Italian invention. The best-known work in the genre is probably Carlo Ginzburg's *The Cheese and the Worms,* a study of the cosmology of a heretical sixteenth-century miller

---

49. This is made clear in Lepetit's introduction (1995b). Lepetit, who seems to have been the leading spirit in this burst of epistemological reexamination, met an untimely death in a traffic accident shortly after the publication of this book.

(1980). But, as Edoardo Grendi, another prominent Italian microhistorian, argues, the movement is quite diverse in its intellectual styles and its epistemic objects (1996). Ginzburg, he points out, is mainly interested in micro-reconstructions of cultural relations (see also Ginzburg 1983), while others, including Giovanni Levi (1988), are more interested in micro-reconstructions of social relations. Giovanni Levi points out that micro-history arose within the Italian left in the 1970s and 1980s, a period of "crisis for the prevailing optimistic belief that the world would be rapidly and radically transformed along revolutionary lines" (Levi 1991, 94). The microhistorians, according to Levi, turned away from the "great Marxist or functionalist systems" by reducing the scale of their observation of historical processes so as to obtain "a more realistic description of human behavior." They saw social action as "the result of an individual's constant negotiation, manipulation, choices and decisions in the face of a normative reality which, though pervasive, nevertheless offers many possibilities for personal interpretations and freedoms" (95). It was only by excavating very local histories and recounting them in exquisite detail that this limited but real human social freedom could be demonstrated, or, for that matter, that the true nature of social constraints could be understood. Although micro-history has been most fully developed in Italy, the fascination for reduction of scale and elaboration of very local historical detail has been an international phenomenon during the era of the cultural turn, with notable examples in France, the United States, England, and Germany alike.[50]

An example of the Annales historians' engagement with microhistory was a seminar on "microhistory and the microsocial," which brought together historians and anthropologists at the École des Hautes Études en Sciences Sociales in the early 1990s, and which gave rise to a book entitled *Jeux d'échelles: La micro-analyse à l'expérience* (Scales in Play: An Experiment in Micro-analysis) (Revel 1996a). The significance of this effort is underlined by the fact that it was edited by Jacques Revel—editor-in-chief of the *Annales* from 1975 to 1980, and a long-time member of its editorial committee, who in 1996 was president of the EHESS—and also contains a contribution by Bernard Lepetit, then the *Annales* editor-in-chief. The book's chapters consist of papers initially presented at the seminar and revised after extended discussion, together with contributions by the Italian microhistorians Giovanni Levi and Edoardo Grendi; it is therefore very much a

---

50. See Le Roy Ladurie (1975), Farge (1986), Darnton (1983), Davis (1983), Sabean (1984), Steedman (1986), Lüdtke (1995).

collective product.[51] Microhistory, it seems clear, fits perfectly the Annales historians' current concern—obsession, almost—with dereification of categories. As Revel puts it in his introduction, the "primary merit" of microanalysis is that it "helps us to grasp better the entanglement of social logics—and also to resist the temptation to reify actions and relations and the categories that enable us to think them" (Revel 1996b, 13). The hope is that by returning to the smallest social units and studying them in detail, it will be possible to grasp the logic of social processes in general. "The wager of microsocial analysis—its experimental choice, if you wish—is that the most elementary experience, that of the small group, even the individual, is the most clarifying—because it is the most complex and because it is inscribed in the largest number of different contexts" (Revel 1996c, 30). Revel holds out the possibility that microhistory may, paradoxically, be the best way to understand even the most far-flung and large-scale processes. Micro history assumes "that each historical actor participates, directly or indirectly, in processes—and hence is inscribed in contexts—of variable dimensions and levels, from the most local to the most global. What the experience of an individual, a group, or a space allows us to grasp is a particular modulation of history as a whole" (26). As Revel sees it, at least, an interest in microhistory does not necessarily imply a retreat from the Annales' long-standing goal of understanding big social processes. It might, rather, be a case of what the French call reculer pour mieux sauter—stepping back to take a better leap forward. But if Revel's formulation indicates a continued interest in global as well as local practices, it is not immediately clear precisely how microhistory will enable us to grasp large-scale or global processes—such as the dynamics of capitalist development or international military rivalries.

Although Revel's version of a redefined Annales history retains the school's ambitions to a global and a total history—a history that embraces macro- as well as microprocesses and attempts to integrate them into a holistic account—nothing I have seen in the Annales' recent historiographical debates indicates how such ambitions might actually be carried out. My own impression is that the current insistence on beginning with microprocesses, whether in the form of conventions arising from the interaction of Boltanski and Thévenot's competent actors or Italian-style

---

51. It is interesting that three of the five historians who participated in the seminar (Simone Cerutti, Maurizio Gribaudi, and Sabina Loriga) were Italians who teach at the EHESS. The others were Revel and Lepetit.

microhistory, leaves the dynamics of large-scale social processes effectively
out of reach. Here I would concur with the judgment of Gareth Stedman
Jones, in his astute review of *Les formes de l'expérience:*

> The danger of a view of history that not only rejects the role of the economy
> or other forms of structural determination, but also substitutes for the reg-
> ularities of discourse the creativity of idiolects and the microscopic varieties
> of situational semantics is that the resulting ensemble will be too boneless
> to fulfill the rudimentary requirements of historical explanation. Too great
> an emphasis upon the resources and competence of actors in the face of
> structures, and too insistent a focus upon the freedom offered by their lim-
> inal location between contradictory belief systems, can lead to the disap-
> pearance from view of a whole range of historical phenomena to which this
> voluntaristic approach offers little guidance. (Stedman Jones 2002, 103)

As I see it, what history needs is a means of grasping the ongoing dialectic
between small-scale and large-scale processes. The current thinking at the
Annales seems to have worked out only one half of this necessary dialectic.

It is too early to know whether the Annales school's redefinition of the
object and methods of history will have a major effect on the way historical research is carried out in France. As is often the case in attempts to theorize practices of social research, the new theorization may be primarily
a self-conscious codification and formulation of practices already in use
rather than an effort to blaze a genuinely new trail. But it certainly is clear
that French historians have not escaped the rash of theoretical argumentation and reassessment that has swept through the historical profession
in the United States and Britain. The timing has been later — mainly in the
1990s rather than the 1980s — and the issues have been different as well:
the turn to cultural history seems not to have caused much disquiet, and
Annales historians, even if their work is largely on cultural issues, continue
to identify themselves unproblematically as social historians. Nor have the
French debates carried the political valences so palpable in Britain and
the United States. Yet, despite these differences, the French case seems consonant with much of the interpretation I elaborated in my consideration
of American developments. The rise of a cultural history more attuned to
nostalgia than to identity politics makes sense as a response to the particular French experience of post-Fordism. And the widespread retreat from
grand narrative and reified historical processes, although it took a different form in France than in the British and American cases, is certainly familiar. The turn to Boltanski and Thévenot's sociology of action and to the

techniques of microhistory evince the same distrust of structural thinking, the same desire to reconstruct historical reasoning from the bottom
up, as the American and British cultural turns—or as, in a very different
mode, social network methodology, rational choice analysis, or microeconomics in American sociology, political science, and economics. What
Jacques Revel observed about historians in the late 1970s and the 1980s
seems to hold for thinkers all across the human sciences and on both sides
of the Atlantic: "The doubts that . . . spread through our societies, confronted as they were by forms of crises that they could not comprehend,
nor even, in many cases, describe, has certainly contributed to the diffusion
of a conviction that the project of an overall intelligibility of the social had
to be, at least provisionally, put in brackets" (Revel 1996c, 18). The disar-
ticulation and gradual recomposition of the world political-economic order between the early 1970s and the 1990s seems to have dissolved what
had previously been taken as the axiomatic solidity of social and economic
structures. It has left social scientists, historians included, scrambling to
rebuild their epistemologies, ontologies, and methods of work from the
bottom up.

But as I see it, the rethinking of historical concepts and methods, in all
its national variants, has tended to suffer from a common defect. It has re-
treated from macro-causation in general and from consideration of the dynamics of capitalism in particular—and has done so during the very time
when the dynamics of capitalism have demonstrated a renewed ability to
disrupt profoundly and refigure fundamentally our own social, political,
and cultural lives. More disturbingly, the particular form of the historians'
retreat—their new passion for the small, the local, the elementary, the culturally constructed—appears, for all its intellectual excitement, to share a
certain logic with the processes of deregulation and ever-rising economic
flexibility characteristic of contemporary capitalism. The conclusion I
reached on the basis of my largely autobiographical reflections about the
American case seems to me essentially valid for the British and French cases
as well. To do clearheaded and efficacious work in historical studies today,
we must develop a critical awareness of the potential complicities between
current forms of thought and current forms of capitalist social relations.

TOWARD A RECONSTITUTION OF THE SOCIAL

Precisely what the implications of such a critical awareness might amount
to is, of course, a matter for discussion and debate. I would submit that
American cultural historians need to reconsider the consequences of our

general abandonment of social history. As I have stated above, cultural history in the United States generally displaced social history without much
argument, largely because so many social historians, myself included, had
themselves taken the cultural turn and therefore put up no intellectual
resistance. Yet some of social history's virtues remain as important as ever.
For example, its insistence on examining the experiences of ordinary
people seems highly relevant in the context of sharply rising economic and
political inequality in the contemporary world. Our turn away from the
poor and disadvantaged was overdetermined, a consequence at once of our
growing historiographical preference for rich textual sources and of dis-
appointing political defeats of popular movements we had sympathized
with — for example, first-world labor movements put on the defensive
by the flight of industrial production to the periphery and third-world
peasant movements wiped out by the global marginalization of peasant
agriculture. But shouldn't the continued worsening of inequality in the
present spark our sympathies for and curiosity about the processes of dis-
possession and the experiences of the dispossessed, both in the present
and in the past?

Likewise, social history's claim that quantitative methods were an indispensable addition to the historian's toolkit continues to make sense.
This is true for the familiar reason that quantification gives us important
and unique forms of access to the historical experiences of otherwise un-
documented categories of people. But an ability to manipulate numerical
evidence seems particularly relevant in a moment like the present, when
the world is being rapidly transformed by seemingly anonymous and un-
planned structural shifts that cannot be recognized, let alone explicated,
without recourse to some serious counting. Examples would be the rapid
displacement of manufacturing by "service" industries in contemporary
European and American cities, a change that has transformed the nature
of both "working classes" and "elites," or the astounding rise of trading in
monetary futures, which has made it possible for entire countries, like Indonesia in 1998 or Argentina in 2002, to be plunged into sudden poverty as
a result of currency speculation in the metropoles of world capitalism. The
undeniable value of numerical assessments for grasping such fundamental
processes in the present ought to make us suspect that quantitative methods might be useful for grasping historical transformations in the past as
well.

Finally, social history always insisted that socioeconomic structures and
processes mattered deeply. In the heady 1960s or the confusing and con-

tradictory 1970s, it seemed possible to imagine that the idea of economic determinism had been an illusion. But the last two decades have made it clear that we are in the grip of a powerful reordering of world capitalism and that changes in economic forms and forces have had an immense impact on contemporary life. This certainly doesn't mean that we should return to some crude notion of economic determinism—after all, the worldwide economic transformation itself was crucially shaped by discursive changes in economic and political ideologies and imaginaries. But it certainly should reanimate the question of how both present and past lifeworlds are related to forms of production, exchange, and economic governance. For all these reasons, social history—in some form—seems as essential as ever.

There is reason to think that I am not alone in this opinion; as usual, my own changes of mind seem to be more or less in tune with the thinking of other American historical scholars. Lynn Hunt, who seems to have a peculiar genius for sniffing out changes in the historians' Zeitgeist, recently edited, with Victoria Bonnell, a new stock-taking collection of essays entitled *Beyond the Cultural Turn: New Directions in the Study of Society and Culture*. Published exactly a decade after Hunt's collection on *The New Cultural History*, which celebrated historians' embrace of culture, *Beyond the Cultural Turn* is rather more ambivalent. Bonnell and Hunt point out in their introductory essay that the authors represented in the collection, who "have all been profoundly influenced by the cultural turn," nevertheless "refuse to accept the obliteration of the social that is implied by the most radical forms of culturalism or post-structuralism. The status or meaning of the social may be in question . . . but life without it has proved impossible" (Bonnell and Hunt 1999, 11). A similar shift seems to be signaled by a change in the human sciences' leading buzzword—from "postmodernism" in the late 1980s and early 1990s to "globalization" in the late 1990s and early 2000s. Both "postmodernism" and "globalization" may be impossibly vague terms, and they may often be pointing at more or less the same set of very heterogeneous phenomena. But the shift from a term with basically epistemological meanings to one with substantive historical meanings seems to me another manifestation of a latent desire for a return to more social or socioeconomic interpretations of the contemporary predicament.

But if social history needs to be revived, I don't believe this is possible without substantially reinventing it. Neither I nor others who share my views advocate a return to social history as it was practiced in the 1970s. I have no desire to revive the "new social history's" uncritical objectivism, its

presumptive preference for quantitative data, its default economic determinism, or its blindness to questions of meaning. I continue to believe, as
I did in the 1970s, that the cultural turn is in itself an immensely positive
intellectual development for historical studies. But existing cultural or linguistic models have so far proved inadequate to the intellectual challenges
posed by worldwide capitalist structural transformation. The pressing and
difficult task facing us in the present, as I see it, is to regain a more robust
sense of the social, but to do so precisely on the richer and more supple
epistemological terrain opened up by the cultural turn. In this essay I have
focused on diagnosis, on probing and characterizing our current historiographical condition. The remainder of this book, by demonstrating the
compatibility of structural thinking with an emphasis on culture, contingency, and agency, attempts to respond to this looming historiographical
challenge—by providing a theoretical language transcending the antinomy of social and cultural history.

3

THREE TEMPORALITIES
Toward an Eventful Sociology

Historical approaches have made important strides in American sociology over the last three decades. Through most of the 1960s, sociology in the United States was utterly dominated by research on contemporary America. But the civil rights and antiwar movements made graduate students trained in the 1960s and early 1970s far more interested than their elders in questions of social change. Rather than seeking timeless laws of the operation of American society—which was implicitly equated with society in general—a new generation began to ask how the world's different societies have been transformed under the impact of capitalism and Western domination. The ideas pioneered by such intrepid historical explorers as Barrington Moore (1966), Charles Tilly (1964), and Immanuel Wallerstein (1974a) were consequently taken up by scores of young sociologists in the 1970s and 1980s.[1]

By the early 1980s, historical sociology was recognizable as a major node of growth in the profession. Its prominence has been institutional-

A shorter version of this chapter was published with the same title in *The Historic Turn in the Human Sciences*, ed. Terrence J. McDonald. Copyright © 1996 by the University of Michigan Press; reprinted with the permission of the University of Michigan Press. I would like to thank Nick Dirks, Larry Griffen, and Sherry Ortner for valuable comments on earlier versions of this chapter.

1. My contention that sociology's historic turn had its origin in a particular moment of domestic and world politics is corroborated by the fact that the work of such liberal historical sociologists as Reinhard Bendix (1956, 1964) and Neil Smelser (1959) has had far less influence on the current generation than that of Moore, Tilly, and Wallerstein. For an interesting autobiographical account of the impact of 1960s politics on a young sociologist, see Theda Skocpol (1988–89).

ized by the formation of two historically inclined official sections of the American Sociological Association (ASA): a Comparative Historical Sociology Section, which a sociologist friend aptly characterizes as "left Weberian," and a Political Economy of the World System Section, which is predominately Wallersteinian.[2] Although it is unlikely that historical approaches will ever become dominant in the discipline, their growing prominence has significantly changed the contours of American sociology.

The leading manifestos and programmatic statements of historical sociologists have generally been concerned with methodological issues and above all with comparative method (e.g., Stinchcombe 1978; Skocpol and Somers 1980; Skocpol 1984; Tilly 1984). The title "Comparative Historical Sociology," adopted by the historical sociologists as the label for their ASA section, is emblematic: it places as much emphasis on comparative method as on historical subject matter. In this respect, historical sociologists reveal themselves to be in the mainstream of American sociology. By stressing comparative method, they participate eagerly in the discipline's obsessive concern to justify itself as a science. Comparative method, after all, is the standard alternative to mainstream statistical methods when the number of cases is insufficiently large. This mode of self-presentation has helped to make historical research acceptable to the rest of the profession. Historical sociology, this rhetoric implies, poses no particular theoretical or epistemological threat; it is simply the sociology of the past, carried on by means as close as feasible to the sociology of the present.

It is not hard to see why historical sociologists have been so self-conscious about method. After all, they have virtually always had to make careers in departments where they were surrounded by skeptical positivists vigilantly on guard against humanistic tendencies. The emphasis on methodology has surely helped historical sociology to establish its secure beachhead in the profession. But it has also served to obscure some of the potentially radical implications of sociology's "historic turn" (Calhoun 1996). I believe that historical sociology is now sufficiently secure to risk examining some of these implications in public. In this spirit, I will here attempt to spell out what I see as deep but as yet largely unvoiced challenges that historical sociology poses to the disciplinary mainstream.

2. I owe the "left Weberian" tag to Terry Boswell. At the beginning of its existence, the Comparative Historical Sociology section of the ASA was explicitly Weberian in its orientation. Beginning in 1983, a new group of scholars seized control of the section and pointed it in the direction of macropolitical sociology of the nation-state. It should be noted that some of the remaining sections of the ASA, especially those devoted to political sociology and cultural sociology, include many sociologists who do historical work.

Until recently, few historical sociologists have had much to say about what makes their sociology *historical*. If historical sociology is merely the sociology of the past, it is valuable above all because it increases the available number of data points. Many social processes require a significant period of time to work themselves out. If we investigate such processes only in the present, we not only risk studying incomplete sequences but greatly restrict the number of cases. But is history just a matter of more data points? Doesn't making sociology historical imply introducing ideas of temporality that are radically foreign to normal sociological thinking?[3] I maintain that the answer to this question depends on how temporality is conceptualized. The currently dominant modes of conceptualizing temporality in historical sociology—what I will call "teleological" and "experimental" temporality—minimize the challenge to mainstream sociology. But a third, currently subordinate, conceptualization—what I will call "eventful" temporality—is potentially much more subversive.[4] I will argue that the dominant teleological and experimental concepts of temporality are seriously deficient, indeed actually fallacious, and that historical sociology needs to adopt the much more subversive eventful notion of temporality, which sees the course of history as determined by a succession of largely contingent events.

TELEOLOGICAL TEMPORALITY

Sociology was born under the sign of teleology. The great nineteenth-century founders, for example, Comte, Marx, Durkheim, Spencer, and Tönnies, saw history as the temporal working out of an inherent logic of social development—from religious to metaphysical to scientific eras, from feudalism to capitalism to socialism, from mechanical to organic solidarity, or ever-increasing individuation, or from *Gemeinschaft* to *Gesellschaft*. For these social theorists, history was shaped by transhistorical progressive laws. The direction and meaning of history were a consequence not of the largely contingent events that made up the surface of history but of long-term, anonymous causal forces, of which particular historical events were at best manifestations. The waning of the nineteenth century's virtually

3. Exceptions to sociologists' silence about this issue include Abbott (1988, 1991, 2001), Hall (1984), Aminzade (1992), and Griffin (1992, 1993).

4. The term "eventful" is an Anglicization of the French *événementiel*. The term *histoire événementielle* was used widely by French historians of the Annales school, but it is particularly associated with Fernand Braudel, who contrasted *histoire événementielle* with *histoire structurelle* and *histoire conjoncturelle* (1958, 1966). For Braudel, *histoire événementielle* was largely a term of abuse. My attempt to rehabilitate the term follows Marshall Sahlins (1991). I have, however, anglicized the word differently than has Sahlins, whose *evenemential* seems to me distinctly non-English.

universal faith in progress has gradually resulted in an abandonment of explicit teleology in sociological thought. But weaker forms of teleology are still very much with us.

A teleological explanation is the attribution of the cause of a historical happening neither to the actions and reactions that constitute the happening nor to concrete and specifiable conditions that shape or constrain the actions and reactions but rather to abstract transhistorical processes leading to some future historical state. Events in some historical present, in other words, are actually explained by events in the future. Such explanatory strategies, however fallacious, are surprisingly common in recent sociological writing and are far from rare in the works of social historians. They are implied, for example, by the common practice of labeling political or social movements as backward-looking and forward-looking. "Backward-looking" movements, in normal usage, are those that value some aspect of a given period's life and culture that the analyst, with her or his twenty-twenty hindsight, regards as doomed to the dustbin of history, whereas "forward-looking" movements are those valuing aspects of a period's life and culture that turned out to have a bright future. The simple act of labeling movements in this way contains an implicit teleological explanation of their histories.[5] Likewise, the term *modern* often serves as a label for those processes or agents that are deemed by the analyst to be doing the work of the future in some present, while *traditional* labels those equally current forces in the present that the analyst regards as doing the work of the past. The entire modernization school of social science was based on such a teleological conceptualization of temporality. But the teleological fallacy is also widespread in the work of many historical sociologists who regard their work as arising out of an uncompromising critique of modernization theory. I will try to demonstrate this claim by briefly examining the work of two historical sociologists who were particularly influential in overthrowing the theoretical approaches of the modernization school and

5. Sometimes the judgments embodied in the usage of the backward-/forward-looking dichotomy are moral rather than merely anachronistic, with "forward-looking" meaning that which all "progressives" should favor and "backward-looking" meaning that which they should abhor. Least common is the literal and in my opinion quite acceptable usage that would designate as "backward-looking" only those movements that explicitly pattern themselves on what they regard as a past historical condition and as "forward-looking" those that pattern their actions on an imagined future. The dichotomy has, however, been so spoiled by teleological usages that employing it literally for such supposedly "forward-looking" but actually backward-looking movements as the Renaissance or such supposedly "backward-looking" but actually forward-looking movements as early utopian socialism would merely breed confusion.

replacing them with those of contemporary historical sociology: namely, Immanuel Wallerstein and Charles Tilly.

IMMANUEL WALLERSTEIN AS SOCIAL ASTRONOMER

Wallerstein is by far the clearer case. In his multivolume history of the modern world-system, Wallerstein proves himself no less anxious than other sociologists to find a secure scientific warrant for his knowledge. But because his object of study is vast and singular—the capitalist "world-system"—the usual quantitative and experimental scientific models are hardly appropriate; there are no other units with which the modern world-system could appropriately be compared. Wallerstein discussed this dilemma in the introduction to his first volume. He worried out loud that there was "only one instance" of his "unit of analysis" and that if this were true he might be reduced to merely writing its history. But he "was not interested in writing its history"; he wanted to discover its *laws*:

> Can there be laws about the unique? In a rigorous sense, there of course cannot be. A statement of causality or probability is made in terms of a series of like phenomena or like instances. . . . There had only been one "modern world." Maybe one day there would be discovered to be comparable phenomena on other planets, or additional modern world-systems on this one. But here and now, the reality was clear— only one. (Wallerstein 1974a, 7)

Wallerstein rescued the scientific status of his enterprise by an inspired analogy. If the capitalist world-system is one of a kind, Wallerstein reasoned, its study can be modeled on a fully recognized and powerful natural science that investigates the unique development of a singular system: astronomy, or more precisely, cosmology, that branch of astronomy that studies the physical universe as a whole. "What," Wallerstein asked himself, "do astronomers do?"

> As I understand it, the logic of their arguments involves two separate operations. They use the laws derived from the study of smaller physical entities, the laws of physics, and argue that (with perhaps certain specified exceptions) these laws hold by analogy for the system as a whole. Second, they argue *a posteriori*. If the whole system is to have a given state at time *y*, it most probably had a given state at time *x*. (7)

This analogy with cosmology, I would argue, crucially shaped Wallerstein's intellectual project, although it did so in part by creative misapplication. It suggested a close relationship between part and whole, where

laws found in investigations of local phenomena are also assumed to operate at the level of the whole. This key assumption—that local and global
processes partake of the same causalities—was profoundly enabling. It
provided Wallerstein with a powerful unified perspective, one that authorized him to see all sorts of local events in various times and places as
determined not by the accidents of local conditions but by the dynamics of
the world economy of which they were a part. I believe that it was above
all this unique perspective, this ability to see the dynamic of the whole at
work in the dynamics of the parts, that established Wallerstein's reputation as a great historical sociologist and that attracted an entire school of
followers.

But in applying the astronomers' assumption about the uniformity of
causalities to the world-system, Wallerstein reversed the direction of the
part-whole relationship. In astronomy, the physical principles discovered
in studies of small-scale earthbound matter, whether these be Galileo's
laws of falling bodies or the findings of contemporary particle physics, are
assumed to apply equally to cosmic matter—to the orbits of planets or to
nuclear reactions in stellar cores. Indeed, such laws are assumed to operate
at the level of the universe as a whole: the great cosmological question of
whether the universe will expand indefinitely or eventually collapse in on
itself hinges on calculations of the aggregate gravitational pull of the entire
mass of matter in the cosmos. Astronomy today, as at the time of Newton,
remains an example of reductionist science at its most awesomely successful. In contemporary astronomy, the key to the dynamics of the infinitely
large is found in the dynamics of the infinitely small.

But Wallerstein rejects models, whether derived from behaviorist psychology or microeconomics, that would explain the dynamics of the world-
system by the principles governing its smallest entities—human individuals. Nor does he argue that the dynamics of local communities provide the
key to understanding the development of world society. His point is precisely the opposite: that the fates of local communities are determined not
by local causes but by the operation of global, system-level causes. The key
to understanding the history of Poland or Peru is to recognize their place
in the world-systemic division of labor—as peripheral societies dependent
on the core. But once we have begun to explain spatially and temporally localized events as a consequence of their place in a totality of world evolution, we are perilously close to teleological explanation.

Wallerstein's misapplied astronomical analogy also encouraged teleology in another, more direct, way. He felt authorized by astronomy to argue

a posteriori, to argue back from the recent or current state of the capitalist world-system to its prior state. Most spectacularly, the astronomers project the current velocities of galaxies backward to argue for the existence of a "big bang" at the beginning of time, a primal cosmic event that determined the subsequent character and evolution of the physical universe. Wallerstein the social astronomer devises what in effect is a big bang theory of the origins of capitalism. A European economy already in crisis as a consequence of the disintegration of feudalism was decisively launched on a new and inexorable dynamic by the European geographical expansion known as "the great discoveries." The discoveries, according to Wallerstein, established the key economic, geographical, and political relationships on which the subsequent development of capitalism has been predicated—a spatially differentiated world economy too large to be controlled by any of the competing political units of which it was composed (38).

Once again, Wallerstein's misapplication of the analogy with astronomy has served him both well and badly. I am convinced that the particular economic-geographical-political dynamic identified by Wallerstein is indeed crucial in the development of world capitalism and that it was decisively set in motion by the discoveries. But Wallerstein's vision of all the subsequent development of capitalism as somehow inherent in his initial big bang warps his understanding both of the discoveries and of subsequent developments. His work contains some astute eventful analysis of the political and economic history of Europe in his period, although his rhetoric suppresses the narrative's eventful qualities. His discussions of how marginal and tiny Portugal became the initiator of the voyages of discovery (50–52), of how the Hapsburgs attempted but failed to gain a political hegemony that would encompass the world economy (165–80), or how the Dutch Revolt made possible the development of crucial new commercial and financial institutions in the Netherlands (199–214) are actually full of contingency, unanticipated consequences, and fateful choices. But in Wallerstein's analysis, the contingencies, choices, and consequences are foreordained by the necessity built into the world-system from the moment of its creation. Hidden behind Wallerstein's big bang theory is a far more interesting account of how the crucial but open-ended event of the discoveries initiated a long chain of subsequent open-ended events that eventually and far from inevitably led to the emergence of a capitalist world economy.

What makes the astronomers' a posteriori reasoning scientifically acceptable is the plausibility of the assumption that just as the laws of physics hold true across space they also hold true across time. If the laws of motion, gravity, and high-energy physics can be projected backward in time, then it is possible to deduce the timing and characteristics of the big bang that propelled the universe into its current dynamics or the state of the universe ten minutes after the big bang or a hundred billion years from now. But we know that human beings and the societies they create are far more perverse than physical matter. Humans, unlike planets, galaxies, or subatomic particles, are capable of assessing the structures in which they exist and of acting—with imperfectly predictable consequences—in ways that change them. While there certainly are turning points or crucial events in human history, there cannot be big bangs. To construct historical arguments on an analogy with astronomy results in a teleology in which some crucial past events are misconstrued as a pure origin that contains the entire future of the social system *in potentia* and in which the partially contingent events that occur subsequently are robbed of their efficacy and reduced to the status of markers on the road to the inevitable future.

CHARLES TILLY AND THE MASTER PROCESSES OF HISTORY

Teleology plays a far less obvious role in Tilly's work than in Wallerstein's. Nevertheless, I shall try to demonstrate that two of his most influential contributions—his book on the Vendée rebellion and his work on the history of French collective violence—contain strong doses of teleological temporality.[6] This might seem particularly curious in the case of the *The Vendée*, which focuses on a particular event, the great counterrevolutionary revolt that erupted in western France in 1793. But Tilly's book is not a narrative history of the revolt. In fact, his argument is introduced by a very effective polemic against the sociological naivete of the countless existing narrative histories (1964, 6–13). Whereas these narrative histories spoke about the cause of the revolt by rather cavalierly invoking the presumed motives of the rebels, Tilly insisted on asking properly sociological causal questions. He wanted to know what it was about the social organization of the Vendée region that led to a revolt there. Tilly's principal analytical device was to compare two adjacent areas in western France, the Val-Saumurois, which supported the revolution, and the Mauges, which supported the counterrevolution. The principal sociological concept he used to analyze the difference in the social organization of these two areas was

6. Tilly (1964, 1969, 1972a, 1972b, 1977, 1981, 1986); Tilly, Tilly, and Tilly (1975).

"urbanization," which in Tilly's somewhat expanded usage was "a collective term for a set of changes which generally occur with the appearance and expansion of large-scale coordinated activities in a society" (16). Urbanization hence implied not just the growth of cities but an "increased involvement of the members of rural communities in sets of activities, norms, and social relationships that reach beyond the limits of their own localities" (11–12).

Tilly argued that the crucial difference between the Mauges and the Val-Saumurois was the extent and the recentness of their urbanization. The Val-Saumurois was "thoroughly and evenly urbanized" (57); even its rural inhabitants had long lived in sizeable, agglomerated villages and sold their produce in regional and national markets. This thorough and even urbanization made the Val-Saumurois well adapted to the more rational and centralized bourgeois regime introduced by the revolution. The Mauges, by contrast, was much less urbanized, but it had experienced very rapid urbanization—especially in the form of rural textile manufacturing—in recent decades. This recent but incomplete urbanization made the social organization of the Mauges far less uniform and led to intense confrontations when the revolution shifted power to the urban bourgeoisie and its agents in the countryside.

Tilly's analysis of how the different forms of social organization of these two regions led to different political and social experiences in the revolution is superb. But his sociological interpretation of these differences is marred by a gratuitous introduction of teleological temporality. For Tilly, The Mauges and the Val-Saumurois represent different points on a single developmental continuum, from less to more urbanized. His procedure, as he puts it, is one "of comparing communities at roughly the same point in time *as if* they were at different stages of progression from a common origin" (12). The obvious advantage of this procedure is its generalizability. It means that differences found between two regions are not just a local peculiarity but are comparable to differences in level of urbanization in other places and times. Introducing a single continuum makes it possible to envisage this local study as one contribution to a general scientific sociological account of the effects of urbanization on politics.

The problem is that the difference between the social organization of the Val-Saumurois and that of the Mauges is demonstrably not a matter of different stages in a single master process. The contrasting forms of social organization that Tilly attributes to differences in a progressive development—large nucleated villages surrounded by open fields in the Val-

Saumurois as against more isolated small villages and hamlets scattered over hedged fields in the Mauges—were actually constant and virtually unchanging features of the rural environment. The line dividing the Val-Saumurois from the Mauges was an ancient territorial division between what Marc Bloch characterized as distinct "agrarian civilizations" whose characteristics were already in place by the early Middle Ages (Bloch 1970). Tilly, in short, committed the fallacy of transmuting a fixed socio-geographical difference in social organization into putative stages in the linear development of the abstract master process of urbanization.

Tilly's use of urbanization as a linear teleology did not actually spoil his comparative study of the political effects of regional social structures, but it did misrepresent the book's contribution—by casting its subject as a lo-cal instance of a universal social process. By doing so, it left unvoiced what I regard as the book's most original accomplishment: its acute analysis of how variations in local social structures made possible a smooth transition from old regime to revolutionary government in the Val-Saumurois but enabled the French Revolution to reconfigure and give new meaning to ex-isting social networks and social cleavages in the Mauges, touching off an escalating and unpredictable chain of confrontational events that culmi-nated in a massive and durable shift in collective identities. It hid a mas-terwork of eventful sociology behind a veil of misconstrued universalizing science.

One might object that The Vendée was Tilly's first book and that his mature work avoids these youthful errors. After all, he subsequently aban-doned his overly abstract concept of urbanization, breaking it down into the two more specific notions of state centralization and capitalist devel-opment. But in his long and evolving project on French collective violence, which he took up after finishing The Vendée, he essentially retained that book's teleological fascination with underlying master processes, while abandoning its superb but insufficiently voiced eventful analysis. Charmed by his own universalizing rhetoric, he pursued the notion that acts of po-litical contestation arise from gradual evolutionary changes in large and anonymous social processes rather than the alternative theme that changes in political regimes reconfigure and give new meaning to existing social networks and cleavages, thereby creating new collective identities.

Tilly argued in his various books and articles on collective violence in France that the change in forms of violence over the last three centuries—in brief, a change from "reactive," backward-looking, locally oriented violence to "proactive," forward-looking, and nationally oriented violence—was the consequence of the gradual and inexorable rise of state centralization and

capitalism.[7] Such an argument is not necessarily teleological. Teleology is
not implied, for example, when Tilly argues that changes in the targets and
goals of violent protest arise in part from the particular and changing nature of the state presence in localities. But the argument frequently takes
on a teleological quality, largely because the asserted causes—capitalist
development and state centralization—occur offstage, outside of Tilly's
texts, where they are essentially assumed as ever-present and ever-rising
forces, a kind of eternal yeast.[8] The violent incidents that Tilly describes in
great number thus figure only as consequences of invisible but ever present causes; they are not *events* in the full sense because they are only effects,
never causes, of change. A particularly clear indication that Tilly abandoned eventful analysis in his later work on French collective violence is his
denial that even the historians' megaevent, the French Revolution, significantly transformed the nature of collective violence: in his account, it
merely caused a certain acceleration of already existing trends (Tilly 1977,
1986). Thus, in spite of the inspired eventful analysis contained in *The
Vendée*, the dominant rhetoric of Tilly's work on French collective violence
did not break with a teleological conceptualization of temporality.

THEDA SKOCPOL AND EXPERIMENTAL TEMPORALITY

If Wallerstein and Tilly exemplify the continuing grip of teleological temporality in historical sociology, Theda Skocpol is the leading prophet and
exemplar of experimental temporality. In *States and Social Revolutions*,
Skocpol explicitly embraces the standard "scientific" methodology of mainstream American sociology, extending it to historical studies. "Comparative historical analysis," she asserts,

> is distinctively appropriate for developing explanations of macro-historical
> phenomena of which there are inherently only a few cases. This is in con-
> trast to more plentiful and manipulable kinds of phenomena suitable for
> experimental investigations, and in contrast to other phenomena where
> there are the large numbers of cases required for statistical analyses. Com-
> parative historical analysis is, in fact, the mode of multivariate analysis to
> which one resorts when there are too many variables and not enough cases.
> (Skocpol 1979, 36)

7. Tilly's terminology shifted more than once over the nearly two decades he devoted to this
project, but the underlying categorization of violence has remained essentially constant. For a
fuller discussion, see Sewell (1990a).
8. Conscience dictates that I attribute this felicitous term to Carl Schorske, who applied it to
the ever-rising bourgeoisie in a lecture on European intellectual history which I heard as a graduate student at Berkeley in the 1960s.

Skocpol applies her comparative method to the three great social revolutions of modern times — the French, the Russian, and the Chinese. Her analysis attempts to set up comparative "natural experiments" capable of sorting out the causal factors that explain the occurrence of social revolutions. She explores the histories of the French, Russian, and Chinese revolutions but also of two major political crises that never became revolutions (the Prussian Reform Movement of 1807–14 and the Japanese Meiji Restoration of 1868–73) and of two political revolutions that did not become social revolutions (the English Civil War and Glorious Revolution of 1640–88 and the German Revolution of 1848–50). On the basis of her comparative investigation of these seven cases, Skocpol develops a powerful and sophisticated theory of the causes of social revolutions. She begins by noting that the pre-revolutionary French, Russian, and Chinese states had all fallen behind their rivals in military competition. This gave rise to attempts to catch up by instituting far-reaching administrative, economic, and fiscal reforms. But reforms were resisted in all three states by the dominant landlord class, which had a firm enough foothold in the state to block, slow, or subvert the reforms. The consequence was a deep fiscal and political crisis that was broken only by a revolution. These considerations led Skocpol to posit two conditions for social revolution: the existence of a state that fell behind rival states in military competition and a dominant class of landlords who were sufficiently powerful to block state-initiated reforms. She strengthened this specification of causes by examining the Prussian and Japanese cases. In both cases the states were driven into crisis by failure in military competition, but because the Prussian and Japanese dominant classes had little political leverage against the state, reformers from within the state apparatus managed to revitalize the states without the intervention of political revolution.

But Skocpol also finds another necessary condition for the occurrence of social revolutions. Fiscal crises based on military backwardness and exacerbated by the resistance of recalcitrant landlords may have been enough to touch off political revolutions, but for these to become social revolutions — that is, to bring about a transformation of the country's class structure — something more was required: a massive uprising of the peasant class. Social revolutions, therefore, also required the existence of well-organized and autonomous peasant communities capable of taking advantage of the breakdown of state authority that resulted from political revolution. Once again, Skocpol shows how this condition was present in her three cases but absent in the seventeenth-century English and mid-nineteenth-century German revolutions, which never advanced from political to social revolutions. In short, Skocpol uses a quasi-experimental, inductive method to discover the three factors necessary for social revolutions: (1) military backwardness, (2) politically powerful landlord classes, and (3) autonomous peasant communities. As I understand the argument, these factors are conceptualized in this order: factor one induces a political crisis; the addition of factor two turns the political crisis into a political revolution; and the further addition of factor three turns the political revolution into a social revolution.

The explanation Skocpol develops by considering these seven cases is extremely powerful and, quibbling aside, quite convincing. But the power of her explanation cannot derive, as Skocpol claims, from her application of quasi-experimental inductive method. As Michael Burawoy has pointed out (1989), a careful examination of Skocpol's logic and evidence indicates that her explanation is by no means proven by the "natural experiments" carried out in her book. In fact, her evidence fails in more than one way. First, as Burawoy remarks, the seventeenth-century English and mid-nineteenth-century German cases actually seem to refute the first stage of her causal theory in that they were genuine political revolutions that were not provoked by military failures: the English Revolution of 1640 certainly arose out of a fiscal crisis but not a fiscal crisis that was provoked by military reverses, and the German Revolution of March 1848 was provoked by neither military reverses nor fiscal crisis. Skocpol's comparisons actually demonstrate that far-reaching political revolutions may arise in the absence of both of her first two factors (Burawoy 1989, 767–68).

Second, the array of cases compared by Skocpol does not demonstrate that the full sequence of three factors is necessary to produce a social revolution. To do so, Skocpol would have had to find a case in which military failure and landlord resistance led to political revolution but in which a social revolution failed to develop due to the absence of autonomous peasant communities. But she had no such case: The Meiji Restoration and the Prussian Reform Movement had only the first factor, the English Revolution only the second, and the German Revolution of 1848 none of the three. On the basis of Skocpol's evidence, it remains logically possible that a combination of military backwardness and a powerful landlord class was by itself sufficient to produce a social revolution.

Indeed, Skocpol's analysis of the Chinese Revolution could actually be read as supporting this proposition. There, a social revolution took place in a country where only the first two of Skocpol's conditions were initially present. Skocpol treats the case as confirming her theory. As she tells the story, the peasantry's lack of autonomy from landlords long prevented the political revolution initiated in 1911 from becoming a social revolution. It was only after 1940 that the Chinese Communists organized an autonomous peasantry in the districts they controlled, thereby creating the agrarian striking force necessary to carry through a social revolution (Skocpol 1979, 252–62). But this argument is actually highly ambiguous. One could just as easily say that the long standoff between state and landlords, exacerbated by the Japanese invasion in 1935, created the conditions for a successful social revolution in the areas that the Kuomintang could no longer control. The creation of peasant communities autonomous from landlords was, in this alternative telling, less a precondition for social revolution than a consequence of a locally successful Communist-led social revolution touched off by a collapse of the stalemated state in the wake of military failure.

These two flaws in Skocpol's argument invalidate her claim to having confirmed empirically her theory of social revolutions. She has not shown either that political revolutions are explained by a combination of military reverses and effective landlord resistance to reforms or that autonomous peasant communities are necessary for a political revolution to be transformed into a social revolution. It is true that these flaws are not intrinsic to the comparative method per se. Skocpol is working on such a rare phenomenon that she has been unable to amass an array of cases sufficient to test out all the logical possibilities inherent in her theory. It is, perhaps, embarrassing that she jumped to conclusions unwarranted by a strict evaluation of the comparative evidence, but it is hardly fatal for the method she espouses. A historical sociologist working on a somewhat more common phenomenon could surely devise more adequate empirical tests (see, e.g., Paige [1978], who statistically analyzed a large number of cases of agrarian revolts). Of course, limiting ourselves to more tractable phenomena would save the comparative method only at a very high cost, inasmuch as it would restrict sociology's ability to say anything valid about rare but world-shaping events like social revolutions. The evidence and arguments presented in *States and Social Revolutions* hardly justifies Skocpol's confidence that comparative historical analysis is a panacea for sociologists working on problems where "there are too many variables and not enough cases" (Skocpol 1979, 36).

Nor do Skocpol's logical difficulties end here. The most troubling flaws of quasi-experimental comparative method come not from the difficulty of amassing enough cases, which effects only some research problems, but from the unhistorical assumptions about temporality that strict adherence to experimental logic requires. The experimental conception of temporality, I shall argue, is inseparable from conventional comparative method, and it can be imposed only by what Burawoy aptly dubs "freezing history"— and, I would extend the metaphor, by cutting up the congealed block of historical time into artificially interchangeable units.

In order for Skocpol's revolutions to be subjected to her comparative method, they must be conceptualized as analogous to separate "trials" of an experiment. This means that the trials must be both equivalent and independent. The principle of equivalence implies that each new trial (in this case, new revolution) be a genuine replication of earlier trials, with all relevant variables held constant. This implies definite assumptions about temporality. The relevant temporality in experimental logic is purely internal to the trial: the posited causal factors must exist prior to their posited consequence. By contrast, the external temporality of historical time—whether one trial precedes or follows another and by how much— must, by definition, be considered irrelevant in order to meet the requirement that experimental trials be strictly equivalent.

This requirement that trials be equivalent poses a considerable difficulty for Skocpol's arguments about the causes of social revolutions. In order to use inductive comparison, Skocpol must assume that her three great social revolutions are in fact a uniform class of objects governed by identical causal laws. But this is a highly dubious assumption, in part because new classes, class relations, and political institutions arise over time. This, in turn, might well alter the conditions necessary and sufficient for social revolution. To take a pertinent example, the Industrial Revolution intervened between the French Revolution and the Russian Revolution, giving rise to a new industrial proletariat. One might consequently assert, with some plausibility, that the revolt of the Petersburg and Moscow proletariat was a necessary condition for social revolution in Russia in 1917, even if it was not a condition for the French Revolution in 1789. But, as Burawoy points out, Skocpol cannot consider this possibility without breaking the crucial assumption of equivalence between the revolutions. Thus, instead of examining empirical evidence about the role of the industrial proletariat in Russia, she dismisses the possibility out of hand on the grounds that because a proletarian revolt was not necessary in her other two causes it cannot have been necessary in Russia either (Burawoy 1989, 769; Skocpol 1979, 113). The assumption of equivalence, which is a logical foundation of

Skocpol's comparative method, does not allow her to pursue questions about how events intervening between revolutions might affect their occurrence and outcome.[9]

The second fundamental assumption of experimental logic, that experimental trials must be independent of one another, also poses serious problems for Skocpol's analysis. For trials to be independent, the outcome of any given trial must have no effect on the outcome of a subsequent trial.[10] But it is absurd to assume that earlier revolutions had no influence on later revolutions. After all, the leadership of the Bolshevik party self-consciously patterned its own revolutionary efforts on what it regarded as the lessons of the French Revolution, and the Chinese Communists not only modeled themselves explicitly on the Bolsheviks but received direct aid from them. Once again, this assumption can only be sustained by "freezing" and "cutting up" history, by treating the histories of the three revolutions as if they took place in isolation from one another rather than as a sequence of historically connected events. In short, Skocpol's comparisons are fundamentally deficient logically if viewed from the perspective of experimental method. They fail both the requirement of equivalence and the requirement of independence.

Although it may occasionally be possible to identify a universe of historical objects that simultaneously satisfies the assumptions of equivalence and independence, such occasions are likely to be unusual. With rare exceptions, attempts to assure equivalence in historical cases will actually result in decreasing the independence between cases—and vice versa. The obvious way to assure independence is to compare phenomena that are widely separated in space and time. One can be reasonably sure, for example, that any similarities between royal ceremonies in eighteenth-century Japan and ancient Mesopotamia cannot be accounted for by imitation. But the very remoteness that assures independence makes the assumption of equivalence impossible to sustain. In societies with radically different economies, systems of social stratification, religious beliefs, conceptions of gender, and so on, how could we ever be confident that the relevant differences have been controlled for?

9. This unwillingness to consider intervening events also gets her into muddy water in her discussion of why the French Revolution consolidated private property when the Russian and Chinese revolutions abolished it (see Sewell 1985a, 59).

10. For example, if performing an experiment on the effects of fertilizer on corn yields increases the concentration of helpful soil bacteria on a plot of land, a second trial on that plot will not be independent of the first because the fact that a prior trial has been carried out there will have a positive effect on crop yields.

It was for precisely this reason that Marc Bloch, in his seminal article on comparative history, cautioned against studying "societies so widely separated in time and space that any analogies between them . . . can obviously not be explained either by mutual influence or by a common origin" (Bloch 1967, 46).[11] Bloch believed that such comparisons were too imprecise and therefore opted for a parallel study of societies that are at once neighboring and contemporary, exercising a constant mutual influence, exposed throughout their development to the action of the same broad causes, and owing their existence in part to a common origin. Bloch preferred comparisons of neighboring societies essentially on the grounds that in such societies the assumption of equivalence could reasonably be approximated (47). I suspect that Bloch, as usual, made the wiser choice. But his choice obviously moves comparative history further from the no less logically necessary assumption of independence between the cases. Because the societies Bloch studied exercised a "constant mutual influence" on one another, it is extraordinarily difficult to determine whether a similar outcome in two cases resulted from a posited set of internal causal factors or from the play of influence. With rare exceptions, equivalence between historical cases is bought only at the price of decreasing independence, and vice versa. This paradox, I submit, makes history a singularly uncompromising territory for the kind of rigorous experimental induction that Skocpol advocates, but cannot really practice, in *States and Social Revolutions*.

It is remarkable, in view of the logical and empirical failure of Skocpol's program of experimental induction, that her analysis of social revolutions remains so powerful and convincing. This implies that, as was true of both Wallerstein and Tilly as well, something important and valuable is accomplished in the book that remains unvoiced in its explicit theoretical and methodological statements.[12] I would contend that much of this unvoiced work occurs in her handling of events. The bulk of her book is composed not of a rigorous weighing of comparative evidence but of carefully constructed causal narratives specifying how social revolutions are brought about in her three cases. Skocpol's best statement of her narrative strategy is, symptomatically, tucked away in a footnote, where she complains that "social-scientific analyses of revolutions almost *never* . . . give sufficient

---

11. For an exposition of Bloch's comparative method that espouses the sort of experimental logic I have criticized here, see Sewell (1967).

12. Once again, my assessment runs closely parallel to Burawoy's conclusion (1989, 778) that Skocpol's work is at its most powerful precisely when it deviates from her announced methodology.

analytic weight to the conjunctural, unfolding interactions of originally separately determined processes" (Skocpol 1979, 320).

Specifying the "conjunctural, unfolding interactions of originally separately determined processes" is the distinctive narrative strategy of her book. It is distinct not only from the usual strategy of sociologists but from the usual strategy of historians as well. Sociological analyses of revolutions tend to emphasize the primacy of some single cause of revolutions, systematically subordinating other causes to the chosen explanatory factor. Historical analyses typically attempt to recount the course of a revolution in some semblance of its original complexity, discussing different causal features of the revolutionary process only as they make themselves felt in the unfolding of the story. The problem with the historical strategy is that crucial causal processes tend to get lost in a muddle of narrative detail and are seldom separated out enough to make their autonomous dynamics clear. The trouble with the sociological strategy is that although it successfully specifies the causal dynamics of one factor, it tends either to conflate other causal factors with the chosen cause (as Marxian treatments of revolution have often viewed the state as merely an expression of class power) or to treat them as mere background (as most studies of revolution have done with the international military setting). Skocpol's strategy is an inspired compromise. It appropriates the power of the sociological strategy but applies it to not one but several distinct causal processes. Yet by emphasizing "conjunctural, unfolding interactions" it also appropriates the historical strategy's concern with events, sequence, and contingency. Quite apart from considerations of comparative experimental induction, Skocpol has elaborated in *States and Social Revolutions* an extremely effective strategy for what might be dubbed multiple causal narrative.[13] She has, to put it differently, worked out a kind of incipient theory of revolutionary process, of how events, by straining or rearranging structures, open the door to further transformative events. But this significant rhetorical and theoretical innovation is never signaled in her introduction or conclusion and is only formulated in passing in a footnote in the third chapter. Skocpol's misplaced obsession with quasi-experimental comparative method has virtually obscured her highly original contribution to eventful sociology.

13. Perhaps the best previous model of such a multiple causal narrative is Lefebvre ([1949] 1971), which recounts how four distinct revolutions—an aristocratic revolution, a bourgeois revolution, a municipal revolution, and a peasant revolution—combined to make what we call the French Revolution of 1789. One wonders how much influence this book had on Skocpol's thinking.

Skocpol's formal comparative method, with its experimental conception of temporality, makes little contribution to her innovations in eventful sociology. Nevertheless, I believe that serious comparative thinking played a crucial role in developing her incipient theory of revolutionary process. The formal logic of comparative method has been developed exclusively as a means of assessing the empirical accuracy of theoretical propositions—to deal with the phase of scientific research that Lakatos (1978) has termed the "context of justification." I suspect, however, that the most important role of comparison in *States and Social Revolutions* was actually in the "context of discovery"—that phase of research concerned with generating theoretical ideas. Skocpol's own description of the history of her project suggests as much. She began, she tells us, with the history of the Chinese Revolution, then found that the Chinese development suggested unsuspected analogies with the French case and finally used an analytic scheme worked out from the Chinese and French cases to interpret Russian history (Skocpol 1979, xii–xiii). One suspects that this mutual reading of each of the cases in terms of the others continued and kept spiraling back: that, for example, Trotsky's emphasis on backward Russia's unsuccessful military competition with the European powers must have suggested parallels in the crisis of the French old regime or that Georges Lefebvre's analyses of the crucial contribution of aristocratic resistance and peasant revolts to the French Revolution must have thrown a sharp light on the roles of landlords and peasants in Russia and China (Trotsky 1932; Lefebvre [1949] 1971, 1973).

I suspect that Skocpol formulated and deepened her interpretations of key revolutionary events by just such a process of critically extending narratives from each of the cases to each of the others. A rough causal logic certainly guided such analogical extensions: if attempts to reform the sprawling agrarian state of imperial Russia arose in response to the threat of German military prowess, is it not likely that comparable attempts to reform a roughly similar French state might have arisen from repeated defeats at the hands of England? But Skocpol's presentation of comparative method as a means of testing already formulated general propositions gets it the wrong way around. It would be more accurate to say that comparison generated propositions whose potential generality was tested by their ability to illuminate the conjunctural unfolding of analogous causal processes in the three cases. Had the crucial question really been whether Skocpol's posited causes were present or absent in an array of cases, there would have been no need to write a long book; a brief article with a few simple tables would have sufficed. What persuades Skocpol's reader is not the formal logic of a tabular array. It is the fact that all three revolutions can be *narrated* convincingly in terms of the operation of analogous causal processes, which in practice means above all that narratives based on these analogies make sense of the numerous details that otherwise would seem purely accidental. The "proof" is less in the formal logic than in the successful narrative ordering of circumstantial detail. The true payoff of Skocpol's comparative history, then, is not the rigorous testing of abstract generalizations but the discovery of analogies on which new and convincing narratives of eventful sequences can be constructed.[14]

EVENTFUL TEMPORALITY

Eventful temporality recognizes the power of events in history. Social life may be conceptualized as being composed of countless happenings or encounters in which persons and groups of persons engage in social action. Their actions are constrained and enabled by the constitutive structures of their societies. Most happenings, as I shall argue in chapter 8, reproduce social and cultural structures without significant changes (see also Giddens 1984). Events may be defined as that relatively rare subclass of happenings that significantly transforms structures. An eventful conception of temporality, therefore, is one that takes into account the transformation of structures by events.

The eventful conception can be clarified by its contrasts with the experimental and teleological conceptions. The experimental conception rests on two fundamental assumptions: a uniformity of causal laws across time and a causal independence of every sequence of occurrences from previous and subsequent occurrences. The eventful conception of temporality denies both of these assumptions. Rather than assuming causal independence through time, it assumes that events are normally "path dependent," that is, that what has happened at an earlier point in time will affect the possible outcomes of a sequence of events occurring at a later point in time. However, path dependence does not necessarily imply that causal structures change over time. In fact, the notion of path dependence was initially formalized by economists, who argued, for example, that different but equally rational choices among alternative technologies at one point in time would imply a divergence in choices at later times even un-

14. This critique of conventional comparative method owes much to conversations with Rebecca Scott and Peggy Somers.

der the standard economists' causal assumption that all actors at all points in time pursue their advantage rationally (Arthur 1988). A fully eventful conception of temporality must also deny the assumption that causal structures are uniform through time. Events must be assumed to be capable of changing not only the balance of causal forces operating but the very logic by which consequences follow from occurrences or circumstances. A fully eventful account of the fate of the nobles in the French Revolution, for example, would have to argue that nobles lost power not only because the loss of some of their assets—land, tax privileges, feudal dues, offices—reduced their resources relative to those of other classes but also because the rules of the social and political game were radically redefined, making what had previously been a prime asset—their noble status—into a powerful liability by the time of the Terror. In this case and, I would argue, in general, events bring about historical changes in part by transforming the very cultural categories that shape and constrain human action. Because the causalities that operate in social relations depend at least in part on the contents and relations of cultural categories, events have the power to transform social causality.[15]

An eventful concept of temporality, then, assumes a causal dependence of later occurrences on prior occurrences and assumes that social causality is temporally heterogeneous, not temporally uniform. Eventful temporality therefore differs fundamentally from experimental temporality. It also differs from teleological temporality. Teleological and eventful temporality share an assumption of path dependence, but teleological temporality denies temporal heterogeneity or at least general temporal heterogeneity. (Stage theories, one of the subtypes of teleological theories, assume causal homogeneity within stages but may accept radical heterogeneity between stages.) However, teleological and eventful concepts of temporality differ most sharply on the question of contingency. Teleological temporality is compatible with a certain contingency at the surface of social relations, but it is incompatible with the assumption of radical contingency that I regard as fundamental to eventful temporality. For example, a teleological Marxian account might argue that the particular situation in which a conflict between workers and bourgeois occurs may affect the outcome of their struggle and may even result in a local victory for a retrograde form of social organization, say, for handicraft over factory production. But no com-

15. This has been demonstrated most eloquently, and with greatest theoretical clarity, by the works of Marshall Sahlins (1981, 1985, 1991), which I discuss in chapter 7.

bination of such local victories can "turn back the clock" definitively. The built-in directionality of underlying causal forces guarantees that local variations are mere surface perturbations with no long-term effect on the course of history.

By contrast, an eventful concept of temporality assumes that contingency is global, that it characterizes not only the surface but the core or the depths of social relations. Contingent, unexpected, and inherently unpredictable events, this view assumes, can undo or alter the most apparently durable trends of history. This does not, of course, imply that human societies are in permanent and universal flux, that social change is easy to accomplish, or that historical changes display no regularities. I am not arguing that capitalism or the global division of labor or sexual inequality would go away if only we wished it or that history is a tale told by an idiot. History displays both stubborn durabilities and sudden breaks, and even the most radical historical ruptures are interlaced with remarkable continuities. To say that events are transformations of structures implies precisely that the structures that emerge from an event are always transformations of preexisting structures. An assumption of global contingency means not that everything is constantly changing but that nothing in social life is ultimately immune to change.

The eventful conception of temporality, then, assumes that social relations are characterized by path dependency, temporally heterogeneous causalities, and global contingency. This is close to the implicit intellectual baggage of most academic historians. Yet most historians take the effectivity of events so much for granted that their accounts of events tend to lack a theoretical edge. Marshall Sahlins, citing Ruth Benedict's aphorism that if deep-sea fish could speak the last thing they would name is water, points out that historians "live in the narrative element" and consequently are remarkably unselfconscious about the event as a theoretical category (Sahlins 1991, 15). My own experience testifies to this dictum. Even as a "social historian" critical of old-fashioned "narrative history," I too swam in the narrative element. It was only sustained encounters with sociological and anthropological discourse, much of it undertaken as a member of an academic sociology department, that made me recognize events as a category in need of theoretical work.

Sociologists, even those whose work contains exemplary analyses of events, are by and large equally unconscious of the event as a theoretical category—as the writings of Wallerstein, Tilly, and Skocpol testify. There are, however, some whose work clearly demonstrates in practice the profound significance of events. In the remainder of this essay I will analyze two such works: *Armies of the Poor* by Mark Traugott (1985) and *Reds or Rackets?* by Howard Kimeldorf (1988). I do not think that either Traugott or Kimeldorf makes much progress toward elaborating the event as a theoretical category. But both of them deploy the highly developed methodological consciousness typical even of nonmainstream sociologists to demonstrate to skeptical readers that events mattered crucially in the cases they are investigating. Although their work does not itself develop a theoretical argument about events, it can be used to develop and illustrate such an argument.

TRAUGOTT'S ORGANIZATIONAL HYPOTHESIS

Traugott's book may be characterized as a study of the differential effect of a great event, the French Revolution of 1848, on two groups of French workers: those enrolled in the government's unemployment relief organization, the National Workshops, who formed the core of the great workers' revolt of June 1848, and those recruited into the paramilitary Mobile Guard, who were instrumental in suppressing it. Traugott's task is to explain why workers associated with these two organizations wound up on opposite sides of the barricades. The leading explanation of their divergent political trajectories has been Marx's. Marx claimed that the Mobile Guard had no scruples about shooting down the proletarian insurrectionaries because it had been recruited exclusively from the rootless *lumpenproletariat*, the scum of the urban poor. Traugott spends much of his book—and doubtless spent even more of his research time—subjecting this argument to a painstaking quantitative test, which shows that the pre-February occupations of the June rebels and the Guardsmen were in fact virtually identical (Traugott 1985, 67–77). The divergent political behavior of Guards and Workshop members cannot be explained by differences in their class backgrounds.

The failure of this standard sociological explanation led Traugott to what he calls the "organizational hypothesis"—that the divergent actions of the guardsmen and the insurrectionaries were the result not of characteristics of their pre-1848 lives but of their collective experiences between February and June 1848 (83). Traugott tests this hypothesis by means of a "paired comparison" of the organizational histories of the Mobile Guard and the National Workshops. There are many parallels between the two institutions: both were improvised in response to working-class pressures after the February Revolution, and both were intended by the Provisional

Government simultaneously to be a means for alleviating unemployment and for co-opting potentially rebellious workers so as to moderate their political sentiments (115). Moreover, both institutions were deeply mistrusted by the conservative bourgeoisie, which feared they would become hotbeds of socialist agitation. By means of his paired comparison, Traugott shows that both were initially highly successful co-optive institutions and that the National Workshops became a nursery of rebellion only when they were organizationally decapitated by a hostile government.

Traugott's organizational analysis borrows from Katherine Chorley's *Armies and the Art of Revolution* (1943). By April 1848 the initially ragtag Mobile Guard had met Chorley's three crucial conditions for successful military repression of a revolutionary movement: a unified corps of officers, effective isolation from the civilian population, and prompt attention to practical grievances in the ranks. The Mobile Guard's officer corps was supplied by the regular army and supplemented by carefully managed elections from the ranks. By April it became a highly professional and unified body. The guardsmen were isolated from the civilian population because they were housed in barracks, usually not in their own neighborhoods. One practical grievance—a long delay in the provision of uniforms—seriously threatened to undermine the guardsmen's morale, but it was resolved well before June. Hence the potentially unruly Mobile Guard was molded into a disciplined military force that was willing to face down fellow workers in several confrontations in April and May—and to shoot them down when the insurrection broke out in June (Traugott 1985, 86–113).

Although the National Workshops were not a military force, Traugott uses Chorley's model in his analysis of their organizational history as well. The Workshops were actually organized on a military model—with squads, brigades, and companies and a uniformed officer corps. Emile Thomas, the youthful director of the Workshops, assured the unity of his officer corps by recruiting its upper echelons from students at the École Centrale des Arts et Manufactures, a national engineering school of which he was an alumnus. Lower-level officers were chosen by election from the ranks but subjected to close administrative supervision. The unified officer corps not only enabled Thomas to maintain firm administrative control of the Workshops but contributed to his personal popularity in the ranks. Thomas was less successful in his efforts to overcome practical grievances—mainly because the Workshops were never supplied with enough meaningful work to occupy their full contingent of unemployed laborers (about 120,000 by June). Nor could members of the workshops be separated fully from the general population—they made up about a third of the working class of Paris and continued to live in their own neighborhoods. But Thomas did his best, insisting that members report to their brigades every day, whether they had work or not, and posting them to peripheral locations when there were demonstrations or political troubles. He also established a National Workshops political club, attempting with considerable success to isolate Workshop members from the political clubs of their neighborhoods (148–65).

This surprisingly effective isolation, together with the unity of the officer corps and Thomas's personal popularity, assured the Workshops' political moderation until nearly the end of May and might have done so indefinitely had the government not decided to sack Thomas and phase out the Workshops. This drove the elected squad and brigade leaders to the left, released them from the political and organizational tutelage of Thomas and his loyal schoolmates, and transformed them from conduits of moderation into a revolutionary cadre (165–68). When the full destruction of the Workshops was announced on June 21, they led their squads and brigades in armed revolt. In short, members of the National Workshops and the Mobile Guard took opposite sides in June not because of divergent class backgrounds but because of the divergent organizational histories of the two institutions in the course of political events.

Traugott justifiably concludes that the "organizational hypothesis" best explains the observed behavior. But the term *organizational hypothesis,* in my opinion, does not capture adequately the nature of Traugott's theoretical argument. The term implies that the organizational hypothesis is just another sociological hypothesis, that he is simply asking his reader to consider another explanatory factor parallel to class background, income, religious preference, or cohort. In fact, he is asking for something much more radical: that sociologists entertain a new and essentially eventful form of explanatory argument. The organizational explanation of why the National Workshops rebelled and the Mobile Guard put down the rebellion is a causal narrative of how these institutions were shaped through time, and it has a characteristically eventful temporality. It incorporates path dependency: the timing of incidents crucially affects their consequences. The fact that the Mobile Guard's deeply felt grievance about lack of uniforms had been rectified well before June assured the Guard's loyalty to the government. Had a revolt broken out before the resolution of this grievance it is uncertain whether the Guard would have followed orders to march against fellow workers. Traugott's temporality is also causally heterogeneous. Consider the role of the Workshops' squad and brigade leaders, who formed the leadership cadre of the insurrection. Their positions of leadership were produced by Emile Thomas's paternalist strategy of cultivating their personal and political loyalties and integrating them tightly into the Workshops' officer corps. This paternalism had the intended effect of assuring the moderation of the Workshop members as long as Thomas and his schoolmates ran the organization. But when Thomas was sacked, the squad and brigade leaders were also in position to organize the rank and file's resistance to the closing of the Workshops, by armed revolt if necessary. Paradoxically, the organizational structure erected by Thomas to ensure the workers' moderation had the effect of exacerbating the crisis when it came. In brief, the creation of this working-class organizational infrastructure changed the causal dynamics of the situation, greatly amplifying the extent, intensity, and effectiveness of resistance to the government's closing of the Workshops.

It should be clear that the temporality of Traugott's account is interlaced with contingency. Like classical narrative historians, Traugott emphasizes the importance of significant persons. The Workshops were organized as they were largely because of the personal decisions of Emile Thomas, and his removal from the directorship was a decisive cause of their radicalization. A forceful and magnetic person like Thomas, placed in a position of strategic importance, can have a remarkable effect on the course of history. Conscious choice also figures importantly in Traugott's account. Thomas purposely drew his officer corps from his schoolmates so as to enhance its solidarity. The conservative government purposely provoked a crisis by abolishing the Workshops. For all these reasons, the course of events Traugott analyzes is contingent, not necessary. Had the government maintained the Workshops in existence and kept Thomas as their director, the insurrection probably would never have happened. Had someone less capable been chosen as director, the revolt would probably have been less effective, but it might well have happened considerably earlier.

Traugott's embrace of eventful temporality does not mean that he has abandoned sociology for narrative history. He is driven to eventful explanation by the austere logic of his sociological method, and he carefully specifies the structural limits within which timing, personality, choice, and contingency operate. Although he comes down in this case for eventful rather than etiological explanations, he does so not to dismiss etiological factors but to specify their mode of effectuation. Class, as he points out, may have an influence, but "any class-based propensities of actors are conditioned by a set of contingent organizational forces" (184). He is arguing not that history is a sequence of pure contingencies but that "an intervening [I would add eventful] level of analysis must demonstrate by what mechanisms macrosociological structures are converted into forms of consciousness and the probability of collective action" (189). Traugott's book, with its careful methodology and its focus on the relationship between structures and events, points the way toward an *eventful* sociology that remains an eventful *sociology*.

KIMELDORF'S MULTIPLE REGISTERS OF CAUSATION

Kimeldorf's book is a study of the divergent political evolution of longshoremen's unions in New York City and on the West Coast from the 1930s through the 1950s. Kimeldorf, like Traugott, uses a strategy of paired comparison, combines narrative history with structural analysis, and provides powerful arguments for the significance of events in the shaping of workers' politics. Kimeldorf attempts to explain why East Coast and West Coast dockworkers, who did similar work under similar technological and economic conditions, nevertheless formed sharply contrasting labor unions, the durably socialist International Longshoremen's and Warehousemen's Union (ILWU) on the West Coast and the politically conservative and chronically racket-ridden International Longshoremen's Association (ILA) on the East Coast.

Kimeldorf's explanation of the difference between the New York and West Coast unions is complex, multicausal, and irreducibly historical. He shows that the differences cannot be attributed to any single, underlying factor, and that their historical roots go back well before the 1930s. The explanatory factors are of several different types. First, the recruitment and the cultures of the labor forces differed substantially. A high proportion of the West Coast longshoremen were recruited from the lumbering and seafaring industries, which because of their work structures very commonly give rise to high levels of worker solidarity and class conflict, and certainly did so on the American West Coast in the early twentieth century. This labor force, whose prior work experience already inclined it to labor militancy, was widely but only temporarily organized by the radical Industrial Workers of the World (IWW) in the 1910s and 1920s. By the 1930s West Coast dockworkers already had been exposed to a radical work culture that made them ready to heed Harry Bridges's call (Kimeldorf 1988, 20–37). These predisposing factors were entirely absent among the New York dockworkers, where the labor force was recruited from two successive

peasant immigrant groups, the Irish and Italians, who, by the 1930s, had
established ethnically divided enclaves on the docks. Moreover, the political and work culture was far more conservative, dominated by the Catholic
Church in the case of the Irish and by an exploitative (sometimes Mafia-
ridden) padrone system in that of the Italians (37–50).

These differences in labor recruitment were reinforced by differences
in the ecology of the shipping business and consequently in the class capacities of shipping capitalists. On the West Coast, three American companies dominated the carrying trade, and they were consequently able to
carry on a particularly ferocious and ultimately radicalizing battle against
longshoremen's unions. In New York, the carrying trade was divided between a larger number of American and European companies and a large
government-owned line. This divided employer class was unable to sustain a unified front against longshore unions, and the companies therefore
negotiated separate deals with different union locals (60–75). There were
consequently structural factors of a demographic, cultural, and economic
nature that made radical unionism more likely on the West Coast than in
New York.

But while these structural factors might have been sufficient to rule out
radical unionism on the New York docks, they were hardly sufficient to
guarantee it on the West Coast. In a chapter entitled "The Strategic Pivot,"
Kimeldorf moves from relatively stable structural conditions to more contingent conjunctural and volitional causes. The conjuncture, largely shared
by the two coasts, was the Depression and the new political climate and
nationwide labor militancy it engendered. But the radical potential of this
period was seized successfully on the West Coast and missed in New
York largely because of the very different strategies of the two areas' Communist Parties. In San Francisco, which became the center of radical longshore unionism, the local Communists ignored the national party's strategy of supporting separate left-wing unions, opting to develop a leftist
force within the existing moderate union instead. The consequence was
that the Communists and allied left-wingers such as Bridges were in a position to assume leadership in the dramatic and violent strike of 1934 and
move the rank and file definitively to the left (81–92). By contrast, the New
York party stuck obstinately to an utterly unsuccessful policy of separate
left unionism and was thereby deprived of any chance to play a radicalizing role in the New York strike movements of the same year (92–97). Finally, the dramatic radicalization of the West Coast union was rendered
enduring by the cultural codification of the "Big Strike" and "Bloody

Thursday" (July 5, 1934), which was embodied in a highly self-conscious cohort of "'34 men" who remained a solid block of support for the leftist leadership right through the 1950s and whose prestige among the rank and file created a pervasively leftist and militant work culture on the docks (100–110).

Kimeldorf's book, as I read it, provides a potentially generalizable model of explanation or interpretation in historical sociology, but that model remains largely implicit rather than theoretically voiced. The implicit model not only specifies multiple causes but sorts out what might be characterized as different registers of causation: preexisting structural conditions (cultural, social, demographic, and economic); conjunctural conditions (such as the generalized labor militancy of the 1930s); and contingent strategic or volitional actions. In certain respects, this recapitulates Fernand Braudel's distinction between three different types of histories based on three different scales of duration: structural history, associated with the study of geological, geographic, social, and mental structures that change only glacially; conjunctural history, associated with the study of economic and demographic cycles with durations of decades rather than centuries; and eventful history, associated with what he tended to regard as the ephemera of politics and to disdain as mere froth on the waves of history (Braudel 1958, 1966). Although the time scales of Braudel's and Kimeldorf's histories are very different, both schemes tackle the crucial question of sorting out social processes with very different temporal rhythms. But whereas Braudel's three types of histories remain in their own distinct causal universes, Kimeldorf's registers of causation are brought together in the event, where the action of human subjects can reconfigure preexisting structures and conjunctures — by, for example, forming the solid block of influential '34 men who maintained the leftism of the ILWU. Theorized as I have advocated here, Kimeldorf's account suggests a way of joining structure, conjuncture, and events in a common causal universe, one that centers on acting human subjects.

Kimeldorf's discussion of how the Big Strike and the '34 men attained mythic stature raises another important theoretical issue, but once again the issue is not clearly voiced (Kimeldorf 1988, 109–10). The myth of the Big Strike arose in part from the actions of '34 men, who continually reasserted a moral authority within the union. But the cult of '34 was also fostered by official union policy, which prescribed annual work stoppages on July 5 to commemorate the union's formative battle. The Big Strike, in other words, not only was an objectively important event in the formation of a radical union but was also constructed as a subjectively important event by the radical union in subsequent months and years. This issue, which Kimeldorf discusses almost in passing, actually raises two fundamental theoretical points about events. First, Kimeldorf's account implies that the question of how events are retrospectively appropriated to institute and reproduce structures is just as important for historical sociology as the question of how conjunctures and strategic action makes transformative events possible in the first place.[16] Second, the case of the '34 men shows that events transform structures largely by constituting and empowering new groups of actors or by reempowering existing groups in new ways.

AN EVENTFUL SOCIOLOGY?

Traugott and Kimeldorf have written exemplary historical sociologies in the eventful mode. The temporalities sketched out in their books are path dependent, causally heterogeneous, and contingent, and reconfiguration of structures by social action is at the core of their explanatory models. Their books stand as an implicit challenge not only to mainstream sociology but also to mainstream historical sociology. But the challenge remains all too implicit. Although the theoretical modesty of these books is one of their most attractive rhetorical features, it nevertheless has limited their impact by causing them to be classified as little gems of sociological craftsmanship rather than as field-transforming blockbusters. My effort in this essay has been to point out the largely unvoiced theoretical implications of these books and to show why their arguments actually constitute a deeper challenge to the reigning "scientific" orthodoxy of sociology than those of the far more assertive historical sociologists who work in the teleological and experimental modes.

Eventful sociology of the sort produced by Traugott and Kimeldorf challenges the "scientific" orthodoxy on several fundamental questions. It implicitly suggests that sociology's epic quest for social laws is illusory, whether the search is for timeless truths about all societies, ineluctable trends of more limited historical epochs, or inductively derived laws of certain classes of social phenomena. Social processes, it implies, are inherently contingent, discontinuous, and open-ended. Big and ponderous social processes are never entirely immune from being transformed by small alterations in volatile local social processes. "Structures" are constructed by

16. For an illuminating study of the political and cultural construction and reconstruction of events, see Coronil and Skurski (1991).

human action, and "societies" or "social formations" or "social systems" are continually shaped and reshaped by the creativity and stubbornness of their human creators.

All of this implies that adequate eventful accounts of social processes will look more like well-made stories or narratives than like laws of physics. An eventful historical sociology would come to resemble history ever more closely. It is worth noting, in this connection, that both Traugott's and Kimeldorf's books read much like works by social historians. Traditionally, historical sociologists have regarded historians as useful drones more than as genuine intellectual collaborators. Historians would do the tedious work of collecting archival data and producing narratives; historical sociologists would utilize the narratives as raw material for their grander and more theoretically sophisticated analyses. The current generation of historical sociologists has already followed historians into the archives. If they are to construct an eventful sociology, they will increasingly have to look to historians and their narratives for theoretical inspiration as well.

Yet if historical sociology should be involved in more and deeper conversations with history, it will almost certainly continue to be recognizable as sociology. It is important to note that Traugott's and Kimeldorf's narratives and my theorizations of them retain sociology's traditional concern with cause. This is so even if they inflect the usage of cause and causality from the highly abstract and generalizing conceptualizations common in "scientific" sociology toward their more singular and contingent usages in ordinary speech, where giving a causal account of something usually means telling a story about how it came to be. Traugott's and Kimeldorf's work shows that a concern with causal regularities of a recognizably sociological sort is crucial to elaborating a convincing narrative of why things happened as they did. Without Traugott's careful quantitative test of the etiological explanation of differences between the Workshops and the Guards, his eventful explanation in terms of organizational histories would have been merely plausible rather than compelling. And Kimeldorf's analysis of the structural differences between the East and West Coast shipping industries and of the different social origins of East and West Coast dockworkers establishes the ground on which the different strategies of organizers operated. The accounts elaborated by both Traugott and Kimeldorf combine diverse causal registers and diverse temporal rhythms. They continue to use conventional structural or etiological strategies of explanation, but these strategies are subsumed in their work within a larger eventful explanatory framework.

This selective appropriation of conventional sociological arguments and methods seems to me the proper strategy. I believe that historical sociology—perhaps sociology as a whole—should be remade in an eventful mode, and I believe that such a remaking would constitute a radical departure from current practices. But I also believe that a reconfiguration of sociology could only succeed by appropriating and subsuming existing modes of sociological analysis, just as Traugott and Kimeldorf appropriate and subsume structural and etiological causality. In this spirit, I have tried, in my own critiques of Wallerstein, Tilly, and Skocpol, to show that adopting an eventful approach would not require jettisoning all works that have employed teleological or experimental conceptions of temporality. Instead, I have tried to show how classical teleological and experimental studies might be rethought, seeking out the valuable eventful analyses that have up to now been masked by misconstrued scientific rhetoric. I think we need to rehabilitate such works as *The Modern World System*, *The Vendée*, and *States and Social Revolutions* as rhetorically flawed masterworks of eventful sociology. Likewise, rather than rejecting comparative method, we need to strip it of inappropriate scientific rhetoric and rethink it as a means of theorizing causal narratives through looping contexts of discovery. The construction of an eventful sociology will require a collective rethinking of the discipline by many scholars. Success in this venture, in my opinion, will hinge on a closer intellectual collaboration of sociologists with historians, anthropologists, political scientists, and others who are themselves engaged in parallel rethinkings.

I would suggest that enlightening analogies with the eventful sociology I have been advocating in this essay might be found in at least one branch of contemporary natural science: paleontology. I am hesitant to make this suggestion, because I believe that the development of the social sciences has been bedeviled from the beginning by attempts to adopt the methods and explanatory strategies of supposedly higher or more mature scientific disciplines. But the analogy with paleontology—more specifically, with the version of paleontology set forth by Steven Jay Gould in *Wonderful Life* (1989)—seems particularly compelling. The stories of animal evolution that Gould recounts in this book are resolutely narrative and contingent. Indeed, he hails contingency as "the central principle of all history"—including, of course, natural history (283). A historical explanation, he goes on, "does not rest on direct deductions from laws of nature, but on an unpredictable sequence of antecedent states, where any major change in any step of the sequence would have altered the final result. This final result is therefore dependent, or contingent, upon everything that came before—the unerasable and determining signature of history" (283). The analogy with natural history as elaborated in *Wonderful Life* is made all the more attractive by Gould's own insistence that scientists need to consider literary and historical narratives as models for their own investigation of evolutionary biology. Remarking that "the theme of contingency, so poorly understood and explored by science, has long been a mainstay of literature" (285), Gould recommends such novels as *Fatal Inversion* by Barbara Vine [Ruth Rendell] (1987) and *Galapagos* by Kurt Vonnegut (1985) as exemplary texts on the nature of history.

Citing paleontology as a scientific warrant for eventful sociology might effectively serve the usual purpose of keeping mainstream colleagues at bay by showing that one's work falls within the sacred precinct of science. After all, the tactic of claiming proper scientific cover for one's procedures may sometimes be unavoidable—especially when the person adopting the rhetorical shield is untenured. But the beauty of invoking the paleontological analogy is that *this* ritual bow toward science also serves the purpose of challenging the conventional assumptions not only of sociology but of science itself. Here is an authentic, exact, and flourishing natural science whose model of explanation resembles that of history and fiction rather than physics. To cite the paleontological model is to argue for the diversity of modes of knowing—as Gould's own plea for a "new taxonomic arrangement of plurality among the sciences" makes clear. Gould argues that "we shall never be able to appreciate the full range and meaning of science until we shatter the stereotype of ordering by status [with physics at the top] and understand the different forms of historical explanation as activities equal in merit to anything done by physics or chemistry" (281). Carefully constructed causal narrative, Gould insists, has as much right to claim the laurels of science as mathematical deduction and statistical calculation. This surely is as true for sociology as it is for biology.

POSTSCRIPT: MACROHISTORY AND EVENTFUL TEMPORALITY

I have long been aware that the argument presented in this chapter has a logical flaw. The flaw is that both of my examples of eventful sociology are studies of social processes relatively limited in time and space. These examples therefore cannot demonstrate that eventful forms of analysis are necessary for understanding large-scale or "macrohistorical" processes. A defender of what I characterize as teleological or experimental forms of temporal argument might well agree that local historical episodes like the Parisian June Days of 1848 and the formation of the radical San Francisco longshoremen's union in the 1930s are inherently susceptible to eventful analysis, but that this is so only because of their limited spatial and temporal scope. When a social change is limited to a particular time and place, so the argument would go, it is hardly surprising that local particularities strongly influence the outcome. But when the changes in question are larger in scale and span a longer period, the perturbations introduced by events will tend to be ironed out and underlying or general causal relations will manifest themselves. This argument derives its plausibility, I believe, from a kind of analogy with standard statistical methodology. Firmer statistical conclusions can be reached on the basis of a large number of cases than on the basis of a few because purely idiosyncratic variations in the cases will tend to be averaged out, enabling the underlying statistical regularities to emerge. Similarly, in macro-level processes—which are in a sense composed of a multitude of micro-level processes—the more fundamental tendencies at work in a situation will win out. If we want to explain why the San Francisco docks produced "Reds" and the New York docks produced rackets, we need to look at peculiarities of events on the San Francisco and New York waterfronts, but if we want to explain why there was a general surge of unionization in America in the 1930s, or why trade unions arise in industrialized countries more generally, we must look at more general causal factors. Likewise, a sociological explanation of the June Days or the Vendée revolt might indeed require eventful analysis, but this would not be true of a study of the entire course of the French Revolution from 1786 to 1815, let alone of the worldwide rise of capitalism between 1500 and 1800. The implication of this reasoning is that although eventful analysis may be appropriate to the type of temporally and spatially limited questions typically favored by historians, truly *sociological* analyses, aiming to establish general laws or robust generalizations, will be required when the topic is the sort of macro-sociology favored by historical sociologists ever since Weber.

What is needed to refute such an argument is a work of sociology that successfully and consistently employs eventful temporal assumptions at a macro time scale. I shall argue in this postscript that Michael Mann's impressive, indeed, daunting, *The Sources of Social Power* (1986, 1993), which traces the changing forms of social power from prehistory to World War I, is precisely such a work. Mann's arguments demonstrate that social temporality is eventful at even the most macro of all historical levels, in the centuries-long process of the development of world civilizations. This is particularly evident in his first volume, which traces the development of the various forms of social power over the millennia stretching from prehistory to the eve of the Industrial Revolution.

Mann's account indicates that the emergence of the social forms we call "civilization"—the cluster of innovations that includes cities, writing, states, extensive division of labor, and permanent social stratification— was a striking example of eventful temporality on the macro time scale. These social forms emerged first in Mesopotamia in the early fourth millennium B.C., but also are generally considered to have appeared independently in Egypt later in the fourth millennium B.C., in the Indus valley in the third millennium B.C., in China in the second millennium B.C., in the valley of Mexico in the first millennium A.D., in the central Andes in the second millennium A.D., and, perhaps (the independence of this case is disputed), in Minoan Crete in the second millennium B.C. The emergence of civilization, according to Mann, was contingent, not necessary. Settled agriculture, the technical prerequisite for the emergence of civilization, had been present for several millennia before civilization appeared. Archeological remains make it clear that relatively complex social units capable of coordinating the labor of large numbers of people—we might think of them as proto-states—emerged repeatedly and over an immense geographical sweep in prehistory, but that such developments almost never led to a breakthrough to civilization. Examples of such archeological remains would be the great stone monuments at Stonehenge in England or on Easter Island, or the massive earthworks that dot indigenous North America. None of these could have been built without a considerable and sustained concentration of labor, which implies the existence of a relatively centralized authority structure of some sort (1986, 63–64). Yet it was only in five or six cases in the entire experience of humankind that the emergence of such levels of social coordination proved irreversible, leading to the development of the historical civilizations. The archeological record seems to indicate that human societies advanced to what in retrospect looks like the edge of civilization countless times without making the leap. Why was the breakthrough to civilization so rare?

Mann's answer to this question stresses the contingency of the emergence of civilization. It appears that one can speak of a general dynamic of social evolution operating in Paleolithic human societies, one that resulted in a development from hunter-gatherer societies to agricultural and herding societies, and that frequently gave rise to what he calls rank-stratified

societies with embryonic states and social hierarchies—such as those observed by early European travelers or later anthropologists in parts of
southern and eastern Africa or Polynesia. But these rank-stratified societies showed no general tendency to develop further into civilizations. Indeed, it was far more common for them to rise and fall over time, decaying
into the seemingly "lower" form of egalitarian kin-centered or village-
centered societies. The general tendency seems to have been one of evolution up to a certain level of complexity and then a cyclical pattern, stopping
short of the emergence of cities, writing, states, extensive division of labor,
and permanent social stratification. The reason for this seemingly stunted
pattern, Mann hypothesizes, is that the monarchs or chieftains in such social orders lacked the power resources to impose enduring authority over
their subordinates or to establish systems of stratification that permanently denied resources to the less favored categories. This is because the
ruled normally had the option of *escape* from the emerging authority relations, either by physical flight to areas beyond the would-be despot's control or by switching their loyalty to an alternative chief who would offer
them better conditions. Unless the subordinate groups could be physically
caged, prevented somehow from moving elsewhere when disgruntled, the
systematic oppressions without which civilization was impossible could
not develop.

It was only in a tiny handful of cases, when rank societies emerged in
spatial locations where populations could be *encaged*, that people could be
induced or forced to submit to the permanent authority of a monarch or
an aristocracy. It was for this reason that most pristine civilizations—this
was true of Mesopotamia, Egypt, the Indus valley, and China—emerged
in flood-fertilized river valleys. Such valleys could support a denser population than other areas. And once irrigation was introduced, the population could get so dense and so dependent on the peculiarities of irrigated
agriculture that the possibility of escape was effectively closed off. This
was especially true when, as in Mesopotamia, Egypt, and the Indus Valley,
the surrounding unirrigated regions were relatively arid and therefore incapable of supporting anything like the population densities of the river
valleys. The population was therefore encaged, having no possibility of
escape when certain families, clans, or dynasties managed to obtain and
enforce rights to expropriate a portion of the agricultural surplus. Once a
surplus could be accumulated in the hands of ruling groups, it became possible to build larger cities, palaces, temples, and fortifications, and for
specialized classes of craftsmen, priests, and administrators to emerge. In

such circumstances, writing was invented—initially, it would seem, to keep track of the complicated flow of resources. The emergence of civilizations was made possible only by quite contingent environmental conditions that encaged the population, and the development of collective powers and productivity by means of civilization further enhanced the initial caging. But it was also true that the power techniques made possible by the initial caging—for example, more refined handicrafts, superior military organization, identification of gods with authority structures, storage and redistribution of surplus grain, administration of tribute and enforcement of property rights by means of writing—eventually became so formidable that they could be employed to encage populations and increase collective power resources even in regions where the initial environmental conditions were absent. Thus civilization, initiated as a consequence of the contingent encaging of a few river-valley populations, could spread to Anatolia, Persia, the Eastern Mediterranean, the Indian subcontinent, Japan, North Africa, South-East Asia, or Europe, and eventually to the entire world.

At first glance, this account might seem similar to Wallerstein's "big bang" theory of the emergence of capitalism, where an initial breakthrough leads to an ineluctable evolutionary development. But there are fundamental differences. In the first place, there was not one big bang but five or six, and the trajectories of the different pristine civilizations were quite variable—ranging from the Indus Valley civilization, which seems to have been remarkably unchanging for several centuries and then collapsed without a trace, to China and Mesopotamia, which proved to be highly dynamic and expansive, although in very different ways. A second, more fundamental, difference has to do with spatial assumptions. Wallerstein tells us that he was driven to his concept of the "modern world-system" by the recognition that nation-states, which most social scientists take as their units of analysis under the label of "societies," were not independently evolving wholes but always part of a larger complex. His solution to this problem was to identify the larger "world-system," rather than the nation-state components, as the evolving and bounded "society" (1974, 7). Wallerstein rejected the sociologists' tacit assumption that "society" is equivalent to the nation-state, but he nevertheless projected many of the characteristics of the nation-state-society—its boundedness, its singularity, its lawfulness, its evolutionary tendencies—onto the wider geographical scale of the world-system.

Mann, who also recognizes the inadequacy of the social scientists' im-

plicit equation of the society with the nation-state, takes a much more radical position: that unitary "societies" simply do not exist, or exist only as a
limiting case. Societies, he writes, "are not unitary. They are not social systems . . . ; they are not totalities. . . . Because there is no system, no totality, there cannot be 'subsystems,' 'dimensions,' or 'levels' of such a totality. . . . Because there is no bounded totality, it is not helpful to divide
social change into 'endogenous' and 'exogenous' varieties. Because there is
no social system, there is no 'evolutionary' process within it." What we call
societies are in fact "constituted of multiple overlapping and intersecting
sociospatial networks of power" (1986, 1). Mann specifies four distinct
forms of power—ideological, economic, political, and military. These four
types of networks of power rarely coincide spatially, and are, in any case,
normally internally heterogeneous and spatially uneven as well (22–28).
There have been a few rare historical instances when these diverse sociospatial networks of power have largely coincided, resulting in a reasonably well-bounded and largely unitary society. The modern nation-state
has come closer to this unitary type than most previous social formations,
although their boundedness has always been more an ideological claim
than an organizational reality. In fact, the best historical example of a unitary society may well be one of the earliest civilizations, Egypt under the
Old and Middle Kingdoms. There the narrow irrigated trench formed by
the Nile, which was surrounded by virtually uninhabited deserts, made
possible a unified, formally despotic, and remarkably unchanging society,
one in which all four types of network of social power tended to coincide
spatially (108–15). This splendid isolation was ended only when Egypt was
impinged upon by the more expansive form of civilization originating in
Mesopotamia and by the rising maritime civilizations of the Phoenicians
and Greeks. It was, thus, only at the dawn of civilization and in the absolutely unique ecological situation of the Nile Valley that such a bounded
society with such isomorphic power-networks could exist. The norm has
been something very different: societies that are "confederal" rather than
unitary and in which power-networks are diverse, overlapping, and non-
isomorphic (16–17).

   It should be obvious that a conception of societies as concatenations of
overlapping organizational networks, rather than as tightly integrated social systems, builds in the possibility of contingent temporal conjunctures
between such networks—which in turn builds in the possibility of historical transformations. Mann's conceptualization of the spatial form of
social relations, in other words, is closely connected to his thinking about

the temporalities of social life. His arguments about historical change in civilizational development consistently hinge precisely upon changing conjunctures between spatially distinct power networks. One type of conjunction that figures prominently in Mann's account is relations between the political and military cores of various civilizations and the "marcher lords" that typically spring up on the civilizations' peripheries. The marcher lords—whether pastoralists on the edges of Mesopotamian or Chinese civilizations or Germanic tribes on the borders of the Roman Empire—were on the one hand essential allies of the rulers of the civilizational core and at the same time dangerous rivals who appropriated power techniques from the core that could be turned against them in moments of political disarray. But the effects of marcher lord triumph over the core have also varied from case to case. In Mesopotamia, from the time of Sargon of Akkad (around 2300 B.C.) at least through the Kassite dynasty some one thousand years later, a succession of imperial decay, marcher lord conquest, and imperial restructuring resulted in a gradually ascending spiral of power development (130–68); in China, after about A.D. 1000, the victorious marcher lords were quickly Sinicized and ritually endowed with the "Mandate of Heaven," leading to a pattern more cyclical than ascending (501–2); in Rome the victory of the Germanic barbarian tribes resulted in a total collapse of imperial power and in sustained economic and social devolution, at least in the Western half of the Empire (292–95). Although marcher lords were troublesome everywhere, the effects of their relations with the civilizational core depended on the particular ecologies, organizational forms, military technologies, and ideologies operating in each case.

A second type of historical conjuncture of organizational networks is what Mann calls the development of interstitial ideologies, ideologies that are elaborated along networks distinct from but nevertheless dependent upon the official circuits of political power. Examples are the flowering of universalistic scientific and philosophical speculation in a Greek civilization politically organized into scores of independent but commercially interlinked city-states (206–7, 211–16); the rise of Hinduism and caste organization in an India chronically divided into rival kingdoms (348–63); and the rise and spread of Christianity through the medium of urban trading networks in the aristocratic and despotic Roman Empire (301–35). If the spatio-temporal dynamics of civilizational cores and marcher lords took a core-periphery form, the rise of interstitial ideologies had to do with the elaboration over essentially the same civilizational space of distinctly shaped, if overlapping, power networks. And the historical destiny of these interstitially developing ideologies was, obviously enough, extremely various. According to Mann's account, Hinduism helped constitute an exceptionally static Indian civilization, Christianity contributed to the undermining of Rome and then became the integument of an exceptionally dynamic European civilization, and Greek thought served, successively and in part simultaneously, as a crucial element of the Roman elite ideology, the philosophical framework of Christian theology, and the foundation of dynamic scientific development in Arabic and then European thought.

It should be evident from the examples I have cited that Mann's macrohistory is consistent with what I have called an eventful conception of temporality. His macrohistory certainly assumes global contingency. Indeed, it shows how contingencies arise over and over again out of unevenly developing, overlapping, and non-isomorphic power networks. It also incorporates path dependency, with the subsequent history of civilizations fundamentally conditioned by developments that arose from previous contingencies. And his causalities are temporally heterogeneous. For example, a level of popular discontent that would have resulted in the collapse and dissipation of centralized power resources before the effective encagement of the population would have no such effect once the power networks that constitute "civilization" had been formed. Or, when Sargon of Akkad showed that a standing army of 5,400 men, properly deployed, could effectively subdue the whole of Mesopotamia, military power became for the first time, and remained for well over a millennium, the leading edge of civilizational development (133–55).

As can be seen by both of these examples, Mann has a very strong sense of the irreversibility of historical time. Indeed, this leads him to a trenchant critique of many of his fellow historical sociologists, who, he claims, treat as equivalent regimes that come from very different eras with different levels and dynamics of power development (167–74). The problem, he says explicitly, is that the historical sociologists are not sufficiently historical. "My criticism of the methodology of the comparative sociology of ancient empires," he says, "is not the 'typical historian's' objection that every case is unique. Though this is true, it does not preclude comparison and generalization. It is rather that comparative analysis should also be *historical*. Each case *develops* temporally, and this dynamic must itself be part of our explanation of its structure" (173–74). Although Mann uses comparison—very deftly, in my opinion—throughout his study, he properly insists that he is above all a *historical* rather than a *comparative* sociologist. He employs comparison not to establish causal laws that hold across a variety of supposedly equivalent cases, but to find analogies that help him to better theorize and explain the historical developments in each case. Thus, for example, he uses studies of the logistics of Roman and Macedonian armies to work out the possibilities and limitations of military power in the earlier Akkadian armies (139–40). And he establishes the unique dependence of the Greek hoplite military formation on the political and social solidarity of the polis by showing that unlike virtually all previous and subsequent military innovations—he mentions Sargon's commissary, the chariot, cavalry with saddle and stirrups, the Swiss pike phalanx, and gunpowder—this one could not be taken up by those against whom it was devastatingly employed, in this case the Persians (202). Mann, in my opinion, employs comparison in the way I argue it should be used: to generate propositions whose potential generality is tested by their ability to illuminate the conjunctural unfolding of analogous causal processes in the cases at hand.

Mann's *The Sources of Social Power* demonstrates to my satisfaction that an eventful conception of temporality is no less necessary for studies of macrohistory than for studies of much more local developments. But, as we should expect, it also suggests some questions and perspectives not raised by the Traugott and Kimmeldorf books. First, as I have already mentioned, Mann's study points out the interconnections between conceptualizations of time and of space. He convinces me that an eventful conception of temporality implies a conception of social space made up of multiple, uneven, overlapping, and non-isomorphic networks rather than of social systems. Second, by greatly stretching out the time scale of historical sociology, Mann's study raises questions about the key category of events. He certainly does recognize the macro-sociological significance of certain happenings that historians would immediately recognize as events, such as Sargon's conquest of Sumerian Mesopotamia or the defeat of the Persians by the Greeks at Thermopylae. But when one is dealing with millennial time-scales, some of what historians or sociologists might think of as gradual processes or trends begin to look like events. Examples would be the initial caging of populations that led to the emergence of civilization in the first place, or the development of iron smelting in Anatolia, Europe, and the Mediterranean, processes that took centuries to accomplish but that marked decisive breaks with previous history and brought about contingent but profound and irreversible structural transformations. This implies that the temporality of the theoretical category "event" is not self-

evident but rather must be constructed theoretically in relation to the
time-scale of the processes being studied.

A third and final issue raised by Mann's work concerns the directionalities of historical change. Historians, in particular, are very chary about at-
tributing long-term directionalities because doing so seems to smack of the
evolutionary teleology so common in nineteenth-century thought and still,
as I have argued, all too present in contemporary historical sociology.
Mann is a thoroughgoing critic of evolutionary theories of history, in part
because he feels that such theories by definition assume bounded unitary
societies or social systems as their units. But Mann's distaste for evolutionary theories does not mean that he avoids questions of directionality. Indeed, one of his major questions is how power resources *develop*, both
within given civilizations and over the history of mankind as a whole. He
attempts to give this question a sustained answer in the final chapter of volume I, entitled "Patterns of World-Historical Development in Agrarian
Societies" (518–41). First, he sees a general tendency for power resources to
increase, at least since the initial breakthrough to civilization. Over the
course of the millennia since that time, power resources have both tended
to spread over wider areas (as they are copied by those on the margins) and
to increase in both intensive and extensive reach. The tendency to develop
was not monotonic and there were certainly major centuries-long setbacks
in given regions of the world, but on the whole human power has tended
to grow—as is evidenced by the general long-run upward tendency of
global population even before the demographic spurt that accompanied
the Industrial Revolution. This is due largely to the fact that "once invented, the major infrastructural techniques seem almost never to have
disappeared from human practice" (534). Social power, Mann tells us, cu-
mulated over time.

However, the patterns of power development differed profoundly in
dynamics and rythms in different times and places. "Historical accidents"
continually deflected development from any given path (531–32). There are
distinct shapes to history "only because real men and women *impose* patterns. They attempt to control the world and increase their rewards within
it by setting up power organizations of varying but patterned types and
strengths. These power struggles are the principal patternings of history,
but their outcomes have often been close-run" (532). The patterns that result from such struggles vary both over time and over space. In the end,
Mann's book, like so many others, is searching for the macrohistorical sociologist's golden fleece, the reason why capitalism and industrialization

emerged in the West. He is, therefore, particularly sensitive to the different levels and kinds of developmental dynamics in different civilizations—the dynamism of early Mesopotamia by comparison with the extraordinary stability of early Egypt or the social stasis of caste-ridden India versus the long-term economic dynamism of feudal Europe. His analyses of the various civilizations' developmental tendencies are fascinating, rich, and consistently eventful. I, for one, am skeptical of certain aspects of his account of the rise of European power—which would be a subject for quite another essay. But Mann absolutely convinces me that an eventful sociology should not, indeed *must* not, eschew the issue of the developmental dynamics of societies. This immense and immensely important question must be wrested from teleological theories and subjected, as Mann has attempted to do in this brave and powerful book, to genuinely historical and eventful analyses.

⫷4⫸

A THEORY OF STRUCTURE

Duality, Agency, and Transformation

"S tructure" is one of the most important and most elusive terms in the vocabulary of current social science. The concept is central not only in such eponymous schools as structural functionalism, structuralism, and post-structuralism, but in virtually all tendencies of social scientific thought. But if social scientists find it impossible to do without the term "structure," we also find it nearly impossible to define it adequately. Many of us have surely had the experience of being asked by a "naive" student what we mean by structure, and then finding it embarrassingly difficult to define the term without using the word "structure" or one of its variants in its own definition. Sometimes we find what seems to be an acceptable synonym—for example, "pattern"—but all such synonyms lack the original's rhetorical force. When it comes to indicating that a relation is powerful or important it is certainly more convincing to designate it as "structural" than as "patterning."

The term structure empowers what it designates. Structure, in its nominative sense, always implies structure in its transitive verbal sense. Whatever aspect of social life we designate as structure is posited as "structuring" some other aspect of social existence—whether it is class that structures

This chapter was originally published with the same title in the *American Journal of Sociology* 98 (1992): 1–29. This chapter benefited, during its many revisions, from the careful reading and constructive criticism of a large number of friends and colleagues. Although I have sometimes failed to heed their good advice, I am grateful to Elizabeth Anderson, Jeffrey Alexander, Ronald Aminzade, Renee Anspach, Terry Boswell, Peggy Evans, Neil Fligstein, Steven Gudeman, Ronald Herring, Ronald Inden, David Laitin, Barbara Laslett, Michael Kennedy, Sherry Ortner, Sylvia Pedraza, Joan Scott, Ellen Sewell, Theda Skocpol, Ann Swidler, John Urry, Loïc Wacquant, and several anonymous reviewers.

politics, gender that structures employment opportunities, rhetorical conventions that structure texts or utterances, or modes of production that
structure social formations. Structure operates in social scientific discourse as a powerful metonymic device, identifying some part of a complex
social reality as explaining the whole. It is a word to conjure with in the
social sciences. In fact, structure is less a precise concept than a kind of
founding or epistemic metaphor of social scientific—and scientific—discourse.[1] For this reason, no formal definition can succeed in fixing the
term's meaning: the metaphor of structure continues its essential if somewhat mysterious work in the constitution of social scientific knowledge
despite theorists' definitional efforts.

There are, nevertheless, three problems in the current use of the term
that make self-conscious theorizing about the meanings of structure seem
worthwhile. The most fundamental problem is that structural or structuralist arguments tend to assume a far too rigid causal determinism in social life. Those features of social existence denominated as structures tend
to be reified and treated as primary, hard, and immutable, like the girders
of a building, while the events or social processes they structure tend to be
seen as secondary and superficial, like the outer "skin" of a skyscraper, or as
mutable within "hard" structural constraints, like the layout of offices on
floors defined by a skeleton of girders. What tends to get lost in the language of structure is the efficacy of human action—or "agency," to use the
currently favored term. Structures tend to appear in social scientific discourse as impervious to human agency, to exist apart from, but nevertheless to determine the essential shape of, the strivings and motivated transactions that constitute the experienced surface of social life. A social
science trapped in an unexamined metaphor of structure tends to reduce
actors to cleverly programmed automatons. A second and closely related
problem with the notion of structure is that it makes dealing with change
awkward. The metaphor of structure implies stability. For this reason,
structural language lends itself readily to explanations of how social life is
shaped into consistent patterns, but not to explanations of how these patterns change over time. In structural discourse, change is commonly located
outside of structures, either in a telos of history, in notions of breakdown,
or in influences exogenous to the system in questions. Consequently, mov-

1. The term "structure" seems to play an essentially identical role in the natural sciences. Such
usages originated, as far as I am aware, in seventeenth- and eighteenth-century botany, from
which they spread to other natural and social sciences (see Foucault 1971, 132–38).

ing from questions of stability to questions of change tends to involve awkward epistemological shifts.

The third problem is of a rather different order: the term structure is used in apparently contradictory senses in different social scientific discourses, particularly in sociology and anthropology. Sociologists typically contrast "structure" to "culture." Structure, in normal sociological usage, is thought of as "hard" or "material" and therefore as primary and determining, whereas culture is regarded as "soft" or "mental" and therefore as secondary or derived. By contrast, semiotically inclined social scientists, most particularly anthropologists, regard culture as the preeminent site of structure. In typical anthropological usage, the term structure is assumed to refer to the realm of culture, except when it is modified by the adjective "social." As a consequence, social scientists as different in outlook as Theda Skocpol and Marshall Sahlins can be designated as "structuralists" by their respective disciplines. Sociologists and anthropologists, in short, tend to visualize the nature and location of structure in sharply discrepant, indeed mutually incompatible, ways.[2]

In view of all these problems with the notion of structure, it is tempting to conclude that the term should simply be discarded. But this, I think, is impossible: structure is so rhetorically powerful and pervasive a term that any attempt to legislate its abolition would be futile. Moreover, the notion of structure does denominate, however problematically, something very important about social relations: the tendency of patterns of relations to be reproduced, even when actors engaging in relations are unaware of the patterns or do not desire their reproduction. In my opinion, the notion of structure neither could nor should be banished from the discourse of social science. But it does need extensive rethinking. This chapter will attempt to develop a theory of structure that overcomes the three cardinal weaknesses of the concept as it is normally employed in social science. The theory will attempt (1) to recognize the agency of social actors, (2) to build the possibility of change into the concept of structure, and (3) to overcome the divide between semiotic and materialist visions of structure. My strat-

2. This bifurcation of the meaning of structure especially inhibits communication between two groups of social scientists whose current projects seem convergent but who have thus far paid little attention to one another: the growing band of sociologists who are examining the cultural dimensions of social life and the anthropologists who are insisting on the importance of power and practice in understanding culture. For an assessment of the mushrooming field of cultural sociology, see Lamont and Wuthnow (1990). For trends in current anthropology, see the remarks of Ortner (1984, 144–60).

egy will be to begin from what I regard as the most promising existing formulations—Anthony Giddens's notion of "the duality of structure" and, at a later point in the argument, Pierre Bourdieu's concept of habitus—and to develop a more adequate theory by means of critique, reformulation, and elaboration.[3]

THE DUALITY OF STRUCTURE: A CRITIQUE AND REFORMULATION OF GIDDENS'S THEORY

The most sustained effort at reconceptualizing structure in recent social theory has been made by Anthony Giddens, who has been insisting since the mid-1970s that structures must be regarded as "dual" (Giddens 1976, 1979, 1981, 1984). By this he means that they are "both the medium and the outcome of the practices which constitute social systems" (Giddens 1981, 27). Structures shape people's practices, but it is also people's practices that constitute (and reproduce) structures. In this view of things, human agency and structure, far from being *opposed*, in fact *presuppose* each other. Structures are enacted by what Giddens calls "knowledgeable" human agents (i.e., people who know what they are doing and how to do it), and agents act by putting into practice their necessarily structured knowledge. Hence, "structures must not be conceptualized as simply placing constraints on human agency, but as enabling" (Giddens 1976, 161). This conception of human agents as "knowledgeable" and "enabled" implies that those agents are capable of putting their structurally formed capacities to work in creative or innovative ways. And if enough people, or even a few people who are powerful enough, act in innovative ways, their action may have the consequence of transforming the very structures that gave them the capacity to act. Dual structures therefore are potentially mutable. It is no accident that Giddens calls his theory "the theory of structuration," indicating by this neologism that "structure" must be regarded as a process, not as a steady state.

As a theoretically self-conscious social historian, I find Giddens's notion of the duality of structure particularly congenial. Much of the best social history of the past forty years has adopted an implicit theoretical

3. It is not my purpose to develop a full critique or appreciation of Giddens or Bourdieu. The critical literature on both is growing rapidly. Held and Thompson (1989) and Bryant and Jary (1991) include not only a wide range of critiques of Giddens's work by prominent scholars but also useful bibliographical listings of previous critiques. On Bourdeiu, see DiMaggio (1979), Brubaker (1985), Lamont and Lareau (1988), Wacquant (1989), and Calhoun, LiPuma, and Postone (1993). Wacquant (1989) provides extensive references to critical works on Bourdieu.

strategy quite consistent with Giddens's theory. Social historians have significantly altered in practice the sociological and anthropological concepts
of structure that they began to borrow so avidly in the 1960s and 1970s. Although they were probably writing more from professional instinct than
from considered theoretical scruples, social historians have demonstrated
how, in a great variety of times and places, structures are in fact dual: how
historical agents' thoughts, motives, and intentions are constituted by the
cultures and social institutions into which they are born, how these cultures and institutions are reproduced by the structurally shaped and constrained actions of those agents, but also how, in certain circumstances,
the agents can (or are forced to) improvise or innovate in structurally
shaped ways that significantly reconfigure the very structures that constituted them. Giddens has arrived at his position by way of a theoretical critique intended to reconcile phenomenology, interactionism, and ethno-
methodology with Marx, Durkheim, and Weber; he has shown little
interest in the work of social historians. Yet I believe that Giddens's notion
of the duality of structure underwrites theoretically what social historians
(and in recent years many historical sociologists and historical anthropologists as well) do in practice.

What Is Structure?

But in spite of its promise, Giddens's theory suffers from serious gaps and
logical deficiencies that have persisted through the theory's all-too-
frequent restatements. Most strikingly, "structure"—the central term of
Giddens's theory—remains frustratingly underspecified. Unlike most social scientists, he does not leave the term completely undefined and simply
allow it to do its accustomed magical work in his readers' minds. Especially
in *Central Problems in Social Theory* (1979), he discusses "structure" at some
length. But I do not think that the concept of structure he elaborates there
or elsewhere is sufficiently clear or robust to serve as the foundation of a
theoretical system.

Giddens defines structure formally in several places, including in the
glossary to *The Constitution of Society*:

> *Structure.* Rules and resources, recursively implicated in the reproduction of
> social systems. Structure exists only as memory traces, the organic basis of
> human knowledgeability, and as instantiated in action. (1984, 377)

This far-from-crystalline definition requires some exegesis. The terms
"rules and resources," in spite of their deceptive simplicity, are quite ob-

scure and will have to be discussed at length. Let us therefore begin with
the rest of the definition, which is arcanely worded but relatively straightforward in meaning. By "social systems" Giddens means empirically observable, intertwining, and relatively bounded social practices that link persons across time and space. Social systems would encompass what most
social scientists mean by "societies" but would also include social units
greater (e.g., the capitalist world system) or more limited (e.g., the neighborhood community) in scope than the nation-state. Social systems, according to Giddens, have no existence apart from the practices that constitute them, and these practices are reproduced by the "recursive" (i.e.,
repeated) enactments of structures. Structures are not the patterned social practices that make up social systems, but the *principles* that pattern
these practices. Structures, therefore, have only what he elsewhere terms
a "virtual" existence (e.g., 1984, 17). Structures do not exist concretely in
time and space except as "memory traces, the organic basis of knowlede-
ability" (i.e., only as ideas or schemas lodged in human brains) and as they
are "instantiated in action" (i.e., put into practice).

Structures as Rules

Structures, then, are "virtual" and are put into practice in the production
and reproduction of social life. But of what do these structures consist?
According to Giddens's definition, they consist of "rules and resources."
Giddens's notion of rules is largely derived from French structuralism.
This is especially clear in *New Rules of Sociological Method* and *Central Problems in Social Theory*. In both of these he relies heavily on a typically structuralist analogy with Saussurian linguistics. Giddens likens his own distinction between structure and practice to the Saussurian distinction
between *langue* and *parole*. According to this analogy, structure is to practice as *langue* (the abstract rules that make possible the production of
grammatical sentences) is to *parole* (speech, or the production of actual
sentences; 1976, 118–22). Hence structure, like *langue*, is a complex of rules
with a "virtual" existence, while practice, like speech, is an enactment of
these rules in space and time. For a French structuralist, structure is a complex of such rules. For example, structure may refer to the set of rules that
enables binary oppositions to be ordered into myths (Lévi-Strauss 1963a).
In *Central Problems in Social Theory* (1979, 62–64), Giddens affirms the similarity of his concept of structure to that of Lévi-Strauss. But he also
attempts to distinguish himself from the French structuralists, in part by
insisting that, because structures "bind" time and space, they must be con-

ceptualized as including not only rules but *resources* as well (1979, 63–64). However, Giddens leaves his discussion of rules dangling, and he fails to give examples of rules that underlie any actual social practices. All we know from *Central Problems in Social Theory* is that rules are virtual and that they somehow generate social practices and social systems.

In *The Constitution of Society*, a later statement of his theory, Giddens retreats even farther from a Lévi-Straussian conception of rules. Now taking his cue from Wittgenstein, Giddens there defines rules simply but, in my opinion, with great promise: "Let us regard the rules as generalizable procedures applied in the enactment/reproduction of social life" (1984, 21). This definition of rules as generalizable procedures could of course include Lévi-Straussian transformation rules, but it also implies the possibility of rules of a wide range of types. Giddens, however, does not give examples or develop typologies of the sorts of generalizable procedures he has in mind. Consequently, his conception of rules is, if anything, more impoverished in *The Constitution of Society* than it was in *Central Problems in Social Theory*, which at least implied an analogy with Lévi-Strauss. However, I think his Wittgensteinian definition of rules as generalizable procedures can be used as a foundation for a more robust conception.

Throughout his theory, Giddens places a great deal of weight on the notion that actors are *knowledgeable*. It is, presumably, the knowledge of rules that makes people capable of action. But Giddens develops no vocabulary for specifying the *content* of what people know. I would argue that such a vocabulary is, in fact, readily available, but is best developed in a field Giddens has to date almost entirely ignored: cultural anthropology. After all, the usual social scientific term for "what people know" is "culture," and those who have most fruitfully theorized and studied culture are the anthropologists. Claude Lévi-Strauss, the one anthropologist Giddens has taken seriously, is virtually unique in his fixation on very deep or general structures. His attempt, ultimately, is to reach by successive abstractions the structure of the human brain itself. Even some of the structuralist anthropologists who have been most profoundly influenced by Lévi-Strauss (see, e.g., Sahlins 1976, 1981, 1985) have been far more interested in applying Lévi-Strauss's method of seeking out recurrent patterns of binary oppositions in order to specify the assumptions, practices, and beliefs of particular peoples than in tracing such oppositions back to the structure of "the savage mind" or the human brain.

Rather than staying at the deep structural level preferred by Lévi-Strauss, I think we should, like most anthropologists, think of rules as existing at various levels. Rules nearer the surface may by definition be more "superficial," but they are not necessarily less important in their implications for social life. "The rules of social life" should be thought of as including all the varieties of cultural schemas that anthropologists have uncovered in their research: not only the array of binary oppositions that make up a given society's fundamental tools of thought, but also the various conventions, recipes, scenarios, principles of action, and habits of speech and gesture built up with these fundamental tools.[4] Indeed, the term "rules" is probably not quite the right word, since it tends to imply something like formally stated prescriptions — the sorts of things spelled out in statutes, proverbs, liturgies, constitutions, or contracts.[5] What I mean to get at is not formally stated prescriptions but the informal and not always conscious schemas, metaphors, or assumptions presupposed by such formal statements. I would in fact argue that publicly fixed codifications of rules are actual rather than virtual and should be regarded as *resources* rather than as rules in Giddens's sense. Because of this ambiguity about the meaning of the word "rules," I believe it is useful to introduce a change in terminology. Henceforth I shall use the term "schemas" rather than "rules" — even though this destroys the pleasing alliteration of Giddens's "rules and resources" formula.

The various schemas that make up structures are, to quote Giddens, "generalizable procedures applied in the enactment/reproduction of social life." They are "generalizable" in the sense that they can be applied in or extended to a variety of contexts of interaction. Such schemas or procedures — whether rules of etiquette, or aesthetic norms, or such recipes for group action as the royal progress, grain riot, or democratic vote, or a set of equivalences between wet and dry, female and male, nature and culture, private and public, or the body as a metaphor for hierarchy, or the notion that the human being is composed of a body and a soul — can be used not only in the situation in which they are first learned or most conventionally applied. They can be generalized — that is, transposed or extended — to new situations when the opportunity arises. This *generalizability or transposability* of schemas is the reason they must be understood as virtual. To say that schemas are virtual is to say that they cannot be reduced to their

4. It is not possible here to list a representative example of anthropological works that elaborate various "rules of social life." The most influential formulation of the anthropological concept of culture is probably Geertz (1973). For a superb overview of trends in cultural anthropology, see Ortner (1984).

5. For a particularly convincing critique of the notion of "rule," see Bourdieu (1977, 1–29).

existence in any particular practice or any particular location in space and time: they can be actualized in a potentially broad and unpredetermined range of situations.

I agree with Giddens, then, that the rules or schemas making up structures may usefully be conceptualized as having a "virtual" existence, that structures consist of intersubjectively available procedures or schemas capable of being actualized or put into practice in a range of different circumstances. Such schemas should be thought of as operating at widely varying levels of depth, from Lévi-Straussian deep structures to relatively superficial rules of etiquette.

Structures as Resources

Surely part of Giddens's nervousness about embracing Lévi-Strauss's conception of structure is that he wishes to distance himself from Lévi-Strauss's sublime indifference to questions of power, domination, and social change — indeed, to questions of social practice more generally. Presumably it is largely for this reason that Giddens insists that structures are not merely rules, but rules and resources, or "rule-resource sets" (1984, 377). But Giddens's concept of resources is even less adequately theorized than his concept of rules.[6] I agree with Giddens that any notion of structure that ignores asymmetries of power is radically incomplete. But tacking an undertheorized notion of resources onto an essentially rule-based notion of structure succeeds merely in confusing things.

In *Central Problems in Social Theory*, Giddens (1979, 92) defines resources as "the media whereby transformative capacity is employed as power in the routine course of social interaction." Unless I am missing some subtlety, this obscurely worded definition could be rendered in ordinary English as "resources are anything that can serve as a source of power in social interactions." This seems to me an unexceptional and theoretically uninformative statement of what we usually mean by social resources. Besides this anodyne definition, almost all he tells us about resources is that they can be classified into two types, authoritative and allocative. In *Central Problems in Social Theory*, he defines "authorization" as those "capabilities which generate command over persons" and "allocation" as those "capabilities which generate command over *objects* or other material phenomena" (1979, 100). Hence, authoritative resources should be human resources and allocative resources nonhuman resources — which once again seems unexceptional.

6. Giddens's concept of rules has occasionally been criticized, most recently by Thompson (1989), but to my knowledge no one has systematically criticized his paired concept of resources.

A THEORY OF STRUCTURE

I believe that Giddens's classification of resources is potentially useful, but that it needs to be reformulated and put into ordinary English. Resources are of two types, human and nonhuman. Nonhuman resources are objects, animate or inanimate, naturally occurring or manufactured, that can be used to enhance or maintain power; human resources are physical strength, dexterity, knowledge, and emotional commitments that can be used to enhance or maintain power, including knowledge of the means of gaining, retaining, controlling, and propagating either human or nonhuman resources. Both types of resources are media of power and are unevenly distributed. But however unequally resources may be distributed, some measure of both human and nonhuman resources are controlled by all members of society, no matter how destitute and oppressed. Indeed, part of what it means to conceive of human beings as *agents* is to conceive of them as *empowered* by access to resources of one kind or another.

Structures as Schemas and Resources

Reformulating Giddens's concept of resources does not make it clear how resources and schemas combine to form structures. Here the most glaring problem is Giddens's definition of structures as "virtual." As we have seen, this makes perfect sense for structures conceptualized as rules or schemas. But are *resources* also virtual? It is surprising that Giddens does not seem to have considered the point. The notion of a virtual resource seems particularly doubtful in the case of nonhuman (or in Giddens's terms "allocative") resources. Nonhuman resources would surely include such things as factories owned by capitalists, stocks of weapons controlled by kings or generals, land rented by peasants, or stacks of Hudson Bay blankets accumulated by Kwakiutl chiefs. It is clear that factories, armaments, land, and Hudson Bay blankets have had a crucial weight in shaping and constraining social life in particular times and places, and it therefore seems sensible to include them in some way in a concept of structure. But it is also hard to see how such material resources can be considered as "virtual," since material things by definition exist in space and time. It is, moreover, only in particular times, places, and quantities that such material objects can serve as resources.

The case of human resources is only a little less clear. By definition, human bodies, like any other material objects, cannot be virtual. But what about knowledge and emotional commitments, the mental aspects of human resources? Examples might be the Roman Catholic priest's power to consecrate the host and hear confession, children's sense of obligation towards their mothers, or the fear and reverence that subjects feel for their king. Unlike factories or Hudson Bay blankets, such resources are not material, or at least not in the same sense. Nevertheless they seem to me actual as opposed to virtual. They exist in what Giddens calls "time-space"; they are observable characteristics of real people who live in particular times and congregate in particular places. And it is their actualization in people's minds and bodies that make them resources. It is not the disembodied concept of the majesty of the king that gives him power, but the fear and reverence felt for him by his actual subjects.

If I am right that all resources are actual rather than virtual, Giddens's notion of structure turns out to be self-contradictory. If structures are virtual, they cannot include both schemas and resources. And if they include both schemas and resources, they cannot be virtual. He, and we, cannot have it both ways. But which way should we have it? The simplest way of conceptualizing structure would be to return to Giddens's starting point in structuralism and to assert that structure refers only to rules or schemas, not to resources, and that resources should be thought of as an *effect* of structures. In this way, structures would retain their virtual quality, and concrete distributions of resources would be seen not as structures but as media animated and shaped by structures, that is, by cultural schemas.

It is not unreasonable to claim that human resources are the products of schemas. A given number of soldiers will generate different amounts and kinds of military power depending on the contemporary conventions of warfare (such as chivalric codes), the notions of strategy and tactics available to the generals, and the regimes of training to which the troops have been subjected. The priest's power to consecrate the host derives from schemas operating at two rather different levels. First, a priest's training has given him mastery of a wide range of explicit and implicit techniques of knowledge and self-control that enable him to perform satisfactorily as a priest. And second, he has been raised to the dignity of the priesthood by an ordination ceremony that, through the laying on of hands by a bishop, has mobilized the power of apostolic succession and thereby made him capable of an apparently miraculous feat—transforming bread and wine into the body and blood of Christ. Fear and reverence for kings are manifestations of fundamental notions about the cosmic function of kingship, notions that are woven into a multitude of discourses and ceremonies at all levels of society; similarly, obligations felt by children toward their mothers are based in notions of the bonds of nature, of nurturance, and of obedience that are encoded in multiple routines of family life and in sermons, adages, novels, and works of political theory. Human resources, these examples suggest, may be thought of as manifestations and consequences of the enactment of cultural schemas.

But while we might reasonably speak of human resources as generated by rules or schemas, it is harder to see how nonhuman resources could be conceived of as so generated. Factories, land, and Hudson Bay blankets have material qualities that are certainly not generated by schemas. But it is also true that their condition as resources capable of producing and reproducing disparities in social power is not wholly intrinsic in their material existence. What they amount to as resources is largely a consequence of the schemas that inform their use. To take perhaps the most obvious case, an immense stack of Hudson Bay blankets would be nothing more than a means of keeping a large number of people warm were it not for the cultural schemas that constituted the Kwakiutl potlatch; but given these schemas, the blankets, given away in a potlatch, became a means of demonstrating the power of the chief and, consequently, of acquiring prestige, marriage alliances, military power, and labor services (Boas 1966; Sahlins 1989). In this case, the schemas constituting the potlatch determined the specific value, extent, and effects of Hudson Bay blankets as a resource. But I would argue that this is true of nonhuman resources in general. For example, the extent and kinds of resources generated by a factory will depend on whether it is owned by an individual capitalist or by a workers' cooperative—in other words, on rules defining the nature of property rights and of workplace authority. The resources gained by peasants from the land they use will be determined by the conventions of land tenure, the exigencies of customary law, the sets of obligations owed to kinsmen, and the agricultural techniques employed. Examples could be multiplied at will. Nonhuman resources have a material existence that is not reducible to rules or schemas, but the activation of material things as resources, the determination of their value and social power, is dependent on the cultural schemas that inform their social use.

It is clear, then, that resources can plausibly be thought of as effects of cultural schemas. It therefore would certainly be possible to clean up Giddens's concept of structure by defining structure as schemas with a purely virtual existence, and resources not as coequal elements in structure but as media and outcomes of the operation of structure. But notice that if we adopt this definition, the rhetorical power of the term structure insinuates a single direction of causality. That which is termed structure is, by this act of denomination, granted power over that which is not termed structure.

Stocks of material goods and people's knowledge and emotional commitments become inert, mere media for and outcomes of the determinative operations of cultural schemas. If we insist that structures are virtual, we risk lapsing into the de facto idealism that continually haunts structuralism however much its exponents—for example, Lévi-Strauss (1966, 130)—protest their materialist credentials and intentions. Schemas—mental structures—become the only form-giving entity, and agents become agents of these mental structures, actors who can only recite preexisting scripts. To define structures in this way threatens, in short, to deny their duality, and consequently, to annihilate the central premise of Giddens's theory.

The Duality of Schemas and Resources

If the duality of structure is to be saved—and as far as I am concerned the notion of duality of structure is the main attraction of Giddens's theory—we must take the other alternative and conceive of structures as having (appropriately) a *dual* character. Structure, then, should be defined as composed simultaneously of schemas, which are virtual, and of resources, which are actual.

If structures are dual in this sense, then it must be true that schemas are the effects of resources, just as resources are the effects of schemas. This seems to me a reasonable claim, one whose plausibility can be demonstrated by a few examples. A factory is not an inert pile of bricks, wood, and metal. It incorporates or actualizes schemas, and this means that the schemas can be inferred from the material form of the factory. The factory gate, the punching-in station, the design of the assembly line: all of these features of the factory teach and validate the rules of the capitalist contract. Or take the priest's performance of the Mass. When the priest transforms the host and wine into the body and blood of Christ and administers the host to communicants, the communicants are suffused by a sense of spiritual well-being. Communion therefore demonstrates to the communicants the reality and power of the rule of apostolic succession that made the priest a priest. In short, if resources are instantiations or embodiments of schemas, they therefore inculcate and justify the schemas as well. Resources, we might say, are *read* like texts, to recover the cultural schemas they instantiate. Indeed, texts—whether novels, or statute books, or folktales, or contracts—are resources from the point of view of this theory. They, too, are instantiations of schemas in time-space that can be used by actors to generate power.

If resources are effects of schemas, it is also true that schemas are effects of resources. If schemas are to be sustained or reproduced over time—and without sustained reproduction they could hardly be counted as structural—they must be validated by the accumulation of resources that the enactment engenders. Schemas not empowered or regenerated by resources would eventually be abandoned and forgotten, just as resources without cultural schemas to direct their use would eventually dissipate and decay. Sets of schemas and resources may properly be said to constitute *structures* only when they mutually imply and sustain each other over time.

THE TRANSFORMATION OF DUAL STRUCTURES: OUT OF BOURDIEU'S HABITUS

A definition of structure as made up of both schemas and resources avoids both the material determinism of traditional Marxism and the ideal determinism of traditional French structuralism. But how it can enhance our ability to understand transformations of structures is not immediately apparent. Indeed, one could argue that if the enactment of schemas always creates resources that inculcate the schemas, schemas and resources should simply reproduce each other without change indefinitely. The claim that dual structures engender stasis is far from fanciful; such an argument has in fact been made with great panache in Pierre Bourdieu's widely influential discussion of what he calls "habitus" in *Outline of a Theory of Practice* (1977). Any attempt to argue that duality of structure improves our ability to understand social transformations must confront this argument.[7]

Duality and Stasis

Although he uses a different terminology, Bourdieu has powerfully illustrated the mutually sustaining relationship between schemas and resources (what he calls "mental structures" and "the world of objects"). For

7. Some of Bourdieu's more recent work, esp. *Homo Academicus* (1988), which is a study of the French professoriat in the events of 1968, deals more directly with change. I do not think, however, that Bourdieu has considered the question of how habitus itself might *generate* change. In *Homo Academicus*, e.g., change arises from sources external to the habitus he is analyzing—fundamentally from the immense rise in the population of students in French universities in the 1960s. The concept of habitus is used to argue that the professors' response to the crisis was wholly determined by their location in the "academic field." *Homo Academicus* seems to indicate that Bourdieu has not overcome the lack of agency inherent in the concept of habitus elaborated in *Outline of a Theory of Practice*.

example, his well-known discussion of the Kabyle house shows how the design of the house and the placement of objects in it reproduces fundamental Kabyle cultural oppositions, such as those between high and low, male and female, fire and water, and light and dark, and thereby patterns all activities conducted in the house in terms of such oppositions. Bourdieu remarks that "all the actions performed in a space constructed in this way are immediately qualified symbolically and function as so many structural exercises through which is built up practical mastery of all the fundamental schemes" (1977, 91).

The house is given its shape by the application of schemas ("mental structures" in Bourdieu's vocabulary), and the house in turn inculcates these schemas by assigning tasks, objects, persons, and emotional dispositions to differently coded spaces. As Bourdieu puts it, in his characteristically ornate and paradoxical style,

> The mental structures which construct the world of objects are constructed in the practice of a world of objects constructed according to the same structures. The mind born of the world of objects does not rise as a subjectivity confronting an objectivity: the objective universe is made up of objects which are the product of objectifying operations structured according to the very structures which the mind applies to it. The mind is a metaphor of the world of objects which is itself but an endless circle of mutually reflecting metaphors. (Bourdeiu 1977, 91)

In many respects, Bourdieu's "theory of practice" is fully compatible with the conception of the duality of structure for which I am arguing in this paper. Bourdieu recognizes the mutual reproduction of schemas and resources that constitutes temporally durable structures—which he calls "habitus." His discussion of habitus powerfully elaborates the means by which mutually reinforcing rule-resource sets constitute human subjects with particular sorts of knowledge and dispositions. Moreover, Bourdieu's Kablye subjects are not cultural dopes. They are endowed with the capacity to engage in highly autonomous, discerning, and strategic actions (see, e.g., Bourdieu's discussion of gift exchange and matrimonial strategies [4–10 and 32–53]). Bourdieu's Kabyles would seem to be exactly the sort of knowledgeable actors called for by Giddens's theory.

Yet Bourdieu's habitus retains precisely the agent-proof quality that the concept of the duality of structure is supposed to overcome. In Bourdieu's habitus, schemas and resources so powerfully reproduce one another that even the most cunning or improvisational actions undertaken by agents necessarily reproduce the structure. "As an acquired system of generative schemes objectively adjusted to the particular conditions in which it is constituted, the habitus engenders all the thoughts, all the perceptions, and all the actions consistent with those conditions and no others" (95). Although Bourdieu avoids either a traditional French structuralist ideal determinism or a traditional Marxist material determinism, he does so only by erecting a combined determinism that makes significant social transformations seem impossible.

But is this powerful implication of stasis really warranted? After all, the Kabyle society in which Bourdieu carried out his fieldwork produced a momentous anticolonial revolution shortly after Bourdieu returned to France to analyze his data. It seems to me that, in spite of his devastating attacks on Cartesian and Lévi-Straussian "objectivism" (1–30), Bourdieu's own theory has fallen victim to an impossibly objectified and overtotalized conception of society. Only in the idealized world constructed by the social scientific observer could habitus engender "all the thoughts, all the perceptions, and all the actions" consistent with existing social conditions "and no others." In the world of human struggles and stratagems, plenty of thoughts, perceptions, and actions consistent with the reproduction of existing social patterns fail to occur, and inconsistent ones occur all the time.

Why Structural Change Is Possible

It is, of course, entirely proper for Bourdieu to insist on the strong reproductive bias built into structures—that is the whole point of the structure concept and part of what makes the concept so essential for theorizing social change. After all, as Renato Rosaldo (1980) and Marshall Sahlins (1981, 1985) have brilliantly demonstrated, the same reproductive biases of structures that explain the powerful continuities of social relations also make it possible to explain the paths followed in episodes of social change. What gets Bourdieu off the track is his unrealistically unified and totalized concept of habitus, which he conceptualizes as a vast series of strictly homologous structures encompassing all of social experience. Such a conceptualization, which Bourdieu in fact shares roughly with many structurally inclined theorists, cannot explain change as arising from within the operation of structures. It is characteristic that many structural accounts of social transformation tend to introduce change from outside the system and then trace out the ensuing structurally shaped changes, rather than showing how change is generated by the operation of structures internal to a society. In this respect, Marshall Sahlins's (1981) analysis of how Cap-

tain Cook's voyages affected the Hawaiians is emblematic. It is my conviction that a theory of change cannot be built into a theory of structure unless we adopt a far more multiple, contingent, and fractured conception of
society—and of structure. What is needed is a conceptual vocabulary that
makes it possible to show how the ordinary operations of structures can
generate transformations. To this end I propose five key axioms: the multiplicity of structures, the transposability of schemas, the unpredictability
of resource accumulation, the polysemy of resources, and the intersection
of structures.

The multiplicity of structures. Societies are based on practices that derive
from many distinct structures, which exist at different levels, operate in
different modalities, and are themselves based on widely varying types and
quantities of resources. While it is common for a certain range of these
structures to be homologous, like those described by Bourdieu in *Outline
of a Theory of Practice*, it is never true that all of them are homologous. Structures tend to vary significantly between different institutional spheres, so
that kinship structures will have different logics and dynamics than those
possessed by religious structures, productive structures, aesthetic structures, educational structures, and so on. There is, moreover, important
variation even within a given sphere. For example, the structures that
shape and constrain religion in Christian societies include authoritarian,
prophetic, ritual, and theological modes. These may sometimes operate in
harmony, but they can also lead to sharply conflicting claims and empow-
erments. The multiplicity of structures means that the knowledgeable social actors whose practices constitute a society are far more versatile than
Bourdieu's account of a universally homologous habitus would imply: social actors are capable of applying a wide range of different and even incompatible schemas and have access to heterogeneous arrays of resources.

The transposability of schemas. Moreover, the schemas to which actors
have access can be applied across a wide range of circumstances. This is actually recognized by Bourdieu, but he has not, in my opinion, drawn the
correct conclusions from his insight. Schemas were defined above as generalizable or transposable procedures applied in the enactment of social
life. The term "generalizable" is taken from Giddens; the term "transposable," which I prefer, is taken from Bourdieu.[8] At one point Bourdieu

8. To generalize a rule implies stating it in more abstract form so that it will apply to a large
number of cases. The verb "transpose" implies a concrete application of a rule to a new case, but
in such a way that the rule will have subtly different forms in each of its applications. This is implied by three of the *Oxford English Dictionary*'s definitions: "To remove from one place or time to

defines habitus as "a system of lasting transposable dispositions which, integrating past experiences, functions at every moment as a *matrix of perceptions, appreciations, and actions* and makes possible the achievement of infinitely diversified tasks, thanks to analogical transfers of schemes permitting the solution of similarly shaped problems" (1977, 83).

The slippage in this passage occurs in the final phrase, "permitting the solution of similarly shaped problems." Whether a given problem is shaped similarly enough to be solved by analogical transfers of schemes cannot be decided in advance by social scientific analysts, but must be determined case by case by the actors, which means that there is no fixed limit to the possible transpositions. This is in fact implied by the earlier phrase, "makes possible the achievement of infinitely diversified tasks." To say that schemas are transposable, in other words, is to say that they can be applied to a wide and not fully predictable range of cases outside the context in which they are initially learned. This fits with what we usually mean by knowledge of a rule or of some other learned procedure. In ordinary speech one cannot be said to really *know* a rule simply because one can apply it automatically to repeated instances of the same case. Whether we are speaking of rules of grammar, mathematics, law, etiquette, or carpentry, the real test of knowing a rule is to be able to apply it successfully in *unfamiliar* cases. Knowledge of a rule or a schema by definition means the ability to transpose or extend it—that is, to apply it creatively. If this is so, then *agency*, which I would define as entailing the capacity to transpose and extend schemas to new contexts, is inherent in the knowledge of cultural schemas that characterizes all minimally competent members of society.[9]

The unpredictability of resource accumulation. The very fact that schemas are by definition capable of being transposed or extended means that the resource consequences of the enactment of cultural schemas is never entirely predictable. A joke told to a new audience, an investment made in a new market, an offer of marriage made to a new patriline, a cavalry attack made on a new terrain, a crop planted in a newly cleared field or in a familiar field in a new spring—the effect of these actions on the resources of

---

another; to transfer, shift," "to alter the order of or the position of in a series . . . to interchange," and, in music, "to put into a different key." *Transposer,* in French (which was of course the language in which Bourdieu wrote), also has an even more appropriate meaning: "faire changer de forme ou de contenu en faisant passer dans un autre domaine" (to cause something to change in form or content by causing it to pass into another domain, *Le Petit Robert* [1984, s.v. "transposer"]). I would like my use of *transpose* to be understood as retaining something of the French meaning.

9. Here my thinking has been influenced by Goran Therborn (1980, esp. 15–22).

the actors is never quite certain. Investment in a new market may make the entrepreneur a pauper or a millionaire, negotiations of a marriage with a new patriline may result in a family's elevation in status or its extinction in a feud, planting a new crop in the familiar field may result in subsistence, starvation, or plenty. Moreover, if the enactment of schemas creates unpredictable quantities and qualities of resources, and if the reproduction of schemas depends on their continuing validation by resources, this implies that schemas will in fact be differentially validated when they are put into action and therefore will potentially be subject to modification. A brilliantly successful cavalry attack on a new terrain may change the battle plans of subsequent campaigns or even theories of military tactics; a joke that draws rotten tomatoes rather than laughter may result in the suppression of a category of jokes from the comedian's repertoire; a succession of crop failures may modify routines of planting and plowing.[10]

The polysemy of resources. The term polysemy (or multiplicity of meaning) is normally applied to symbols, language, or texts. Its application to resources sounds like a contradiction in terms. But, given the concept of resources I am advocating here, it is not. Resources, I have insisted, embody cultural schemas. Like texts or ritual performances, however, their meaning is never entirely unambiguous. The form of the factory embodies and therefore teaches capitalist notions of property relations. But, as Marx points out, it can also teach the necessarily social and collective character of production and thereby undermine the capitalist notion of private property. The new prestige, wealth, and territory gained from the brilliant success of a cavalry charge may be attributed to the superior discipline and élan of the cavalry officers and thereby enhance the power of an aristocratic officer corps, or it may be attributed to the commanding general and thereby result in the increasing subordination of officers to a charismatic leader. Any array of resources is capable of being interpreted in varying ways and, therefore, of empowering different actors and teaching different schemas. Again, this seems to me inherent in a definition of agency as the capacity to transpose and extend schemas to new contexts. Agency, to put it differently, is the actor's capacity to reinterpret and mobilize an array of

---

10. Although Marshall Sahlins (1981, 1985) does not explicitly include resources in his definition of structure, my argument here runs closely parallel to his. Sahlins argues that "in action in the world — technically, in acts of reference — the cultural categories acquire new functional values" because the categories are "burdened with the world" (1985, 138). This burdening of categories with the world is a matter of schemas being changed by the unanticipated effects of action on the resources that sustain the schemas. See the discussion of Sahlins in chapter 7, below.

resources in terms of cultural schemas other than those that initially constituted the array.

The intersection of structures. One reason arrays of resources can be interpreted in more than one way is that structures or structural complexes intersect and overlap. The structures of capitalist society include both a mode of production based on private property and profit and a mode of labor organization based on workplace solidarity. The factory figures as a crucial resource in both of these structures, and its meaning and consequences for both workers and managers is therefore open and contested. The intersection of structures, in fact, takes place in both the schema and resource dimensions. Not only can a given array of resources be claimed by different actors embedded in different structural complexes (or differentially claimed by the same actor embedded in different structural complexes), but schemas can be borrowed or appropriated from one structural complex and applied to another. Not only do workers and factory owners struggle for control of the factory, but Marx appropriates political economy for the advancement of socialism.

Structures, then, are sets of mutually sustaining schemas and resources that empower and constrain social action and that tend to be reproduced by that social action. But their reproduction is never automatic. Structures are at risk, at least to some extent, in all of the social encounters they shape — because structures are multiple and intersecting, because schemas are transposable, and because resources are polysemic and accumulate unpredictably. Placing the relationship between resources and cultural schemas at the center of a concept of structure makes it possible to show how social change, no less than social stasis, can be generated by the enactment of structures in social life.

AGENCY

Such enactments of structures imply a particular concept of agency — one that sees agency not as opposed to, but as constituent of, structure. To be an agent means to be capable of exerting some degree of control over the social relations in which one is enmeshed, which in turn implies the ability to transform those social relations to some degree. As I see it, agents are empowered to act with and against others by structures: they have knowledge of the schemas that inform social life and have access to some measure of human and nonhuman resources. Agency arises from the actor's knowledge of schemas, which means the ability to apply them to new contexts. Or, to put the same thing the other way around, agency arises from the actor's control of resources, which means the capacity to reinterpret or mobilize an array of resources in terms of schemas other than those that constituted the array. Agency is implied by the existence of structures.

I would argue that a capacity for agency—for desiring, for forming intentions, and for acting creatively—is inherent in all humans. But I would also argue that humans are born with only a highly generalized capacity for agency, analogous to their capacity to use language. Just as linguistic capacity takes the form of becoming a competent speaker of some particular language—French, or Arabic, or Swahili, or Urdu—agency is formed by a specific range of cultural schemas and resources available in a person's particular social milieu. The specific forms that agency will take consequently vary enormously and are culturally and historically determined. But a capacity for agency is as much a given for humans as the capacity for respiration.

That all humans actually exercise agency in practice is demonstrated to my satisfaction by the work of Erving Goffman (1959, 1967a). Goffman shows that all members of society employ complex repertoires of interaction skills to control and sustain ongoing social relations. He also shows that small transformative actions—for example, intervening to save the face of an interactant who has misread the situation—turn out to be necessary to sustain even the most ordinary intercourse of daily life (Goffman 1967b). Once again, knowledge of cultural schemas (in this case of interaction rituals) implies the ability to act creatively. Actors, of course, vary in the extent of their control of social relations and in the scope of their transformative powers, but all members of society exercise some measure of agency in the conduct of their daily lives.

It is equally important, however, to insist that the agency exercised by different persons is far from uniform, that the agency differs enormously in both kind and extent. What kind of desires people can have, what intentions they can form, and what sort of creative transpositions they can carry out vary dramatically from one social world to another depending on the nature of the particular structures that inform those social worlds. Without a notion of heaven and hell a person cannot strive for admission into paradise; only in a modern capitalist economy can one attempt to make a killing on the futures market; if they are denied access to the public sphere, women's ambitions will be focused on private life. Agency also differs in extent, both between and within societies. Occupancy of different social positions—as defined, for example, by gender, wealth, social prestige, class, ethnicity, occupation, generation, sexual preference, or education—gives people knowledge of different schemas and access to different kinds and amounts of resources and hence different possibilities for transformative action. And the scope or extent of agency also varies enormously between different social systems, even for occupants of analogous positions. The owner of the biggest art gallery in St. Louis has far less influence on American artistic taste than the owner of the biggest gallery in Los Angeles; the president of Chad has far less power over global environmental policy than the president of Russia. Structures, in short, empower agents differentially, which also implies that they embody the desires, intentions, and knowledge of agents differentially as well. Structures, and the human agencies they endow, are laden with differences of power.

Finally, I would insist that agency is collective as well as individual. I do not agree with Barry Hindess (1986) that the term "agent" must be applied in the same sense to collectives that act as corporate units in social life—political parties, firms, families, states, clubs, or trade unions—as it is applied to individuals. But I do see agency as profoundly social or collective. The transpositions of schemas and remobilizations of resources that constitute agency are always acts of communication with others. Agency entails an ability to coordinate one's actions with others and against others, to form collective projects, to persuade, to coerce, and to monitor the simultaneous effect of one's own and others' activities. Moreover, the extent of the agency exercised by individual persons depends profoundly on their positions in collective organizations. To make the extreme case, a monarch's personal whims or quarrels may affect the lives of thousands (see, e.g., Sahlins 1991). But it is also true that the agency of fathers, executives, or professors is greatly expanded by the places they occupy in patriarchal families, corporations, or universities and by their consequent authority to bind the collectivity by their actions. Agency, then, characterizes all persons. But the agency exercised by persons is collective in both its sources and its mode of exercise. Personal agency is, therefore, laden with collectively produced differences of power and implicated in collective struggles and resistances.

VARIETIES OF STRUCTURES

The concept of structure I elaborate in this chapter is very general and therefore could be applied to structures of widely differing character—ranging in import from structures that shape and constrain the development of world military power to those that shape and constrain the joking practices of a group of Sunday fishing buddies or the erotic practices of a single couple. This immense range in the scope and character of the structures to which this article's concepts can be applied is appropriate, given the premise that all social action is shaped by structures. But it suggests a need for some means of distinguishing the character and dynamics of different sorts of structures. I will offer no detailed typology—both because space is short and because I feel that typologies should arise out of concrete analyses of social change and reproduction. Instead, I shall simply indicate two important dimensions along which structures vary: depth, which refers to the schema dimension of structures, and power, which refers to the resource dimension. I shall try to demonstrate that thinking in terms of depth and power can help to illuminate the very different dynamics and durabilities of three important types of structures: those of language, states, and capitalism.

Depth has long been a key metaphor of linguistic and structuralist discourse. To designate a structure as "deep" implies that it lies beneath and generates a certain range of "surface" structures, just as structures underlie and generate practices. In structuralist discourse, deep structures are those schemas that can be shown to underlie ordinary or "surface" structures, in the sense that the surface structures are a set of transformations of the deep structures. Thus the structural schemas for the performance of a fertility ritual may be shown to be particular transformations of a deeper set of oppositions between wet and dry or male and female that also underlie structures informing other institutionally distinct practices—from house-building, to personal adornment, to oratory. Consequently, deep structural schemas are also pervasive, in the sense that they are present in a relatively wide range of institutional spheres, practices, and discourses. They also tend to be relatively unconscious, in the sense that they are taken-for-granted mental assumptions or modes of procedure that actors normally apply without being aware that they are applying them.

Different structures also vary enormously in the resources, and hence the power, that they mobilize. Military structures or structures shaping state finance create massive concentrations of power, whereas the grammatical structures of a language or the structures shaping schoolchildren's play create much more modest power concentrations. Structures also differ in the kinds of power they mobilize. For example, the power created by apostolic succession is based primarily (although far from exclusively) on persuasion, while that created by the military government of a conquering army is based primarily on coercion.

Language

I believe that thinking about structures in terms of their depth and power can lead to insights about the structures' durability and dynamics. Consider, for example, linguistic structures, which scholars in many disciplines have used as the prime example of structure in general. Linguistic structures, which of course tend to be remarkably durable, actually fall at extremes on the dimensions of both power and depth. Linguistic structures are unusually deep. Intricate phonological, morphological, syntactical, and semantic structures underlie every sentence. Sentences, in turn, are aggregated into meaningful utterances or texts in accord with the discursive structures of rhetoric, narrative, metaphor, and logic. And all of these layered linguistic structures underlie the multitude of structures that rely at least in part on speech and writing—which is to say the immense preponderance of all structures.

Yet the *power* of linguistic structures is unusually slight. The enactment of phonological, morphological, syntactical, and semantic structures in speech or writing in itself has relatively modest resource effects. It confirms the speaker's membership in a linguistic community and reinforces the schemas that make the generation of grammatical sentences possible. Assuming that an utterance is made to other competent speakers of the language, the speaking of a grammatical sentence in itself creates no significant power disparities but rather establishes an equality among the conversants. Language, of course, serves as a medium for all kinds of enactments of power relations, but at the level of phonology, morphology, syntax, and semantics, it is as close as we are likely to get to a neutral medium of exchange. This relative neutrality with respect to power helps to account for the other peculiarity of linguistic structures: their extraordinary durability. If the enactment of linguistic schemas serves only to sustain the linguistic empowerment of speakers without sharply shifting resources toward some speakers and away from others, then no one has much incentive to engage in innovations that would transform linguistic structures.

If it is true that linguistic structures are much less implicated in power relations and much deeper and more durable than most structures, it follows that we should be wary of the widespread tendency to use linguistic structures as a paradigm for structures in general. Although the elegance of the linguistic model may set an enviable standard, structures that operate nearer the surface of social life and that are more directly implicated in power relations may have very different principles and dynamics. One danger that arises from accepting the linguistic model uncritically is a tendency to think of structures as composed purely of schemas, while ignoring the resource dimension. In studying the syntactic structures of languages, where the enactment of schemas has minor power consequences, it does not matter much if the resource aspect of structure is neglected. But when we try to make sense of the arenas of life more permeated by power relations, it may be downright crippling to apply the linguistic analogy and conceptualize structures purely as schemas.

States

Particularly poor candidates for the linguistic analogy would be state or political structures, which commonly generate and utilize large concentrations of power and which are usually relatively near the surface of social life. State and political structures are consciously established, maintained, fought over, and argued about rather than taken for granted as if they were unchangeable features of the world. Although one might initially imagine that large power concentrations would tend to assure a structure's durability, this may not actually be true. Although centralized states with immense coercive power impose high costs on those who would challenge them, it is far from clear that centralized and coercive states have generally proved more durable than relatively decentralized or uncoercive states. Compare, for example, Britain and France between 1750 and 1850, the United States and Germany from 1870 to 1950, Costa Rica and Nicaragua, El Salvador, or Guatemala since World War II, or India and China over the same time span. Even the relatively stable states are subject to periodic structural transformations. Although the United States has had a single constitution since 1789, it has experienced a succession of fundamental political crises that produced at least five sharply distinct party systems over the past two centuries (Burnham 1967). One might argue that state structures are relatively mutable precisely because their massiveness (power) and obviousness (lack of depth) of their resource effects make them natural targets for open struggles.

But if most political structures are characterized by both high power and low depth, an inverse relationship between power and depth is by no means necessary. There are some political structures with immense power implications that are nevertheless relatively deep, that have become "second nature" and are accepted by all (or nearly all) political actors as es-

sentially power-neutral, taken-for-granted means to political ends. Such
structures also appear to be unusually durable. This would appear to be
true of political structures as diverse as the American constitutional system, the French public bureaucracy, or the English community legal structures whose persistence Margaret Somers (1986) has traced from the fourteenth to the mid-nineteenth century. Durability, then, would appear to be
determined more by a structure's depth than by its power.

Capitalism

How do structures with huge power effects become or remain deep? One
would normally expect the massiveness of the effects to make social actors
aware of and willing to contest the schemas and resource accumulations of
those structures. I will approach this question by examining the case of
capitalism, a spectacular case of a power-laden yet long-enduring structure. Capitalism is, of course, highly dynamic. Yet it is commonly maintained that the past two hundred fifty to three hundred years (if not the
entire period since the sixteenth century, according to Wallerstein [1974])
constitutes a unified capitalist era with a continuous dynamic of capital accumulation guided by an enduring core structure, or what in Marxian parlance is called the capitalist mode of production.

Marx himself noted the extraordinarily dynamic and changeable character of capitalist development, but he saw the change converging on a
single form: the large-scale, mechanized factory staffed by an increasingly
homogenous proletariat. Recent developments have tended to make the
changeability of capitalism seem more radical and permanent. Far from
registering the onrush of the classic factory, the current era of world economic growth has been characterized by an increasing use of subcontracting, sweatshops, outsourcing, and "cottage industry," and by the burgeoning of services at the expense of manufacturing. At the same time, scholars
are increasingly pointing out the unevenness, contingency, and openness
of development patterns under capitalism, whether in the past (Samuel
1977; Sabel and Zeitlin 1985; see also chap. 10, below) or in the present and
future (Piore and Sabel 1984). Sabel (1988) has even suggested that forms
of economic change in the so-called capitalist era are so indeterminate that
the very concept of capitalism, with its implication of underlying regularity, is misleading and should be abandoned. I think Sabel is right as far as
he goes: a wide variety of institutional arrangements and property relations are compatible with "capitalism," and never in its history has capitalism obeyed uniform "laws of motion." Capitalist development has always

been a messy and uneven affair. But I think that the messiness has been at the level of secondary or surface structures and that beneath the surface mutability lies a far more stable deep structure of schemas that are continually reinforced by flows of resources—even on occasions when the surface structures are revolutionized.

Unlike most Marxians, I see the core schemas not as those defining the wage-labor relationship but as those governing the conversion of use value into exchange value.[11] The core procedure of capitalism—the conversion of use value into exchange value or the commodification of things—is exceptionally transposable. It knows no natural limits; it can be applied not only to cloth, tobacco, or cooking pans, but to land, housework, bread, sex, advertising, emotions, or knowledge, each of which can be converted into any other by means of money. The surface instability of capitalism arises precisely from this interconvertibility, which encourages holders of resources to trade them for other resources as relative values change and which always makes it possible for resources not previously treated as commodities to enter the circuit of monetized exchanges. To put it otherwise, the commodity form, by making almost all resources readable as exchangeable commodities, organizes a virtually universal intersection of structures, which means that changes in one structure—an increased or decreased accumulation of resources or a new procedure—can affect an indefinitely vast number of other structures that intersect through the medium of money. Changes at any point in the circuit of exchange will give rise to resource effects and innovations elsewhere. And these changes are not necessarily constrained to follow any particular institutional form, so long as they are profitable. Thus the rise of the automobile industry stimulated the simultaneous development of rubber plantations based on indentured or forced labor, automobile assembly operations based on immense factories staffed by wage-earning proletarians, and a proliferation of repair shops run by self-employed petty capitalists.

But this chronic instability or unpredictability of capitalism's surface structures actually reinforces its deeper structures. An alteration anywhere along the vast chain of commodity exchanges is a new incitement to invest; the logic inherent in the commodity form makes any new array of resources or new procedure a potential opportunity for profit. And of course any new investment results in further changes. Even investments that fail create new

---

11. John Roemer (1982) has proved to my satisfaction that capitalist exploitation can occur in the absence of wage labor.

opportunities that can be seized by following the normal procedures of capitalist investment and exchange—when a firm goes under there is plant and equipment to be brought up at bargain prices, a residual market for the firm's former competitors to exploit, and so on. Consequently, the procedures themselves are remarkably impervious to—indeed, paradoxically, are reinforced by—the failures of particular capitalist enterprises or industries. The displacement of handweavers by the power loom or of coal by petroleum may have destroyed skills, wrecked businesses, or blighted the economies of certain localities. But it simultaneously proved that following the logic of the commodity form creates wealth for those who do so, and even—over the long run and in spite of important local exceptions—for the capitalist economy as a whole. In some cases, structures can combine depth with great power and, consequently, can shape the experiences of entire societies over many generations.

CONCLUSION

Beginning from the premise that structure is an unavoidable epistemic metaphor in the social sciences, I have tried to specify how that metaphor should be understood. Structures, I have argued, are constituted by mutually sustaining cultural schemas and sets of resources that empower and constrain social action and tend to be reproduced by that action. Agents are empowered by structures, both by the knowledge of cultural schemas that enables them to mobilize resources and by the access to resources that enables them to enact schemas. This differs from ordinary sociological usage of the term because it insists that structure is a profoundly cultural phenomenon and from ordinary anthropological usage because it insists that structure always derives from the character and distribution of resources in the everyday world. Structure is dynamic, not static; it is the continually evolving outcome and matrix of a process of social interaction. Even the more or less perfect reproduction of structures is a profoundly temporal process that requires resourceful and innovative human conduct. But the same resourceful agency that sustains the reproduction of structures also makes possible their transformation—by means of transpositions of schemas and remobilizations of resources that make the new structures recognizable as transformations of the old. Structures, I suggest, are not reified categories we can invoke to explain the inevitable shape of social life. To invoke structures as I have defined them here is to call for a critical analysis of the dialectical interactions through which humans shape their history.

⫷5⫸

THE CONCEPT(S) OF CULTURE

The aim of this chapter is to reflect upon the concept—or more properly the concepts—of culture in contemporary academic discourse. Trying to clarify what we mean by culture seems both imperative and impossible at a moment like the present, when the study of culture is expanding explosively in virtually all fields of the human sciences. Although I glance at the varying uses of the concept in a number of disciplines, my reflection is based above all on the extensive debates that have occurred in anthropology over the past two decades—debates in which some have questioned the very utility of the concept.[1] I feel strongly that it remains as useful, indeed essential, as ever. But given the cacophony of contemporary discourse about culture, I also believe that the concept needs some reworking and clarification.

The current volatility of the culture concept stands in sharp contrast with the situation in the early 1970s, when I first got interested in a cultural approach to social history. At that time it was clear that if you wanted to learn about culture, you turned to the anthropologists. And while they by no means spoke in a single voice, there was a widespread consensus both about the meaning of culture and about the centrality of the culture con-

A version of this chapter was originally published with the same title in *Beyond the Cultural Turn: New Directions in the Study of Culture and Society*, ed. Victoria E. Bonnell and Lynn Hunt. Copyright © 1999 by The Regents of the University of California; reprinted with the permission of University of California Press. I would like to thank Anne Kane, David Laitin, Claudio Lomnitz, Sherry Ortner, Bill Reddy, Marshall Sahlins, Paul Seeley, Ann Swidler, and Lisa Wedeen for their valuable comments on earlier versions of this chapter.

1. For a discerning analysis of this debate, see Brightman (1995).

cept to the anthropological enterprise. I began borrowing the methods and insights of cultural anthropology as a means of learning more about nineteenth-century French workers. Cultural analysis, I hoped, would enable me to understand the meaning of workers' practices that I had been unable to get at by using quantitative and positivist methods — my standard toolkit as a practitioner of what was then called "the new social history."[2] I experienced the encounter with cultural anthropology as a turn from a hard-headed, utilitarian, and empiricist materialism — which had both liberal and *marxisant* faces — to a wider appreciation of the range of human possibilities, both in the past and in the present. Convinced that there was more to life than the relentless pursuit of wealth, status, and power, I felt that cultural anthropology could show us how to get at that "more."

Anthropology at the time had a virtual monopoly on the concept of culture. In political science and sociology, culture was associated with the by then utterly sclerotic Parsonian theoretical synthesis. The embryonic "cultural studies" movement was still confined to a single research center in Birmingham. And literary studies were still fixated on canonical literary texts — although the methods of studying them were being revolutionized by the importation of "French" structuralist and post-structuralist theory. Moreover, the mid-1960s to the mid-1970s were the glory years of American cultural anthropology, which may be said to have reached its apotheosis with the publication of Clifford Geertz's phenomenally influential *The Interpretation of Cultures* in 1973. Not only did anthropology have no serious rivals in the study of culture, but the creativity and prestige of cultural anthropology were at a very high point.

As I have noted in chapter 2, during the 1980s and 1990s the intellectual ecology of the study of culture was transformed by a vast expansion of work on culture in a wide range of academic disciplines and specialties. The history of this advance differs in timing and content in each field, but the cumulative effects are undeniable. In literary studies, which were already being transformed by French theory in the 1970s, the 1980s marked a turn to a vastly wider range of texts, quasi-texts, para-texts, and text analogues. If, as Derrida (1976) declared, nothing is extratextual ("il n'y a pas de hors-texte"), literary critics could direct their theory-driven gaze upon semiotic products of all kinds — legal documents, political tracts, soap operas, histories, talk shows, popular romances — and seek out their inter-

2. One outcome of these efforts was Sewell (1980).

textualities. Consequently, as such "new historicist" critics as Steven Green-blatt and Louis Montrose recognize, literary study is increasingly becoming the study of cultures.[3] In history the early and rather self-conscious borrowing from anthropology was followed by a theoretically heterogeneous rush to the study of culture, one modeled as much on literary studies or the work of Michel Foucault as on anthropology.

In the late 1970s, an emerging "sociology of culture" began by applying standard sociological methods to studies of the production and marketing of cultural artifacts—music, art, drama, and literature. By the late 1980s, the work of cultural sociologists had broken out of the study of culture-producing institutions and moved toward studying the place of meaning in social life more generally. Feminism, which in the 1970s was concerned above all to document women's experiences, has increasingly turned to analyzing the discursive production of gender difference. Since the mid-1980s the new quasi-discipline of cultural studies has grown explosively in a variety of different academic niches—for example, in programs or departments of film studies, literature, performance studies, or communications. In political science, which is well known for its propensity to chase headlines, interest in cultural questions has been revived by the recent prominence of religious fundamentalism, nationalism, and ethnicity, which look like the most potent sources of political conflict in the contemporary world. This frenetic rush to the study of culture has everywhere been bathed, to a greater or lesser extent, in the pervasive trans-disciplinary influence of the French post-structuralist trinity of Lacan, Derrida, and Foucault.

It is paradoxical that as discourse about culture becomes ever more pervasive and multifarious, anthropology, the discipline that invented the concept—or at least shaped it into something like its present form—is somewhat ambivalently backing away from its long-standing identification with culture as its keyword and central symbol. For the past two decades, anthropology has been rent by a particularly severe identity crisis, which has been manifested in anxiety about the discipline's epistemology, rhetoric, methodological procedures, and political implications.[4] The reasons for the crisis are many—liberal and radical guilt about anthropology's association with Euro-American colonialism, the disappearance of

3. A good introduction to this current of scholarship is Veeser (1989).
4. The most celebrated expression of this angst is the collective volume edited by Clifford and Marcus (1986).

the supposedly "untouched" or "primitive" peoples who were the favored subjects for classical ethnographies, the rise of "native" ethnographers who contest the right of European and American scholars to tell the "truth" about their people, and the general loss of confidence in the possibility of objectivity that has attended post-structuralism and postmodernism. As anthropology's most central and distinctive concept, "culture" has become a suspect term among critical anthropologists—who claim that both in its academic usages and in the way it has been picked up in public discourse, talk about culture tends to essentialize, exoticize, and stereotype those whose ways of life are being described and to naturalize their differences from white middle-class Euro-Americans. If Geertz's phrase "The Interpretation of Cultures" was the watchword of anthropology in the 1970s, Lila Abu-Lughod's "Writing Against Culture" (1991) more nearly sums up the mood of the late 1980s and the 1990s.

As Robert Brightman points out in his superb commentary on the recent disputes about culture in anthropology, the anthropological critics of the 1980s and 1990s have exhibited widespread "lexical avoidance behavior," either placing the term culture in quotation marks when it is used, refusing to use culture as a noun while continuing to use it as an adjective (as in "cultural anthropology"), or replacing it with alternative lexemes such as "habitus," "hegemony," or "discourse" (1995, 510). This emerging anthropological tabu about using the term culture seems to me mistaken on two counts. First, it is based on the implicit assumption that anthropology "owns" the lexeme and that it is therefore responsible for any abuses that might be perpetrated by means of the term. Second, it assumes that anthropological abstention from the use of the lexeme will magically abolish such abuses. The truth is that the term culture has escaped all possibility of control by anthropologists: whatever lexical practices the anthropologists may adopt, talk about culture will continue to thrive, in both abusive and acceptable ways, in a wide range of other academic disciplines and in ordinary language as well. Moreover, as Brightman again points out, even the critical anthropologists find it impossible to give up the *concept* of culture, as opposed to the lexeme. James Clifford's lament that "culture is a deeply compromised concept that I cannot yet do without" (1988a, 10) seems emblematic of the unresolved ambivalence: the concept is compromised and he hopes in the future to do without it, but because it continues to perform valuable intellectual work the fateful act of renunciation is indefinitely deferred. If, as I believe, Clifford is right that we cannot do without a concept of culture, I think we should try to shape it into one we can

work with. We need to modify, rearticulate, and revivify the concept, retaining and reshaping what is useful and discarding what is not.

WHAT DO WE MEAN BY CULTURE?

Writing in 1983, Raymond Williams declared that "culture is one of the two
or three most complicated words in the English language" (1983; see also
1958). Its complexity has surely not decreased since then. I have neither the
competence nor the inclination to trace out the full range of meanings of
culture in contemporary academic discourse. But some attempt to sort out
the different usages of the word seems essential. We should begin by distinguishing two fundamentally different meanings of the term.

In one meaning, culture is a theoretically defined category or aspect of
social life that must be abstracted out from the complex reality of human
existence. Culture in this sense is always contrasted to some other equally
abstract aspect or category of social life that is not culture—for example,
to economy, or politics, or biology. To designate something as culture or as
cultural is to claim it for a particular academic discipline or subdiscipline—
for example, anthropology or cultural sociology—or for a particular style
or styles of analysis—for example, structuralism, ethno-science, compo-
nential analysis, deconstruction, or hermeneutics. Culture in this sense—
as an abstract analytical category—only takes the singular. Whenever we
speak of "cultures," we have moved to the second fundamental meaning.

In its second meaning, culture stands for a concrete and bounded world
of beliefs and practices. Culture in this sense is commonly assumed to belong to or to be isomorphic with a "society" or with some clearly identifi-
able subsocietal group. We may speak of "American culture" or "Samoan
culture," or of "middle-class culture" or "ghetto culture."[5] The contrast in
this usage is not between culture and not-culture but between one culture
and another—between American, Samoan, French, and Bororo cultures,
or between middle-class and upper-class cultures or ghetto and mainstream cultures.

This distinction between culture as theoretical category and culture as
concrete and bounded body of beliefs and practices is, as far as I can dis-

5. The two types of meanings I have distinguished here can be overlaid, so that the cultural
aspects of the life of a people or a social group are distinguished from the noncultural aspects of
its life. Hence, "Balinese culture" may be contrasted to "Balinese society" or "the Balinese economy." In anthropological usage, however, "culture" also is commonly used to designate the whole
of the social life of a given people, so that "Balinese culture" becomes a synonym for "Balinese society" rather than a contrastive term.

cern, seldom made. Yet it seems to me crucial for thinking clearly about cultural theory. It should be clear, for example, that Ruth Benedict's concept of cultures as sharply distinct and highly integrated refers to culture in the second sense while Claude Lévi-Strauss's notion that cultural meaning is structured by systems of oppositions is a claim about culture in the first sense. Their theories of "culture" are, strictly speaking, incommensurate; they refer to different conceptual universes. Failure to recognize this distinction between two fundamentally different meanings of the term has real consequences for contemporary cultural theory; some of the impasses of theoretical discourse in contemporary anthropology are attributable precisely to an elision of the two. Thus, a dissatisfaction with "Benedictine" ethnographies that present cultures as uniformly well bounded and coherent has led to what seem to me rather confused attacks on "the culture concept" in general—attacks that fail to distinguish Benedictine claims about the tight integration of cultures (1934) from Lévi-Straussian claims about the semiotic coherence of culture as a system of meanings (1963a, 1966). Conversely, anthropologists who defend the culture concept also tend to conflate the two meanings, regarding claims that cultures are rent with fissures or that their boundaries are porous as implying an abandonment of the concept of culture altogether.

Here, I will be concerned primarily with culture in the first sense—culture as a category of social life. One must have a clear conception of culture at this abstract level in order to deal with the more concrete theoretical question of how cultural differences are patterned and bounded in space and time. Once I have sketched out my own ideas about what an adequate abstract theory of culture might look like, will I return to the question of culture as a bounded universe of beliefs and practices—to the question of cultures in the Benedictine sense.

CULTURE AS A CATEGORY OF SOCIAL LIFE

Culture as a category of social life has itself been conceptualized in a number of different ways. Let me begin by specifying some of these different conceptualizations, moving from those I do not find especially useful to those I find more adequate.

Culture as learned behavior. Culture in this sense is the whole body of practices, beliefs, institutions, customs, habits, myths, etc. built up by humans and passed on from generation to generation. Culture, in this usage, is contrasted to nature: it is possession of culture in this sense that distinguishes us from other animals. When anthropologists were struggling to establish that differences between societies were not based on biological differences between their populations—that is on race—a definition of culture as learned behavior made sense. But now that racial arguments have virtually disappeared from anthropological discourse, a concept of culture so broad as this seems impossibly vague; it provides no particular angle or analytical purchase on the study of social life.

A narrower and consequently more useful conceptualization of culture emerged in anthropological discourse during the second quarter of the twentieth century and has been dominant in the social sciences generally since World War II. It defines culture not as all learned behavior but as that category or aspect of learned behavior that is concerned with *meaning*. But this concept of culture-as-meaning is in fact a family of related concepts; meaning may be used to specify a cultural realm or sphere in at least four distinct ways, each of which is defined in contrast to somewhat differently conceptualized noncultural realms or spheres.

Culture as an institutional sphere devoted to the making of meaning. This conception of culture is based on the assumption that social formations are composed of clusters of institutions devoted to specialized activities. These clusters can be assigned to variously defined institutional spheres—most conventionally, spheres of politics, economy, society, and culture. Culture is the sphere devoted specifically to the production, circulation, and use of meanings. The cultural sphere may in turn be broken down into the subspheres of which it is composed: say, of art, music, theater, fashion, literature, religion, media, and education. The study of culture, if culture is defined in this way, is the study of the activities that take place within these institutionally defined spheres and of the meanings produced in them.

This conception of culture is particularly prominent in the discourses of sociology and cultural studies, but it is rarely used by anthropologists. The roots of this meaning probably reach back to the strongly evaluative conception of culture as a sphere of "high" or "uplifting" artistic and intellectual activity, a meaning that Raymond Williams tells us came into prominence in the nineteenth century (1983, 90–91). But in contemporary academic discourse, this usage normally lacks such evaluative and hierarchizing implications. The dominant style of work in American sociology of culture has been demystifying: its typical approach has been to uncover the largely self-aggrandizing, class-interested, manipulative, or professionalizing institutional dynamics that undergird prestigious museums, artistic styles, symphony orchestras, or philosophical schools. And cultural studies, which has taken as its particular mission the appreciation of cultural forms disdained by the spokesmen of high culture—rock music, street fashion, cross-dressing, shopping malls, Disneyland, soap operas—employs this same basic definition of culture. It merely trains its analytical attention on spheres of meaning production ignored by previous analysts and regarded as debased by elite tastemakers.

The problem with such a concept of culture is that it focuses only on a certain range of meanings, produced in a certain range of institutional locations—on self-consciously "cultural" institutions and on expressive, artistic, and literary systems of meanings. This use of the concept has a certain complicity with the widespread notion that meanings are of minimal importance in the other "noncultural" institutional spheres: that in political or economic spheres, meanings are merely superstructural excrescences. And since institutions in the political and economic spheres control the great bulk of society's resources, the concept of culture as a distinct sphere of activity may in the end simply confirm the widespread social-scientific presupposition that culture is merely froth on the tides of society. The rise of a cultural sociology that limited itself to studying "cultural" institutions effected a partition of subject matter that was very unfavorable to the cultural sociologists. Indeed, it is only the supercession of this restrictive concept of culture that made possible the explosive growth of the subfield of cultural sociology in the past two decades.

Culture as creativity or agency. This usage of culture has grown up particularly in traditions that posit a powerful "material" determinism—most notably Marxism and American sociology. Over the past four decades or so, scholars working within these traditions have carved out a conception of culture as a realm of creativity that escapes from the otherwise pervasive determination of social action by economic or social structures. In the Marxist tradition, it was probably E. P. Thompson's *The Making of the English Working Class* (1963) that first conceptualized culture as a realm of agency and it is particularly English Marxists—for example, Paul Willis in *Learning to Labor* (1981)—who have elaborated this conception. But the defining opposition on which this concept of culture rests—culture vs. structure—has also become pervasive in the vernacular of American sociology. One clear sign that American anthropologists and sociologists have different conceptions of culture is that the opposition between culture and structure—an unquestioned commonplace in contemporary sociological discourse—is nonsensical in anthropology.

In my opinion, identifying culture with agency and contrasting it with structure merely perpetuates the same determinist materialism that "culturalist" Marxists were reacting against in the first place. It exaggerates both the implacability of socioeconomic determinations and the free play of symbolic action. Both socioeconomic and cultural processes are blends of structure and agency. Cultural action—say performing practical jokes or writing poems—is necessarily contrained by cultural structures, such as existing linguistic, visual, or ludic conventions. And economic action—such as the manufacture or repair of automobiles—is impossible without the exercise of creativity and agency. The particulars of the relationship between structure and agency may differ in cultural and economic processes, but assigning either the economic or the cultural exclusively to structure or to agency is a serious category error.

This brings us to the two concepts of culture that I regard as most fruitful and that I see as currently struggling for dominance: the concept of culture as a system of symbols and meanings, which was hegemonic in the 1960s and 1970s, and the concept of culture as practice, which has become increasingly prominent in the 1980s and 1990s.

Culture as a system of symbols and meanings. This has been the dominant concept of culture in American anthropology since the 1960s. It was made famous above all by Clifford Geertz, who used the term "cultural system" in the titles of some of his most notable essays (1973e, 1973h, 1983b, 1983c). The concept of cultural system was also elaborated by David Schneider (1968, 1976), whose writings had a considerable influence within anthropology but lacked Geertz's interdisciplinary appeal. Geertz and Schneider derived the term cultural system from Talcott Parsons's usage, according to which the cultural system, a system of symbols and meanings, was a particular "level of abstraction" of social relations. It was contrasted to the "social system," which was a system of norms and institutions, and to the "personality system," which was a system of motivations (Parsons 1959).[6] Geertz and Schneider especially wished to distinguish the cultural system from the social system. To engage in cultural analysis, for them, was to abstract the meaningful aspect of human action out from the flow of concrete interactions. The point of conceptualizing culture as a system of symbols and meanings is to disentangle, for the purpose of analysis, the semiotic influences on action from the other sorts of influences—demographic, geographical, biological, technological, economic, and so on—that they are necessarily mixed with in any concrete sequence of behavior.

Geertz's and Schneider's post-Parsonian theorizations of cultural systems were by no means the only available models for symbolic anthropol-

6. Geertz and Schneider were both students of Talcott Parsons and Clyde Kluckhohn in the Harvard department of social relations, and they taught together during the 1960s at the University of Chicago, then the epicenter of cultural anthropology.

ogy in the 1960s and 1970s. The works of Victor Turner, whose theoretical origins were in the largely Durkheimian British school of social anthropology, was also immensely influential (1967, 1969). Claude Lévi-Strauss and his many followers provided an entire alternative model of culture as a system of symbols and meanings—conceptualized, following Saussure, as signifiers and signifieds. Moreover, all these anthropological schools were in a sense manifestations of a much broader "linguistic turn" in the human sciences—a diverse but sweeping attempt to specify the structures of human symbol systems and to indicate their profound influence on human behavior. One thinks above all of such French "structuralist" thinkers as Roland Barthes ([1957] 1972), Jacques Lacan (1977), or the early Michel Foucault (1971). What all of these approaches had in common was an insistence on the systematic nature of cultural meaning and the autonomy of symbol systems—their distinctness from and irreducibility to other features of social life. They all abstracted a realm of pure signification out from the complex messiness of social life and sought to specify its internal coherence and deep logic. Their practice of cultural analysis consequently tended to be more or less synchronic and formalist.

Culture as practice. The past decade and a half has witnessed a pervasive reaction against the concept of culture as a system of symbols and meanings, which has taken place in various disciplinary locations and intellectual traditions and under many different slogans—for example, "practice," "resistance," "history," "politics," or "culture as toolkit." Analysts working under all these banners object to a portrayal of culture as logical, coherent, shared, uniform, and static. Instead they insist that culture is a sphere of practical activity shot through by willful action, power relations, struggle, contradiction, and change.

In anthropology, Sherry Ortner remarked on the turn to politics, history, and agency in anthropology in 1984, suggesting Pierre Bourdieu's (1977) key term "practice" as an appropriate label for this emerging sensibility. Two years later the publication of James Clifford's and George Marcus's collection *Writing Culture* (1986) announced to the public the crisis of anthropology's culture concept. Since then, criticisms of the concept of culture as a system of symbols and meanings has flowed thick and fast. The most notable work in anthropology has argued for the contradictory, politically charged, changeable, and fragmented character of meanings—both meanings produced in the societies being studied and meanings rendered in anthropological texts. Recent work in anthropology has in effect recast culture as a performative term.

Not surprisingly, this emphasis on the performative aspect of culture is compatible with the work of most cultural historians. Historians are generally uncomfortable with synchronic concepts. As they took up the study of culture, they subtly—but usually without comment—altered the concept by stressing the contradictoriness and malleability of cultural meanings and by seeking out the mechanisms by which meanings were transformed. The battles in history, discussed at length in chapter 2, have been over a different issue; they have pitted those who claim that historical change should be understood as a purely cultural or discursive process against those who argue for the significance of economic and social determinations or for the centrality of concrete "experience" in understanding it.[7]

Sociologists, for rather different reasons, have also favored a more performative conception of culture. Given the hegemony of a strongly causalist methodology and philosophy of science in contemporary sociology, cultural sociologists have felt a need to demonstrate that culture has causal efficacy in order to gain recognition for their fledgling subfield. This has led many of them to conceptualize culture so that it can be constructed as a collection of variables whose influence on behavior can be rigorously compared to that of such standard sociological variables as class, ethnicity, gender, level of education, economic interest, and the like. The consequence has been a move away from earlier Weberian, Durkheimian, or Parsonian conceptions of culture as rather vague and general "value orientations" to what Ann Swidler has termed a "toolkit" composed of a "repertoire" of "strategies of action" (1984). For many cultural sociologists, then, culture is not a coherent system of symbols and meanings, but a diverse collection of "tools" that, as the metaphor indicates, are to be understood as means for the performance of action. Because these tools are discrete, local, and intended for specific purposes, they can be deployed as explanatory variables in a way that culture conceived as a translocal, generalized system of meanings cannot.

CULTURE AS SYSTEM AND PRACTICE

Much of the theoretical writing on culture during the past two decades has assumed that a concept of culture as a system of symbols and meanings is at odds with a concept of culture as practice. System and practice approaches have seemed incompatible, I think, because the most prominent practitioners of the culture-as-system-of-meanings approach effectively marginalized consideration of culture-as-practice—if they didn't preclude it altogether.

7. See chapter 2, above, esp. note 29, and Appleby, Hunt, and Jacob (1994, 198–237).

This can be seen in the work of both Clifford Geertz and David Schneider. Geertz's analyses usually begin auspiciously enough, in that he frequently explicates cultural systems as means of resolving a puzzle aris- ing from concrete practices—a state funeral, trances, a royal procession, cockfights. But it usually turns out that the issues of practice are princi- pally a means of moving the essay to the goal of specifying in a synchronic form the coherence that underlies the exotic cultural practices in question. If Geertz marginalized questions of practice, Schneider, in a kind of re- ductio ad adsurdum, explicitly excluded them, arguing that the particular task of anthropology in the academic division of labor was to study "culture as a system of symbols and meanings in its own right and with ref- erence to its own structure," leaving to others—sociologists, historians, political scientists, or economists—the question of how social action was structured (1976, 214). A "cultural account," for Schneider, should be lim- ited to specifying the relations among symbols in a given domain of mean- ing—which he tended to render unproblematically as known and accepted by all members of the society and as possessing a highly determinate for- mal logic (see, e.g. 1968).

Nor is the work of Geertz and Schneider unusual in its marginalization of practice. As critics like James Clifford (1986) have argued, conventional modes of writing in cultural anthropology typically smuggle highly debat- able assumptions into ethnographic accounts—for example, that cultural meanings are normally shared, fixed, bounded, and deeply felt. To Clif- ford's critique of ethnographic rhetoric, I would add a critique of ethno- graphic method. Anthropologists working with a conception of culture- as-system have tended to focus on clusters of symbols and meanings that can be shown to have a high degree of coherence or systematicity—for ex- ample, those of American kinship or Balinese cockfighting—and to pres- ent their accounts of these clusters as examples of what the interpretation of culture in general entails. This practice results in what sociologists would call sampling on the dependent variable. That is, anthropologists who belong to this school tend to select symbols and meanings that clus- ter neatly into coherent systems and pass over those that are relatively fragmented or incoherent, thus confirming the hypothesis that symbols and meanings indeed form tightly coherent systems.

Given some of these problems in the work of the culture-as-system school, the recent turn to a concept of culture-as-practice has been both understandable and fruitful—it has effectively highlighted many of that school's shortcomings and made up some of its most glaring analytic defi- cits. Yet the presumption that a concept of culture as a system of symbols and meanings is at odds with a concept of culture as practice seems to me perverse. System and practice are complementary concepts: each presupposes the other. To engage in cultural practice means to utilize existing cultural symbols to accomplish some end. The employment of a symbol can be expected to accomplish a particular goal only because the symbols have more or less determinate meanings—meanings specified by their systematically structured relations to other symbols. Hence practice implies system. But it is equally true that the system has no existence apart from the succession of practices that instantiate, reproduce, or—most interestingly—transform it. Hence system implies practice.[8] System and practice constitute an indissoluble duality or dialectic; the important theoretical question is not whether culture should be conceptualized as practice or as a system of symbols and meanings, but how to conceptualize the articulation of system and practice.

THE AUTONOMY OF CULTURE

Let me begin this task by stating some assumptions about practice. I assume that human practice, in all social contexts or institutional spheres, is structured simultaneously both by meanings and by other aspects of the environment in which they occur—by, for example, power relations or spatiality or resource distributions. Culture is neither a particular kind of practice nor practice that takes place in a particular social location. It is, rather, the semiotic dimension of human social practice in general. I further assume that these dimensions of practice mutually shape and constrain each other but also that they are relatively autonomous from each other.[9]

The autonomy of the cultural dimension of practice can also be understood by thinking about culture as a system. The cultural dimension of

8. Readers of Marshall Sahlins (esp. 1985, 136–56) should find this formulation familiar.

9. By speaking of *dimensions* of social life that are *relatively* autonomous from each other, I do not mean to imply that these are in some sense *prior* to culture or entirely independent of it, as the anthropologist Richard Handler imagined in his review essay on the volume in which this chapter originally appeared (2002, 1516). As I try to spell out more fully in the final chapter of this book, I in fact agree with Handler that all social action is culturally constituted. But I do not agree with Handler's implicit claim (one very common among anthropologists) that a cultural account is therefore a sufficient explanation of social life. From the fact that all social action is meaningful, it does not necessarily follow that social action is shaped by *nothing but* meaning. Other orders of constraints and pressures (for example, abundance or scarcity of resources, gross disparities of coercive force, or the spatial locations and physical mobilities of actors and resources), which may themselves be the outcomes of semiotically motivated action, regularly influence social action in ways that escape the awareness of actors and are not easily accounted for by semiotic analysis alone. I think a program of cultural research that attempts to utilize and

practice is autonomous from other dimensions of practice in two senses. First, culture has a semiotic structuring principle that is different from the political, economic, or geographical structuring principles that also inform practice. Hence, even if an action were almost entirely determined by, say, overwhelming disparities in economic resources, those disparities would still have to be rendered meaningful in action according to a semiotic logic — that is, in language or in some other form of symbols. For example, an impoverished worker facing the only manufacturer seeking laborers in his district will have no choice but to accept the offer. Yet in accepting the offer she or he is not simply submitting to the employer, but entering into a culturally defined relation as a wage worker. Second, the cultural dimension is also autonomous in the sense that the meanings that make it up — although influenced by the context in which they are employed — are shaped and reshaped by a multitude of other contexts. The meaning of a symbol always transcends the particular context, because the symbol is freighted with its usages in a multitude of other instances of social practice. Thus, our worker enters into a relationship of "wage worker" that carries certain recognized meanings — of deference, but also of independence from the employer and perhaps of solidarity with other wage workers. These meanings are carried over from the other contexts in which the meaning of wage work is determined — not only from other instances of hirings but from statutes, legal arguments, strikes, socialist tracts, and economic treatises. They enter importantly into defining the local possibilities of action, in this case perhaps granting the worker greater power to resist the employer than the local circumstances alone would have dictated.

To understand fully the significance of this second sort of autonomy, it is important to note that the network of semiotic relations that make up culture is not isomorphic with the network of economic, political, geographical, social, or demographic relations that make up what we usually call a "society." A given symbol — mother, red, polyester, liberty, wage-labor, or dirt — is likely to show up not only in many different locations in a given institutional domain (motherhood in millions of families) but in a variety of different institutional domains as well (welfare mothers as a potent political symbol, the mother tongue in linguistic quarrels, the Mother of God in the Roman Catholic Church). Culture may be thought of as a

---

grapple with the insights of, say, economic or geographical or demographic analysis, will be stronger than one that ignores or disdains all analytical traditions other than the semiotic. For an earlier and somewhat different exposition of this point, see Sewell (1993).

network of semiotic relations cast across society, a network with a different shape and different spatiality than institutional, or economic, or political networks.[10] The meaning of a symbol in a given institutional location may therefore be subject to redefinition by dynamics entirely foreign to that institutional domain or spatial location: thus, for example, in the 1950s a particular political meaning of the symbol "red" became so overpowering that the Cincinnati Reds baseball team felt the need to change its name to "the Redlegs." It is this fact that makes possible—indeed virtually guarantees—that the cultural dimension of practice will have a certain autonomy from its other dimensions.

If culture has a distinct semiotic logic, this implies that it must in some sense be coherent. But it is important not to exaggerate or misspecify the coherence of symbol systems. I assume the coherence of a cultural system to be semiotic in a roughly Saussurian sense: that is, that the meaning of a sign or symbol is a function of its network of oppositions to or distinctions from other signs in the system. This implies that users of culture will form a semiotic community—in the sense that they will recognize the same set of oppositions and therefore be capable of engaging in mutually meaningful symbolic action. To use the ubiquitous linguistic analogy, they will be capable of using the "grammar" of the semiotic system to make understandable "utterances."

It should be noted, however, that this conception actually implies only a quite minimal cultural coherence—one might call it a thin coherence. The fact that members of a semiotic community recognize a given set of symbolic oppositions does not determine what sort of statements or actions they will construct on the basis of their semiotic competence. Nor does it mean that they form a community in any fuller sense. They need not agree in their moral or emotional evaluations of given symbols. The semiotic field they share may be recognized and used by groups and individuals locked in fierce enmity rather than bound by solidarity, or by people who feel relative indifference toward each other. The posited existence of cultural coherence says nothing about whether semiotic fields are big or small, shallow or deep, encompassing or specialized. It implies only that if meaning is to exist at all, there must be systematic relations among signs and a group of people who recognize those relations.

That this Saussurian conception implies only a thin cultural coherence seems consonant with certain deconstructionist arguments. The entire

10. On the spatial aspect of culture, see Lomnitz-Adler (1991).

thrust of deconstruction has been to reveal the instability of linguistic meaning. It has located this instability in the signifying mechanism of language itself—claiming that because the meaning of a linguistic sign always depends on a contrast with what the sign is opposed to or different from, language is inevitably haunted by the traces of the very terms it excludes. Consequently, the meaning of a text or an utterance can never be fixed; attempts to secure meaning can only defer, never exclude, a plethora of alternative or opposed interpretations.

Cultural analysts who—like me—wish to argue that cultural systems are powerfully constraining have often drawn back from deconstructionist arguments in horror. I think this is a major mistake; indeed, I would maintain that a broadly deconstructionist understanding of meaning is essential for anyone attempting to theorize cultural change. Deconstruction does not deny the possibility of coherence. Rather, it assumes that the coherence inherent in a system of symbols is thin in the sense I have described, and it demonstrates over and over that what are taken as the certainties or truths of texts or discourses are in fact disputable and unstable. This seems entirely compatible with a practice perspective on culture. It assumes that symbol systems have a (Saussurian) logic but that this logic is open ended, not closed. And it strongly implies that if a given symbol system is taken by its users to be unambiguous and highly constraining, this fact cannot be accounted for by the system's semiotic qualities alone, but must result from the way semiotic structures are interlocked in practice with other structures—economic, political, social, spatial, etc.[11]

Thus far in this section I have mainly been talking about culture as system. But what I have said has implications for how we might conceptualize culture as practice. First, the conception of culture as semiotic implies a particular notion of cultural practice. To engage in cultural practice is to make use of a semiotic code to do something in the world. People who are members of a semiotic community are capable not only of recognizing statements made in a semiotic code (as I have pointed out above) but of using the code as well, of putting it into practice. To use a code means to attach abstractly available symbols to concrete things or circumstances

---

11. This is not, of course, the usual conclusion arrived at by deconstructionists, who would insist that these "other structures" are no less textual than semiotic structures and that making sense of them is purely a matter of intertextuality. This epistemological and ontological difference between my position and that of deconstruction should make it clear that I am appropriating from deconstruction specific ideas that I find useful rather than adopting a full-scale deconstructionist position.

and thereby to posit something about them. As I argued in chapter 4, to be able to use a code (or a schema) means more than being able to apply it mechanically in stereotyped situations. It also means having the ability to elaborate it, to modify or adapt its rules to novel circumstances.

What things in the world *are* is never fully determined by the symbolic net we throw over them—this also depends upon their preexisting physical characteristics, the spatial relations in which they occur, the relations of power with which they are invested, their economic value, and, of course, the different symbolic meanings that may have been attributed to them by other actors. The world is recalcitrant to our predications of meaning. Hence, as Marshall Sahlins has pointed out, every act of symbolic attribution puts the symbols at risk, makes it possible that the meanings of the symbols will be inflected or transformed by the uncertain consequences of practice. Usually, such attributions result in only tiny inflections of the meaning of symbols. But on some occasions—for example when Hawaiian chiefs used the category of tabu to enforce a chiefly monopoly on trade with Western merchants—novel attributions can have the result of transforming the meaning of a symbol in historically crucial ways (Sahlins 1981, 67–72; 1985, 136–56).

Part of what gives cultural practice its potency is the ability of actors to play upon the multiple meanings of symbols—thereby redefining situations in ways that they believe will favor their purposes. Creative cultural action commonly entails the purposeful or spontaneous importation of meanings from one social location or context to another. I have recently worked on a telling example of the importation of meaning. The men and women who captured the Bastille in July 1789 were unquestionably characterizable as "the people" in the common sense of "the mob" or the "urban poor." But Parisian radicals and members of the French National Assembly played on the ambiguity of the term "the people" to cast those who took the Bastille also as a concrete instance of the abstract category of "the people" who were said to be sovereign in radical political theory. Importing the association between the people and sovereignty from the context of political theory into that of urban crowd violence had the not inconsequential effect of ushering the modern concept of revolution into the world (see chapter 8, below).

CULTURES AS DISTINCT WORLDS OF MEANING

Up to now, I have been considering culture only in its singular and abstract sense—as a realm of social life defined in contrast to some other noncultural realm or realms. My main points may be summarized as follows: culture, I have argued, should be understood as a dialectic of system and practice, as a dimension of social life autonomous from other such dimensions both in its logic and in its spatial configuration, and as possessing a real but thin coherence that is continually put at risk in practice and therefore subject to transformation. Such a theorization, I maintain, makes it possible to accept the cogency of recent critiques and yet to retain a workable and powerful concept of culture that incorporates the achievements of the cultural anthropology of the 1960s and 1970s.

But it is probably fair to say that most recent theoretical work on culture, particularly in anthropology, is actually concerned primarily with culture in its pluralizable and more concrete sense — that is, with cultures as distinct worlds of meaning. Contemporary anthropological critics' objections to the concept of culture as system and their insistence on the primacy of practice are not, in my opinion, really aimed at the concept of system as I have outlined it above — the notion that the meaning of symbols is determined by their network of relations with other symbols. Rather, the critics' true target is the idea that cultures (in the second, pluralizable, sense) form neatly coherent wholes: that they are logically consistent, highly integrated, consensual, extremely resistant to change, and clearly bounded. This is how cultures tend to be represented in the classic ethnographies — Mead on Samoa, Benedict on the Zuni, Malinowski on the Trobriands, Evans-Prichard on the Nuer, or, for that matter, Geertz on the Balinese. But recent research and thinking about cultural practices, even in relatively "simple" societies, has turned this classical model on its head. It now appears that we should think of worlds of meaning as normally being contradictory, loosely integrated, contested, mutable, and highly permeable. Consequently the very concept of cultures as coherent and distinct entities is widely disputed.

Cultures are contradictory. Some authors of classic ethnographies were quite aware of the presence of contradictions in the cultures they studied. Victor Turner, for example, demonstrated that red symbolism in certain Ndembu rituals simultaneously signified the contradictory principles of matrilineal fertility and male bloodletting. But he emphasized how these potentially contradictory meanings were brought together and harmonized in ritual performances (1967, 41–43). A current anthropological sensibility would probably emphasize the fundamental character of the contradictions rather than their situational resolution in the ritual. It is common for potent cultural symbols to express contradictions as much as they express coherence. One need look no farther than the central Christian symbol of the Trinity, which attempts to unify in one symbolic figure

three sharply distinct and largely incompatible possibilities of Christian
religious experience: authoritative and hierarchical orthodoxy (the Father), loving egalitarianism and grace (the Son), and ecstatic spontaneity
(the Holy Ghost). Cultural worlds are commonly beset with internal contradictions.

Cultures are loosely integrated. Classical ethnographies recognized that societies were composed of different spheres of activity—for example, kinship, agriculture, hunting, warfare, and religion—and that each of these
component parts had its own specific cultural forms. But the classical
ethnographers typically saw it as their task to show how these culturally
varied components fit into a well-integrated cultural whole. Most contemporary students of culture would question this emphasis. They are more
inclined to stress the centrifugal cultural tendencies that arise from these
disparate spheres of activity, to stress the inequalities between those relegated to different activities, and to see whatever "integration" occurs as
based on power or domination rather than on a common ethos. That most
anthropologists now work on complex, stratified, and highly differentiated societies, rather than on the "simple" societies that were the focus of
most classical ethnographies, probably enhances this tendency.

Cultures are contested. Classical ethnographies commonly assumed, at
least implicitly, that a culture's most important beliefs were consensual,
that they were agreed upon by virtually all of a society's members. Contemporary scholars, with their enhanced awareness of race, class, and gender, would insist that people who occupy different positions in a given social order will typically have quite different cultural beliefs or will have
quite different understandings of what might seem on the surface to be
identical beliefs. Consequently, current scholarship is replete with depic-
tions of "resistance" by subordinated groups and individuals. Thus James
Scott (1985) detects "hidden transcripts" that form the underside of peasants' deference in contemporary Malaysia, and Marshall Sahlins (1981, 46)
points out that it was Hawaiian women who most readily violated tabus
when Captain Cook's ships arrived—because the tabu system, which classified them as profane (noa) as against the sacred (tabu) men "did not sit
upon Hawaiian women with the force it had for men." Cultural consensus,
far from the normal state of things, is a difficult achievement and when it
does occur it is bound to hide suppressed conflicts and disagreements.

Cultures are subject to constant change. Cultural historians, who work on
complex and dynamic societies, have generally assumed that cultures are far
from unchanging. But recent anthropological work on relatively "simple"

societies also finds them to be remarkably mutable. For example, Renato Rosaldo's study (1980) of remote Ilongot headhunters in the highlands of Northern Luzon demonstrates that each generation of Ilongots constructed its own logic of settlement patterns, kinship alliance, and feuding—logics that gave successive generations of Ilongots experiences that were probably as varied as those of successive generations of Americans or Europeans between the late nineteenth and late twentieth centuries.

Cultures are weakly bounded. It is extremely unusual for societies or their cultural systems to be anything like isolated or sharply bounded. Even the supposedly simplest societies have had relations of trade, warfare, conquest, and borrowing of all sorts of cultural items—technology, religious ideas, political and artistic forms, and so on. But in addition to mutual influences of these sorts, there have long been important social and cultural processes that transcend societal boundaries—colonialism, missionary religions, interregional trading associations and economic interdependencies, migratory diasporas, and, in the current era, multinational corporations and transnational nongovernmental organizations. Although these trans-societal processes are certainly more prominent in more recent history than previously, they are hardly entirely new. Think of the spread of such "world religions" as Islam, Christianity, Hinduism, or Buddhism across entire regions of the globe or the development of extensive territorial empires in the ancient world. I would argue that social science's once virtually unquestioned model of societies as clearly bounded entities undergoing endogenous development is as perverse for the study of culture as for the study of economic history or political sociology. Systems of meaning do not correspond in any neat way with national or societal boundaries—which themselves are not nearly as neat as we sometimes imagine. Anything we might designate as a "society" or a "nation" will contain, or fail to contain, a multitude of overlapping and interpenetrating cultural systems, most of them either subsocietal or trans-societal or both.[12]

In summary, all of the assumptions of the classic ethnographic model of cultures—that cultures are logically consistent, highly integrated, consensual, resistant to change, and clearly bounded—seem to be untenable. This could lead to the conclusion that the notion of coherent cultures is purely illusory: that cultural practice in a given society is diffuse and decentered; that the local systems of meaning found in a given population do not them-

---

12. Arjun Appadurai's work on recent forms of trans-national cultural forms has been particularly influential (1991, 1996).

selves form a higher-level, society-wide system of meanings. But such a conclusion would, in my opinion, be hasty. Although I think it is an error simply to assume that cultures possess an overall coherence or integration, neither can such coherences be ruled out a priori.

HOW COHERENCE IS POSSIBLE

Recent work on cultural practice has tended to focus on acts of cultural resistance, particularly on resistance of a decentered sort—those dispersed everyday acts that thwart conventions, reverse valuations, or express the dominated's resentment of their domination.[13] But it is important to remember that much cultural practice is concentrated in and around powerful institutional nodes—including religions, communications media, business corporations, and, most spectacularly, states. These institutions, which tend to be relatively large in scale, centralized, and wealthy, are all cultural actors; their agents make continuous use of their considerable resources in efforts to order meanings. Studies of culture need to pay at least as much attention to such sites of concentrated cultural practice as to the dispersed sites of resistance that currently predominate in the literature.[14]

Even in powerful and would-be totalitarian states, centrally placed actors are never able to establish anything approaching cultural uniformity. In fact, they rarely attempt to do so. The typical cultural strategy of dominant actors and institutions is not so much to establish uniformity as it is to organize difference. They are constantly engaged in efforts not only to normalize or homogenize but also to hierarchize, encapsulate, exclude, criminalize, hegemonize, or marginalize practices and populations that diverge from the sanctioned ideal. By such means, authoritative actors attempt, with varying degrees of success, to impose a certain coherence onto the field of cultural practice.[15] Indeed, one of the major reasons for dissident anthropologists' discomfort with the concept of culture is that it is so often employed in all of these ways by various powerful institutional actors—sometimes, alas, with the help of anthropologists.

The kind of coherence produced by this process of organizing difference may be far from the tight cultural integration depicted in classical ethnographies. But when authoritative actors distinguish between high

13. For a critical discussion of such work, see Ortner (1995).
14. For a fascinating study of state cultural practices, see Wedeen (1999).
15. This characterization seems to me to be roughly consonant with a Gramscian idea of hegemony (1971a). For a two quite different Gramscian cultural analyses of politics, see Stuart Hall (1988) and Laitin (1986).

and low cultural practices or between those of the majority ethnicity and minorities or between the legal and the criminal or the normal and the abnormal, they bring widely varying practices into semiotic relationship — that is, into definition in terms of contrasts with one another. Authoritative cultural action, launched from the centers of power, has the effect of turning what otherwise might be a babble of cultural voices into a semiotically and politically ordered field of differences. Such action creates a map of the "culture" and its variants, one that tells people where they and their practices fit in the official scheme of things.

The official cultural map may, of course, be criticized and resisted by those relegated to its margins. But subordinated groups must to some degree orient their local systems of meaning to those recognized as dominant; the act of contesting dominant meanings itself implies a recognition of their centrality. Dominant and oppositional groups interact constantly, each undertaking its initiatives with the other in mind. Even when they attempt to overcome or undermine each other, they are mutually shaped by their dialectical dance. Struggle and resistance, far from demonstrating that cultures lack coherence, may paradoxically have the effect of simplifying and clarifying the cultural field.

Moreover, dissenting or oppositional groups work to create and sustain cultural coherence among their own adherents, and they do so by many of the same strategies — hierarchization, encapsulation, exclusion, and the like — that the authorities use. Once again, it is notable that the concept of culture is as likely to be deployed politically by dissident groups as by dominant institutions, and with many of the same exclusionary, normalizing, and marginalizing effects as when it is deployed by the state. To take an obvious example, dissident nationalist and ethnic movements nearly always involve attempts to impose standards of cultural purity on those deemed members of the group and to use such standards to distinguish between those who are and are not group members.

None of this, of course, implies that cultures are always, everywhere, or unproblematically coherent. It suggests, instead, that coherence is variable, contested, ever-changing, and incomplete. Cultural coherence, to the extent that it exists, is as much the product of power and struggles for power as it is of semiotic logic. But it is common for the operation of power, both the efforts of central institutions and the acts of organized resistance to such institutions, to subject potential semiotic sprawl to a certain order: to prescribe (contested) core values, to impose discipline on dissenters, to describe boundaries and norms — in short, to give a certain focus to the production and consumption of meaning. As cultural analysts we must acknowledge such coherences where they exist and set ourselves the task of explaining how they are achieved, sustained, and dissolved.

It is no longer possible to assume that the world is divided up into discrete "societies," each with its corresponding and well-integrated "culture." I would argue forcefully for the value of the culture concept in its nonpluralizable sense, but the utility of the term in its pluralizable sense appears to me more open to legitimate question. Yet I think that the pluralizable concept of culture also gets at something we need to retain: a sense of the particular shapes and consistencies of worlds of meaning in different places and times and a sense that in spite of conflicts and resistance these worlds of meaning somehow hang together. Whether we call these partially coherent landscapes of meaning "cultures" or something else— worlds of meaning, or ethnoscapes, or hegemonies—seems to me relatively unimportant so long as we know that their boundedness is only relative and constantly shifting. Our job as cultural analysts is to discern what the shapes and consistencies of local meanings actually are, and to determine how, why, and to what extent they hang together.

6

HISTORY, SYNCHRONY, AND CULTURE
Reflections on the Work of Clifford Geertz

Clifford Geertz is surely the most influential American anthropologist of his generation. Although others—for example, Marshall Sahlins or Victor Turner—may rival his standing within anthropology, none approaches his influence on readers outside his home discipline.[1] As Renato Rosaldo once remarked, Geertz has become the "ambassador from anthropology."

The ambassador's slot was already in existence when Geertz emerged as an anthropological superstar in the early 1970s. It had previously been occupied by Ruth Benedict and Margaret Mead. Mead, whose ambassadorial service overlapped with Geertz's, had gained a huge popular following, writing a regular column in *Redbook* and dispensing advice in various media on topics as wide-ranging as the nuclear arms race, juvenile delinquency, world hunger, and sex education. Geertz's ambassadorial role has been much closer to that of Ruth Benedict, who, like Geertz, was more interested in the bearing of anthropology on issues of social and moral philosophy than on current social problems. Like Geertz, Benedict was a gifted literary stylist with a penchant for ethnographic *contes philosophiques*—her superb essays on the Zuni, Dobu, and Kwakiutl in *Patterns of Culture*

This chapter was originally published as "Geertz, Cultural Systems, and History: From Synchrony to Transformation," in *Representations* 59:35–55. Copyright © 1997 by the Regents of the University of California; reprinted with the permission of the University of California Press.

1. For example, a quick check of the 1995 *Social Sciences Citation Index* (1996) indicates that Marshall Sahlins was cited slightly more often than Geertz in anthropology journals, but that Geertz received more than twice as many citations overall (roughly 350 as opposed to 150), including citations in journals in fields as far flung as agriculture, nursing, environmental studies, business, social work, information science, gerontology, and public relations.

are surely among the classics of a genre that Geertz has subsequently made his own. But Geertz and Benedict have been ambassadors to somewhat different publics. *Patterns of Culture* (1934), in particular, was intended for and read by the educated public at large (see also Benedict 1946). Geertz may well have been aiming for such a public, but his major impact has actually been on practitioners and students of other academic disciplines — the social sciences, literary studies, philosophy, and beyond.[2]

Geertz's rise to ambassadorial dignity has given him an iconic status in the American academy. This has also made him vulnerable to iconoclasm, particularly in his home discipline of anthropology, where he is a favorite target of critique among anthropologists of the most varied intellectual provenance — he has been attacked by positivists, postmodernists, and materialists alike.[3] The positivists criticize Geertz for abandoning the scientific values of "predictability, replicability, verifiability, and law-generating capacity" in favor of the more "glamorous" or "alluring" qualities of interpretive method.[4] The postmodernists, by contrast, reproach him for not pushing his interpretive method far enough — in particular for failing to subject his own interpretive ethnographic practice to critical interpretation (Crapanzano 1986; Clifford 1988b; Watson 1989, 1991). The materialists, finally, criticize him for his neglect of history, power, and social conflict (Roseberry 1982; Asad 1982 and 1993, esp. ch. 1).

This rather edgy relationship between Geertz and his anthropological colleagues is in sharp contrast to his relationship with historians, who embraced his ambassadorial efforts early and warmly. Historians have generally simply quoted him favorably and then gone about applying his meth-

2. This difference between Benedict's and Geertz's audiences probably reflects the changing contours of American intellectual life more than it does their own specific proclivities: the community of lay public intellectuals for whom Benedict could write in the 1930s hardly exists in the present — it has increasingly been either snuffed out by the rampant commercialization of the media or engulfed by universities.

3. Again a comparison with Marshall Sahlins is revealing. Sahlins is as frequently cited as Geertz by anthropologists and his work is highly controversial. See especially the exchange between Obeyesekere (1992) and Sahlins (1995). Yet the eleven annual volumes of *Anthropological Literature* published between 1984 and 1994 list twenty-four critical works on Geertz and only ten on Sahlins.

4. The quotations are from Shankman (1984, 264, 270), which is the most systematic critique from a positivist perspective. As is the norm in this journal, the article itself is followed by comments from an assortment of scholars and a response by the author. Five of the fifteen published comments (those of Erika Bourguignon, Linda Connor, John R. Cole, A. D. Fisher, and Robin Riddington) indicate that Shankman's positivist distrust of Geertz is far from unique among anthropologists. Shankman's thorough bibliography is a good guide the critical literature on Geertz as of 1984.

ods or ideas in their own work.[5] Of course, historians are generally far less prone than anthropologists to engage in theoretical disputes, and it is also true that Geertz does not serve as a marker in generational struggles among historians. Moreover, the history profession has never had many convinced positivists nor, at least until very recently, many convinced postmodernists. Nevertheless, it seems odd, on reflection, that some version of the materialist critique of Geertz has not been embraced by more historians.

The materialist critique, as elaborated for example by William Roseberry in "Balinese Cockfights and the Seduction of Anthropology" (1982), should be quite compatible with the theoretical and methodological commitments of most social and cultural historians. Roseberry argues that Geertz, by conceptualizing culture as a text, adopts an effectively idealist position, separating cultural products from their historical production and from the relations of power and domination in which they are necessarily enmeshed. He points out that Geertz fails to indicate how the contemporary Balinese cockfight has been shaped by gender relations, by the legal regulations of the Dutch colonial and Indonesian states, or by the changing politics of Balinese status formation—all of which are referred to, but never really taken up, in Geertz's text.[6] The cockfight, Roseberry asserts, "has gone through a process of creation that cannot be separated from Balinese history," but in Geertz's account it is in fact separated from that history by being treated as a text (1022). Rather than conceptualizing culture as a text, Roseberry suggests, we should think of it "as material social process," as "production" rather than as a "product," constantly asking how, by whom, and for what ends it is being produced (1023–24). This, Roseberry asserts, would "move cultural analysis to a new level" and would render "the old antinomies of materialism and idealism irrelevant" (1026–27).

Most of Roseberry's specific criticisms of Geertz's cockfight essay are bound to resonate with historians' predilections. However, his proposal that we overcome the "antinomy between the material and the ideal" by adopting a "materialist" concept of culture (1024) hardly seems promising: one doesn't normally overcome an antinomy by simply embracing one of

5. Walters (1980) gives an account of Geertz's early reception by historians.

6. Roseberry's critique (1982, 1020–23) centers on Geertz's "Deep Play: Notes on the Balinese Cockfight" (1973b). This article is the sole or primary example discussed in a number of critical articles devoted to Geertz, including those by Clifford and Crapanzano cited above. Although there is far more to Geertz than the cockfight article, there is a certain poetic justice in critics treating as a synechdochic representation of Geertz an article in which he claims that the cockfight synechdochically represents Balinese culture.

the antinomic poles.[7] But on closer inspection the issue of materialism vs. idealism is quite beside Roseberry's real point, which has more to do with diachrony vs. synchrony. The problem is not a matter of Geertz's metaphysical commitments—indeed, I shall later argue that his materialist metaphysical credentials are impeccable—but of his methodological practices. By treating a cultural performance as a text, Roseberry points out, one fixes it and subjects it to a synchronic gaze, bracketing the question of the processes that produced it in order to work out its internal logic.

I would argue that every cultural analysis *necessarily* entails a synchronic moment of this sort, but I would also argue that the synchronic moment should be dialectically related to an equally necessary diachronic moment. And I agree with Roseberry that Geertz's practice of cultural interpretation too often slights the diachronic—that, as I would put it, in Geertz's work the necessary dialectic between synchronic and diachronic tends to be seriously truncated. A number of Geertz's essays, including the cockfight article, feature an event in real historical time, in which particular individuals in specific social and political relations engage in interested social action—in this case a police raid that scatters observers of a village cockfight. But introduction of such temporal and social particulars serves Geertz as a literary device to move the essay to the real goal: specifying the synchronic and aesthetically satisfying coherence that underlies the cultural practice in question. Geertz does not usually circle back from the synchronic analysis to enrich our understanding of the contingent historical circumstances or structured social tensions that produced the cultural performance in the first place.[8] Thus, although I believe that Roseberry's invocation of the problem of materialism and idealism is confused, I find his critique of Geertz considerably more troubling than those of the pos-

7. For a discussion of Roseberry consonant with mine, see Dirks (1996).
8. The only exception that comes to mind is an article written early in Geertz's career, which treats a politically fraught funeral:"Ritual and Social Change: A Javanese Example" (1973i). This article was written in 1959, before Geertz had freed himself from his Parsonian heritage, at a time when he was preoccupied with the problematic of modernization. Although it is now fashionable to equate modernization theory with an unreflexive teleology, Geertz used it in this article and in a number of his early works to examine the contradictions of a Javanese society that, in the 1950s, was experiencing the throes of transition from colony to independent state. See, e.g., Geertz (1963a, 1963b, 1965). In an exceptionally subtle critical evaluation of Geertz's work, Diane J. Austin-Broos points out the contrast between Geertz's early work on Java, which was undertaken from a modernization perspective but treated culture as ambiguous and manipulable, and his later work on Bali and Morocco, which is characterized by a"new stillness" that results from"the rendering of life as aesthetic" (Austin-Broos 1987, 156).

itivists or the postmodernists. It gets at precisely the kinds of weaknesses
that are bound to seem serious to a social historian.

GEERTZ AND HISTORIANS

Yet social historians, myself included, have been enormously responsive to
Geertz's work. Roseberry's critique therefore poses a paradox: why should
so many historians, who are professionally concerned with questions of
change over time, be so strongly influenced by an anthropologist whose
work is insistently synchronic?

In her pathbreaking article on "The Traffic in Women," Gayle Rubin
thanks her undergraduate teacher Marshall Sahlins for what she calls "the
revelation of anthropology" (1975, 157). The phrase is apt. The revelation,
I take it, is that our world is contingent rather than necessary; that there
exist forms of life radically different from ours that are nonetheless fully
human, and that, consequently, our own future is potentially more open
than we usually imagine. This is the perennial message of anthropology to
the world, and its delivery is the core duty of its long-standing ambassadorial function, certainly as carried out by Benedict, Mead, and Geertz. Indeed, I suspect that virtually all anthropologists were initially "allured" or
"seduced" into their field by the exhilaration of discovering simultaneously
the radical otherness and human comprehensibility of exotic cultures.
Most have learned in the course of their professional training to suppress
this initial thrill of recognition-in-difference, to replace it with an effort to
encompass exotic facts in supposedly universal but actually very Western
scholarly codes. Geertz, like Benedict before him, has striven to keep alive
and to communicate to his readers the revelation of anthropology. It is precisely this quality that has made him so effective as an ambassador.

If historians have been particularly susceptible to Geertz's charms, it is
partly because history is built on an analogous seduction. In the pasts they
study, historians find worlds structured differently from ours, worlds where
people's motives, senses of honor, daily tasks, and political calculations
are based on unfamiliar assumptions about human society and the cosmic
order. Many of the greatest works of history—for example, Jacob Burckhardt's *The Civilization of the Renaissance in Italy* (1958), Johan Huizinga's *The
Waning of the Middle Ages* (1954), Marc Bloch's *Feudal Society* (1964), E. P.
Thompson's *The Making of the English Working Class* (1963), Emmanuel Le
Roy Ladurie's *Montaillou* (1978)—reveal to us worlds hardly less strange
than Bali, Zuni, or the Trobriands. History, like anthropology, specializes

in the discovery and display of human variety, but in time rather than in space. It reveals that even our own ancestors lived lives stunningly different from ours. Geertz's brand of anthropology, which attempts to plumb the cultural logic of exotic societies, was thus prealigned with an important form of historical sensibility.

Anthropology had an additional claim on history as it was being practiced in the early 1970s, when Geertz published *The Interpretation of Cultures*. Geertz's emergence as an academic superstar took place at a time when social history was reaching for dominance in the history profession. The rise of social history introduced fundamental changes to the field: a shift from the study of high politics and the actions of political and cultural elites to the study of social structures and the actions of ordinary people. In the United States, the first wave of social history was marked above all by the borrowing of theories and methods (particularly quantitative methods) from sociology, but by the early 1970s a second generation of American social historians, myself among them, were beginning to feel that purely quantitative approaches could never grasp adequately the textures and meanings of ordinary people's lives (see chap. 2 above). Anthropology, as practiced by Geertz, seemed to offer a means of reaching deeper. Like social history, it was focused not on the practices of political leaders and intellectuals but on those of ordinary people. And it revealed—in their rituals, social conventions, and language—lives rich with complex symbolism and overflowing with meaning.

But anthropologists had a huge advantage over historians when it came to studying the kinds of people whose thoughts and deeds are seldom recorded in writing. They could live with them, learn their languages, engage them in conversation, observe their rituals, and participate in their daily routines. Historians working on peasants, workers, slaves, women, or colonized peoples were limited to what was written down and saved in archives or libraries—often not in such people's own words but in those of their "betters" or governors. But here Geertz's particular theory of culture gave historians reason for hope—and for emulation. Geertz continually stressed that meaning was not locked away in actors' heads but was embodied in publicly available symbols. He insisted that the symbol systems that make up a culture "are as public as marriage and as observable as agriculture" (1973h, 91). Good ethnographic field workers, Geertz told us, do not achieve some miracle of empathy with the people whose lives they briefly and incompletely share; they acquire no "preternatural capacity to think, feel, and perceive like a native" (1983e, 56). The ethnographer does

not "perceive what his informants perceive. What he perceives, and that
uncertainly enough, is what they perceive 'with'—or 'by means of' or
'through.'" He or she does this "by searching out and analyzing the symbolic forms—words, images, institutions, behaviors—in terms of which,
in each place, people actually represented themselves to themselves and to
one another" (58).

It should be apparent that such a conceptualization of the study of culture is epistemologically empowering to social historians. It is obvious that
those of us who study the dead cannot hope to share their experiences directly, as a naive ethnographer might imagine she or he directly shares the
experiences of her or his "natives." But some of the symbolic forms through
which the dead experienced their world are available to us in surviving
documents—often piecemeal and second hand, to be sure, but by no
means beyond recovery. Geertz's particular conceptualization of culture as
made up of publicly available systems of symbols provided an important
epistemological guarantee to social historians. It powerfully authorized
the use of anthropological methods in studies of past societies.

THE USES OF SYNCHRONY

The vein of anthropological revelation opened up to historians by Geertz's
methods was essentially synchronic in character. What Geertz analyses
most brilliantly, or describes most thickly, are what he frequently called
"cultural systems" (1973e, 1973h, 1983b, 1983c). To portray an ensemble of
symbols and the practices in which they are employed as a cultural system
is to trace out how these symbols and practices mutually sustain each
other as an integrated whole. For instance, the cultural system of a religion
is composed of two complementary symbolic orders—an ethos (a people's
"moral and aesthetic style and mood") and a worldview ("their picture of
the way things in sheer actuality are")—that mutually imply one another
(1973h, 127). Thus, for Navahos, "an ethic prizing calm deliberateness, untiring persistence, and dignified caution complements an image of nature
as tremendously powerful, mechanically regular, and highly dangerous."
And for Hindus "a transcendental moral determinism in which one's social
and spiritual status in a future incarnation is an automatic outcome of the
nature of one's action in the present, is complemented by a ritualistic duty-
ethic bound to caste" (130). Religions, in short, mutually tune a people's
conceptions of the real with their conceptions of the appropriate way to
live. It is this mutual reinforcement that gives them their systemic character. But such systems of mutual implication are by no means limited to the

sphere of religion. Geertz argues in "Person, Time, and Conduct in Bali" that Balinese naming practices fit tightly with Balinese modes of calendrical reckoning and that both reinforce a particular mode of conduct; the three symbolic domains "are hooked together by a definable logic" (1973g, 404). Again and again, whether the subject is religions, conceptions of persons, hermaphrodism, aesthetic practices, cockfights, ideologies, state funerals, or royal progresses, Geertz's version of cultural analysis constantly returns to the trope of culture as interlaced and mutually sustaining systems of meaning.

Analyzing culture in this way is a synchronic intellectual operation. Although a synchronic description or analysis is often glossed as a "snapshot" that "freezes" time or as a "slice" of time, this is not quite right. Such a description is, rather, one in which time is *suspended* or *abolished* analytically so that things that actually occur in the flow of time are treated as part of a uniform moment or epoch in which they simply coexist. Just as "synoptic" means that all views are present in a single glance, as in one of those Renaissance paintings in which the far flung scenes of a saint's life and martyrdom are depicted in a single continuous landscape, so "synchronic" means that different times are present in a continuous moment. To put it otherwise, in synchronic description, acts of cultural signification, rather than being treated as a temporal sequence of statement and counterstatement or as linked by causal chains of antecedent and consequence, are seen as a mutually defined and mutually sustaining universe of (at least momentarily, until the analytic spell breaks) unchanging meaning.

Such a procedure of suspending time would appear on the surface to be unhistorical, but this is not necessarily the case. The term "historical" actually has two quite distinct meanings in contemporary speech. On the one hand, it has the obvious adjectival meaning derived from its root "history"—that is, it designates happenings that take place over time, as in "historical sequence," "historical continuity," or "historical narrative." But historical also implies "in the past," standing at a distance from the contemporary world, as in "historical novel," "historical costume," or "historical significance." I would actually argue that this is the primary meaning of the term in both everyday and academic language, since it is only when connected to nouns that themselves imply temporal flow, like sequence, continuity, or narrative, that "historical" implies the continuous passage of time. Consequently, when we admonish someone to "think historically," we give an ambiguous message. We might mean "recognize more consciously and explicitly the 'pastness' of the past you are thinking about." Or we might mean "place the happening you are thinking about in a temporal sequence of transformations." Or we might mean both.

These two meanings of "historical" and "history"—what we might call "history as temporal context" and "history as transformation"—are the synchronic and diachronic faces of history. History as temporal context is historical in the sense that it is placed in some past era, but it is concerned not with the process of change during that time but with the distinct character and atmosphere of what we might call a *block* of time. Indeed, we convince our readers—and ourselves—that we have truly understood the pastness of that time by showing how a wide range of different beliefs, practices, judgments, and forms of action were linked by some common but now foreign logic.

Both history as transformation and history as context are recognized in the practice and training of professional historians. We would regard as incompetent any historian not capable of arguing in both modes. But as in ordinary language, it is actually the synchronic mode that is privileged in historical judgments, not the diachronic. A historical work that makes no effort (or only the most passing effort) to explicate or explain a historical transformation but portrays effectively the context of some past lifeworld can be hailed as a masterpiece. Think of Louis Namier's *The Structure of Politics at the Accession of George III* (1929), Emmanuel Le Roy Ladurie's *Carnival in Romans* (1979) the already mentioned works by Huizinga (1954) or Burckhardt (1958), or Robert Darnton's essay on "The Great Cat Massacre" (1983)—a work that was strongly influenced by Geertz. By contrast, a history that recounted a series of changes over time but failed to indicate the distance of the lifeworld being described from the present would be dismissed out of hand as "anachronistic"—the historian's equivalent of the anthropologist's "ethnocentric" and perhaps the most damning term in the historian's lexicon of judgment.

It is significant that "anachronism," which means "in the wrong time" is an indispensable term in the historian's vocabulary and has unambiguously negative connotations, whereas "achronism," a perfectly good word that means "without time," has no negative connotations—indeed, is not a part of the historian's critical vocabulary at all. Here, as any good Geertzian would expect, the language used by historians tells us something about the shape and meaning of their lifeworld.[9] It tells us, perhaps surprisingly,

---

9. On the use of academic languages of judgment to understand the preoccupations of different disciplines, see Geertz (1983f, 157–58).

that adequately realized synchrony is more important to good historical analysis than adequately realized diachrony. In the eyes of professionals, it is more important for a historian to know how to suspend time than to know how to recount its passage. Geertz's synchronic methods, therefore, may be just what historians need.

But if historians' language indicates that they value synchronic adequacy over diachronic adequacy, most also care about history as transformation. Here Geertz is of little direct assistance, but indirectly his synchronic methods remain extremely valuable.[10] I would argue that the study of history as transformation has typically been haunted by an excess of diachrony. It is not without reason that insurgent social historians, whether the American "new social historians" or the French historians of the Annales school, consistently defined themselves against "narrative history" (see chap. 2 above). And even though it was the social historians (and their successors the cultural historians) who won these battles, historians' long-standing habit of trying to narrate themselves out of tight conceptual spots has hardly disappeared. If I think of the many history articles I have advised journals not to publish in the course of my long service as a peer reviewer, their most common failing by far was attempting to solve—or to avoid—a conceptual problem by retreating to the obvious archival sources and stringing together a narrative of "what actually happened." My ethnographic research in the daily routines of "historyland," in other words, tells me that leaving the synchronic element out of historical analysis—neglecting to pause long enough to work out the structure of a given historical moment—remains an extremely common failing of historical research and writing.[11]

A proper appreciation of synchrony is the secret ingredient of effective diachronic history. I would argue that no account of a historical transformation can be cogent unless it performs a dialectical oscillation between synchronic and diachronic thinking. We should, in my opinion, pay more literal attention to the word "transform," whose two roots—"trans" and "form"—signal precisely the necessary joining of diachrony and synchrony. Unless we can represent to ourselves and our readers the *form* of

---

10. In fact, his early monographs on Indonesian modernization, cited in note 8, might have been of direct assistance. But they were so similar in style to studies already being done by social historians that they were not much noticed. It was the later, more synchronic, essays that captured historians' imaginations.

11. The invocation of "historyland" is of course a reference to the immortal Bernard Cohn's "History and Anthropology: The State of Play" (1980).

HISTORY, SYNCHRONY, AND CULTURE   185

life in one historical moment or era, unless we can describe systematically the interlocking meanings and practices that give it a particular character, how are we to explain its *trans*formation—or, for that matter, even to recognize when and how it has been transformed? A typical account of historical change shows how initial changes in some particular sector or sectors of a lifeworld have ramifying effects on others, with the ultimate consequence that the lifeworld as a whole is cast into a different shape. An account of this sort can only be convincing if the pre-transformation interrelationships have already been cogently demonstrated: otherwise the claims about ramifying effects of initially local changes will seem insubstantial. No account of change will be judged deep, satisfying, rich, or persuasive unless it is based on a prior analysis of synchronic relations.

In short, the fact that Geertz's work is so resolutely synchronic hardly makes his work irrelevant to historians. Indeed, its most signal virtue for historians may be its cultivation of a synchronic sensibility. If the trope of the cultural system, the image of deep play, or the ideal of thick description can enable historians to suspend time more effectively—and consequently to portray past lifeworlds and their transformations with greater clarity, complexity, consistency, or depth—then they have been far from foolish to take seriously even Geertz's most unrelentingly synchronic work.

CULTURAL SYSTEMS AS A MATERIAL FACT

Geertz's concept of the cultural system posits a very tight fit between publicly available clusters of symbols and the moods, motivations, affects, and activities that these symbols shape. It is this assumed tightness of fit that makes his theorization of culture problematic for explaining cultural change. Geertz never explicitly raises the question of why cultural systems determine human behavior so closely. But I think the basic assumptions can be found in two essays written in the 1960s: "Religion As a Cultural System" (1973h) and, especially, "The Growth of Culture and the Evolution of Mind" (1973d), one of the most brilliant and underappreciated essays in *The Interpretation of Cultures*. In these essays, Geertz argues that cultural patterning must be understood as an analogue of genetic programming.

Although I disagree with Geertz's conclusions about the overwhelmingly determining character of cultural systems, I regard his extended meditation on the relationship of genes and symbols as the necessary starting place for any theory of culture. This meditation, moreover, provides the vindication of Geertz's materialist metaphysical credentials that I promised earlier. It does so by demonstrating that "mind"—seemingly a suspiciously "idealist" concept—has a substantial biological basis in human evolution. I will therefore present Geertz's fundamental theory of the symbolic patterning of behavior in some detail in this section, before going on to criticize and modify it the next. "Systems or complexes of symbols," Geertz writes in "Religion as a Cultural System,"

> are extrinsic sources of information. By "extrinsic," I mean only that—unlike genes, for example—they lie outside the boundaries of the individual organism as such in that intersubjective world of common understandings into which all human individuals are born, in which they pursue their separate careers, and which they leave persisting behind them after they die. By "sources of information," I mean only that—like genes—they provide a blueprint or template in terms of which processes external to themselves can be given a definite form. As the order of bases in a strand of DNA forms a coded program, a set of instructions, or a recipe, for the synthesis of the structurally complex proteins which shape organic functioning, so culture patterns provide such programs for the institution of the social and psychological processes which shape public behavior. (1973h, 92)

This analogy between genes and culture is not a mere metaphor, Geertz claims: it has a basis in the biology of human evolution:

> [The] comparison of gene and symbol is more than a strained analogy of the familiar "social heredity" sort. It is actually a substantial relationship, for it is precisely because of the fact that genetically programmed processes are so highly generalized in [humans], as compared with lower animals, that culturally programmed ones are so important; only because human behavior is so loosely determined by intrinsic sources of information that extrinsic sources are so vital. (92–93)

Human culture, or systems of symbols, provide a supplementary source of information that is not just a convenience to humans but a physiological necessity of our biological endowment.

As against an earlier view that culture arose in human evolution only after the huge cerebral cortex had developed, Geertz, following the lead of such anthropologists as S. L. Washburn and W. W. Howells, argues persuasively that culture and the human brain must have evolved in tandem. In the Pleistocene period, early hominids began to manufacture and use primitive tools and, relatedly, to engage in symbolic communication. Evolutionary pressures then selected for the kinds of neural structures that made such behavior possible, thereby enabling more sophisticated cultural patterns to develop, which in turn increased the selective pressures favoring cerebral development. Eventually, when the growing forebrain had allowed culture to accumulate to the point that "its role as an adaptive factor dominated its role as a selective one," the organic changes in neural structures effectively ceased. From that time forward, having long since acquired language, religion, moral regulation, and the incest tabu, *Homo sapiens* has remained neurologically more or less constant. It was, in short, the development of culture that called into existence the large forebrain which distinguishes our nervous system from that of the earliest hominids (1973d, 69).

Not only did culture and the large forebrain evolve together, but they remain organically linked today. "Man's nervous system does not merely enable him to acquire culture, it positively demands that he do so if it is to function at all" (68). Culture, extrinsic information coded in symbols, is a condition of our viability as a species. This is true because the large and astoundingly complex human brain does not respond to stimuli by producing specific behavioral responses, but rather with highly general affects:

> The lower an animal, the more it tends to respond to a "threatening" stimulus with an intrinsically connected series of performed activities which taken together comprise a comparatively stereotyped . . . "flight" or "fight" response. Man's intrinsic response to such a stimulus tends to consist, however, of a diffuse, variably intense, "fear" or "rage" excitability accompanied by few, if any, automatically preset, well-defined behavioral sequences. Like a frightened animal, a frightened man may run, hide, bluster, dissemble, placate, or, desperate with panic, attack; but in his case the precise patterning of such overt acts is guided predominantly by cultural rather than genetic templates. (75)

The only way for humans to produce specific behavior appropriate to the challenges thrown up by their environment is to use the manifold cultural codes that their peculiar neural structure has made possible. Because humans' genetically programmed responses are so generalized, they need the extrinsic information supplied by culture in order to accomplish the diverse tasks of life—whether those be responding to threats, constructing shelter, reproducing the species, seeking companionship, killing other species for food, or constructing political regulations. Humans proceed, and can *only* proceed, by gathering and manipulating information (including information about how to gather information) which is stored not in the physiological structure of the body but in the intersubjective space of human signifying practice and in the objects—books, maps, clothing, tools, sacred goods, illustrations, the built environment—that give it material form.

Intellectually unviable without culture, humans would be emotionally unviable as well. Geertz remarks that "man is the most emotional, as well as the most rational animal" (80).[12] He might have added the most emotional *because* the most rational. The emotional diffuseness or uncertainty of the human neural response to stimuli is the flip side of the existence of the complex neural apparatus that makes us capable of reasoning. The response to stimuli *can* be diffuse because our reasoning brain makes possible tremendous and adaptively useful flexibility in how we deal with a problem; it *must* be diffuse if we are to deal with a problem flexibly rather than in a stereotyped fashion. But this makes the human "a peculiarly high-strung animal," subject to all sorts of emotional excitement but without in-built patterns to guide responses to the excitement (80). It is cultural patterns that provide the necessary control of emotionally upsetting stimuli. They give "specific, explicit, determinate form to the general, diffuse, ongoing flow of bodily sensation," thereby "imposing upon the continual shifts in sentience to which we are inherently subject a recognizable, meaningful order, so that we may not only feel but know what we feel and act accordingly" (80).

This provision of specific form for diffuse and unsettling human emotion is, according to Geertz, precisely what religions are about. They provide us with conceptions and practices that enable us to live with the ever-present threat of chaos. In "Religion as a Cultural System," Geertz specifies three sources of such threat: events or problems that seem beyond our powers of explanation, suffering that seems impossible to endure, and ethical paradoxes that seem impossible to resolve. What religious symbolism does is not to deny the existence of the uncanny, of suffering, or of evil, but to provide concepts that make them thinkable (such as divine mystery, imitation of Christ, or original sin) and ritual practices that give them an experiential reality (such as the Eucharist, extreme unction, or penance). Religious doctrine, mirrored and experienced in ritual acts, does not, for example, spare us from suffering: it teaches us "how to suffer, how to make of physical pain, personal loss, worldly defeat, or the helpless contemplation of others' agony something bearable, supportable—something, as we say, sufferable" (1973h, 104). In short, our neural organization necessitates as well as makes possible the shaping of both our cognitive and emotional lives by systems of symbols.

12. Geertz quotes this phrase from Hebb and Thompson (1954).

This account of the evolutionary origins and the biological necessity of human culture is a brilliant piece of materialist argumentation. It transcends the material/ideal dichotomy not by some verbal formula, but by a substantial, scientifically based account of the inescapable complementarity of "material" and "ideal" in the human condition. It enables us to recognize the simultaneous rootedness of culture (or "mind") in bodily needs and its irreducibility to bodily needs. It enables us to pursue the autonomous logic of cultural systems without worrying that we are becoming "idealists" and therefore losing touch with the "real" world. If Geertz is right, as I firmly believe he is, semiotic systems are not unworldly or ghostly or imaginary; they are as integral to the life of our species as respiration, digestion, or reproduction. Materialists, this suggests, should stop worrying and love the symbol.

HOW CULTURAL SYSTEMS CHANGE

The theory of culture Geertz builds on this impressive ontological foundation provides wonderful tools for analyzing synchronic cultural relations, but clumsy tools for explaining cultural change. This means that a historian who wants to take advantage of Geertz's synchronic insights but also wants to investigate cultural transformations must modify Geertz's concepts in practice. This is precisely what historians—or historically inclined anthropologists—ought to expect: after all, virtually none of the social theory we use in our work has been developed to deal with problems of historical change. The overriding problem posed by most social theory has been accounting for social order or structure. This is true, for example, not only of Geertz, but of nearly all of anthropology before 1980; of the entire Durkheimian tradition; of Claude Lévi-Strauss, Roland Barthes, Michel Foucault, and Pierre Bourdieu; of Talcott Parsons, Robert Merton, and Erving Goffman. And even those theorists who have made the explanation of change a central problematic—principally Karl Marx, Max Weber, and such successors as Louis Althusser, Jürgen Habermas, or Immanuel Wallerstein—have usually employed notions of temporality so teleological that their concepts must be extensively revised to be useful to historians.[13]

What is needed is a theoretical critique that acknowledges and em-

13. I have made attempts at such revisions in chapters 3 and 4, above. So has Marshall Sahlins (e.g. 1981, 1985). The work of classical social theory that most fully embodies what I regard as a historian's appreciation of contingency is Max Weber's The Protestant Ethic and the Spirit of Capitalism (1958). But even here the possibility of contingency gives way to teleology; once capitalism is established it becomes, in Weber's memorable phrase, an "iron cage" (181).

braces what is most valuable in Geertz—for example, his epistemology of ethnographic research, his powerful sense of synchronic relations, and his ontological founding of the concept of culture in human biology—but that modifies his theories so as to make the possibility of change in cultural systems not an afterthought or an externality, but integral to the very notion of culture.[14]

A useful starting point for such a critique is Geertz's famous statement that symbols are both "models of" and "models for" reality. They are "models for" in the sense that they are templates for the production of reality—whether architectural ideals that guide the construction of houses or male- and female-coded forms of public behavior that guide the construction of men and women. But they are at the same time "models of" reality: the architectural principles used to construct houses are also used to make sense of or judge existing buildings, and the difference between men's and women's public behavior is taken as an index of the difference between the sexes. This double quality of symbols, Geertz points out, makes them different from genes, which are only models for, not models of (1973h, 93).

This is an exceptionally fruitful observation, but in my opinion Geertz fails to exploit some of its most interesting implications. He concludes that the "model of" and "model for" doubleness of symbols means that they give "objective cultural form to social and psychological reality both by shaping themselves to it and by shaping it to themselves" (93). He assumes, in other words, that the models of the social world will simply reflect back the reality that models for the social world have produced—and, correlatively, that models for the social world will simply produce in the world the "realities" that models of the social world describe. He assumes a relationship of mirroring or circularity, of complementarity and mutual tuning.

What Geertz fails to explore is that the doubleness of symbols also raises the possibility of a *disjunction* between their "model of" and "model for" aspects, a disjunction that opens up for actors a space for critical reflection about the world. The disjunction could open up on either of the symbol's two sides. To say that symbols are models of reality means that they

---

14. Geertz's most recent book, *After the Fact: Two Countries, Four Decades, One Anthropologist* (1995), is much more concerned with issues of diversity, power, struggle, and social transformation than were either *Interpretation of Cultures* or *Local Knowledge*. A kind of poetic autobiographical meditation on changes in anthropology and the world over the course of Geertz's career, it takes up these issues obliquely in the course of the narrative rather than addressing them head on. But as I read it, the book is actually quite compatible with the critiques and revisions of his earlier theories that I spell out here.

are the product of humans' attempts to make sense of or represent the world. The "model of" dimension of the symbol implies active human thought or consciousness, the very process of intellection that our large brains and diffuse responses to stimuli render both possible and impera- tive. This process of representation of course employs the symbols made available by the culture, but these symbols may be used in a creative or open-ended fashion. One makes sense of and evaluates buildings by using the existing store of architectural principles, but doing so might lead the evaluator to discover, to formally elaborate, and to integrate into architec- tural theories hitherto unrecognized principles that she discovers in the buildings being evaluated. The result may be a change in architectural principles (see Venturi et al. 1977). Because the world is always far more manifold than our representations of it, the representations are always po- tentially susceptible to change.

There is also a possibility of disjunction on the "model for" side. "Social reality," as Geertz would insist, is produced by shaping human action in the world according to cultural templates. But the world may prove quite re- calcitrant to our attempts to shape it. After all, every attempt to apply a template takes place in a situation not quite the same as those in which the template was initially constructed. Hence, even if we assume that people always try to reproduce conscientiously that which they have known, what they actually produce is bound to vary — sometimes significantly — from what is intended. An attempt to produce men and women whose forms of public behavior fit the existing pattern may prove impossible if new forms of employment open up for women — say, in spinning mills — in which ex- isting "feminine" forms of public behavior are no longer adequate. When this happens, a gap opens up that can only be closed by some change in the gender coding of forms of public behavior (see Dublin 1979). Because the world so frequently resists our attempts to shape it, cultural symbols that model the world (in both senses) are, once again, susceptible to change.[15]

What this implies is that we cannot unproblematically assume that the "model of" and "model for" aspects of symbols or symbol systems will au- tomatically mirror each other. That they frequently do so, or even that hu- mans normally attempt to make them do so, may well be true; I am no less

15. Here my arguments are very close to and have been strongly influenced by those of Mar- shall Sahlins: "The worldly circumstances of human action are under no inevitable obligation to conform to the categories by which certain people perceive them. In the event they do not, the received categories are potentially revalued in practice, functionally redefined" (1981, 67). See chapter 7 below.

inclined than Geertz to believe that people normally attempt to impose coherence on their world. But as the notional examples given above would seem to indicate, this attempt to impose coherence can be a force for *transformation* of cultural systems no less than a force for stability. The double character of symbols, far from constituting a guarantee of stability, guarantees that whatever stability is achieved can only be impermanent.

Geertz's ideas about the relations between culture and human neural structure may also be interpreted as implying a certain potential for instability in cultural systems. They do so because they imply considerable variation among individuals in response to a given problem. Because humans react to environmental stimuli in diffuse or general rather than in specific biologically programmed fashions, they must search for extrinsic information in order to find solutions to challenges. In some cases, cultural codes are so highly stereotyped that this search for information will be very brief, determinate, and uniform for all persons facing the same stimuli. But this is certainly not always the case. Because initial neural responses are diffuse, because there is often ambiguity about what cultural code might apply, and because there is considerable flexibility about precisely how it might be applied, any stimulus is likely to be met by a significant range of responses, some of which might be quite innovative. If for some reason an innovative response gains salience—for example, because it is particularly successful in dealing with the problem at hand or because the person who responds innovatively is powerful or influential—the cultural codes might be permanently altered. The kind of reproductive mirroring of cultural pattern and social action that Geertz implicitly assumes as the norm may indeed be the norm. But Geertz's explicit ontological model of human cognitive activity seems to imply that significant departures from reproductive mirroring are bound to occur as well.

A similar point might be made about the emotional implications of Geertz's model of the person. He stresses that humans are peculiarly high strung, that without the assistance of cultural patterns a human "would be functionally incomplete . . . a kind of formless monster with neither sense of direction nor power of self-control, a chaos of spasmodic impulses and vague emotions" (1973h, 99). Geertz moves from this insight about the fundamental emotional instability of the human condition to an account of how culture provides the controls that are somatically lacking. He points out, very astutely, in my opinion, that the control does not always or even primarily take the shape of repression, but rather of channeling emotions into knowable forms—whether the flamboyant courage of the

Plains Indian, the Manus' guilt-ridden compunctiousness, or the quietism of the Javanese.

But if the organic human emotional response to the environment is so diffuse and unstable, it hardly seems plausible that even the culturally thick, aesthetically appealing, and affectively powerful patterns of emotional self-expression that Geertz analyses in so many of his articles could consistently generate patterns of behavior that are genuinely constant over time.[16] Instead, one might expect the fundamentally vagrant quality of human emotion to lead to occasional experimentation with new forms of emotional patterning, to periodic dissatisfaction with existing moral and religious systems, and to spasmodic bouts of intense political, religious, and artistic activity. Here, as Geertz himself so often does, we might turn to the theoretical legacy of Max Weber, who insisted on the crucial role of charisma in certain cases of profound historical change. The emergence of prophets, heroes, congregations of disciples, or bands of revolutionaries can harness diffuse emotional energies into specific, historically potent social forces.[17] Both the emotional and cognitive dimensions of Geertz's theory of mind imply that cultural systems will not be reproduced automatically. An animal so high-strung and so prodigiously talented as the human being is bound to produce significant episodes of cultural transformation.

One reason Geertz's cultural systems appear impervious to change is that few of his works explore differences or variations in the beliefs, values, or idioms embraced by different groups within societies. On this question, the practices of cultural anthropologists have diverged sharply from Geertz's over the past two decades: examination of cultural difference has become one of their major preoccupations. Probably the most important source of the interest in difference has been feminist anthropology, which has problematized the apparent unity of cultural systems by demonstrating that cultures look very different from the perspective of women than from that of men.[18] But the interest in difference has also been central to "reflexive anthropology," which has advocated the ethnographic representation of multiple voices, and to the anthropology of colonialism, which

16. For such analyses, see, e.g., Geertz (1960, 1968, 1973b, 1973c, 1973g, 1973j, 1983c, 1983d, 1983e).

17. See Weber (1958 and 1978, esp. 1:241–54, 2:1111–56). Emile Durkheim ([1912] 1965) also has extremely interesting things to say about the role of emotion in social life. For an attempt to use some of Durkheim's insights in the analysis of cultural transformation, see chapter 8 below. For a sustained argument about the place of emotions in history, see Reddy (2001).

18. Four examples among many are Wiener (1976), Abu-Lughod (1986), Martin (1987), Ortner (1996).

has focused on the freighted cultural negotiations between European rulers and their colonial subjects.[19] Social historians, of course, have been interested in questions of difference for some time: "history from below," as practiced ever since the 1960s, explicitly endeavored to rescue the voices of the poor and marginalized and to relate their cultural experiences to those of the dominant classes.[20] Indeed, the more recent anthropological practices of multivocality have surely been influenced in part by the example of social history.[21]

As much of this anthropological and historical work demonstrates, cultural change often arises out of conflict, communication, rivalry, or exchange between groups with different cultural patterns and social relations. Group difference implies the possibility of conscious challenges to practices or values that might otherwise be reproduced automatically, and of continual negotiations or struggles about meanings. Moreover, internal social differentiation also makes possible the development in specific social niches of new cultural complexes. It is usually the case that cultural innovations do not take place uniformly over an entire society, but are concentrated in or originate from specific social and geographical locations. The possibility of a workers' revolt, which haunted European politics for the better part of the nineteenth and twentieth centuries, initially arose out of a very particular dispute between weavers and silk merchants in Lyon in 1831; the cultural innovations we think of as the Renaissance were remarkably concentrated in the town of Florence; the early twentieth-century transformation of Sherpa Bhuddism was initiated by a handful of wealthy traders and monks.[22]

Geertz certainly does not deny the existence or the significance of internal difference, but he usually brackets such difference in his texts. The difference he emphasizes is that *between* societies or peoples—between "the Plains Indian's bravura, the Hindu's obsessiveness, the Frenchman's rationalism, the Berber's anarchism, the American's optimism" (1973f, 53). It is remarkable how frequently Geertz makes assertions about "the Balinese," "the Javanese," "the Berbers," "the French," "the Hindus," "the Manus,"

---

19. The best known manifesto of reflexive anthropology is Clifford and Marcus (1986). See also Marcus and Fischer (1986). The pioneering anthropologist of colonialism is Cohn (1987, 1996).

20. Perhaps the most celebrated examples are Thompson (1963) and Genovese (1974).

21. On history from below and anthropology, see Rosaldo (1990).

22. On the significance of Lyon in the development of workers' revolts, see Sewell (1980, 206–7). On Sherpa religion, see Ortner (1989).

or "the Zuni" without considering the possibility that there are culturally important differences within these categories—of outlook, belief, and comportment, or of wealth, gender, power, and status.

Yet here again, there are theoretical resources in Geertz's work for conceptualizing cultural difference at the intra-society as well as inter-society level. For example, Geertz argues that the sort of cultural diversity that makes possible such different lifeworlds as those of the Plains Indians, the Hindus, the Manus, and the French is a consequence of humans' inescapable reliance on extrinsic cultural codes. Although the neural equipment of humankind is everywhere essentially the same, the cultural codes that provide our minds with specific content is fundamentally diverse. "To be human," Geertz states, "is thus not to be Everyman; it is to be a particular kind of man and of course men differ: 'Other fields,' the Javanese say, 'other grasshoppers.'" According to Geertz, it is the anthropologist's particular calling to study the different modes of being human; it is only by understanding the particulars of these forms of life that "we shall find out what it is, or can be," to be human (53).

To this I would add three points. First, the cultural production of different forms of life takes place at many levels, not just at the level of the "society" or the "people." Differences between the forms of life of peasants and landlords, workers and students, men and women, priests and nobles, or slaves and masters are as legitimate an object of anthropological scrutiny as those between "societies." Second, examining the relations between such different categories of people—whether of conflict, domination, exchange, emulation, or self-conscious differentiation—is a crucial task for cultural analysis. And third, the value of studying relations between categories of people is as great for what we conventionally label "societies" as for classes, genders, or status groups. "Societies" are themselves interpenetrating and mutually constituting social categories, in this respect analogous to the classes, genders, or status groups that constitute them. And they too are animated by relations of conflict, domination, exchange, emulation, and self-conscious differentiation with one another.

Geertz actually provides a good metaphor for the sort of dynamic, relational, differentiated cultural analysis I am advocating here. In "Thick Description: Toward an Interpretive Theory of Culture," he explicates and draws lessons from the tangled Moroccan story of the Jewish peddler Cohen, a tribe of Berber horsemen, and a French colonial official—a story whose "confusion of tongues" he takes as paradigmatic for the situation facing the ethnographic interpreter (1973j, 9). In this instance, the confu-

sion of tongues arises from the encounter of three "peoples" in the traditional anthropological sense: Jews, Berbers, and French. But the metaphor
could easily be extended. Analogous cultural misunderstandings, conflicts,
and negotiations occur all the time among people who share language, religion, territory, or a sense of ethnic identity but differ in status, gender,
class, age, power, caste, or occupation. And it is precisely in these various
episodes of confusion of tongues — where social encounters contest cultural meanings or render them uncertain — that cultural systems are transformed. Once we admit social diversity, we can no longer see cultural systems as always self-reinforcing: instead, they must also be seen as sites of
conflict, dialogue, and change.

To make sense of historical transformations, then, we must adopt a different theory of culture than Geertz's. But unlike Roseberry and many
other of Geertz's anthropological critics, I think we would be gravely mistaken to respond by rejecting his theory outright. Instead, I think we
should *appropriate* his theoretical categories — engaging them, weighing
their strengths and weaknesses, reworking them from within, but also
supplementing them where necessary with foreign grafts. There is still
enough untapped richness, insight, and analytical power in Geertz's work
to make it a continuing inspiration for historical analysis.

A THEORY OF THE EVENT

Marshall Sahlins's "Possible Theory of History"

In the ordinary language of the human sciences, the expression "theory of the event" is an oxymoron. Events, by definition, are unique and contingent happenings and are subject to the vagaries of human will. They therefore hardly seem a proper subject for a social science that sees its task as the discovery of general social laws. In the traditional division of labor in the human sciences, events were relegated to history, which specialized precisely in recounting the unique and contingent. Even the rise of social history—which by the end of the 1970s had become the dominant form of historical scholarship nearly everywhere—did not lead to the development of a systematic theoretical approach to events. Social historians defined themselves above all in opposition to the previously dominant narrative political history, and they consequently disdained the study of events. The structure-event contrast, which had traditionally distinguished the social sciences from history, was thus replicated within the discipline of history, where it distinguished social history from narrative history. For Fernand Braudel, the leader of the enormously influential French Annales school of social historians, the history of events (*l'histoire événementielle*) was mere froth on the waves of history. The history that really mattered was *l'histoire structurelle*, which studied geographical, ecological, and mental "structures of long duration" (*structures de longue durée*)

This chapter was originally published in German as "Eine Theorie des Ereignisses. Überlegungen sur 'Möglichen Theorie der Geschichte' von Marshall Sahlins," in *Struktur und Ereignis*, ed. Andreas Suter and Manfred Hettling, Sonderheft 19 of *Geschichte und Gesellschaft: Zeitschrift für Historische Sozialwissenschaft*. Copyright © 2000 by Vandenhoeck and Ruprecht, Göttingen; reprinted with the permission of Vandenhoeck and Ruprecht.

and *l'histoire conjoncturelle*, which studied the shifting conjunctures of economy and demography (Braudel 1958, 1966).

It is true that few historians still cleave to Braudel's hard anti-evenementalism. The "return of the event" was announced as early as 1974 (Nora 1974) and by the end of the 1970s a number of historians once associated with something like the Braudelian position had either explored particular events in lavish detail or declared their interest in a more narrative and less structural form of historical writing (e.g., Duby 1973; Le Roy Ladurie 1975, 1979; Stone 1979). But this return to writing about events has not, at least until very recently (e.g., Suter 1997), led historians to reflect upon the event as a theoretical category.

By far the most impressive and systematic theoretical discussion of the event has, instead, taken place in a very different and perhaps surprising disciplinary location: in the work of the structuralist anthropologist Marshall Sahlins. That Sahlins's theory has not been more generally recognized by historians reflects one of the history profession's most unfortunate and most ingrained professional traits: great power chauvinism. Sahlins's theory arose out of his work on the ethnographic history of Polynesia, safely out of the view of historians of Europe or America, or, for that matter, of most historians of the great non-Western civilizations in Asia and the Middle East.[1] Sahlins's theory is, in my opinion, brilliant, elegant, widely generalizable, and eminently useful for historians. I regard it as the necessary starting point for any theorization of events. In this article I shall begin with an exposition of Sahlins's theory as I understand it, and will then suggest some elaborations, critiques, and modifications.

Structural anthropology is, at first glance, a surprising source for a theory of events. Indeed, the epistemological conventions of structuralism would seem virtually to rule out the study of rapid and turbulent historical change. Structure is, as I have remarked in chapter 4, a powerful, pervasive, and constitutive metaphor in the human sciences; it implies permanence, order, and solidity. In its various uses in the human sciences (and for that matter in the natural sciences) structure signifies the stable principle of order that underlies the surface multiplicity of phenomena. It represents one of the major strivings of the sciences: the attempt to reduce the apparent chaos of the world to relatively simple and comprehensible models or rules. Events, which are turbulent and chaotic, are conventionally

---

1. Two European historians who have appreciated the significance of Sahlins's work are Peter Burke (1987, 1992) and Andreas Suter (1997).

contrasted to structure, and they tend to be denigrated in the comparison. Sahlins notes:

> For a certain anthropology, as for a certain history, it seemed that "event" and "structure" could not occupy the same epistemological space. The event was conceived as antistructural, the structure as nullifying the event. . . . Indeed, the table of oppositions that could be constructed from Annales texts would be worthy almost of the cosmological dualisms of certain Amazonian peoples. Structure is to the event as the social to the individual, the essential to the accidental, the recurrent to the idiosyncratic, the visible to the invisible, the lawful to the aleatory, the quotidian to the extraordinary, the silent to the audible, the anonymous to the authored, the normal to the traumatic, the comparable to the unique. (1991, 38–40)

Sahlins, to his credit, does not simply abandon the contrast between structure and event. After all, it is the powerfully recurrent or structured character of social existence, the strong tendency of social relations to be reproduced, that makes the event an interesting and problematic category in the first place. But Sahlins recasts the meaning of the contrast, attempting to transform the unequal and radical *opposition* between structure and event, which makes the two categories hostile and mutually incomprehensible, into a more balanced *relation*, in which each category implies and requires the other. Sahlins might be characterized as a structuralist of the Lévi-Straussian school who is trying to create a theory of cultural change without abandoning his structuralism. He has attempted to revise the structuralist common sense by giving structuralism a kind of American pragmatist inflection, one that focuses on social actors doing things with structural categories. Events, in Sahlins's reformulation, are transformations of structure, and structure is the cumulative outcome of past events.

Sahlins points out that events are recognizable as such only within the terms provided by a cultural structure. Events can be distinguished from uneventful happenings only to the extent that they violate the expectations generated by cultural structures. The recognition of the event as event, therefore, presupposes structure. Moreover, what consequences events will have depends on how they are interpreted, and that interpretation can only be made within the terms of the cultural structures in place. What an event will be, how it will run its course, depends on how it is implicated in the structure. Sahlins calls this "the constitution of historical events by cultural structures" (1991, 42). But if structures define and shape

events, it is also true that events (re)define and (re)shape structures. A society's cultural structure is a product of the events through which it has
passed.

SAHLINS'S "POSSIBLE THEORY OF HISTORY"

A number of Sahlins's writings from 1980 to the mid-1990s focused on the
relationship between structure and event (Sahlins 1981, 1985, 1989, 1990,
1991, 1994, and 1995; Kirch and Sahlins 1992). In his conclusion to *Islands
of History*, he sets forth what he terms "a possible theory of history, of the
relation between structure and event" (1985, 138). This "possible theory"
has two fundamental propositions. The first is that *"the transformation of
a culture is a mode of its reproduction"* (1985, 138). By this paradoxical phrase,
Sahlins means that unexpected happenings—like expected happenings—
are appropriated and can only be appropriated and acted upon by people
in terms of their existing cultural categories. Sahlins elaborates this notion
by considering a particularly spectacular case: the arrival of Captain Cook
in Hawaii. The gist of his argument is that Cook and the English were received in Hawaii in accordance with the categories of Hawaiian mythical
history. They were seen as beings from Kahiki, the "invisible lands beyond
the horizon," and hence as divine. In Hawaiian culture, the physical arrival
of divine beings was extraordinary but not unprecedented: according to
myth, both the current Royal line and the kings they deposed were divine
beings who had also arrived by sea from distant lands.[2]

The supposition that Cook was a god was enhanced by an additional

2. It should be noted that Sahlins's interpretation of Cook's encounter with the Hawaiians
has been sharply challenged by Gananath Obeyesekere (1992). According to Obeyesekere, the
notion that Hawaiians regarded Captain Cook as a god was purely a European invention, one
based on long-standing myths about the inferiority and gullibility of savages that were shared by
European explorers and landlubbers alike. Obeyesekere argues that Hawaiians dealt with Europeans more in a pragmatic than a mythological register, and that the ceremony interpreted by
Sahlins as the deification of Cook was in fact a rite intended to install him as a chief within the
Hawaiian scheme. This was probably motivated, Obeyesekere hypothesizes, by the desire of
the king of Hawaii to create an alliance with Cook in his wars against Maui. Cook was eventually integrated into the Hawaiian system as a god, but only after his death, as was the case for
Hawaiian royalty. Sahlins has, to my satisfaction, effectively refuted Obeyesekere's major claims
(Sahlins 1995). Although the issues at dispute between the two protagonists are significant, I do
not think that the outcome of their scholarly duel matters much for the arguments I am making
here. Obeyesekere, no less than Sahlins, sees the Hawaiians as making sense of and interacting
with the Europeans in terms of their own cultural categories; the difference is that he thinks they
treated Cook as a chief rather than as a god. Moreover, Obeyesekere, unlike Sahlins, has little to
say about the longer-term transformative effects of the event, which is my principal interest in
Cook and the Hawaiians.

coincidence: his second landing on Hawaiian shores, in January 1779, took place during the four-month Makahiki festival. During the rainy Hawaiian winter, the god-chief Lono arrived by sea to reclaim the land as his own, restoring its fertility and suspending the cult of the rival god Ku, which notably included human sacrifice. Because Ku was the god of warfare and was closely associated with the ruling line of Hawaiian chiefs, the four-month ritual cycle of Makahiki represented the temporary eclipse of the arts of war by those of peace. At the end of this festival period, Lono's warriors and the warriors of the king engaged in a mock battle, after which the Lono image was dismantled, the cult of Ku restored, and the warlike ways of the kings resumed (Sahlins 1981, 17–20; 1985, 116–20).

When Cook arrived at Kealakekua Bay in January 1779, he and his ships were received with great and joyous ceremony and Cook himself was led through elaborate rites that, in Sahlins's interpretation, identified him as the god Lono. Some days later, Cook unwittingly obliged the Hawaiians' expectations by departing, as Lono should, at the end of the Makahiki period—just as the king was recommencing the Ku cult and ritually regaining possession of his kingdom. But a less happy coincidence soon intervened: Cook's ship sprung a mast and he and his men returned a few days later to obtain a replacement. This time his appearance on the shore signified not the expected return of the peaceful Lono but an unwelcome threat—might not Lono-Cook overthrow the king and take power himself, as the king's own mythical ancestors had once done? In an atmosphere of mutual suspicion and hostility, the situation rapidly deteriorated. The Hawaiians committed a series of thefts, and Cook retaliated by going ashore with a body of marines to take the king hostage. This led to a confrontation on the beach in which Cook's outnumbered men were sent scurrying to a waiting boat and the captain was killed by a dagger thrust and then fallen upon by more than a hundred Hawaiians.

But Cook's death did not end the matter. Precisely what happened to his body is uncertain. Two days after Cook's death, two priests of Lono stole out to one of the ships and turned a piece of his body over to the British, asking when Lono "would come again?" (Sahlins 1981, 24). A few days later, what were apparently the rest of Cook's bones were returned, and the British ceremonially consigned them to the waters of the bay. But by the early nineteenth century, the priests of Lono were carrying what they claimed to be Cook's bones around the island in the annual Makahiki festival—in a sennit casket of the sort used to carry the remains of apotheosized chiefs. Once Cook was dead, he was appropriated by Hawaii's

rulers as an ancestral spirit—most notably by Kamehameha, who succeeded to the kingship of the island of Hawaii shortly after Cook's murder.
As the inheritor of the sacrifice of Cook, Kamehameha's mana, according
to Sahlins, "had become British" (1981, 26). This was true both ritually and
practically. Kamehameha venerated Cook's memory and his relics, and he
also undertook a policy of friendship with the British and other Europeans, guaranteeing their safety and promoting their commerce with the
islands. His promotion of European trade brought him enough guns,
ships, and European advisors to conquer the entire Hawaiian archipelago
and subject it to his unified rule.

The intrusion of Europeans into the islands was certainly a transformative event in the history of Hawaii. But how the intrusion affected
Hawaii, what its specific historical consequences were, resulted not simply
from the brute force or technological superiority of the Europeans. Europeans, their actions, and their material goods were appropriated in Hawaiian cultural terms, absorbed into a Hawaiian scheme of myth and practice.
This is the sense in which, as Sahlins puts it, "the transformation of a culture is a mode of its reproduction" (1985, 138).

This brings us to the second proposition of Sahlins's "possible theory."
This is that *in action in the world—technically, in acts of reference—the cultural
categories acquire new functional values*" (1985, 138). It follows from Sahlins's
first proposition ("the transformation of a culture is a mode of its reproduction") that to act in the world is always to perform an act of reference,
that "human social experience is the appropriation of specific percepts by
general concepts"—in the case at hand, of a British sea captain by Hawaiian notions of divinity (1985, 145). But this necessary practical classification
of the objects of perception and action into our existing categories puts the
categories at risk. If a deceased British sea captain is adopted as the favored
god of a Hawaiian king, this changes the sorts of mana available to kings.
Integrating Cook into the Hawaiian pantheon domesticated Cook in important ways. It not only made the potentially threatening appearance of
white men with huge ships, metal tools, and firearms thinkable, but made
these novel happenings susceptible to manipulation and calculation according to a Hawaiian logic. Having domesticated European mana through
the person of Captain Cook, Kamehameha could confidently trust European traders, protect them against theft and fraud, and could also prohibit
others from gaining certain fruits of this trade, which included firearms
and warships. These crucial European goods resulted in a remarkable ac-

cumulation of mana in the person of Kamehameha, who performed the unprecedented feat of conquering all the Hawaiian islands. To return to the language of Sahlins's second proposition: Kamehameha's "act of reference"—adopting Cook as a personal god—gave the Hawaiian concept of mana novel referents and therefore changed its meaning. "The cultural categories," as he puts it, "acquire new functional values. Burdened with the world, the cultural meanings are thus altered" (1985, 138).

It is, of course, particularly easy to see how transformations in cultural structures result from spectacular events like the first appearance of Europeans in Hawaii. But unexpected actions on the part of beings of any kind—of those categorized as women, or men, or chiefs, or fish, or rain, or plows, or dreams, or democracies, or verbs, or deaths—set in motion the same logic of cultural transformation. After all, it is true in general that, as Sahlins remarks, "the world is under no obligation to conform to the logic by which some people conceive of it" (1985, 138). Meaningful action in the world, which always includes an implicit or explicit act of reference, puts cultural categories at risk because the world is capable of subverting or contradicting the meanings that presume to describe it. This Sahlins calls the objective risk of the categories in action.

The categories also undergo a subjective risk—because they are used "by acting subjects in their personal projects" (1985, 149–50). To explicate this subjective risk, Sahlins develops a semiotic theory of interest. The term "interest," he notes, is derived from the Latin *inter est*, which means "it makes a difference" (1985, 150). If the meaning of a cultural sign, in Saussurian linguistics, is determined by its differential relation to other signs in the collective symbolic scheme, the interest of a sign is determined by the difference it makes in the life schemes of a particular subject—life schemes in the double sense of the person's unique sequence of experiences and of her or his current plans or intentions (1981, 68–69; 1985, 150). Undertaking an action always subjects a sign or cultural category to the plans or intentions of the person who acts. Actions, as we have seen, are acts of reference, but they are also acts of reference *by a person*, which means that the act inflects the meaning of the sign in accord with the interest of the actor. If the inflection succeeds, as when the Hawaiian monarch extended the concept of "tabu" to give himself and his followers a monopoly over European trade goods, the meaning of the category, and the meanings of all categories defined in relation to that category, are altered (1981, 71). Events transform the meanings and relations of cultural cate-

gories not only because the world fails to conform to categorical expectations, but because actors bend categories to their own ends in the course
of action.

This is a brief exposition of Sahlins's "possible theory." In my opinion,
Sahlins's theory introduces precisely the right objects of theoretical investigation: *structures*, which shape the world in their image; *events*, which,
although they are shaped by structures, transform the structures that
shaped them; a balky *world*, which is under no obligation to behave as our
categories tell us it should, and *subjects*, whose interested and creative actions are the human stuff of events. I believe that Sahlins's theory is extraordinarily fruitful; that it has important implications for thinking
about all kinds of events, in all areas of the world, and all historical eras.
Such a simple, elegant, and generalizable theory should have long since
broken out of the "islands of history" to be widely adopted by scholars
working on history's continents, metropoles, and empires—but it has not.
This is due in part, as I have remarked above, to the apparent marginality
of precolonial Hawaii to a history dominated by great power chauvinism.
But I also think there are certain intrinsic features of Sahlins's theory that
might reduce its attractiveness to historians. The elaborations and modifications I suggest in this chapter are intended, among other things, to
make the theory more attractive to mainline (or mainland) historians. I
might point out in passing that an effort at elaboration and modification
of the theory seems authorized by Sahlins's own uncharacteristic hesitancy in putting his theory forward, a hesitancy revealed in the phrase
"possible theory."

WHAT ARE STRUCTURES?

I believe that the best place to begin is with the concept of structure.
Sahlins's own concept is distinctly structuralist, firmly in the tradition of
Saussurian linguistics and Lévi-Straussian anthropology. Two features of
his usage make this clear. First, Sahlins employs the term structure in the
singular rather than in the plural. This implies that a given society has one
overarching system of meanings, a cultural system in the strong sense. According to this conception, all cultural meanings everywhere in a society
are bound tightly into a network of mutual definition. Second, structure
means cultural or symbolic structure. Although Sahlins is keenly aware of
how resources, including material resources, limit or shape social action,
he does not designate material circumstances as structure or part of structure, as they would be in normal sociological or Marxian usage of the term.

Sahlins does deviate from a Lévi-Straussian structuralist conception by emphasizing what Anthony Giddens calls the "duality" of structure. Rather than seeing structure as a sort of extra- or superhuman agency that imposes social behavior on hapless actors from the outside, Sahlins, like Giddens, makes it clear that structure is the outcome as well as the source of social conduct, that it enables as well as constrains, and above all that it can be transformed by human social practice (Giddens 1976, 1979, 1984).

I heartily endorse Sahlins's recognition of the duality of structure, but I dissent from the more conventionally structuralist features of his usage. I shall attempt to demonstrate that his conception of structure as singular and as exclusively symbolic results in theoretical and interpretive conundrums, and that these could be resolved, or at least ameliorated, by adopting the rather different concept of structure I have outlined in chapter 4, which sees structures as plural rather than singular and as being composed not just of cultural schemas but of mutually reinforcing sets of cultural schemas and material resources. I will be arguing, in effect, that accomplishing the sort of pragmatist inflection of structuralism that Sahlins envisages requires a more far-reaching modification of the concept of structure than he has yet undertaken—one that, appropriately enough, places structures more emphatically in the world of material practice.

IS STRUCTURE SINGULAR?

I am convinced that a plural rather than a singular conception of structure is absolutely crucial for a plausible theory of events. The notion that structure is singular for a whole society poses a number of problems, not the least of which is how to determine where one society and its cultural structure ends and the next begins. This problem is not so evident when the society in question is small in scale, relatively undifferentiated, and located on an isolated cluster of islands. But in the ethnically diverse, multireligious, spatially sprawling, mobile, and highly differentiated social formations that make up virtually all of the contemporary world and most of the world available to us in the historical record, boundaries are notoriously difficult to delineate.

Consider an immigrant Bengali chemical engineer who lives and works in Houston—hardly a freak in the contemporary world. Such a person participates simultaneously in an American culture, a Bengali culture, and an international scientific and engineering culture—among others. Each of these cultural structures or systems has its own language, sets of symbolic distinctions, schemes of hierarchical judgment, modes of authority,

and so on, but none of them has clear geographical or sociological boundaries—precisely because some persons inhabit all of them simultaneously
and blend or mix them in the course of their daily activities. Attempting to
retain a singular concept of structure in such circumstances would require
awkward and arbitrary choices. One could posit some vast globe-spanning
cultural structure with local cultural differences encoded as hierarchically
imbedded substructures, but such a concept of structure would have to be
either so vague and distended as to not count as a structure in any meaningful sense or be so minutely complex and full of epicycles as to be unus-
able in practice. Alternatively, one could maintain that American culture,
Bengali culture, and engineering culture are actually separate entities that
have only external relations with each other. But this would require carv-
ing our Bengali engineer from Houston into three separate noncommunicating consciousness that accidentally meet in his or her body. One could
think about cultural structures in this way—indeed, one might read the
structuralists and post-structuralists who proclaimed the death of the
subject as saying precisely that the person is a humanist illusion and that
subjects are nothing more than carriers of or sites for structures that determine their utterances or activities. But this would nullify the American
pragmatist (and humanist) thrust of Sahlins's project, which is to modify
structuralism by including within its perview intelligent and suffering human persons who transform structures by their effectual actions.

I believe that if Sahlins's theory is to be applicable not only to the "islands
of history" but to the continents, metropoles, and empires as well, structure
must be conceptualized as plural. Cultural structures, in my opinion,
should not be seen as corresponding to distinct "societies"—because it is so
often impossible to specify where one society or culture ends and the next
begins—but rather as corresponding to spheres or arenas of social practice
of varying scope that intertwine, overlap, and interpenetrate in space and
time. This would mean that for any given geographical or social unit, the
relevant structures would always be plural rather than singular.

A singular conception of structure is awkward not only for societies
that are complex, mobile, and geographically contiguous with other societies, but even for relatively well-bounded and isolated societies like the
Hawaiian islands before Cook's arrival. This is true in part because a singular conception of structure makes it difficult to explain where events
come from. Notice that Sahlins's paradigm case, the coming of Captain
Cook to Hawaii, avoids this problem because it involved a collision of two
cultures hitherto isolated from one another. When British and Hawaiians

met, the blatant contradictions between their cultural structures set off a stream of remarkable events. But in the absence of what (literally, from the Hawaiian point of view) we may call the *deus ex machina* of inter-societal contact, it is hard to see how a single overarching cultural structure will generate the differences, the shocks, and the novelties of reference that give rise to transformative events.

Sahlins's theory of interest, which asserts that persons occupying different positions in a system will understand and be motivated by the structure differently, moves toward one possible answer to this objection. In his Hawaiian example, Sahlins notes that women played an especially prominent role in the acts of tabu violation that eventually led to the collapse of the tabu system. For example, during Cook's sojourn in Hawaii and during subsequent visits by Europeans, commoner women repeatedly ignored the occasional tabus on the sea by swimming out to the ships at night to engage in sexual commerce with the sailors. While on the ships they also not only ate with their sailor paramours (Hawaiian women were forbidden to eat in the presence of men), but ate such tabued foods as plantains and pork—and with considerable gusto, according to the Europeans' chronicles (Sahlins 1981, 47–49). Indeed, it was a chiefly woman, Kaahahumanu, the powerful widow of Kamehameha, who engineered the public and ceremonial tabu violation that, in 1819, put an end to the tabu system for once and for all (63). Hawaiian women's particular willingness to violate tabus, Sahlins remarks, arose from the fact that

> the tabu did not sit upon Hawaiian women with the force it had for men. . . . The tabu as it affected women was rather the negative image of the consecrated status of men and gods: functioning to protect the sanctity of divine beings and things rather than a positive condition, state or attribute of women themselves. (46–47)

Women's personal and emotional commitment to the tabu system was far less powerful than men's, and they were therefore more willing than men to engage in acts of violation. This difference in perspective on a feature of the cultural structure endowed women with different interests than men. So, by analogy, any culturally marked difference in social position could give rise to differences in interest, and hence to potentially disruptive inflections of the meanings of cultural categories.

However, one wonders if this perspectival difference in interests is really sufficient to explain the novel actions of the Hawaiian women. If, as Sahlins seems to suggest, the tabu system is the master code in the cultural structure of Hawaii and that code defines women only negatively, where did women get the sense of self and the plans for social action that allowed them to engage in subversive and potentially dangerous episodes of tabu violation? One plausible response would be to retain Sahlins's singular usage, but to propose a more deconstructionist or post-structuralist image that would insist on the instability, contradictions, gaps, and fissures in structure. Specifically, in the case of Hawaiian women one could argue that while the tabu system defined women negatively, it defined them negatively in relation to the positively marked categories of men, chiefs, and gods. One might argue in the deconstructionist mode that the negative definition of women inevitably contained traces of the excluded positively defined categories, and that the trace identities with men, chiefs, and gods had the potential to endow women with capacities that are explicitly denied to them. Hence, when breaches occurred in the ordinary and expected course of social relations, these trace identities could be activated in powerful and subversive ways.

But however salutary such a post-structuralist inflection may be, I also think that structures need to be seen as multiple in the quite different sense that different institutional realms, operating at varying social and geographical scales, operate according to different symbolic or cultural logics.[3] Although I am ignorant of Hawaiian history and ethnography beyond what I have learned from Sahlins's work, it is surely not plausible that Hawaiian women's only social definition was as a negative category in the system of tabu relations. Surely women were also defined in quite different ways in other institutional realms—for example, in agricultural and craft production, in their families or households, and in their relations with other women. Of course, these institutional realms and the cultural structures that informed them can only have been relatively autonomous. Relations between men and women, both as categories in public ritual situations and as husbands and wives or brothers and sisters in families, were powerfully structured by the tabu definitions, according to which women are to men as commoners are to chiefs and as humans are to gods. But tabu relations surely did not exhaust the cultural categories of Hawaiian families. I assume that there must have been forms of cooperation, play, authority, and division of labor characteristic of Hawaiian families or households in general that were patterned according to rules quite different from those of tabu. Likewise, interactions among Hawaiian commoner women,

3. For a brilliant development of this point, see Swidler (2001).

all of whom were defined as noa rather than tabu, must have been structured primarily by principles other than those of the tabu system.

Societies should be conceptualized as the sites of a multitude of overlapping and interlocking cultural structures. These structures are only relatively autonomous, in that they contain meanings and symbols shared by other structures—as, for example, both the cultural structures pertaining to family relations and those pertaining to public ritual relations included notions of tabu. But however relative, the autonomy is also real: the cultural structure of family relations is by no means reducible to that of tabu relations. The different structures that shape a society in fact overlap or interlock in more than one way—they contain common symbols, they refer or lay claim to common objects, and they coexist in and hence inform the subjectivities of the same persons. Structures also may exist at quite different levels or scales. The tabu system encompasses all Hawaiians, indeed the entire Hawaiian cosmos. After Cook's arrival, Hawaiian social relations were also affected by a quite different world system of capitalist exchange that spanned vast geographical regions of the globe, but that, in much of the world, governed only a narrow band of human relations. Other structures correspond to broad institutional spheres: the family, priestcraft, chiefly lineages, warfare, or production. But structures also exist at much more microscopic levels—particular work gangs, households, or even diadic friendships develop their own specific cultural structures that are not reducible to the cultural structures operating at more inclusive levels of social relations.

Such a multiple concept of structures is important for two reasons. First, if we assume that subjects are formed by structures, a multiple concept of structure is capable of explaining the existence of persons with widely varied interests, capacities, inclinations, and knowledge. Thus Hawaiian women, in addition to being defined negatively by their relation to the tabu system, or in potentia by traces of the categories from which the tabu system excluded them, were also defined more positively and along quite different axes by their participation in other spheres of social and cultural relations—in teasing relations with brothers, in work relations with other women, in mother-daughter relations, and so on. Second, given that structures overlap, cultural meanings and identities derived from one structure or institutional sphere can be transposed to others. To return to Hawaiian women, it is hard to imagine that the violations of tabu occasioned by the appearance of Europeans were not informed in part by identities, solidarities, and meanings derived from, say, everyday relations among women or relations between sisters and brothers in particular households. With respect to the latter possibility, Sahlins remarks that there were many cases of close male relatives who colluded with women in their sexual commerce with the European sailors, a collusion that must arise at least in part from a sphere of social relations fairly autonomous from tabus (1981, 41–42).

Sahlins himself recognizes in a footnote in a paper on Fijian warfare that some sort of pluralizing of structure is necessary in order to explain the play of difference and the work of mutual redefinitions that is characteristic of the event. "The word 'structure,'" he remarks, "is also an evident oversimplification. We shall see that what is characteristic of the event, or of the incident as event, is the connections it makes between different orders of structure . . . in the culture of a given society" (1991, 86). He goes on to use the locution "orders of structure," fairly frequently in the remainder of the paper. I think, however, that the conception of multiple, overlapping, relatively autonomous, and transposable structures that I have been advocating is superior to the half-hearted compromise implied by "orders of structure." I should say that I am encouraged to advocate a more radical repudiation of the singular structuralist conception of structure by the fact that in the passage marked by the ellipses in the above quotation, Sahlins remarks "alternatively, one could follow Sewell in speaking of different structures," citing a prepublication version of the paper that became chapter 4 of this book. My remarks over the past few pages are an argument as to why one should "follow Sewell" on this issue.

A conception of structures as multiple rather than singular also helps to solve another issue Sahlins raises in a footnote in his paper on Fijian warfare: the difficulty of determining when a happening should be regarded as an event, rather than simply as an incident that reproduces a structure:

> I am aware of the looseness of the formulation of events as acts or incidents that change rather than simply implement structures. . . . There are also practical difficulties in distinguishing acts which reproduce an existing cultural order from those which alter it, insofar as every intelligible act is at once novel and continuous with the order. . . . Cultural orders are event-systems. . . . All this raises problems of the kinds and magnitudes of change necessary to qualify as "event." I deal with certain of these issues concretely only . . . leaving further consideration of the abstract problems to haunt me another time. (1991, 86)

In one respect it is appropriate that this problem should stay around to haunt anyone who embraces the notion of the duality of structure. Structures are made and reproduced by human action, not by God or by Nature. Because a structure is reproduced by enactments, and because the situation in which a structurally shaped enactment occurs is never quite the same as the previous situation, the difference between an act of reproduction and an event is always a difference in degree, not in kind. Distinguishing transformative events from ordinary implementations of structure is necessarily a matter of practical judgment.

However, determining which happenings are to be regarded as events would be a far less haunting affair if structures were conceptualized as multiple rather than singular. If structure is singular, one will constantly be asking whether an incident that has clearly changed the meaning and relations of categories in some particular corner of social relations is important enough to be called an event from the point of view of the cultural structure as a whole. The problem is often intractable, since what unambiguously qualifies as a local structural transformation may actually have the effect of reproducing a structure at a higher level. A divorce or a remarriage that profoundly transforms the culture of a given family will simply reproduce the categories of the American matrimonial system. If structure is regarded as singular, this incident poses an agonizing problem. But if structures are regarded as multiple, the happening is simultaneously an event from the point of view of the local family culture and an implementation of structure from the broader viewpoint.

A conception of structures as multiple, overlapping, and transposable also clarifies the problem of the production of acting subjects, about which Sahlins says relatively little. Sahlins makes certain assumptions about human subjects, all of which I would endorse: that subjects are willful, that they vary, and that they are profoundly shaped by their cultures. But Sahlins spends little time justifying these assumptions or exploring the relations between them. In particular, he has not pondered the possible contradictions between the assumption that people are culturally produced and that they are various. Since the cultural structure of any society is based on distinctions, it follows that different categories of persons identified in the culture will be different from each other — adults from children, men from women, chiefs from commoners, priests from chiefs, and so on. But Sahlins seems also to assume variations within such culturally recognized categories. I would maintain that within-category variation is compatible with an assumption of cultural production of subjects only if the cultural structures that inform subjectivities are conceptualized as multiple. Thus, in addition to being shaped by society-wide definitions of the relation of chiefs, or of women, or of priests to other categories, particular chiefs, women, and priests will also have been shaped by their varying participation in other institutions and bundles of social relationships. Under the assumption of multiple structures, the experiences, capacities, and knowledges of different persons will necessarily vary—because their life histories will yield unique mixes of exposure to different cultural structures, and from different angles of vision. Multiple structures imply varying subjectivities, and hence the varying interests that figure so centrally in Sahlins's account of events.

Moreover, whereas Sahlins clearly assumes that actors are willful, various, and profoundly shaped by their cultures, it is not so clear whether he regards actors as capable of acting creatively. True, they are able to make sense of novel phenomena, but they seem to do so essentially by assigning them to existing categories. Sahlins's Hawaiian actors sometimes seem rather unhesitating and automatic about their acts of reference, especially given the unprecedented and presumably unsettling nature of their situation. A European ship appears on the horizon during the appropriate time for Lono's arrival and Cook is immediately classed as Lono; Cook comes ashore, and the priests unhesitatingly lead him through ceremonies designed to identify him with that god. To be sure, our sources are all written by British sailors, so we are not privy to the perplexities, doubts, arguments, projects and counter-projects that may have emerged among the Hawaiians as they attempted to make sense of Cook's arrival on the scene. But in my opinion Sahlins's account makes the Hawaiians' crucial and risky acts of reference seem too easy, too automatically generated by the structures in place, and makes Hawaiian actors seem insufficiently conscious of the risks or reflective about the possibilities of other acts of reference. Indeed, the term reference seems a bit anemic for the kinds of cultural action that goes on in events. It could be read as implying that people have no sense of distance from their cultural structures, that the only issue is the assignment of the novel phenomenon to the appropriate structural category.

Yet it is not hard to imagine that the appearance of an anomalous phenomenon (and Cook in Hawaii would certainly qualify as anomalous) might result in semiotic actions far more complex than the assignment of the phenomenon to a category. People might also reflect upon the existing categories, suggesting redefinitions of various kinds—for example, the splicing together of previously separate categories, the moving of a category from its place in one structure to a place in another, the collapsing or multiplying of categorical levels, the development of alternative possible schemes of classification, and so on. Moreover, when confronted with the need for action, people might well act ambiguously, trying out more than one form of semantic reference at once, hoping to be guided further by the future behavior of the anomalous phenomenon itself. While one cannot fault Sahlins for not tracing out the semiotic complexities of Hawaiian action—the documents, unfortunately, are silent or virtually silent about these issues—it seems very likely that such complexities in fact lay behind the acts of reference that emerge in the documents.

I would argue that a multiple conception of structures would make subjects' cultural creativity easier to explain. If the cultural structures by which subjectivities are formed are multiple, then so are the subjectivities. Any individual person combines within herself or himself a number of different situational subjectivities, and the motivations, plans for action, and modes of thinking associated with these different subjectivities can never be strictly limited to any particular situation. Because persons, symbols, and objects of cultural reference overlap between structural realms, structurally generated rules, emotions, categories, and senses of self can potentially be transposed from one situation to another. Indeed, if actors commonly have the experience of negotiating and renegotiating the relationships between noncongruent cultural structures, it follows that they should have some intellectual distance on the structural categories themselves, that they should be able to view one set of cultural categories from the point of view of others that are differently organized, to compare and criticize categories and categorical logics, to work out ways of harmonizing or ordering the seemingly contradictory demands of different structural schemes. A multiple conception of structure, consequently, makes human creativity and reflection an integral element in the theory of history, not a philosophically prior metaphysical assumption.

IS STRUCTURE ONLY CULTURAL?

I argue that structures are multiple in the sense that different clusters or systems of cultural meanings inform different realms of institutional practice. This claim actually breaks with classical structuralism in two ways. First, it challenges structuralism's sense of totality by separating the symbols and meanings that structure human practices into relatively autono-

mous and noncongruent local clusters. But, second, it also implies that
the symbols and meanings are defined as much by their local relations to
worldly practice as by their global semiotic relations of similarity and difference. This implies a more substantial link between "structures" and "the
world" than can be comfortably accommodated by traditional structuralism, one that I believe can be clarified by conceptualizing structures as
made up of both cultural schemas and material resources, rather than of
schemas alone.

Although Sahlins does not treat resources as a part of structure, they
nevertheless play crucial roles in several episodes of his "structural history."
This can be illustrated most clearly by revisiting his account of structural
change in Hawaii after the death of Captain Cook. We might begin a discussion of resources with the question of the dead captain's bones, which
were a matter of dispute between the Hawaiians and the English. The
English wanted the bones so that Cook's barbarous death could at least be
appeased by giving his worldly remains a Christian funeral, and they did
consign someone's bones — whose we can only guess — to the waters of the
bay. The Hawaiians regarded Cook's bones as divine, but their use of them
was rather more worldly. By extending to Cook's bones the ritual treatment
accorded to those of deceased chiefs, Cook's mana could be captured for the
royal house, thereby increasing the king's worldly powers. Kamehameha,
who succeeded to the throne shortly after Cook's death, devoted himself
particularly to the cult of the British god Lono-Cook, who, according to a
priest speaking to Lieutenant Peter Puget in 1793, "always accompanied
the king" on his voyages (Sahlins 1981, 26). This royal adoption of the Cook
cult and the resulting access of British mana had important practical consequences for Kamehameha; indeed, it might be maintained that it was
precisely this that enabled him to conquer all the Hawaiian islands and
subject them to his unified rule. Kamehameha, as the privileged possessor
of European mana, set himself up as the protector of foreign shipping and
placed a royal tabu on all trade with Europeans. This assured him access to
European advisors and an effective monopoly over the firearms and ships
he needed to overpower his enemies. By 1812, Kamehameha had parlayed
these advantages into suzerainty of the entire archipelago.

This successful use of tabu to engross trade had an extended but ultimately disastrous history in Hawaii. In the early nineteenth century, when
Hawaiian sandalwood suddenly became a major item in European commerce with China, the value of the trade tabu rose precipitately. Not only
Kamehameha but many of the chiefs who administered his kingdom

and/or held the land and controlled the labor of commoners could gain enormous wealth by forcing gangs of commoners to troop into the forests and cut sandalwood. The exploitation of commoners by landholding chiefs drove them into poverty and exhaustion, probably contributing to the alarming drops in population attendant on the spread of "civilized" diseases like smallpox. The chiefs, meanwhile, accumulated new forms of mana from the commerce with Europeans. They bought vast quantities of European and Chinese luxury goods. They built European-style houses, which they used only for ceremonial occasions, and filled them with clocks, dishes, plate, and figurines. They piled up the finest quality Chinese silks, and American and English ginghams, linens, and woolens in storehouses where they were left to rot. At the same time, Hawaiian chiefs began calling themselves by European names: Billy Pitt, Cox, John Adams, Charley Fox, Thomas Jefferson, and so on. Sahlins sees these seemingly bizarre behaviors as resulting from perfectly logical extensions of existing Hawaiian notions. Traditionally, rulers claimed to rule as the descendants of foreign conquerors and used various means to emphasize symbolically their difference from the common people. To adopt the name Billy Pitt was precisely to assume a foreign, in this case European, identity that marked one off from ordinary Hawaiians. And the advent of massive levels of European trade in the years before the sandalwood forests were exhausted (around 1830) made possible an accumulation of the signs of foreign mana on previously unheard of proportions. The result was a frenzy of conspicuous consumption in a Hawaiian "political economy of grandeur"— one that wound up exhausting and depleting the ranks of commoners and eventually undermining the chiefs, who had accumulated gigantic debts by the time the boom ended. The eventual result was the "land reforms" of the 1850s, which had the effect of dispossessing Hawaiians altogether and turning the land over to American missionaries and traders (Sahlins 1990; Kirch and Sahlins 1992).

Once again, Sahlins uses this story to show how novel happenings are domesticated by the application of existing semiotic schemas. Cook's bones were given the same ritual treatment as those of dead kings or of chiefs defeated and killed in battle; this captured the mana of the dead great one as one's own. Trade with Europeans was coded as a royal affair, in part because the king was the privileged possessor of Cook's European mana, and the royal tabu was therefore extended to cover it. Luxury goods introduced by Europeans were interpreted as signs of chiefly mana and accumulated accordingly. Once again, European novelties were appropriated and shaped by Hawaiian cultural categories, but at the same time the meaning of the Hawaiian cultural categories were transformed by the new realities to which they refer.

But how did this simultaneous appropriation by and transformation of cultural categories take place? Here I want to point to the crucial but theoretically unmarked role played in Sahlins's story by the dynamic, dialectical relationship between schemas and resources. The dialectic may be schematized in three points or moments.

1. *Resources are produced by cultural schemas.* By this I do not mean that cultural schemas create the substances or the human beings that become resources in a given social situation. Rather, I mean that humans' or substances' specific value arises from their categorization within existing cultural schemas. Cook's bones become a powerful source of mana because they are treated according to schemas governing the bones of great chiefs. European trade is categorized as royal and subjected to tabus both because the king's association with Lono-Cook has made him "European"—that is, endowed him with European mana—and because the trade comes from over the water, like royal power itself. Action in the world marks substances or persons as resources with certain values and potentials for social power. It not only places the substances (or persons) in abstract categories that have specific semiotic relations with other categories, but endows them with the real-world powers that are characteristic of other substances (or persons) that belong to the category. Cooks' bones radiate a quality of divinity comparable to those of other divinized chiefs, and mana inheres in European firearms or fancy cloths as it does in certain tabued foods. A successful act of categorization—and categorizations are often disputed—makes things into resources of a specific sort and thereby subjects them to social dynamics characteristic of that category.

2. Nevertheless, *resources are also governed by other dynamics than those they receive from this categorization.* These supplemental dynamics are of two general types: natural and sociocultural. All resources are subject to certain biological or physical limitations and tendencies. Sahlins's story includes two obvious cases of such dynamics. Sandalwood trees are culturally marked as a trade good of particular value and as the property of chiefs or the king. But these markings do not change the fact that the trees reproduce slowly and therefore will eventually be exhausted by unrestrained cutting. Likewise the harvesters—the Hawaiian common people—could be pushed only so hard without suffering rises in mortality and declines in fertility. In addition to these natural dynamics, culturally defined re-

sources were also subject to sociocultural dynamics beyond those arising from their assignment to a particular category. Hawaiians could classify Cook as a god and a source of mana. But the European mana generated by Lono-Cook differed from previous Hawaiian forms of mana because it depended on modes of production and commercial currents—most particularly European and American trade with China—that extended far beyond the Hawaiian archipelago. The European goods that were categorized as indices of mana (for example, warships, guns, plate, crystal, silks, ginghams, clocks) not only had particular physical characteristics (guns were weapons of unprecedented power) but were implicated in cultural schemas and the social dynamics of the emerging world capitalist system. As resources implicated in other cultural universes, they could hardly be governed solely by the Hawaiian schemas of mana and tabu.

3. *The transformation of cultural schemas results from unexpected flows of resources.* This point may be explained by means of a commentary on the second proposition of Sahlins's "possible theory of history": that "in action in the world—technically, in acts of reference—the cultural categories acquire new functional values. Burdened with the world, the cultural meanings are thus altered" (Sahlins 1985, 138). The issue is how we should understand the burdening of cultural categories with the world. I would argue for two elaborations of or amendments to Sahlins's formulation. First, while it is important to understand that action in the world is always an act of reference, this is only a one-sided description of the act. To engage in action is to act linguistically, to designate a thing as belonging to a semantic category—as an instance of "tree," or "god," or "tabu." But this same act is also a marking of a thing in the world as a potential resource for action, as being susceptible to the kinds of social uses characteristic of that category of thing. Meaningful action, then, should be understood as at once a reference in language and a marking of things in the world as potential resources for action. Second, Sahlins's formulation is too synchronic. It is true that the very act of making a reference may be seen as inflecting the meaning of the category to which a thing is referred. Any act of reference changes the empirical contents to which the category refers, and therefore affects the range of characteristics which it may include. But the risk of transformation of cultural categories arises above all from the fact that the things marked as resources in an initial action may be subject over time to other determinations, natural and sociocultural, that will cause them to change significantly in content, in quantity, in value, and in relations. If the Hawaiian categories of mana and tabu were transformed

between the 1790s and the 1830s, it was above all because many of the things marked as resources by their relation to these categories—for example, firearms, European commerce, luxury goods, and sandalwood—were subject to rhythms and valuations unforeseen by the Hawaiian chiefs and priests who so marked them in the 1790s. It was not acts of reference per se that caused categories to be so fatefully transformed, but unpredictable flows or fluctuations of the resources marked by the act of reference.

According to my reading of Sahlins, structural change does not operate on a purely cultural level. It is inextricably wrapped up with the marking, use, and dynamics of resources. For this reason we need to take more literally than Sahlins does his own claim that categories are "burdened with the world." Cultural categories are worldly facts. They burden the world with potentials for human use whenever actors mark things by using them as resources. And they are burdened by the things they mark, dragged into new constellations of meaning when the course of action doesn't go as expected. This does not mean that cultural categories are not also defined by their place in webs of semiotic relations—webs that often reach far beyond the locality where they are burdened with particular worldly referents. Indeed, it is precisely this simultaneous participation in far-flung networks of semiotic implication and in local relations of worldly practice that makes novel acts of reference so risky. The designation of European trade goods as tabued meant that resentments arising out of trade relations could react back on the food tabus distinguishing men from women or commoners from chiefs, indeed on the entire tabu system. The power of Sahlins's own account depends, in my opinion, on an implicit conception of structure that encompasses both schemas and resources. Only such a conception can satisfactorily explain the dialectical relationship between cultural categories and human action in the world.

STRUCTURE AND EVENT

Although I have spent much time in this chapter criticizing certain aspects of Sahlins's theorization of structure, it is important to recognize that we share certain fundamental assumptions. I would state them as follows.

First, historical events should be understood as happenings that transform structures. The reason that events constitute what historians call "turning points" is that they somehow change the structures that govern human conduct. To understand and explain an event, therefore, is to specify what structural change it brings about and to determine how the structural change was effectuated.

Second, the key to an adequate theory of the event is a robust theory of structure. This point may seem paradoxical because "structure" has been understood as an essentially synchronic concept whereas "event" has usually been thought of as preeminently diachronic—as something that can be captured only by means of a detailed narration of happenings in time. But Sahlins's meditation on the coming of Captain Cook to Hawaii shows that to narrate an event meaningfully, the historian not only must recount happenings in time, but must also break from narration—that is, temporarily suspend time in order to analyze, in a synchronic discursive mode, the skein of relationships that define the nature and the potentialities of the objects and persons about which a story may be told. There can be no adequate diachronic narrative of an event without a synchronic understanding of the structures that the event transforms.

Third, I believe that Sahlins has uncovered the fundamental mechanism of structural change: the necessary but risky application of existing cultural categories to novel circumstances, the action of culturally marking things in the world that, at least occasionally, transforms the meanings of the cultural markers and thereby reorients the possibilities of human social action. Clear and simple in the abstract, this mechanism is of course difficult to specify and subject to countless complexities in the actual details of historical change. But Sahlins has provided the crucial service of naming the quarry that we need to capture and of giving us a luminous example—his Hawaiian historical ethnography—of how the hunt can be carried out successfully.

THE STRUCTURE OF THE CONJUNCTURE AND THE CONJUNCTION OF STRUCTURES

Sahlins's historical ethnography possesses a virtue that is much valued by historians: an acute appreciation of the significance of historical detail. The entire thrust of his theory impels us to identify the specific situations in which novel acts of reference (and markings of the world) are made. Even if events in some way mediate or instantiate more gradual changes in larger historical forces (and of course they often do), the social transformations that are effectuated in events depend on the details of what happens in specific times, places, and situations. Hence, details matter: contingent, transient, or seemingly trivial particularities of the situation can have major and lasting effects on subsequent history. The expansion of intensive European navigation into the Pacific was bound to bring Europeans into contact with Hawaiians, and this contact was bound to have a major impact on Hawaiian social relations. But the specific nature and form of the impact depended upon details of the initial encounter. Had Cook's ships sailed into Kealakekua Bay in July instead of December, the fateful assimilation of the British sea captain to the god Lono might never have occurred, since it was normal for Lono to come to Hawaii during the time of Makahiki, but it would have been highly irregular for him to arrive in midsummer. And had Cook not been taken into Hawaiian culture as a god, Hawaiian history over the next half-century of so would have been quite different, as the entire corpus of Sahlins's historical ethnography makes plain.

Sahlins sees this tendency for micro conditions to have macro effects as a characteristic mark of the event. In *Historical Metaphors and Mythical Realities* (1981), Sahlins introduces the paradoxical aphorism "structure of the conjuncture" to designate a peculiar quality of events. He uses this term rather casually, defining it only contextually and in passing, as in the following examples:

> Nothing guarantees that the situations encountered in practice will stereotypically follow from the cultural categories by which the circumstances are interpreted and acted upon. Practice, rather, has its own dynamics—a "structure of the conjuncture"—which meaningfully defines the persons and the objects that are parties to it. (35)
>
> * * * *
>
> The pragmatics had its own dynamics: relationships that defeated both intention and convention. The complex of exchanges that developed between Hawaiians and Europeans, the structure of the conjuncture, brought the former into uncharacteristic conditions of internal conflict and contradiction. (50)
>
> * * * *
>
> The specificity of practical circumstances, people's differential relations to them, and the set of particular arrangements that ensue (structure of the conjuncture) sediment new functional values on old categories. (68)
>
> * * * *
>
> We must bring into account the relations of practice itself, the "structure of the conjuncture." My argument has been that there is a sui generis development of cultural relationships at this level: a working-out of the categories of being and things as guided by interests and fitted to contexts. We have seen that such "working disagreements" may entail some arrangement of conflicting intentions and interpretations, even as the meaningful relationships so established conflict with established relationships. (72)

Writing a decade later, he defines structure of the conjuncture only a little more formally:

> In other studies I have in effect described the evenemential process as a "structure of the conjuncture," meaning the way the cultural categories are actualized in specific context through the interested action of the historic agents and the pragmatics of their interaction. (1991, 80–81)

The term requires some unpacking. Sahlins invokes the structure of the conjuncture to explain why, in events, the "situations encountered in practice" will fail to "stereotypically follow from the cultural categories by which the circumstances are interpreted and acted upon" (1981, 35). Structure of the conjuncture, hence, does not refer to structure in its most ordinary sense, that is, enduring and routinely reproduced relationships. It is, rather, a "pragmatics" or a "dynamics" that, although driven by the "interests" of actors, "defeated both intention and convention." Yet, if structure of the conjuncture does not refer to structure in the usual sense, the term has a certain paradoxical appropriateness. Sahlins is arguing that the dynamics of events are not utterly chaotic, that they exhibit significant regularities, albeit not the regularities that the actors would have expected. The term "structure of the conjuncture" is an attempt to signify that the "conjunctures" we call events are characterized by emergent regularities or logics and are in this sense "structured" in spite of their novelty.

But the neologism "structure of the conjuncture" is reversible and, I believe, gains something from the reversal. The "structure of the conjuncture," as Sahlins conceptualizes it, may be said to arise from a "conjuncture of structures." What makes possible the peculiar dynamic that characterizes events is the conjoining in a given situation of structures that previously either had been entirely disjoint or had been connected only in substantially different ways. When people act in a situation in which previously existing structures are newly conjoined, the consequences of certain of their actions will be deflected from what the actors intend. The situation therefore will have the effect of suppressing certain actions and suggesting new possibilities for the elaboration of others. Note that this novel combination of frustrations and incitements will influence actions predicated on each of the previously disjoint structures simultaneously. The consequence is that all the parties can be expected to engage in experimental transpositions of structurally shaped schemes of actions in a volatile and interactive dynamic. In this sort of situation, where the level of uncertainty is bound to be very high, mutual redefinitions of the situation that significantly restructure practice are likely. And, of course, seemingly minor or contingent details of the situation can have major and enduring consequences.

This may be illustrated once again by Sahlins's Hawaiian example. We have remarked that the utterly contingent fact that Cook's ships arrived at Kealakekua Bay at the beginning of the Makahiki festival made his unexpected appearance codeable as the coming of Lono, thereby inciting Hawaiian priests of the Lono cult to treat him as a god and to perform on his person ceremonies usually performed on an idol. The priests, according to Sahlins, were particularly solicitous of Lono-Cook during his entire stay in Hawaii because they could use the extraordinary fact of Lono's flesh and blood visitation to reinforce their own position in ongoing rivalries with the local chiefs. The British, who needed the supplies that flowed to them from the Lono-priests in the form of gifts, were happy to cooperate. The chiefs, by contrast, were rather more ambivalent in their treatment of Cook, alternating "opportunistically" between "noblesse oblige and stealing" (Sahlins 1995, 70). The consequence was a particular "structure of the conjuncture." As Sahlins puts it,

> Chiefs, priests, and English were all following their received inclinations and interests. The result was a little social system, complete with alliances, antagonisms—and a certain dynamic. The British had been drawn into the schismogenic relation "between the Laity and the Clergy." In the existing ceremonial cum political circumstances, this was not necessarily to their advantage. For, the more the priests objectified themselves as the party of Lono, the more they intimated for Cook the destiny of the king's victim. (1995, 71)

Why did this structure of the conjuncture mark Cook as a potential victim? The king traditionally ended the Makahiki period by coming ashore in the vicinity of the Lono temple, where he staged a ritual battle with Lono's adherents. Then the image of Lono was disassembled—he was, that is to say, ritually killed—and a canoe filled with offerings for Lono was set adrift to Kahiki. Meanwhile, the king recommenced the cult of the war god Ku. In the context of these ritual oppositions, traditionally acted out at the end of the Makahiki period, the three-way interaction of chiefs, priests, and English had the effect of marking Cook as a god who stood in a potentially hostile relation to the Hawaiian king and chiefs. The potential hostility was held in abeyance when Cook and his men—coincidentally, but, from the Hawaiian point of view, appropriately—set off from Hawaii into the open sea at the end of the Makahiki period. But the potential hostility was powerfully actualized when another of history's little accidents, a storm that broke a mast, induced Cook's untimely return to Hawaiian shores a few days after his ceremonious departure. The upshot, of course, was that the flesh-and-blood Lono-Cook suffered the death and dismemberment normally visited on the idol and that his mana was captured by Hawaiian royalty.

Here the structure of the conjuncture was formed by a three-way conjuncture of structures. The preexisting structural tensions between Lono priests and chiefs were exacerbated and given a particular twist by the unexpected appearance of Cook, whose own interests unwittingly drew him into the ritual drama of the Makahiki on the side of the priests—in a role whose significance he could not know, but for which he was singularly suited as a consequence of his own highly ritualized and absolute power as a captain in the British Navy. In the structured improvisations that arose in this complex conjuncture, Cook gained his divinity and lost his life, and the Hawaiians absorbed the presence of ship-borne Europeans into their social world in a way destined to transform it in a particular fashion.

The specific nature of the structure of the conjuncture will, of course, be different in every event. But if Sahlins's theory of the event is correct, it should always involve a novel conjuncture of structures. Hence, we cannot predict in advance what structure of the conjuncture will shape the novel acts of reference that constitute the core of a given event. But we do know what to look for: a conjunction of structures that sets off a synergetic interaction between actors attempting to make structural sense of a highly volatile situation.

A POSSIBLE THEORY OF HISTORY

Sahlins's theory of the event is appropriately open-ended. It is a "possible" theory of history not only in the sense that it might just work, but in the sense that what it specifies is not a collection of iron laws of historical development but a set of possibilities inherent in history generally. It provides a vocabulary and a paradigmatic logic for the historical analysis of events. I have tried to elucidate Sahlins's paradigm, to convey its elegance and power, and also to show how it invites elaboration and modification. Its essential terms are all abstract—structure, event, actor, interest, reference, structure of the conjuncture, and, I would add, schemas, resources, and conjunctions of structures. We might wish for a more elaborated and richer theory of the event than Sahlins provides. But if so, it is our job as students of history to produce one. By reflecting further, on the basis of events that interest us—events with the widest variety of actors, geographical and historical locations, political and cultural dynamics, and temporalities—we should be able to say more about the different ways that conjunctions of structures may give rise to structures of the conjuncture, the different kinds of semiotic acts of reference that reshape structures, the types and relationships of structures that are effected by events, and so on. But it is my contention that Sahlins has provided us with the essential framework for such further reflections. In short, I regard his theory of history as much more than merely *possible*. It is, as I see it, a powerful, generalizable, fruitful, and open-ended theory of historical change. It should be a theory impossible to do without—not just a *possible* but an *indispensable* theory of history.

⊰8⊱

HISTORICAL EVENTS AS
TRANSFORMATIONS OF STRUCTURES
Inventing Revolution at the Bastille

Ever since Herodotus, historians have written about events. Battles, alliances, scandals, conquests, conspiracies, revolts, royal successions, reforms, elections, religious revivals, assassinations, discoveries: momentous events have always been the bread and butter of narrative history. But despite the prominence of events in historical narratives, the event has rarely been scrutinized as a theoretical category. Traditional narrative historians who reveled in the contingency and particularity of events generally refused on principle to engage in explicit theorizing. Meanwhile, historical sociologists, along with the minority of historians who turned to the social sciences in order to escape the hegemony of political narrative, generally disdained the study of mere events and sought instead to discover general causal patterns underlying historical change. This was true of the Annales school in France from the late 1920s forward and of the "new social history" that blossomed in the United States in the 1960s and 1970s. By the 1980s the old antagonisms between narrative history and historical sociology had begun to fade; yet theoretical work on historical events has remained relatively rare.[1] I begin by outlining a theoretical con-

A shorter version of this chapter was published with the same title in *Theory and Society* 25 (1996): 841–81. Copyright © by Kluwer Academic Publishers; published with the kind permission of Springer Science and Business Media. I have had valuable comments on this chapter from Ronald Aminzade, Laura Downs, Muge Goçek, David Laitin, Colin Lucas, Sherry Ortner, Sharon Reitman, Sidney Tarrow, Charles Tilly, and the editors of *Theory and Society*.

1. The rapprochement between social history and narrative may be conveniently marked by the appearance of Stone (1979). Among the scholars who have contributed to a theoretical understanding of events are Abrams (1982, 190–226), Nora (1974), Molino (1986), Abbott (1992), Aminzade (1992), and Griffen (1992, 1993).

ception of the historical event, but then refine the theory by using it to an-alyze particular historical happenings that took place in France in the sum-mer of 1789. I am convinced that an adequate theorization of events can only be built up through a mutual interrogation of theoretical categories and real historical sequences.

EVENTS AS A THEORETICAL CATEGORY

According to standard dictionary definitions, the term event can refer to a happening or occurrence of any kind, but the word is more commonly used to signify an occurrence that is remarkable in some way — one that is widely noted and commented on by contemporaries. Great public ceremo-nies (such as royal entrances or military parades) might be designated as events even though they had no discernable effect on historical change. But when historians argue for the importance of events, they have in mind occurrences that have momentous consequences, that in some sense "change the course of history." It is historical events in this sense that I in-tend to deal with in this article.

Although I agree with traditional narrative historians that events play a crucial role in historical change, my general view of social life is radically at odds with theirs. As should be clear from my arguments in chapter 4 of this book, I insist that social relations are profoundly governed by under-lying social and cultural structures and that a proper understanding of the role of events in history must be founded on a concept of structure. A structural view of social action accounts for what I regard as an outstand-ing general characteristic of social life: that most social practices — whether international diplomacy, petty trade, or popular recreation — tend to be reproduced with considerable consistency over relatively extended peri-ods of time. Of course, all social practices undergo constant revision even in the course of reproduction, and the accumulation of small revisions may eventually result in significant transformations. Yet even when such small and undramatic changes accumulate over time, the overall structural frame-work of social relations tends to be maintained. When changes do take place, they are rarely smooth and linear in character; instead, changes tend to be clustered into relatively intense bursts. Even the accumulation of in-cremental changes often results in a buildup of pressures and a dramatic crisis of existing practices rather than a gradual transition from one state of affairs to another. Lumpiness, rather than smoothness, is the normal texture of historical temporality. These moments of accelerated change, I would argue, are initiated and carried forward by historical events. While the events are sometimes the culmination of processes long underway, I would claim that events typically do more than carry out a rearrangement of practices made necessary by gradual and cumulative social change. Historical events tend to transform social relations in ways that could not be fully predicted from the gradual changes that may have made them possible. As I have pointed out in chapter 1, what makes historical events so important to theorize is that they reshape history, imparting an unforeseen direction to social development and altering the nature of the causal nexus in which social interactions take place. For this reason, a theoretically robust conception of events is a necessary component of any adequate theory of social change.

I argue that events should be conceived of as sequences of occurrences that result in transformations of structures. Such sequences begin with a rupture of some kind—that is, a surprising break with routine practice. Such breaks actually occur every day—as a consequence of exogenous causes, of contradictions between structures, of sheer human inventiveness or perversity, or of simple mistakes in enacting routines. But most ruptures are neutralized and reabsorbed into the preexisting structures in one way or another—they may, for example, be forcefully repressed, pointedly ignored, or explained away as exceptions.[2] But whatever the nature of the initial rupture, an occurrence only becomes a historical event, in the sense in which I use the term, when it touches off a chain of occurrences that durably transforms previous structures and practices.

This happens above all when a rupture in one particular structural and spatial location also produces reinforcing ruptures in other locations. Thus, a fight that breaks out in a neighborhood bar breaks the usual routine of sociability. If it can be resolved by the normal politics of tavern sociability—for example, by having the bouncer eject the aggressor, or by having the combatants duke it out in the back alley—it may have no serious consequences. But if, say, one of the combatants is white and the other black, the initial rupture could be amplified by a rupture in the system of race relations that also structures interactions in the bar, and this could lead to a generalized racial brawl, which could draw in the police, who might commit acts of racial violence, which could touch off a city-wide riot, which in turn could permanently embitter race relations, discredit the mayor and police chief, and scare off private investment—and, of course,

2. For a fascinating account of how potential ruptures are handled in face to face interactions, see Goffman (1967b).

alter the mode of sociability in bars. Because structures are articulated to other structures, initially localized ruptures always have the potential of bringing about a cascading series of further ruptures that will result in structural transformations—that is, changes in cultural schemas, shifts of resources, and the emergence of new modes of power. A single, isolated rupture rarely has the effect of transforming structures because standard procedures and sanctions can usually repair the torn fabric of social practice. Ruptures spiral into transformative historical events when a sequence of interrelated ruptures disarticulates the previous structural network, makes repair difficult, and makes a novel rearticulation possible.

A historical event, then, is (1) a ramified sequence of occurrences that (2) is recognized as notable by contemporaries, and that (3) results in a durable transformation of structures. This conception of historical events retains significant theoretical and methodological ambiguities. But rather than elaborating abstract solutions to such difficulties now, I would prefer to clothe my concept of the event with some empirical detail and then return to theoretical and methodological issues toward the end of this chapter. I shall use as my empirical example a sequence of occurrences that took place in the summer of 1789 in France—what is generally known as the taking of the Bastille. I choose this example not because I regard it as providing an ideal type of historical events in general, but because I believe it raises analytical issues of wide import and because I know enough about the context in which it took place to be confident of my empirical and theoretical judgments about it. It goes without saying that a different example might lead to a significantly different theorization. I intend this study not as a definitive statement of the theory of events, but as an invitation to comparison, elaboration, and critique.

THE FRENCH REVOLUTION AND
THE DISLOCATION OF NORMAL LIFE

The French Revolution began with a local rupture, although in a structural location that was already densely articulated to other structures. In 1786, the comptroller general informed the king that the state was nearly bankrupt. By the early summer of 1789, this crisis of the state's fiscal institutions had become a crisis of the system of social stratification (because fiscal reform would mean stripping the clergy and nobility of one of their major privileges, their immunity from taxation); it had become a crisis of the privileged corporate institutions that were the integument of the social order of old regime France (because their privileges were linked to particular fiscal arrangements); it had become a deep constitutional crisis (because it was unclear which governmental body had the authority to change the system of taxation); and it had also become a crisis of the very principles of the social and political order (because proponents of natural rights, national sovereignty, and civic equality had managed to dominate political discourse and gain a sizeable foothold among the deputies to the Estates General).

I do not recount here how the initial crisis expanded to such proportions—although thinking analytically about the process by which such expansions occur would surely be theoretically illuminating. I focus on a different aspect of the French Revolution and of historical events in general: how the uncertainty of structural relations that characterizes events can stimulate bursts of collective cultural creativity. Here it is important to recognize the internal *temporality* of events. In spite of the punctualist connotations of the term, historical events are never instantaneous happenings: they always have a duration, a period that elapses between the initial rupture and the subsequent structural transformation. During this period, the usual articulations between different structures become profoundly dislocated. Actors, consequently, are beset with insecurity: they are unsure about how to get on with life. This insecurity may produce varying results, sometimes in the same person: anxiety, fear, or exhilaration; incessant activity, paralysis, extreme caution, or reckless abandon. But it almost certainly raises the emotional intensity of life, at least for those whose existence is closely tied to the dislocated structures. And when, as in France in the summer of 1789, the structural dislocation is pervasive and deep, virtually everyone lives on the edge. I examine the effects of such generalized insecurity by concentrating on a period of twelve days stretching from July 12 to July 23. This was an extraordinary period of fear, rejoicing, violence, and cultural creativity that changed the history of the world.

I already indicated some of the reasons why French men and women were living in a state of profound uncertainty by the summer of 1789. The political situation was particularly dislocated and particularly charged. In 1788, after two long years of unsuccessful stratagems, the king was forced to call a meeting of the Estates General, a body made up of elected representatives of the three estates of the realm. The Estates General had not met for 175 years, but according to traditional constitutional theory it had the exclusive right to consent to new taxes. (The three estates were the clergy, the nobility, and the commoners, who were known as the Third Estate.) Calling the Estates General was effectively an admission by the king that royal absolutism was at an end and that some form of representative government was inevitable; it was clear to all that the meeting of the Estates General would result in a new constitutional arrangement. During the electoral campaign for the Estates General, royal censorship was lifted and the country was flooded with political pamphlets of all stripes. The political struggle had begun as a contest between the Crown and the political nation as a whole, but disputes soon broke out between the nobles and commoners, and by 1789 there was a three-sided struggle. The king was attempting to salvage as much royal power as possible, the nobles were trying to gain an independent role in the state, more or less on the model of the English House of Lords, and the Third Estate, which made up more than 95 percent of the population, was also attempting to gain a predominant role for itself (Lefebvre [1949] 1971; Egret 1977).

When the Estates General finally met in May, the delegates of the Third Estate refused to organize themselves as the lower body of a three-part legislature, and their intransigence brought the meeting to a standstill. Finally on June 17, the delegates of the Third Estate took the radical step of declaring themselves to be the "National Assembly," a title which clearly implied that they were the sole legitimate representative of the French people. They invited the delegates of the clergy and nobility to join the Assembly and proceed to the task of regenerating the nation. Initially the king and most of the nobles resisted this move, but after a couple of tense confrontations during the following week, the king effectively recognized the National Assembly and ordered the nobles to join it. But the king seems to have been merely biding his time, or perhaps he changed his mind. In any case, on July 11 Louis XVI dismissed his liberal minister, the Swiss banker Necker, who had good relations with the National Assembly, and began to encircle Paris and Versailles with royal troops. It appeared that he was ready to dissolve the National Assembly, repress the Parisian popular movement, and return to rule by decree. This, in a nutshell, was the political situation that led to the taking of the Bastille.

The dislocations that had occurred in the French state by early July 1789 were particularly sharp. What Leon Trotsky (1932) later called "dual power" had developed: two distinct and conflicting political apparatuses, the monarchy and the National Assembly, claimed to hold legitimate power.[3] It was consequently difficult for an ordinarily prudent individual to know which apparatus to obey. Moreover, the two powers based their

3. Charles Tilly (1993) speaks of these as situations of "multiple sovereignty."

claims on sharply contradictory ideologies. The monarch claimed to rule by the grace of God, a grace conferred upon him by inheritance through the male line and sealed by the religious ritual of coronation. The National Assembly claimed its authority by popular sovereignty, the natural right of the nation's people to choose its own constitution. These two ideologies not only envisaged different kinds of states, but were based on divergent cosmologies and implied sharply different forms of social order. The cosmology of the monarchy was profoundly hierarchical, with order originating in God and cascading downward through the various orders of heavenly beings, to kings, priests, and nobles, thence to commoners, and finally to animals, plants, and inanimate matter. In the language of the old regime, order was indistinguishable from hierarchy (Mousnier 1972; Sewell 1974a; Loyseau 1666, 1994). The implicit cosmology of the National Assembly was sharply different: order originated not in the spiritual realm, but in nature, and nature created all humans equal in rights. Political institutions arose from a social contract, from a rational agreement by the people about the appropriate form of government. The people had no obligation to obey any authorities except those they had chosen for themselves, either directly or through their duly constituted representatives.

The fact that the two contesting powers in the French state legitimated themselves in terms of two sharply contrasting ideologies meant that the uncertainty experienced by ordinary people went beyond the unsettling question of which authorities to obey. Accepting the authority of the National Assembly also might entail accepting a new language of social order, one that had implications for virtually all spheres of social relations. Relations between priests and parishioners, seigneurs and peasants, municipal officials and townsmen, masters and journeymen, husbands and wives, fathers and children: all of these were currently encoded in the hierarchical language of the old regime monarchy. Accepting the legitimacy of the National Assembly therefore might imply redefining and renegotiating these relations in an idiom of natural equality and social contract. This might mean unsettling changes in numerous spheres of daily life. But the practical implications and the scope of the National Assembly's ideology were as yet unclear, not only to ordinary people, but to deputies in the National Assembly itself. As long as the standoff between the king and the Assembly remained unsettled, no one could be entirely sure what actions were safe or dangerous, moral or wicked, advantageous or foolish, rational or irrational.

In the peculiar circumstances of the summer of 1789, these insecurities were joined to a harrowing concern about biological survival. The harvest of 1788 had been disastrously short, and for several months impossibly high bread prices had rendered both poor urban-dwellers and peasants chronically hungry. The coming harvest looked promising, but in mid-July it was still several weeks away, and last year's grain stocks were running dangerously low. Untimely hail or sustained rains could still spoil the crop and plunge the nation into another year of hunger and despair. Thus, in mid-July, at the same time when the political crisis reached its peak, anxiety about subsistence was general. This potent combination of political standoff and economic crisis implied a moral and practical uncertainty that penetrated deeply into daily life.

THE TAKING OF THE BASTILLE

On July 11, when Louis XVI dismissed Necker and began to encircle Paris and Versailles with royal troops, the moment of truth seemed at hand.[4] The National Assembly continued to hold firm, but it was meeting in Versailles, where the king's military might was concentrated, and could easily have been overpowered by royal troops had the king given the order. In Paris, where the population overwhelmingly supported the National Assembly, the level of political mobilization was already unprecedentedly high. Newspapers and pamphlets had flooded the city over the past six months, political clubs had sprung up, and the debates in the National Assembly were discussed in cafés, clubs, public squares, and wineshops all over the city. When the news of Necker's dismissal reached Paris, on the afternoon of the 12th, the population was quickly mobilized. "Patriots" massed in the Palais Royal (not a royal palace, but an enclosed public garden). There they heard Camille Desmoulins declaim, "Citizens, you know that the Nation had asked for Necker to be retained, and he has been driven out! Could you be more insolently flouted? After such an act they will dare anything, and they may perhaps be planning and preparing a Saint-Bartholomew massacre of patriots for this very night!" (Godechot 1970, 187–88). This quotation from Desmoulins demonstrates two things about the agitations in Paris. First, it shows that orators were using a language of popular sovereignty and national will to talk about the crisis (the *Nation* had asked for Necker to be retained and its will had been flouted). Second, the invocation of a Saint-Bartholomew massacre both registers

---

4. My account of the events surrounding the taking of the Bastille is based primarily on Godechot (1970), which is the best single scholarly account.

and propagates the sense of intense insecurity that is palpable in nearly all accounts of these events.

From the Palais Royal, the crowd surged through the city, closing the Opera and theaters, seizing a bust of Necker from a wax museum, and parading into the Tuileries and the place Louis XV (now the place de la Concorde). There the crowd skirmished with a detachment of German mercenaries but were aided by another army unit known as the French Guards, who had already shown strong sympathies with the Parisians and the National Assembly. That evening, mobs broke into gun-shops to arm themselves and smashed and burned the customs posts where dues were assessed on goods coming into the city. Early in the morning they sacked the Saint-Lazare monastery in a search for stored grain. They also forced open the doors of several prisons where, in the words of the newspaper *Les Révolutions de Paris*, they "liberated the prisoners, except for the criminals"—a gesture that seems to suggest an annulling of the king's law (*Les Révolutions de Paris* 1, July 17, 1789, 8). Largely in response to the widespread disorders of July 12, a group of "electors"—those who had chosen Paris's deputation to the Estates General under the city's relatively restricted franchise—met on the 13th and chose an executive committee, which effectively became the municipality of the city. The new municipality's first act was to set up a militia, intended both as a means of defending Paris from royal troops and of maintaining order. It patrolled the streets effectively on the evening of the 13th, but the municipality was far from having enough guns to arm it properly. It was the quest for more arms that led to the Bastille.

On the morning of the 14th, a delegation from the emergency municipality, followed by a crowd of demonstrators, went to the Hôtel des Invalides, on the southwest edge of the city, to demand the arms that they knew to be kept there. The governor of the Invalides temporized, but the crowd soon broke in, and, meeting no significant resistance from the garrison, seized some thirty to forty thousand muskets. It was by this means that the Parisians managed to arm themselves. But the newly armed popular militia remained desperately short of ammunition, which was not stored at the Invalides, so the crowd trekked across the city to the Bastille, directly east of the city center, where a large quantity of powder was known to be kept.

Taking the Bastille was a much more daunting operation than breaking into the Invalides, since the Bastille was an ancient military fortress with thick walls, deep moats, and drawbridges. The story of the operations by

which the besiegers eventually took the fortress has been told many times
and need not be recited here.[5] Suffice it to say that nearly one hundred attackers died in the assault, that the attackers finally succeeded because
they were joined by a unit of the French Guards, which supplied artillery
pieces, and because in the end the defenders, a group of semi-retired veterans, had no stomach for a determined resistance and let down the draw-
bridge. Once inside the Bastille, the crowd freed the few prisoners kept
there—four forgers and three madmen—and removed the barrels of gunpowder they had initially come for. The soldiers who had defended the
fortress were led through the streets to the city hall. On the steps of the city
hall, their commandant, the marquis de Launay, was shot, stabbed, and
beheaded by members of the crowd, who then paraded around the city
with his head on a pike. The crowd also killed Flesselles, an official of the
old municipality who had temporized about arming the militia, and was
therefore suspected of treason. His head was also severed from his body
and paraded about on a pike.

The effect of the occurrences of July 14 was sensational. The king's
troops pulled back from Paris, and the king, recognizing that the troops
could not be trusted to act against the Parisians, ordered them back to the
frontiers, thereby giving up his effort to intimidate the National Assembly.
The Assembly, which had seemed utterly at the king's mercy, emerged tri-
umphant, thanks to the actions of the Parisian people. It was on July 16
that the king decided that conquering Paris was impossible and that flight
to the provinces was pointless and undignified, especially since many of
the cities of the kingdom had already rallied to the Assembly. Instead, he
made a humiliating visit to Paris on the 17th, accompanied by a delegation
from the National Assembly. There he formally assented to the establishment of the new Parisian municipality and the national guard. This ritual
effectively marked the king's capitulation to Paris and the National Assembly. The events of July 14 thus constituted a major turning point in the
French Revolution.

THE BASTILLE AND THE CONCEPT OF REVOLUTION

But why was this complex of events that unfolded in Paris and Versailles
over the week from July 12 to July 17 known, both by contemporaries and
by subsequent historians, by the metonymic title "the taking of the
Bastille"? And why has the capture of this fortress become synonymous

5. Again, the best account is Godechot (1970).

with the French Revolution? The capture of the Bastille was not, in itself, a matter of supreme military importance; Jacques Godechot, who has written the best scholarly account of the attack, thinks that the earlier and bloodless capture of the Invalides was actually the decisive military action, because it established that the royal troops could not be counted on to resist assaults from the Parisian people (1970, 217). It is also true that in many respects the taking of the Bastille marked no great rupture with what Charles Tilly calls the "repertoire of contention" of eighteenth-century urban dwellers (Tilly 1986). Crowd violence, even pitched battles with the military, were hardly unheard of in old regime France. Nevertheless, the taking of the Bastille was immediately weighted with such heavy symbolic significance that it soon came to be seen as the founding action of the French Revolution (Lusebrink and Reichard 1983, 1990). How did this seemingly inflated evaluation of the actions at the Bastille come about?

We are by now used to the notion that revolutions are radical transformations in political systems imposed by violent uprisings of the people. We therefore don't see the extraordinary novelty of the claim that the taking of the Bastille was an act of revolution. Prior to the summer of 1789, the word revolution did not carry the implication of a change of political regime achieved by popular violence. What was going on in France in the spring and summer of 1789 was sometimes spoken of as a revolution, but in the parlance of the time this meant only a great change in the affairs of a state; as it was used before the Bastille, the term revolution could as well have been applied to the coup d'état that Louis XVI was attempting in the days following July 11 as to the Parisian uprising that took place on the 14th (Baker 1990).[6] There was also a fairly extensive preexisting vocabulary to describe events like the assault on the Bastille and the associated disorders in Paris. In ordinary parlance they could have been called by any number of terms: uprising, emotion, revolt, riot, mutiny, insurrection, rebellion, or sedition (Tilly 1986; Sewell 1990a). The "uprising" or "mutiny" of July 14 could also be designated by contemporaries as a "revolution," but this was only because of its effects — the defeat of the king and the reinforcement of the National Assembly — not because it was a self-conscious attempt by the people to impose by force its sovereign will.

Yet in the days that followed, the taking of the Bastille was construed as

6. Baker's essay "Inventing the French Revolution" charts a wide range of transformations of the term revolution in the eighteenth century, and even during the weeks following the taking of the Bastille, but he does not specifically consider when revolution became associated with an act of popular violence.

an act of the people's sovereign will, as a legitimate uprising that dictated the country's political fate. This construal required a dramatic and utterly unforeseen articulation between two modes of activity not previously understood as linked: on the one hand, political and philosophical claims about the sovereignty of the people, of the sort that delegates of the Third Estate used when they declared themselves the National Assembly; on the other, acts of crowd violence of the sort that the Parisian populace used to defend themselves and the National Assembly from the king's troops on July 14. In the excitement, terror, and elation that characterized the taking of the Bastille, orators, journalists, and the crowd itself seized on the political theory of popular sovereignty to explain and to justify the popular violence. This act of epoch-making cultural creativity occurred in a moment of ecstatic discovery: the taking of the Bastille, which had begun as an act of defense against the king's aggression, revealed itself in the days that followed as a concrete, unmediated, and sublime instance of the people expressing its sovereign will. What happened at the Bastille became the establishing act of a *revolution* in the modern sense. By their action at the Bastille, the people were understood to have risen up, destroyed tyranny, and established liberty. To make sense of the taking of the Bastille as a historical event, then, we must determine when, how, and why the happenings of July 14, 1789 came to be understood as a revolution in which the people rose up, expressed its sovereign will, and transformed the political system of the nation—or, to put the same thing a different way, when, how, and why these happenings effected a durable articulation of popular violence and popular sovereignty in the new category of revolution.

THE TEMPORALITY OF THE BASTILLE:
INVENTING REVOLUTION

I have already remarked that events are never instantaneous happenings, that some period of time elapses between the initial rupture and the subsequent structural transformation. Making sense of the taking of the Bastille requires us to reconstruct the sequence of action and interpretation that led from the rupture (the assault on the Bastille, which disrupted existing modes of power and posed a novel challenge to existing claims of political sovereignty) to the new articulation (the encoding of a new conception of revolution, which durably transformed the effective meaning of the sovereignty of the people). While this process began at the Bastille and in the surrounding streets on July 14, it was not until some days later, in the meeting hall of the National Assembly in Versailles, that it can be said to have been definitively achieved.

The first steps toward articulating popular violence and popular sovereignty were made in Paris, if not during the assault, then in actions and commentary immediately afterwards. Certain ritual actions in the events themselves seem to indicate that the crowds claimed to act on behalf of the nation. Thus the popular newspaper *Les Révolutions de Paris* reported that one of the first acts of the men who had captured the Bastille was to seize and display "the sacred flag of the fatherland, to the applause and the transports of an immense crowd of people"(*Les Révolutions de Paris* 1, July 17, 1789, 17). The fact that they claimed the flag as their own, rather than desecrating it, implies that they regarded themselves, rather than the defeated royal troops, as the legitimate armed force of the nation. The display on pikes of the severed heads of de Launay and Flesselles, which seems to mimic the rituals of state exections (Foucault 1977), could be read as implying an assertion of sovereignty. The language employed in contemporary accounts of the events of July 14 also tended to cast the popular violence as an act of the sovereign people. *Les Révolutions de Paris* used the highly charged term "citizens" to designate the attackers, spoke of the hastily improvised urban militia as "soldiers of the nation," and characterized the events as a rising of liberty against despotism.[7] All this implies that the Parisians drew upon the notion of popular sovereignty to assert the legitimacy of the taking of the Bastille.

But simply identifying the attack on the Bastille as an expression of the will of the people did not amount to inventing the modern concept of revolution. A revolution is not just a forceful act that expresses the will of the people, but such an act that puts into place a new political regime. Only when it became clear that the taking of the Bastille had forced the king to yield effective power to the National Assembly could the acts of the Parisian people be viewed as a revolution in this new sense. The epoch-making cultural change — the invention of a new and enduring political category — could therefore only take place in tandem with practical changes in institutional and military power relations. It was in the National Assembly that the new concept of revolution was definitively and authoritatively articulated. As the members of the National Assembly came to realize that the people of Paris had assured them a great victory, they not only began to echo the Parisians' view that the uprising was a blow for liberty against despotism and that it expressed the legitimate wishes of the people, but began

7. The term "citoyen" is used frequently throughout the account. The line about "the soldiers of the fatherland" occurs on 7. The language of liberty and despotism occurs prominently on 18–19.

to cast it as a decisive act of popular sovereignty that rightfully determined the fate of the nation. It took several days of political maneuvering and parliamentary debates for this to happen.

In pre-Bastille political discourse, even the "patriots" regarded popular violence as irrational, blind, and contagious, as a kind of natural disaster virtually impossible to control except by repression. This made it fundamentally incompatible with the sovereign will of the nation, which was regarded as rational, majestic, and generous. When the National Assembly learned of the taking of the Bastille on the evening of the 14th, the deputies did not rejoice that the people had risen up and struck a great blow against the royal forces. According to the minutes of the Assembly, the taking of the Bastille was initially regarded as "disastrous news" which "produced in the Assembly the most mournful impression. All discussion ceased" (*Réimpression de l'Ancien Moniteur*, 158). On the following morning the Assembly talked about what had happened, but its members remained anxious and pessimistic about the probable effects. The marquis de Sillery introduced a motion containing the conventional wisdom: "The massacres that took place yesterday, the Bastille besieged and taken, the bloody executions which resulted, have carried the people to an excess of fury that is very difficult to stop." He went on to charge that the violence had been purposely provoked by the pernicious ministers now in charge of the government so as to convince the king of the need for further armed repression. He, and the Assembly as a whole, worried that the events of July 14 would strengthen the king's hand and undermine the position of the Assembly (155).

It soon became clear, however, that the taking of the Bastille had precisely the opposite effect. By the 16th, the king had ordered the troops away from the capital, dismissed his ministry, and recalled Necker. This unexpected turn doubtless made the Assembly less inclined to bewail the violence and disorder of the Parisian people. Meanwhile, a delegation from the Assembly went to Paris on the afternoon of the 15th and found that far from seething with violent hatred, the capital was bathed in the glow of a joyous and generous patriotism. Mounier, who reported on this visit on the morning of the 16th, described in rapturous tone the delegation's reception in Paris. The Parisians "attempted, by all the most vivid signs of affection, to express the sentiments weighing upon them. It was a great joy for them to shake hands with a member of the National Assembly. . . . Citizens congratulated and embraced one another. All eyes were wet with tears; intoxicated sentiment was everywhere" (163). In this same speech,

Mounier began to rethink the violence of the 14th. "Regrets are surely due for all the troubles that the capital has suffered. May she never again see those terrible moments when the law has lost its empire; but may she never again feel the yoke of despotism! She is worthy of liberty; she has earned it by her courage and energy" (164). Rather than "massacres," and "bloody executions" which "have carried the people to an excess of fury that is very difficult to stop," Mounier spoke of the violence euphemistically as "the troubles that the capital has suffered" and "those terrible moments when the law has lost its empire." Indeed, he hailed it, again euphemistically, as the "courage and energy" that have made Paris "worthy of liberty."

Nor, in Mounier's rendering, does the just and courageous violence of the Parisians presage continuing disorder. "These troubles shall cease; the Constitution will be established; it will console us, it will console the Parisians for all their previous misfortunes." Indeed, the taking of the Bastille, however tragic, must be a source of pride for true patriots:

> Among the people's acts of despair, even while weeping for the death of several citizens, it will perhaps be difficult to resist a sentiment of satisfaction upon seeing the destruction of the Bastille. There, on the ruins of that horrible prison, there will soon be erected, according to the wishes of the citizens of Paris, the statue of a good king, the restorer of the liberty and the happiness of France. (164)

The taking of the Bastille, Mounier wishfully implies, will establish a new era of liberty and happiness, presided over by a good king and a new constitution. Thus, as early as July 16, the taking of the Bastille was spoken of in the National Assembly not only as a justified response of the people to despotic oppression, but as a crucial step toward a new political order. In Mounier's speech we begin to discern not just a new attitude toward the popular violence of July 14, but a sanctioning of the Parisian uprising as a legitimate revolt of liberty against despotism.

Over the course of July 16 and 17, it became ever clearer that the taking of the Bastille was immensely strengthening the position of the National Assembly. These developments must have persuaded many members of the Assembly to concur in Mounier's somewhat ambivalent approval of the popular violence of the 14th. Later on the 16th, shortly after Mounier finished his speech, a sizeable group of deputies of the nobility who had thus far abstained from debates and votes in the Assembly announced that they would henceforth participate fully (166). The victory of the Parisians and the king's decision to send away the troops thus had the effect of persuading the last holdouts for deliberation by order to abandon their passive resistance and cast their lot with the Assembly. That afternoon came the clinching news: the king had agreed to dismiss his ministry, recall Necker, and visit Paris on the following day to demonstrate his acceptance of the new municipality and civic militia. The king's trip to Paris on the 17th was generally interpreted as a ritual of capitulation. Bailly, the new mayor chosen by the Paris municipality and accepted by the National Assembly and the king, greeted the monarch at the Versailles gate with words that indicated as much: "Sire, I bring to your majesty the keys of your good city of Paris; these are the same ones that were presented to Henry IV. He had reconquered his people; here it is the people who have reconquered their king" (173). The king was then received in a joyous ceremony, the high point of which came when the monarch appeared on the balcony of the city hall and placed on his hat the blue, white, and red rosette that had been adopted as the special badge of the Parisian patriots.

By the morning of July 18, the astonishing results of the taking of the Bastille were clear. The troops had been sent back to their barracks in the provinces, Necker had been recalled, the king had essentially capitulated to both Paris and the National Assembly, Paris had a redoubtable urban militia and a new vigorously patriot municipality, and the last of the nobles had ended their boycott and joined in the work the Assembly. Meanwhile, addresses supporting the Assembly came pouring in from the provinces, indicating that its new political supremacy was national, not merely Parisian. The barriers that had kept the National Assembly from its self-appointed task of providing France with a new constitution were suddenly swept away. The Parisian uprising had resulted in a triumph of astounding proportions for the National Assembly, which henceforth became the chief arbiter of the nation's fate.

These developments did not lead the Assembly to undertake an immediate revaluation of the violent actions of July 14. It was not until July 20 that the Assembly spelled out further a conception of the taking of the Bastille as a legitimate popular revolution. The Assembly was driven to this elaboration not by sheer gratitude, but by a practical need to distinguish the just violence of the sovereign people from the unacceptable violence of the dangerous mob. On July 17, the mayor of the nearby town of Poissy asked the Assembly to help it put down disorders there and in the neighboring town of Saint-Germain-en-Laye, where what he termed "a troop of brigands" had killed a miller accused of hoarding grain. The following day, upon learning that another man had been seized by this mob and that his life was in danger, the Assembly sent a deputation of twelve members to save him (174). On the 20th, the deputation related the harrowing tale of how they had braved the howling mob and barely managed to rescue the unfortunate man from hanging (175–76).

This incident inspired the conservative deputy Lally-Tolendal to rise later that day and introduce a motion condemning political violence (181). Lally's proposal raised an immediate storm of protest from legislators who saw it as a thinly veiled attack on the actions of the Parisians at the Bastille; their collective outrage succeeded in getting Lally's motion tabled. In their arguments, they spelled out more explicitly than Mounier had done the thesis that taking the Bastille had been a legitimate action. Robespierre complained that Lally's motion "presents a disposition against those who have defended liberty. But is there anything more legitimate than to rise up against a horrible conspiracy formed to destroy the nation?" (181–82). De Blesau, an obscure deputy from Brittany, warned against "confusing popular riots with legitimate and necessary revolutions, by placing . . . side by side seditious men armed for licence and citizens armed for liberty" (182). Buzot joined in next, claiming that Lally's motion

> proposes to declare as bad citizens and rebels all armed men indiscriminately. Must we then forget the generous courage of the Parisians who, by taking arms, have procured our liberty, have expelled the ministers, have quieted intrigue, have directed the steps of the king into the Assembly? . . . But this is not all; who will tell us that despotism could not be reborn among us? And who will be the guarantor of its complete destruction? If one day it draws together its forces to strike us down, what citizens will arm themselves in time to save the fatherland? (183)

Buzot's remarks are particularly significant. It was, Buzot emphasized, the Parisians' violent action that effected all the salutary changes of the past few days: it was the people of Paris who procured the liberty of the Assembly, expelled the perfidious ministers, quieted intrigue, and forced the king to submit to the Assembly. Moreover, Buzot implies that comparable action might be necessary in the future to save the fatherland from its enemies. This suggests that, for Buzot, the popular violence that occurred at the Bastille had become not only a legitimate occurrence but an example of a category of legitimate occurrences — of necessary violent actions undertaken by the people to crush despotism and establish liberty. It was in this debate on July 20, in short, that the members of the Assembly explicitly stated the notion of a revolution as a legitimate rising of the sovereign people that transformed the political system of the nation.

In the debate of July 20, the patriots had to defend the victors of the
Bastille against the insinuation that they were no better than food rioters.
They did this by defining the taking of the Bastille as a legitimate revolution, arguing that the intervention of the armed people against despotism
was justified. Three days later, on July 23, the Assembly reiterated this definition, but now in order to limit more carefully the circumstances in which
popular intervention was warranted. This was done in response to a new
act of "popular justice" in the capital—one that was disturbingly similar to
an action of July 14. On July 23, Bertier, the former intendant of Paris, who
was widely blamed for food shortages, and his father-in-law Foullon, who
was identified with the minister who had replaced Necker, were arrested
in the suburbs of Paris and brought to the city hall. There an enraged
crowd seized them and treated them much as they had de Launay and
Flesselles on July 14: the crowd killed them and paraded their severed
heads and Bertier's heart on pikes. This mimetic act of popular violence
alarmed the Assembly. But rather than condemning political violence in
general, members of the Assembly attempted to distinguish the justified
violence of July 14 from the unjustified violence of July 23.

The speeches justifying the taking of the Bastille on July 16 and 20 were
abstract in character, referring only to the energy and courage of the Parisians, who took arms or rose up against despotism. The executions of de
Launay and Flesselles—clearly the most troubling of the actions taken by
the Parisians on the 14th—were passed over in silence. But now that the
events of July 14 had been sanctified as a "necessary and legitimate revolution," deputies who wished to condemn the murders of Bertier and
Foullon actually felt constrained to justify the murders of the 14th. Gouy
d'Arcy proclaimed:

> The first blows struck by the people are due to the effervescence necessar-
> ily inspired by the annihilation of despotism and the birth of liberty. It was
> scarcely possible that a people which had just broken the yoke under which
> it had groaned for so long would not immolate to its fury its first vic-
> tims. . . . The governor of a fort taken by assault, of a fort which was the
> abyss of liberty, could hardly have any other fate; fallen into the hands of the
> defenders of liberty, of a numerous people which he had wished to sacrifice
> to despotism, he got what he deserved. (192)

But at a moment when the Parisian people's own generous actions had
brought peace and harmony to the state, "nothing can justify the fury that
has just been expressed against two individuals." Such "bloody and revolt-

ing scenes" must cease; otherwise "the people could get accustomed to these bloody spectacles and make a game of spilling blood. Barbarity could become a habit" (192). Thus the denunciation of the murders of July 23 was accomplished by justifying those of July 14. Even the conservative Malouet denounced the current atrocities by praising the violence of July 14:

> Resistance to oppression is legitimate and honors a nation; licence debases it. A national insurrection against despotism has a character superior to the power of the laws, without profaning their dignity. But even when a great interest has effected a great uprising, the slightest pretext suffices to reawaken the anxieties of the people and lead it to excesses. . . . It is such misfortunes that must now be prevented. (197)

By July 23, the Assembly had so thoroughly accepted the notion that the taking of the Bastille had been a legitimate revolution that even a conservative deputy who wished above all to bring an end to popular violence spoke of the actions of July 14 as "a national insurrection against despotism," and asserted that such an insurrection "has a character superior to the power of the laws." It seems fair to say that by July 23, the place of the Bastille had been firmly established in French political culture. From then on the capture of the fortress was enshrined as the defining event of a *revolution* in the modern sense—a rising of the sovereign people whose justified violence imposed a new political system on the nation.

But if the meaning of the taking of the Bastille was thenceforth relatively fixed, the precise boundaries of the new concept of revolution remained very much in dispute—indeed, they have remained so up to the present. The elaboration of the new concept of revolution and its definitive identification with the taking of Bastille occurred when the National Assembly was forced to delimit ever more strictly what forms of political violence might be deemed legitimate. Once an act of popular violence was recognized as the very foundation of political legitimacy, it became imperative to distinguish that one transcendent founding moment from other violent actions that might on the surface seem comparable; otherwise, the state would be forever vulnerable to the whim of any crowd that claimed to act on behalf of the people. But at the same time, as Buzot pointed out in his speech of July 20, future acts of legitimate revolution could not be ruled out altogether. No one could guarantee that despotism might not be reborn, and should it return another revolution might be necessary. The problem of bringing the revolution to a close was thus posed at the very moment of its birth. Within the semantic and political field created by the concept of revolution, the boundary between legitimate and illegitimate popular violence, between revolution and rebellion, could never be definitively etched.[8]

The event of the taking of the Bastille therefore had powerful lingering effects—indeed, many of its effects linger still. Yet one can say that the duration of the event, defined as the time that lapsed between the rupture and the rearticulation, was some twelve days, from July 12 to July 23. The great rupture occurred in the dramatic action of July 14. Over the next few days, from the 14th to the 17th, the effects on the political conjuncture gradually became clear—the withdrawal of the troops from the Paris area, the recall of Necker, the effective capitulation of the king, the official establishment of the new Parisian municipality and militia, and the rise to supremacy of the National Assembly. The seemingly miraculous victory of the National Assembly caused its orators to reassess their initial opinion that the taking of the Bastille was a lamentable disorder and to accept the Parisians' own characterization of it as an act of legitimate resistance against despotism and a valid expression of the nation's will. They did so somewhat tentatively on July 16, but more firmly on July 20 and 23. By the 20th, the evolution of the balance of political forces had not only made it unthinkable for the Assembly's majority to criticize the violence of July 14, but made it imperative for them to embrace the violence as a foundation of their own authority. It was by this process that the modern concept of revolution definitively entered French political culture, effecting a hitherto undreamed of but henceforth enduring articulation of popular violence to popular sovereignty.

THE BASTILLE AND THE THEORY OF HISTORICAL EVENTS

Over the past several pages, my account of the taking of the Bastille has been primarily narrative in form. Careful reconstruction of narrative is, I submit, an intellectual necessity in any serious analysis of events. But it is also necessary to tack back and forth between narration and theoretical reflection. Let me therefore elaborate some theoretical implications of this account.

HISTORICAL EVENTS REARTICULATE STRUCTURES. In this chapter I am attempting to conceptualize historical events in a particular way: as

---

8. Colin Lucas (1988, 1991) has written with great penetration about the revolutionary conundrum of distinguishing legitimate from illegitimate violence.

dislocations and transformative rearticulations of structures. As I see it, the taking of the Bastille could only become the founding act of the French Revolution—and of the modern concept of revolution in general—because it took place at a time when political structures were massively dislocated. The National Assembly had declared the people's will to be sovereign, but because it was engaged in an inconclusive struggle with the king, it had not yet definitively established its own claim to represent that will. It was because sovereignty was up for grabs that the taking of the Bastille could be interpreted as a direct and sublime expression of the nation's will—that an act of popular violence could be articulated directly with sovereignty to form the new political category of revolution.

HISTORICAL EVENTS ARE CULTURAL TRANSFORMATIONS. The novel articulation that makes this happening a momentous event in world history is an act of signification. Terms—for example "Bastille" and "revolution," but also "people," "liberty," "despotism," and so on—took on authoritative new meanings that, taken together, reshaped the political world. This implies that events are, literally, significant: they signify something new and surprising. They introduce new conceptions of what really exists (the violent crowd as the people's will in action), of what is good (the people in ecstatic union), and of what is possible (revolution, a new kind of regeneration of the state and the nation). The most profound consequence of the taking of the Bastille was, then, a reconstruction of the very categories of French political culture and political action.

This implies that symbolic interpretation is part and parcel of the historical event. It would be artificial and misleading to conceptualize the assault on the Bastille as a brute physical occurrence that, once complete, was mulled over and interpreted. Those who risked (and in some cases lost) their lives to take the fortress did so because they regarded it as an intolerable barrier to their political hopes; their action was already symbolically motivated. And as soon as the fortress had fallen, its captors began to interpret their victory as a blow struck against despotism by the people. Throughout the extraordinary flow of actions, from the first skirmishes on the evening of the 12th to the slaughter of Bertier and Foullon and its condemnation by the Assembly on the 23rd, interpretation of what was happening was a crucial ingredient of what happened, of the sheer factuality of the event.

However, to say that the event of the taking of the Bastille was a cultural transformation and that it arose from interpretive or symbolic action is not to deny that what happened on July 14 also had crucial military and political consequences. Indeed, had these actions not led to the withdrawal of troops from the Paris region and a victory of the National Assembly over the king, the collective euphoria experienced at the taking of the Bastille would not have resulted in the birth of the concept of revolution—even had those who assaulted the Bastille self-consciously regarded themselves as embodying the will of the nation. The cultural transformation effected by this event—as is true of cultural transformations in general—was both stimulated and locked into place by simultaneous shifts both in resources (e.g., the transfer of control of all those guns and ammunition from the royal forces to the Paris militia) and in modes of power (e.g., the formation of the new Paris militia, which made for a new means of resisting the king, and of a new Parisian municipality, which stood in a novel relation to the city's population).

HISTORICAL EVENTS ARE SHAPED BY PARTICULAR CONDITIONS. The taking of an urban fortress does not automatically lead to the invention of the new concept of revolution. It had this result in the summer of 1789 only because of conditions peculiar to the circumstance—and not only the large and general conditions I have discussed above under the rubric of structural dislocations. There were also very local or particular conditions that made possible the outcome that occurred. Marshall Sahlins uses the term "structure of the conjuncture" to refer to the particular meanings, accidents, and causal forces that shape events—the small but locally determining conditions whose interaction in a particular time and place may seal the fates of whole societies (Sahlins 1981). Three particular conditions that obtained in Paris in July 1789 did much to make the taking of the Bastille into a world-shaping event.

    1. First, we can specify a semantic condition that made the new articulation of popular violence and popular sovereignty possible: the longstanding ambiguity of the term le peuple—the people. On the one hand, le peuple could mean the entire French population. It was the people in this highly generalized and somewhat mystical sense that was designated as sovereign in the political theory adopted by the National Assembly. On the other hand, le peuple could mean the ordinary people, commoners as opposed to nobles and clergy, or the poor and vulgar as opposed to the cultured and wealthy. It was, of course, the people in this latter sense who were thought to be capable of acts of crowd violence. The semantic slippage between the two meanings of "the people" made possible an equation of the

people who rose up and took the Bastille (sense two) and the sovereign people choosing the form of government that suited it best (sense one).

2. A second specific condition for the equation of crowd violence at the Bastille with the exercise of the people's will concerns the preexisting meanings of the fortress, which was already a symbol of political injustice. Since the early eighteenth century, publicists and journalists had cast the Bastille as a sinister prison of despotism, where the regime secretly locked up innocent victims and patriotic martyrs (Lusebrink and Reichardt 1983, 1990). Although the attack of July 14 was in fact launched by militiamen with the eminently practical goal of getting ammunition for their muskets, the Bastille's sinister aura meant that the attack could easily be cast as an assault on despotism itself.

This equation of the Bastille and despotism is clear in the earliest accounts of the occurrences of July 14. Thus, *Les Révolutions de Paris* interrupts its story of the attack to paint a portrait of the Bastille as a prison of despotism. "The cells were opened; innocent men were given their liberty, venerable old men astonished to see the light once again." At this point a footnote adds:

> One respectable old man had been shut up for thirty years. It is useless to relate what an immense quantity of pamphlets, what a quantity of books, of registers of imprisonment, of materials for history were found in the Bastille; in brief, among the multiplicity of arms, of flags, it is said that there were also found machines of death unknown to man.

The main text then sums up: "Liberty, august and sainted, has finally been introduced for the first time into this place of horrors, this fearful abode of despotism, of monsters, of crime" (18). This account draws heavily from the conventional black legend of the Bastille as a place where innocent men were sealed off from light for decades, where pamphlets and books critical of the regime were seized and stored, where horrible cruelties were secretly visited on prisoners by means of "machines of death unknown to man." *Les Révolutions de Paris* again invokes the legend of the Bastille on the following page:

> This astonishing fortress, built under Charles V in 1369, and finished in 1383, which that terrifying colossus Louis XIV and Turenne judged impregnable, has thus been taken by assault in four hours, by an undisciplined and leaderless militia, by inexperienced townsmen, supported, to be sure, by a few soldiers of the nation; finally, by a handful of free men. Oh sainted liberty! What is then thy power? (19–20)

If the people were going to rise up against despotism and establish liberty, it is hard to think of a better place to have done this than the Bastille. The Invalides, which was also invaded earlier that day, and whose capture was probably of greater military significance, lacked the Bastille's bad reputation. As a consequence, its capture was hardly heard of in the myth of July 14. No one said "at the Invalides the people rose up and captured liberty." But a similar phrase became a litany about the Bastille.

3. One local condition is rather more generalizable: the assault on the Bastille, unlike that on the Invalides, was a theater of heroism, treachery, and bloodshed. The object was an impregnable fortress, whose commandant was thought to have lured the attackers into an outer courtyard in order to gun them down more efficiently. The operation lasted several hours, it afforded many opportunities for signal bravery under fire, and it brought death to a nearly one hundred assailants and serious wounds to a few score more. It is absolutely crucial to recognize the emotional significance of the bloodshed if we are to understand the unfolding of the event over the following hours and days. The deaths of the assailants made them understandable as martyrs of liberty; the spilling of their blood became a transformative sacrifice, an act of sacred founding violence of the sort analyzed by René Girard in *Violence and the Sacred* (1977). And the deaths of the martyrs was avenged and doubled by the ritual slaughter of de Launay and Flesselles. The people itself, so the symbolism went, convicted these two men of treason to the nation. Here the ghastly detail that their severed heads were displayed on pikes is significant. As readers of Foucault (1977, chap. 2) will recognize, this act mimicked royal rituals of public execution, which often involved the display of body parts; the sovereign people, in a fashion strikingly similar to the king as sovereign, wreaked public and visible vengeance on the body of those who dared to defy its law.

These local conditions, then, constituted the structure of the conjuncture of the taking of the Bastille. The semantic ambiguity of the term "people," the preexisting political meanings of the Bastille, and the dramatic and bloody character of the action itself made it possible for the myth of the Bastille as a revolution of the sovereign people to become the political truth of the incidents of July 14, 1789.

HISTORICAL EVENTS ARE CHARACTERIZED BY HEIGHTENED EMOTION. Most social scientists avoid emotion like the plague. They seem to fear that if they take emotion seriously as an object of study, they will be tainted by the irrationality, volatility, subjectivity, and ineffability that we associate with the term—that their own lucidity and scientific objectivity will be brought into question. But if, as I would maintain, high-pitched emotional excitement is a constitutive ingredient of many transformative actions, then we cannot afford to maintain this protective scientific distance. The transformations that occurred as a consequence of the taking of the Bastille are certainly impossible to explain without considering the emotional tone of the event.

To begin with, the emotional tone of action can be an important sign of structural dislocation and rearticulation. The more or less extended dislocation of structures that characterizes the temporality of the event is profoundly unsettling. It was in part the unresolved dislocations of the spring and summer of 1789 that rendered the Parisians so wrought up by the middle of July; the emotion was then raised to a fever pitch when the king's attempted coup against the Assembly threatened to dash all hopes of reform. The widespread incidents of violence in Paris on the 12th and 13th bear witness to the tension and fear that motivated people to acts of both heroism and butchery on the 14th. And the resolution of structural dislocation—whether by restoring the ruptured articulation or by forging new ones—results in powerful emotional release that consolidates the rearticulation. We have already noted the rapturous reception of the delegation of the National Assembly in Paris on July 15, with its clamorous cheering and spontaneous weeping. It was the delegates' experience of this rapture that first induced them to revalue the events of the 14th as a legitimate revolution.

Emotion not only is an important sign of dislocations and rearticulations, but also shapes the very course of events. This is especially true in moments like the afternoon of July 14, when a large number of people interacted intensively in a restricted space, experiencing the kind of contagious emotional excitement that Emile Durkheim called "collective effervescence." Collective effervescence lifts people out of their ordinary inhibitions and limitations. As Durkheim puts it, "in the midst of an assembly animated by a common passion, we become susceptible of acts and sentiments of which we are incapable when reduced to our own forces" ([1912] 1965, 240).

The powerful emotions introduced by collective effervescence make events markedly unstable. Joy and rage blend into one another, making possible acts of either generosity or savagery. The descriptions in *Les Révolutions de Paris* of the victorious procession from the Bastille to the city hall capture beautifully this supreme and dangerous exaltation. When the victors came forth from the fortress, escorting their captives, they formed a column and exited in the midst of an enormous crowd. Applause, an excess of joy, insults, imprecations hurled at the perfidious prisoners of war, all were mixed together; cries of vengeance and of pleasure leapt forth from every heart. The victors, glorious and covered with honor, carrying the arms and the corpses of the vanquished; the flags of victory; the militia mixed in with the soldiers of the fatherland; the laurels offered to them from all sides; everything offered a terrible and superb spectacle. (19)

This was the prelude to the slaughter of de Launay. When the column arrived at city hall,

the people, impatient to avenge itself, would permit neither de Launay nor the other officers to mount to the tribunal of the city. They were torn from the hands of their victors, trampled under foot one after the other. De Launay was pierced by a thousand blows, his head was severed, and it was placed on the end of a lance with the blood running down on all sides. (19)

This slaughter did not seem to slake the crowd's thirst; the scene of triumph threatened to degenerate into an orgy of bloodshed. When the rest of the soldiers who had defended the Bastille arrived, "the people called for their execution" as well. But then the mood of the crowd suddenly shifted to generosity. The French Guards, who had been escorting these prisoners, "asked for their grace, and upon this request all voices were united and the pardon was unanimous" (19). The volatility that characterizes events in general can sometimes result, as this example implies, from inherently unpredictable shifts in emotions. And its effects on the future can be extremely important: had the killing of de Launay led to a generalized slaughter of the soldiers who had defended the Bastille, the National Assembly might never have embraced the Parisians' actions as a sublime expression of the people's will and the modern category of revolution might never have come into being. Tracking down the causes and character of structural transformations in political events may require us to be particularly sensitive to the emotional tone of action.

HISTORICAL EVENTS ARE ACTS OF COLLECTIVE CREATIVITY. Dislocation of structures, I have tried to suggest, produces in actors a deep sense of insecurity, a real uncertainty about how to get on with life. I think that this uncertainty is a necessary condition for the kind of collective creativity that characterizes so many great historical events. In times of structural dislocation, ordinary routines of social life are open to doubt, the sanctions of existing power relations are uncertain or suspended, and new possibilities are thinkable. In ordinary times, cultural schemas, arrays of resources, and modes of power are bound into self-reproducing streams of structured social action. But in times of dislocation, like the spring and summer of 1789, resources are up for grabs, cultural logics are elaborated more freely and applied to new circumstances, and modes of power are extended to unforeseen social fields. In 1789, new arguments were tried out, new forms of organization were invented, and new ideas circulated in both old and new media and institutions—newspapers, pamphlets, political clubs, wine-shops, public meetings, caucuses, National Assembly debates, and street-corner conversations. Even in moments like this, which combined extraordinary freedom with an unusual sense of practical urgency, creativity was still shaped and constrained by the structurally available forms of thought and practice. But within these limits, the clamorous and multi-sited public sphere that emerged in France in 1789 was a site of remarkable collective creativity.

If the extended structural dislocations of 1789 led to widespread experimentation, the rearticulation of structures was accomplished above all at very particular places and times—at the Bastille and the city hall on July 14, in the reception ceremonies for the delegation from the National Assembly and for the king on July 15 and July 17, and in the meeting hall of the National Assembly on July 16, 20, and 23. These were moments when the pressure of rapidly unfolding actions and the massing of bodies in space led to emotionally charged cultural improvisations that determined the shape of future history. These improvisations were genuinely collective. For example, the notion that the people itself rose up and conquered despotism at the Bastille was not the invention of one particular orator or journalist but a revelation arrived at by a collectivity of actors in the heat of the moment. The itinerary and gestures of the reception ceremonies of July 15 and 17 were made up on the spot. And the speeches that authoritatively established the events of July 14 as a legitimate revolution were not written out the night before, but were improvised by a succession of speakers in the heat of debate—on July 20 in a feverish effort to rebut Lally's blanket censure of political violence, and on July 23 in response to the shocking news of the murders of Bertier and Foullon.

HISTORICAL EVENTS ARE PUNCTUATED BY RITUAL. We usually think of rituals as formalized ceremonies whose gestures and procedures are prescribed in advance and repeated formulaically on many occasions. Events, in sharp contrast, are unique and unpredictable sequences of happenings that must, by definition, be improvised on the spot. It follows that rituals and events ought to be antithetical categories. Yet in the cluster of occurrences known by the metonymic title "the taking of the Bastille," some of the most important episodes had distinctly ritual qualities. Four crucial episodes were especially ritualized in form; first, the procession of the victors of the Bastille from the fortress to the city hall; second, the murder of de Launay and Flesselles; third, the visit of the delegation of the National Assembly to Paris on July 15; and fourth, the reception of the king in Paris on July 17. It will be recognized that these four episodes played a crucial role in transforming the assault on the Bastille into a revolution of the sovereign people. What did their ritual character have to do with their significance in the invention of the French Revolution? And, more generally, how do we account for the intrusion of the supposedly static category of ritual into the quintessentially dynamic category of the event?

One might, of course, ask in what sense the episodes I have identified had a ritual character. Students of ritual disagree about precisely how ritual should be defined; among the characteristics that have been proposed to mark off ritual from other types of social action are the formalization and repetition of gesture, the theatrical character of the action, the invocation of supernatural forces, the demarcation through gesture of sacred from profane persons, places, and activities, and the delineation of particular stages in "the ritual process" (see, e.g., Leach 1968; Turner 1969). My own usage follows that of Catherine Bell, who argues that there can be no general list of characteristics that universally distinguish ritual from nonritual action. Ritual, in her usage, is a mode of acting "that sets itself off from other ways of acting" in such a way that it "aligns one . . . to the ultimate sources of power" (Bell 1992, 140–41). What is ritualistic about the episodes I cite above is (1) that the actions constituting them are marked off as ritual by the actors and (2) that they align everyone present with the newly posited ultimate source of power: the people-as-nation. In these episodes, to quote Bell, "the strategic production of expedient schemes . . . structure[s] an environment in such a way that the environment appears to be the source of the schemes and their values" (140). Let me be more specific.

Once the Bastille had been captured, the elated victors celebrated their feat by spontaneously forming a triumphal procession. They marched through the streets to the city hall displaying trophies of their victory — captured weapons, freed prisoners, flags, and the defeated soldiers — to the assembled public. The triumphal procession was a preexisting military rite, but one that previously had displayed the armed might of the king's army—an army that was celebrating the defeat of foreign enemies but that was always also a means of intimidating the king's subjects. In this case, however, an existing ritual form was adapted to a very different situation: the armed men had *defeated* the king's soldiers and in the procession they displayed themselves as members of the people/nation through whose midst they were marching and whose accolades they accepted. They strategically produced an expedient scheme (the triumphal procession), thereby structuring the environment (the streets mobbed with ordinary citizens) in such a way that it (the assembled people, both marching and looking on) appeared to be the source of the schemes and their values (it was the people whose sovereign power made the triumph and celebration possible). This procession stated in highly dramatic and emotionally powerful terms the identity between the people and the armed force that had taken the Bastille.

In an analogous but more terrifying way, the killing of de Launay and Flesselles was ritualized by parading their severed heads on pikes around the thronged plaza in front of the city hall. By mimicking the old regime magistrates' display of body parts of executed criminals, the slaughter was solemnized and identified as an act of the sovereign—but now of the sovereign people. The cries of approval that arose from the crowd in the plaza dramatically and publicly identified the people with this act of vengeance and justice. The remaining ritualized episodes also used preexisting ritual gestures to establish the sovereignty of the people/nation. The rapturous reception of the National Assembly delegation on the 15th and of the king on the 17th both adapted the form of the royal entry. In royal entries, the king or a prince of the blood would be greeted at the city gate and escorted through a cheering throng by urban officials and dignitaries of the city's various guilds and corporate bodies, who would march in a carefully arrayed hierarchy. But once again the spontaneously invented rituals of July 1789 departed from precedent by symbolically establishing the thronged people as the sovereign from whom power arose. On July 15, the crowds established their ecstatic unity with their representatives—so effectively that Mounier returned to Versailles and praised the Parisian uprising as a legitimate revolt of liberty against despotism. And on the 17th, Bailly engaged in a consummate act of symbolic reversal, greeting the king at the gate of the city according to the traditional protocol, but explicitly reminding him that it was the people who had conquered their king, not vice-versa. The high point of this particular ritual arrived only when, having arrived at the city hall, a site by now indelibly associated with the uprising, the king stepped onto the balcony and publicly placed the insurrection-aries' tricolor rosette on his hat. All of these ritualized episodes placed the various participants in alignment to the new ultimate source of power—whether as members of the sovereign people, as its soldiers, its represen-tatives, or the objects of its wrath. The rituals, I would argue, made pal-pable the notion that the people/nation was indeed sovereign, and that its will was the ultimate arbiter of the affairs of the nation. These largely spontaneous ritualized actions had the effect of concretely articulating the previously far more abstract will of the sovereign people to the violent up-rising of July 14.

To a significant extent, then, the taking of the Bastille was created as a legitimate revolution through the performance of these spontaneous ritu-als. Most scholarly study of ritual focuses on religious rites of one kind or another. In most religious rituals, the participants are collected into a place marked off as sacred and then participate in a series of activities that in-duce a certain emotional state—quiet awe, rapt attention, terror, intense pleasure, or frenzied enthusiasm, as the case may be. In many cases, par-ticipants enter into what Victor Turner has called liminality—a state of "betwixt and between" in which social constraints and hierarchies mo-mentarily evaporate and the celebrants experience a profound sense of community with one another and with the deity or deities. It is the cre-ation of this sense of communitas that gives rituals their psychological and social power (Turner 1969). In episodes like those surrounding the taking of the Bastille, the usual process is reversed: rather than the ritual induc-ing the emotional excitement and the sense of communion, the emotional excitement and sense of communion—what Durkheim would call the col-lective effervescence—induce those present to express and concretize their feelings in ritual. The Parisians who participated in these events were massed in confined spaces, and their emotions were excited by the crowd-ing and by the memory—very recent in the episodes of the 14th, more dis-tant on the 15th and 17th—of the battle fought and the victory won. They were also aware that they were participating in a momentous event, whose outcome could determine their future as individuals and as a nation. Fi-nally, in the very course of the event, they discovered that they were mem-bers of the sovereign people, that their actions constituted a sacred col-lective will that rightfully determined the fate of the nation. They could manifest this state of liminality and communitas only by spontaneously appropriating known ritual forms to create new and powerful rituals of sovereignty. Through these rituals, the Parisians participated in the inven-tion of the modern revolution.

HISTORICAL EVENTS PRODUCE MORE EVENTS. Events are sequences of ruptures that effect transformations of structure. If structures are multiple and overlapping, it follows that any transformation of structure has the potential of touching off dislocations and rearticulations of overlapping or contiguous structures. This cascading character of events can be seen within the series of episodes that I have designated as the overall event of the taking of the Bastille. What happened on the 14th resulted in the strategic retreat of the king and the ecstatic reception of the delegation of the National Assembly in Paris, the Assembly's initial statement of the legitimacy of the violence of the 14th, and the king's ceremonial reconquest by the Parisians on the 17th. But it also led to intensified uncertainty and anxiety in the provinces, and to disturbances like those of the 17th and 18th at Poissy and Saint-Germain-en-Laye, which in turn led to the further justification of the taking of the Bastille as a legitimate revolution. The success of the Parisian insurrection and its explicit justification in the debates of the Assembly also emboldened the Parisian mob to renew its acts of "popular justice" by murdering Bertier and Foullon on the 23rd, which paradoxically led to a further elaboration of the myth of the Bastille as a legitimate revolution so as to condemn as illegitimate the lynching of the 23rd.

I am conceptualizing the taking of the Bastille from a particular perspective: as the historical event that articulates popular violence with the nation's sovereign will in the new concept of revolution. For this reason it is reasonable for me to declare the event completed on July 23. But the cascade of consequences flowing from the actions of July 14 certainly did not stop then. The profound redefinition of sovereignty, the defeat of the king, the victory of the National Assembly, the establishment of a new form of popular urban militia, and the emergence of revolution as a category of political action both raised hopes and accentuated the practical dislocation of social and political structures all over France. It therefore heightened the already pervasive sense of insecurity. I would like to sketch out two of the most spectacular and momentous historical events that flowed from the taking of the Bastille: the vast agrarian panic that historians have come to call "the Great Fear" and the famous legislative session of the night of August 4, which abolished feudalism and privilege and established a new social order based on equality before the law.

The Great Fear was probably the most astonishing mass panic in recorded history. The news of the Paris uprising reached the provinces during the crucial days when the promising crop of 1789 was beginning to ripen in the fields, but in a countryside that was crushed by poverty and crowded with beggars and vagabonds produced by the previous year's disastrous harvest. The panic began independently at several different points in France during the week that followed July 20—that is, within a few days after the arrival of the astounding news from Paris. At each of the points of origin, someone reported seeing troops of brigands advancing into the fields and cutting the standing grain before it could ripen. The result was a wave of panics that extended over most of the surface of the country by the early days of August. The bells in the church steeple would be rung, the villagers would assemble, arm themselves, and march out in pursuit of the imaginary brigands, usually sending a messenger to the adjacent villages to announce the dreadful news. These villages would mobilize in turn and send out their own messengers. Thus the panic might spread a hundred miles or more in the course of a few days.

In a few cases, the peasants, once mobilized, attacked the lords' chateaux and burned the rolls on which their dues and charges were written. According to Georges Lefebvre, who wrote the classic history of the Great Fear, this event persuaded the vast mass of the peasantry that they were threatened by a nation-wide aristocratic plot (Lefebvre [1932] 1973). But Lefebvre's own evidence seems more consistent with the findings of Clay Ramsay, who concluded in his recent study of the Great Fear in the Soissonais that by far the most common outcome was a symbolic reaffirmation of the hierarchical social order of the old regime village community. When the villagers took up arms against the "brigands," they usually called on the local lord or magistrates to constitute and lead their militias. Faced with a kind of peasants' vision of the apocalypse—the harvest unaccountably destroyed by mysterious outsiders—country people turned to their traditional superiors to save the day (Ramsay 1992). The Great Fear probably is better understood as the last hurrah of the rural old regime than as the definitive triumph of the peasant revolution.

But most of the villages where the Great Fear occurred were distant from Paris, and communications were uncertain and irregular. From the perspective of Paris or Versailles, the news was indeed alarming: chateaux in flames, crops destroyed by brigands, armed men everywhere. It was the journalists and legislators in Paris and Versailles, not the peasants in the villages, who darkly attributed the disorders to an aristocratic plot. The legislators feared a general peasant rising against the feudal system, a rising that would threaten not only the lords' seigneuries but rural property in general. The famed legislative session of the night of August 4 was actually based on this misapprehension of what was happening in the countryside.

The enactments of August 4 resulted in part from a legislative conspiracy. A sizeable conclave of patriot deputies determined to appease the peasants by abolishing the feudal system in return for an indemnity to be paid by the peasants. To this end they recruited two great nobles, the vicomte de Noailles and the duc d'Aiguillon, to propose the renunciation of feudal rights. Their speeches electrified the Assembly, and before long even nobles and clerics who had hitherto been hostile to such reforms began to vie with one another by renouncing their own privileges at the altar of the nation, bathed in tears of joy amid the clamorous applause of the Assembly. The session, which lasted nearly until dawn, destroyed the entire tissue of privilege that had constituted the social and political order of the old regime and replaced it with a new social order based on the equality of all citizens before the law. If the taking of the Bastille definitively established the sovereignty of the people/nation, it was on the night of August 4 that France's principles of social organization were finally brought into harmony with the new foundational ideology of natural equality, national sovereignty, and social contract. The night of August 4 effected the definitive rearticulation between the new metaphysical principles of the state and the juridical organization of social life. It finally spelled out the consequences for daily life of the ideology the delegates had adopted implicitly when they declared themselves the National Assembly on June 17 (Kessel 1969; Fitzsimmons 2003).

The Great Fear and the night of August 4, no less than the taking of the Bastille, had all the characteristics of historical events listed above. They rearticulated structures, transformed cultures, were crucially shaped by local conditions, were bathed in powerful emotions, were acts of collective creativity, were punctuated by improvised rituals, and produced yet more events. In all these respects, they could be analyzed in no less detail than I have lavished on the taking of the Bastille. They formed part of an extraordinary series of historical events that, over the summer of 1789, transformed the political and social system of the most populous, most powerful, and most prestigious state in the European world, and that changed forever the horizons of world politics.

TO BECOME DEFINITIVE, REARTICULATIONS OF STRUCTURES MUST GAIN AUTHORITATIVE SANCTION. In the case of the Bastille, the ruptural action took place in Paris rather than Versailles and involved a clash between armed citizens under the improvised banner of an emergency municipality and a minor military detachment of elderly veterans guarding an urban fortress. It was also in Paris that the trope of the sovereign people rising against despotism was first introduced, both in spontaneous rituals and in oral and written discourse. But for this to become the recognized truth of the taking of the Bastille required action by the central governing authorities — the National Assembly and the king, both bystanders on July 14. The taking of the Bastille could only become a legitimate and founding revolution after the ceremonial entries of July 15 and 17, which bound the Parisians to the National Assembly and registered the acquiescence of the king, and the debates in the National Assembly that marked off the violence of July 14 as, in Malouet's words, "a national insurrection against despotism" with "a character superior to the power of the laws." The structural rearticulation could only be definitive when it had been sanctioned at the pinnacle of state authority.

The crucial role of action at the center of the state is even clearer in the case of the Great Fear and the night of August 4. The Great Fear might be characterized as an interrelated series of dispersed and local events. Although these events were of tremendous emotional and political impact in each locality, the structural transformations they effected in the localities — usually the reconstruction of a kind of participatory old regime hierarchy — was ephemeral. The most important long-term effects of the Great Fear in the localities was mediated by action at the center. It was because the Great Fear provoked members of the National Assembly to abolish the feudal system on the night of August 4 that its effects not only on French and world history, but also on local history, were so profound. The night of August 4 resulted in the abolition of serfdom, feudal exactions, provincial and municipal privileges, exclusive hunting rights, venality of office, and tithes, and the confiscation and sale of the vast properties of the church. It was the effects of these reforms that transformed the character of social and political relations in French villages, not the ephemeral resurgence of old regime hierarchical relations that were the immediate result of the Great Fear. Once again, even though the impetus of the events came from a peripheral location, it was their resolution at the center of the state that determined their structural effects.

Because the taking of the Bastille and the Great Fear were above all political ruptures, it should not be surprising that in both cases the authoritative rearticulations were effected at the center of the state. But we should expect the location of rearticulating action to vary with the setting and scope of the event. A religious event might well achieve its authoritative resolution in a religious institutional setting: in, say, a presbytery or a council of bishops. A rupture in kinship relations might be sanctioned by the elders of the clan or by a tacit agreement on the part of the appropriate kinsmen. Where authoritative rearticulations will be achieved depends on what modes of power are activated or challenged by the event in question and on the particular institutional nodes in which the affected power is concentrated. Authoritative rearticulations, however, are likely to take place at power nodes that command an adequate geographic and institutional scope. Given the institutional and geographic cascades that characterize events, this means that even ruptures located primarily outside the sphere of state activity are often resolved only by state action.

HISTORICAL EVENTS ARE SPATIAL AS WELL AS TEMPORAL PROCESSES. We usually think of the event as a temporal category. But it is impossible to analyze an event without encountering spatial processes.[9] This is certainly true of the taking of the Bastille, and of the Great Fear and the Night of August Fourth as well. Let me specify some key spatial dimensions of the taking of the Bastille that seem characteristic of historical events more generally.

1. The actions that determined how structures were transformed were highly concentrated in space. It was spatial concentration that made possible the episodes of "collective effervescence." The exaltation of imagination, the collective creativity, the superheated emotionality, and the spontaneous ritual that marked the occurrences of July 14, 15, 17, and 23 all depended on the massing of large numbers of people into particular spaces—the environs of the Bastille, the place de l'Hotel de Ville, the parade routes along which the delegation of the National Assembly and the king made their way into Paris. These particular spaces, at particular times, constituted crucial nodes in the transformative event known as the taking of the Bastille—crucial because action taken there and then determined the course of subsequent action over long durations and wide geographic scopes. The action of the National Assembly, debating in its meeting place in Versailles, was also concentrated spatially. The fateful outcome of the debates that sanctioned the taking of the Bastille as a legitimate revolution of the sovereign people depended on particular rivalries, alliances, spontaneous flows of debate—and, indeed, on collective effervescence—that were concentrated at a particular moment in a particular building.

2. The intersection of structures that results in cascades of transforma-

9. For elaborations on this point, see Zhao (2001, esp. chap. 8) and Sewell (2001).

tive actions is spatial as well as institutional. The structures that are unevenly articulated into networks have varying and far from congruent spatial scopes. One important reason that some ruptures result in cascades of
further ruptures has to do with spatial scale. A rupture that has consequences outside its initial place of occurrence is far more likely to result in
a transformative cascade than one that is spatially contained. Whether
spread mimetically like the Great Fear, or by immediate or mediated
effects on structures of much wider scope like the assault on the Bastille,
or because they occur initially in socio-spatial locations with great spatial
scope like the night of August 4th, historical events can be defined at least
in part by a prodigious expansion in spatial reach of what are initially local phenomena.

3. All action by definition takes place in a particular spatial location. But
action taken in some locations has only a local scope, while the scope of
other actions is much wider. In part this is because some locations are central nodes in social practices of wide extent. An act taken in the National
Assembly or in the king's chambers may bind people spread over the entire territory of the country. Moreover, because of Paris's position as the
quasi-capital of France, its centrality in French cultural and political life,
and its proximity to the royal government at Versailles, a disturbance that
occurred there had reverberations all over the country. By contrast, an
equally violent event in a remote village would have only a local impact, unless it was nationalized by the Parisian press or led the National Assembly
or the king to take action. The particular shape and dynamic of events—
quite different for the taking of the Bastille, for example, than for the Great
Fear—will depend fundamentally on the evolving spatial scope of its constituent actions.

DEFINING THE BOUNDARIES OF A HISTORICAL EVENT REQUIRES
AN ACT OF JUDGMENT. Historical events have what might be called a
fractal character. An event like the taking of the Bastille might well be said
to be composed of a series of events—among others, the assault on the Invalides, the slaughter of de Launay and Flesselles, the king's entry into
Paris, or the Assembly debate of July 23. And each of these sub-events is itself composed of a series of smaller but significant ruptures. Moreover, the
taking of the Bastille itself is but one episode in the French Revolution,
and the French Revolution but one component of the vast transformation
of forms of government, national boundaries, and modes of warfare that
took place between 1789 and 1815. There is no a priori reason to call the tak-

ing of the Bastille an event and to deny the term to the king's entry into Paris on July 17, or to his actions on the balcony of the city hall that afternoon, or to the French Revolution as a whole. Each of these may be usefully conceptualized as a sequence of ruptures that dislocates and rearticulates structures. Each is a historical event at its own particular scale.

But the complexity of events is not limited to their fractal character. Events are also overlapping and interpenetrating. If it is true that structures form a loosely articulated network, and if we define events as sequences of occurrences that transform structures, then an occurrence like the assault on the Bastille will be implicated in the transformations of a number of different structures, and each of these transformations will have a different spatial and temporal range. Once again, deciding how to bound an event is necessarily a matter of judgement. One may state as a rule of thumb that how an analyst should delimit an event will depend on the structural transformation to be explained. For example, I define the event of the taking of the Bastille as beginning with popular resistance to the dismissal of Necker on July 12 and as ending with the Assembly debates of July 23 that authoritatively interpret the assault on the fortress as a legitimate revolution. I do so because I am focusing on a particular structural transformation: the articulation of popular sovereignty with crowd violence to form the category of revolution. But because this was by no means the only significant transformation to come out of the taking of the Bastille, these are not the only appropriate boundaries of the event. A study focusing on the emergence of the urban militia as a new mode of power—another crucial consequence of the taking of the Bastille—might well fix different beginning and ending dates. Such decisions must be made post hoc: with some confidence when dealing with an event that occurred two hundred years ago and whose consequences have generally been fixed for some time, more tentatively when the consequences of a rupture have only recently begun to appear and when additional, perhaps surprising, consequences may yet emerge.

*   *   *

Just as the taking of the Bastille led to a cascade of further events, so the theoretical reflections touched off by my analysis of that event has led to a cascade of further reflections. And as the analyst must draw an arbitrary boundary to establish analytical closure to an event, so must I bring to a close an essay that still seems to me radically open and unfinished. I believe I have written enough to establish that thinking about historical events as I have done here—that is, treating them as sequences of occurrences that result in durable transformations of structures—is potentially fruitful. Precisely how fruitful can only be determined by future work on other historical events.

POSTSCRIPT

Calculation, Semiosis, and Charisma

I remarked at the conclusion of my essay that it still seemed to me open and unfinished. This postscript is a practical testimony to that observation. At about the time the essay was initially published, I took part in a several-day conference on revolutions that included practitioners of what is called rational choice theory.[10] This encounter provoked me to articulate more clearly the strategic dimensions of my argument—a task that I undertook initially in a memo drafted shortly after the conference. This postscript is a revised version of that memo. It attempts to specify both the value and the limitations of explaining "the invention of revolution at the Bastille" as a consequence of self-interested strategic action.

The "rational choice" perspective in the social sciences is based upon "methodological individualism." It assumes that no social action has been properly explained until it has been reduced to the aggregate effects of individual actions. It further assumes that individuals are "rational maximizers"—that is, that they act strategically so as to maximize their individual interests. It attempts to develop formal mathematical models, generally derived from game theory, to explain why people act as they do. This perspective, which was explicitly borrowed from economics, has become quite common in contemporary sociology and is currently making a robust but increasingly contested bid for methodological dominance in contemporary political science. Given the growing institutional power of rational choice theory, especially in the discipline of political science, it seems worthwhile to assess a strategic approach to what surely must count as a highly significant happening—the emergence of the modern concept of revolution in July 1789.

Rational choice theory has been applied effectively to certain problems in the study of revolutions. For example, Michael Taylor (1988) has shown that an explicit modeling of the individual choice to join or abstain from revolutionary protests can significantly clarify the process by which small

---

10. This was a conference on Social Theory and Revolution, organized by Shmuel Eisenstadt and Björn Wittrock and held in Uppsala in 1995.

and local actions snowball into revolutionary uprisings; and Jack Goldstone (1990, 1994) has shown that rational choice analysis can provide a plausible micro-translation of his macro-historical explanations of revolutionary dynamics. Yet I suspect that many specialists on revolutions would agree with me that even such cogent analyses as these fail to grasp something essential to the revolutionary phenomenon. Taylor and Goldstone focus on the problem of how people choose which side to take when an explicitly revolutionary movement has been launched. They have to assume a high degree of stability in the goals of the contesting forces; otherwise actors would not know what benefits or costs to expect from a victory by the revolutionaries and could not make rational calculations. The problem is that in most revolutions worthy of the name, the goals of the revolution, and for that matter the identities of the actors as well, are significantly transformed in the course of the revolutionary process. What makes the political struggles we call revolutions *revolutionary* is that they fundamentally change the nature of the ideological and institutional alternatives available to members of the polity, and that they do so by elaborating new and surprising political and moral options. To my knowledge, rational choice approaches have not succeeded in formulating, let alone resolving, this crucial problem of revolutionary changes in cultural meanings. One of the merits of my essay on the Bastille is precisely that it attempts to explain one such transformation: the emergence of the modern concept of "revolution." Although my essay uses none of the rhetorical tropes associated with rational choice, it nevertheless does, like most cultural or historical analyses, contain arguments about interest-based calculations—arguments that could, in principle, be cast in rational-choice terms. In this postscript, I pursue such arguments more systematically—in part to clarify my own explanation, in part as a means of assessing the potential contribution of rational choice arguments to the explanation of revolutionary cultural transformations.

Woven into my account of the taking of the Bastille is a story of strategic action on the part of the National Assembly.[11] It goes as follows. The National Assembly was engaged in a high-stakes political game with the

11. In this argument, I am constrained to consider the National Assembly as, in effect, a single actor, even though it was of course made up of a large number of individual actors who, as my account has made clear, often disagreed. But because there are no roll-call data on votes in the Assembly, I cannot disaggregate their actions to work out a more fine-grained interpretation of the genuinely individual political calculations that were undoubtedly going on between July 12 and July 23, 1789. For an example of a more individual-level analysis of what was at least a quasi-revolutionary process, see Ivan Ermakoff's (2000) study of the legislature's decision to accede to regime change in France in 1940, after the defeat by the Germans.

king. At stake was effective sovereignty. The taking of the Bastille introduced a new element into the game—the rebellious Parisian people. Initially the National Assembly was hesitant to embrace the Parisians. This hesitancy was based on several calculations: (1) that the violence that had taken place was likely to prove contagious, (2) that a contagious expansion of popular violence was likely to have the effect of strengthening the hand of the king, who alone had the armed force necessary to put it down, (3) that a strengthened king would be in a position to dominate or dissolve the Assembly, and (4) that the king would be more likely to use force against the Assembly if it embraced the rebellious Parisians than if it did not. (5) Against these considerations must be weighed whatever strength in either military forces or popular support might have been gained by embracing the Parisians. I am sure that a competent formal modeler could render the strategic situation facing the National Assembly as a utility function or functions.

The mournful silence that greeted the initial news of the taking of the Bastille in the Assembly indicates that it found itself in an irresolvable dilemma. It believed that embracing the Parisians by approving of the taking of the Bastille would have negative utility, but also knew that embracing the king against the Parisians would have negative utility. So rather than choosing sides immediately, the Assembly did what any rational actor would do in a situation where neither choice looks promising: it temporized and gathered more information. It did this by sending a delegation to Paris and by sending a series of delegations to the king. This resulted in new information that shifted the "expected utilities" in two ways. First, the delegation to Paris found that the city, rather than being violent and chaotic, was peaceful and orderly. This decreased the perceived likelihood that the violence would be contagious, therefore increasing the perceived likelihood that supporting the Parisians against the king would actually strengthen the Assembly. Second, the delegations to the king found that he did not seem to regard his own position as more powerful. He first removed his troops from Paris, and then effectively renounced the use of force against the Parisians. The information from the delegation to Paris changed the Assembly's calculations because it indicated that contagious violence was not occurring. And the delegations to the royal palace indicated that the king regarded himself as weakened, rather than strengthened, by the Parisian violence. All of this sharply decreased the perceived costs of forming an alliance with the Parisians. Consequently, the Assembly opted to support the Parisians, cementing the alliance by giving the uprising retroactive authoritative legitimation—by recognizing it as an act of the sovereign people.

This argument about strategic calculation certainly packs an explanatory punch. But it does not really get us to our goal, which is to explain the invention and locking into place of the modern concept of revolution. The argument explains why the National Assembly, if it behaves as a rational actor, would initially keep its distance from the Parisians and subsequently form a coalition with Paris against the king. But it surely does not tell us why the Assembly would form the coalition in the way it did—by legitimating an act of popular violence as "a national insurrection against despotism" with "a character superior to the power of the laws." By enunciating this doctrine, the National Assembly did more than cement an alliance with the Parisians: it established a new principle of legitimacy that could, in principle, be used against its own power as much as against the king's. If we take the Assembly's goal as the maximizing of its own power and security, it went irrationally far when it defined the Parisian crowd's action in a way that compromised its own claims to a monopoly on the legitimate representation of sovereignty. In short, an argument based on rational calculation cannot explain why crowd violence and popular sovereignty were articulated in this particular and historically fateful way. In order to explain this articulation, we need to move beyond a purely rational choice framework of explanation. We need to explain why the taking of the Bastille, which was initially understood by the Assembly as an act of potentially contagious license and disorder, could be reinterpreted as a rising of the people against despotism and an exercise of popular sovereignty. Here the initial rational choice explanation needs to be joined to a semiotic explanation, one that proceeds on different premises and by different methods.

A semiotic approach would explain what happened in the Assembly between July 14 and July 23 as a novel code switch followed by a further elaboration of the newly adopted code. The initial response of the Assembly was consistent with a well-established code for interpreting popular violence. This code depended on a generalized elite conception of the people (le peuple) as irrational, unruly, and naturally violent. Thus, when the Parisian populace attacked the Bastille and gruesomely slaughtered its commander, the automatic response of any educated person would have been to condemn the violence and fear its contagious spread. But over the last few decades of the eighteenth century, and at an accelerated rate since the calling of the Estates General, another entirely different discourse de-

veloped that also used the term *le peuple:* the discourse of national or popular sovereignty, which, in June and July 1789, became the chief legitimating discourse of the self-proclaimed National Assembly. In this discourse
the people and the people's will figured in an entirely positive but purely
abstract way, as the principle of sovereignty that underlay a legitimate
state and as the entity that was represented in the National Assembly or
any legitimate government. Far from being a threat to order and morality,
"the people" in this somewhat mystical sense was the very source of order
and morality.

When, as early as July 15, orators in the National Assembly began to
characterize the people who attacked the Bastille as courageous and ener-
getic, and to speak of their action as a blow struck for liberty against despotism, they were seizing on a pregnant ambiguity of the term people.
They were shifting the people's action at the Bastille out of the context of
a discourse on the people's inherent violence and irrationality and into the
context of a discourse on popular sovereignty. Once the shift had been
made, the valence of the people's action was systematically reversed from
negative to positive. And over the course of the next several days, the logical entailments of inserting the taking of the Bastille into the discourse of
popular sovereignty were elaborated, leading to the definition of the violence of July 14 not only as a heroic attack on despotism but as a necessary
national insurrection with an authority superior to the laws. The argument about rational calculation can perhaps explain why the National Assembly chose the second discourse over the first. But it cannot explain why
these two discourses were the available alternatives nor why the choice of
the popular sovereignty discourse led to the elaboration of a concept of
popular revolution that actually diminished the Assembly's claim to be the
sole legitimate interpreter of the national will. Unless the rational choice
argument is joined to a semiotic analysis, this outcome will remain utterly
inexplicable.

But even a combined rational choice and semiotic analysis leaves an explanatory puzzle. Rational choice can explain why the National Assembly
decided to form a coalition with the Parisians against the king. Semiotic
analysis can establish the alternative discursive universes in terms of which
the taking of the Bastille could be evaluated and can explicate the logic of
semiotic elaboration followed once a given discursive universe had been
entered. But neither of these explanatory strategies makes it clear why it
suddenly seemed to the Assembly possible, indeed natural, to speak of an
act of crowd violence in the discursive categories of popular sovereignty.

Here it is important to recognize the novelty of the interpretation elaborated by the Assembly. The idea of revolution as a radical change of political regime was certainly available to political actors in 1789—chiefly from the English "Glorious" Revolution of 1688 and the American Revolution of 1776–83. So was the notion that the regime established by a revolution was to be based on the sovereignty of the nation or the people. But before the taking of the Bastille, the idea that an act of popular violence could be an authoritative expression of the people's will had not been imagined.

To understand why the National Assembly could see this as self-evident in the days after July 14, we need to turn to a third framework of explanation, this one based on Max Weber's (1978, 1:241–25) concept of charisma and Emile Durkheim's ([1912] 1965) concept of collective effervescence. Neither the rational choice nor the semiotic explanatory framework has any way of accounting for the high-pitched emotional excitement that characterized the Bastille episode and many other key revolutionary events. Both frameworks are essentially formal and rationalist, although they posit different notions of rationality and employ different formal methods. Weber and Durkheim, by contrast, both find a place for the power of emotions near the center of their theoretical schemes.

The experience that initially influenced members of the Assembly to rethink the meaning of the Bastille was the visit of a delegation to Paris on July 15. Mounier's account of the visit actually dwelt less on the Paris municipality's new arrangements for assuring law and order or the militia's exemplary discipline than on the emotional tone of the episode. The Parisians, he noted, "attempted, by all the most vivid signs of affection, to express the sentiments weighing upon them. It was a great joy for them to shake hands with a member of the National Assembly. . . . Citizens congratulated and embraced one another. All eyes were wet with tears; intoxicated sentiment was everywhere" (*Réimpression de l'ancien Moniteur*, 163). What Mounier is signaling here is the establishment of an emotional bond between the delegates of the Assembly and the throngs of Parisians who lined their route into the city. As Durkheim would point out, the emotional excitement experienced by both the delegates and the Parisians was in part the consequence of "collective effervescence," the remarkable enhancement of emotion that occurs when a large number of people are crowded into a confined space, especially one that, like the parade route followed by the delegation, was ritually marked off as extraordinary or sacred. The excitement was not merely the mechanical effect of crowding— it is rare for the crowd at Grand Central station during rush hour to erupt in tears of joy. The emotional power of these crowd scenes derived from what Weber would call their charismatic quality—the sense that what was happening somehow touched ultimate sources of order. The joyous mingling of the National Assembly's delegation with the populace of Paris was experienced by both parties as an incarnation of the unity of the sovereign people and its representatives, as a concrete enactment of the mystery that lay at the center of the theory of popular sovereignty. The sense of ecstatic union, which contrasted sharply with the pervasive conflict and tension of the past several months, was obviously a consequence of the taking of the Bastille. It was, I am convinced, this profound emotional experience on the 15th of July—an experience repeated during the king's visit to Paris on the 17th—that made it thinkable for the Assembly to take the novel step of coding a bloody assault on a fortress as a sublime action of the sovereign people, and thereby to introduce into the world a concept of popular revolution that had the potential of undermining its own authority.

Methodological Lessons

It is my experience that practitioners of rational choice theory have only a minor interest in issues of cultural transformation. The problem is not that they ignore culture altogether, but that culture figures in their accounts in a highly limited fashion: usually either as a residual that is invoked when rational choice accounts have been pushed to the limit and still leave something unexplained, or as a framework within which calculations take place, but that is taken as given for the explanatory purpose at hand. At the outside, rational choice arguments may be used to explain the choice between alternative existing frameworks of meaning or to explain the emergence of certain norms that make rational calculation possible. But on what I regard as the crucial question of the emergence of new and structurally crucial cultural frameworks in transformative events, rational choice theory has, as far as I know, remained silent.

The intent of this postscript is to argue both that rational choice analysis—or at least a serious interrogation of the strategic options faced by actors—has something useful to offer in the study of this question and that it is incapable of providing a sufficient answer on its own. In the case of the taking of the Bastille, and I suspect more generally, arguments about rational calculation of advantage need to be joined to arguments about semiotic structures and their transformations and arguments about the socially generated emotional experiences that inspire the invention and elaboration of new cultural meanings. Without taking semiotic structures and socio-emotional dynamics into account, and without recognizing the synergistic interaction between calculation, semiotic structure, and socio-emotional dynamics, it is impossible to explain the emergence of the modern concept of revolution—or, I would maintain, the radical transformation of cultural meanings more generally. In some ways this conclusion is one that practitioners of rational choice have heard many times before and are no doubt tired of hearing: that the fundamental failing of the rational choice perspective is its one-dimensional model of the human actor. I am claiming that because human action during the Bastille episode had crucial semiotic and emotional dimensions, an account based solely on the rational calculation of interests cannot generate an adequate explanation. The major difference between my objection to a purely rational choice account and that usually offered is that mine is posed in empirical rather than merely a priori theoretical terms; it offers a concrete explanatory challenge, not just a philosophical objection.

But if previous experience is any guide, practitioners of rational choice may chose to ignore the challenge on another ground. The response I normally get when I object that rational choice falls grievously short in its attempt to explain some important social transformation is a retreat to a certain abstract model of science. Our goal, the answer usually goes, is not to explain every historical case in its fullness. There are always factors at work in any given case that require explanation by other theories than ours. Indeed, a rational choice explanation will never be able to predict the outcomes of a particular case in all its detail; that is a job for (mere) historians or ethnographers. Science is advanced by not by such ideographic detail work but by building a general body of theory that allows us to make predictions across a wide variety of cases. To do so in a fruitful way we need to restrict our focus to a single set of factors that will be present in the widest range of social settings and that can be compared rigorously across the entire range of possible cases. Our inability to explain fully the National Assembly's response to the taking of the Bastille (or any other particular case) is consequently irrelevant to the forward march of our general science.

But the claim I am making is in fact a general one. I am using the case of the taking of the Bastille to argue that rational choice theory, as currently practiced, lacks the conceptual and methodological tools necessary to explain the emergence and transformation of the cultural frameworks within which calculation takes place. I further suggest that it is not likely to develop such tools from within its own intellectual armory, but can do so only by pursuing a much deeper engagement than it has so far undertaken with existing traditions of cultural analysis. For an approach that regards itself as providing general "Foundations of Sociological Theory" (Coleman 1990), this should be a troubling and challenging diagnosis.

⊰ 9 ⊱

HISTORICAL DURATION AND
TEMPORAL COMPLEXITY
The Strange Career of Marseille's Dockworkers, 1814–70

The last two chapters have been concerned with events—brief and intense sequences of social interaction that have long-lasting effects on the subsequent history of social relations. This chapter continues to explore the textures of what I have called eventful temporality, but it looks at what might be regarded as the opposite problem: how structured patterns of social relations, once established, can sometimes be reproduced with very little change over long periods of time, even in eras of considerable historical transformation. The case I have chosen to look at is particularly interesting because the continuities in question—the economic privileges of Marseille's nineteenth-century dockworkers—were a stunning exception to the general pattern of French labor relations in this era and were maintained at the core of the city's most dynamic industry during a period of exceptionally rapid economic growth. Making sense of this case requires us to sort out the relations among several nonsynchronous but overlapping and mutually implicated temporal processes—from the rhythms of daily life on the waterfront, to the complex and contradictory dynamics of nineteenth-century capitalism, to the institutional history of the dockworkers' trade organization, to the discontinuous sequence of French national regime changes.

The dockworkers (*portefaix*) of Marseille certainly constitute an exceptional case in the history of the nineteenth-century French working class.

A version of this chapter was published as "Uneven Development, the Autonomy of Politics, and the Dockworkers of Nineteenth-Century Marseille," in *American Historical Review* 93 (1988): 604–37. Versions of the chapter have been read and critiqued by Geoff Eley, Jan Goldstein, Howard Kimmeldorf, Bill Reddy, and Joan Scott.

French Revolutionary legislation, particularly the D'Allarde law of March 1791 and the Le Chapelier law of June 1791, abolished the corporate or guild forms of organization that had governed labor relations in the eighteenth century, and the Napoleonic penal code criminalized efforts at labor organization. As I have argued at length elsewhere (Sewell 1980), it was nevertheless common for French workers in the first half of the nineteenth century to form illicit organizations. These were sometimes formed under the institutional cover of mutual benefit societies—associations that were legal, indeed encouraged by both the Napoleonic and Restoration regimes, so long as they did not stray from their mutual insurance functions. Like many other working-class trades, Marseille's dockworkers also formed a mutual benefit society. But in this case the society's "trade union" functions were not hidden: indeed the dockworkers' society was organized openly as a continuation of their Old Regime guild. The publicly registered statutes of their society empowered them to place tight restrictions on entry into the trade, to control all work done on the docks in minute detail, and to maintain wages superior not only to those of other unskilled laborers but to those of virtually all skilled craftsmen as well. In a working-class world populated by shadowy, fragmented, and struggling labor organizations constantly subject to official repression, Marseille's dockworker society operated publicly and self-confidently, tolerated for some four decades by both the local political authorities and the merchants who were the dockworkers' employers.

THE TEMPORALITIES OF LABOR HISTORY

It is obvious that any phenomenon so singular must be explained largely by local and particular causes, and most of this chapter will concentrate on the peculiarities of Marseille's history. But I want to explain this admittedly peculiar case in a way that addresses a much wider set of problems. The most general is the problem of social reproduction—the question, evoked in my opening paragraph, of how given patterns of social relations can be reproduced over time even in the context of environing social changes. For most historians and social scientists, reproduction—what historians tend to call "continuity"—hardly requires explanation: we tend to posit a kind of generalized inertia in social life. The argument for inertia sometimes goes beyond mere unstated assumption. Thus Anthony Giddens, synthesizing arguments by Harold Garfinkel, Erving Goffman, and Bruno Bettleheim, argues that the routinization of activities provides what he calls "ontological security," establishing a taken-for-granted background that makes possible stable identities and self-conscious social action (Giddens 1984, 60–92). But positing this general tendency toward routinization cannot explain how and why some patterns remain constant when much around them is in flux. To explain such differences we must identify both the institutional structures that reinforce reproductive actions and the peculiar ecological situations that shield these institutions from the forces that potentially threaten them with erosion, decay, or disassembly. The study of social reproduction, no less than that of eventful social transformations, must examine local contingencies, path dependencies, and structures of the conjuncture. The conceptual apparatus required to explain transformative events is equally necessary for explaining why transformations fail to occur.

The temporality of any real historical sequence is bound to be complex, in the sense of being a particular combination of many different social processes with varying temporalities. It might be useful to classify these multiple temporalities provisionally into three types: trends, routines, and events. *Trends* are directional changes in social relations, the sort of temporalities that historians typically mark by terms like "rise," "fall," "decline," "stagnation," "growth," and the like. In any given situation, there may be several different trends, with different rhythms, which may be causally related (as were economic growth, urban expansion, maritime trade, and in-migration in nineteenth-century Marseille) or may be quite independent of one another (as were the ebb and flow of Royalist sentiments, the crowding of the old port, and the increase of literacy). *Routines* are more-or-less taken for granted activities that tend, other things being equal, to be repeated indefinitely in unchanged ways. There can be routines of office work, conversation, dock labor, religious practice, leisure, cuisine, or politics. Routines, to use the language introduced in chapter 4, are practical schemas that reproduce structures. Institutions in general might be defined as machines for the production and maintenance of routines. *Events*, as should be clear from the previous two chapters, are temporally concentrated sequences of actions that transform structures. This implies that events are likely to establish new routines and change old ones and to accelerate, reverse, or reorient trends.

Any given historical sequence is likely to combine a plethora of trends, routines, and events. The job of the historian—or the historically minded social scientist—is to figure out how these various temporal processes are related to each other within a real historical sequence. The relations can, in principle, go in any direction. Routines may be subject to trends (routines of dock labor may be intensified over time by the crowding of the port) or changed by events (office work becomes much more bureaucratized when large steamship lines replace sailing ships owned by ever-changing groups of partners). Or the performance of routines might, in certain circumstances, produce trends (careful accounting of a business's profits and losses may tend to produce rising wealth; a too-strict adherence to existing routines of production in a period of technological change may lead to the decline of a firm or an industry). Events may establish or revive routines (by, for example, instituting the dockworkers' society) and may reverse trends (as the volatile politics of the Second Republic reversed the rightward drift of dockworker politics). This chapter will attempt to reconstruct the confluence of trends, routines, and events that explain the "strange career" of Marseille's dockworkers.

But the chapter also has ambitions of another sort. In addition to providing a cogent account of what seems to me the fascinating trajectory of an exceptional group of workers, I wish to use the case of the dockworkers to rethink quite general issues about the temporality of nineteenth-century labor history. Labor historians have long assumed that the history they are recounting has an essentially progressive teleological plot. Just as most political history has been written as the story of the rise of nations (Duara 1995), most labor history—including that written by me (Sewell 1980)—tends to be, in the end, about the rise of the labor movement.[1] The specifics of these broadly teleological accounts have varied considerably. Before the early 1960s, most were written within the mold of a rather crude Marxism—what might be called paleomarxism. The rise of capitalism meant the growth of the factory system of production, and the growth of factories meant the expansion of the factory proletariat and therefore the development of radical and class-conscious labor movements. Although labor movements obviously have a rather cyclical or even punctual history—one that depends on, among other things, both business cycles and the complicated conjunctures of politics—the long-term upward path of the labor movement was understood as determined by the inex-

---

1. This is certainly less true today than it was when I published the first version of this chapter. The most important historiographical effect of the sharp decline of labor movements worldwide since the 1970s has been to decrease the output of scholarship in the field and the prominence of the field within the discipline. It has also, however, given rise to some works that probe the weaknesses of labor movements or trace the history of nineteenth-century deindustrialization. See, for nineteenth-century France, Rancière (1981), Liu (1994), and Johnson (1995). For further thoughts on the state of labor history, see Sewell (1993).

orable rise of the factory system. In spite of defeats and setbacks, the workers' movement—in the words of the *Communist Manifesto*, whose vision underlay this paradigm—"ever rises up again, stronger, firmer, mightier" (Marx and Engels [1848] 1948, 18).

It was only with the publication of E. P. Thompson's *The Making of the English Working Class* in 1963 that this factory-centered model of the dynamics of labor history was definitively driven from the field. Thompson was as convinced as any of his predecessors that the rise of a class-conscious labor movement was the effect of capitalist development, but his picture of both capitalist development and its effects were much subtler and more complicated. Thompson's story centered on handicraft workers, both urban artisans and rural "outworkers." He not only catalogued the bewildering diversity of artisan experience, but demonstrated that these trades frequently suffered from intensified capitalist exploitation during the early nineteenth century even when they were not transformed by factory production. He also recounted how handicraft workers responded to such exploitation with various forms of labor and political militancy. Subsequent research all across Europe and North America has tended to confirm both aspects of Thompson's findings. Artisans formed the vanguard of the nineteenth-century labor movement nearly everywhere, and it was far from rare for artisans' working conditions to be degraded by the multifarious penetration of capitalism—in the form of increasing division of labor, substitution of unskilled for skilled workers in certain phases of the production process, the development of sweatshops or urban putting-out networks, exploitative forms of subcontracting, and so on.[2]

Between the 1960s and the 1980s, labor historians massively shifted their focus from the "dark, satanic mill" to the artisan's workshop.[3] Yet their underlying temporal assumptions changed surprisingly little from the reductionist and teleological model that had prevailed before the publication of Thompson's masterpiece. Although it was no longer possible to see

2. Work on French artisans that explores this problem includes Johnson (1971, 1975, 1979), Aminzade (1979 and 1981, esp. chap. 2), Cottereau (1980), and Faure (1977). For a similar argument about nineteenth-century American workers, see Wilenz (1984).

3. Moreover, labor historians who have studied factory workers and coal miners in recent years have found that these seemingly paradigmatic proletarians were by no means the regimented and uniformly exploited masses posited by the classic account; they formed tightly knit, kin-based communities, they prized their skills, maintained remarkable workplace autonomy, and their relations with employers often took the form of commercial subcontracting rather than straightforward wage labor. See, esp. Reddy (1984) and Harrison (1978).

the rise of the labor movement as an automatic outgrowth of factory industry, the temporality of the old account was often carried over into the
new. As I have argued elsewhere (Sewell 1993, 17–19), this transfer has
been accomplished largely by means of the slippery notion of "proletarianization," which includes under one rubric all changes that decrease workers' control over the process of production. Labor historians have tended
to think of proletarianization as a pervasive, ever-rising master process of
capitalism and to attribute all upsurges of labor radicalism to it. The concept is defined so broadly that some sign of its presence can be found virtually everywhere in the nineteenth century—the growth of factories
here, sweatshops there, exploitative subcontracting in another trade, intensified divisions of labor in a third, the displacement of skilled work by
machinery in yet another. Because these various indices of proletarianization are so widespread, it may seem reasonable to conclude that this process is capable of explaining labor radicalism wherever it appears.

Yet on closer inspection the process of proletarianization was far from
universal. That it may seem so is partly an artifact of labor historians' procedures of research, which necessarily over-represent situations in which
workers were actively resisting capitalist impositions. We tend to learn
about labor relations in a trade mainly at times of strife—above all when
there are strikes or other forms of labor unrest that catch the interest of
the document-generating authorities or the press. Hence we get the impression that workers' wages and conditions of work were always under attack. But this is largely because we have little evidence for the periods,
sometimes very long periods, when trades experienced labor peace.

Single trade case studies, such as Christopher Johnson's pioneering
article (1975) on French tailors in the first half of the nineteenth century,
have shown that the piecemeal proletarianization undergone by artisans
could be economically devastating and have powerfully radicalizing consequences. But no study of a single trade can make the general case for the
importance of proletarianization. If proletarianization resulting from capitalist penetration were truly the major cause of artisan militancy, it should
be the case that militants were drawn above all from trades being degraded
by capitalist penetration. Yet as far as I know, this relationship has never
been systematically demonstrated. Indeed, the contrary can be shown for
the case of Marseille during and after the Revolution of 1848, where politically radical workers were drawn not only from degraded trades but also
from trades that had been essentially unaffected by capitalist penetration
and even those that had been privileged by capitalist development. The

trades most severely affected by capitalist penetration in Marseille in the first half of the nineteenth century were the tailors and the shoemakers. Both had rates of participation in the revolutionary movement that were slightly above the average of Marseille's skilled workers. But their radicalism was distinctly surpassed by that of bakers, housepainters, and stonecutters, whose trades seem to have been largely unaffected by capitalist penetration, and by machinists, whose scarce and avidly sought-for skills made them among the most privileged workers in the city.[4] The case of Marseille suggests that the real effects of capitalist development in the nineteenth century were probably so various that they created no path of working-class economic experience sufficiently general to account adequately for the broad artisan revolts that occurred.

Although I am critical of the implicitly paleomarxist temporal assumptions underlying the proletarianization argument, my own conception of the temporality of capitalism is itself thoroughly Marxian.[5] As I see it, capitalist society has a fundamental dynamic, which I would characterize as the relentless accumulation of capital through the pursuit of profit for profit's sake. But the dynamic of capital accumulation does not generate smooth or steadily "progressive" historical changes; rather, it produces temporal patterns that are contradictory, conflictual, cyclical, and chronically crisis-prone. Specifically, I see capitalist temporality as characterized by *uneven development*. This concept was initially used by Lenin and Trotsky to make sense of the deviations of backward Russia from the supposedly orderly sequence of Western European development. Trotsky (1932) insisted that Russia experienced both uneven and *combined* development: that is, it had modern, technologically advanced large-scale industries side by side with an utterly archaic peasant economy. Indeed, according to Trotsky, it was the particular mixtures resulting from combined development that gave Russia its explosive revolutionary potential. The notion of uneven development has been used widely in Marxian thought, particularly in discussions of national patterns of economic development and underdevelopment. But it can equally well be applied to differences be-

4. These conclusions are drawn from quantitative data on persons arrested for participating in the insurrection that took place in Marseille in June 1848, and on those rounded up as dangerous revolutionaries after Louis Napoleon's coup d'état in December 1851 The documents from which these figures were derived may be found in the Archives Départementales des Bouches-du-Rhône (hereafter, ADBdR): M6/137; M6/100. Analyses of these data are in Sewell (1974b and 1974c, esp. 115–16). On Marseille's shoemakers, see Sewell (1980, 176–77).

5. Two works that have influenced my thinking about this questions are Harvey (1982) and Postone (1993).

tween sectors or regions within a nation or even to different processes within the same industry.[6] I believe that the temporalities of nineteenth-century labor history can be significantly illuminated by a suitably adapted version of the concept.

Although the abstract logic of capitalist development is always the same, opportunities for the pursuit of profit vary enormously over time and space and evolve historically as the capitalist economy itself evolves. It is notorious that capitalist development proceeds not by uniform incremental growth and innovation in all economic sectors or industries simultaneously but by industry-specific spurts: booms in cotton textiles, or shipping, or railroad development, or automobile manufacture, or microelectronics, or financial services. Even within the booming industries, innovation and dynamism rarely affect all processes at once: the timing of innovation was different in cotton spinning than in cotton weaving, in manufacture of locomotives than in manufacture of sleeping cars. One of the consequences of this unevenness has been a species of combined development in the labor force. Growth in the dynamic sector often creates new, highly mechanized, classically "proletarian" industrial specialties, but it also inevitably stimulates employment in less technologically advanced auxiliary sectors, either preexisting or new. The rise of factory spinning multiplies the numbers of both handloom weavers and field slaves; the development of the locomotive calls forth hordes of navvies; automobile factories give rise to repair shops, taxi drivers, and filling stations; computers create keypunch operators and programmers. In nineteenth-century conditions, the establishment of any kind of factory industry inevitably led to a multiplication of handicraft workers whose techniques were slow to change: masons, stonecutters, carpenters, and joiners to build the factories; builders, tailors, shoemakers, butchers, and bakers to house, clothe, and feed their workers. The most advanced techniques developed hand in hand with the most archaic.

In adapting the concepts of uneven and combined development to questions of nineteenth-century labor history, I am following the lead of Raphael Samuel, who employed these terms in his remarkable essay "Workshop of the World: Steam Power and Hand Technology in Mid-Victorian Britain" (1977). Samuel documented in staggering detail the intimate cohabitation of new mechanical techniques, old handicraft skills, and backbreaking manual labor. He did not, however, exploit the possibil-

6. David Harvey (1982), for example, uses it in these ways.

ity for rethinking the temporality of labor history that was implicit in his terminology. He was concerned above all to demonstrate that the advance of machinery in mid-Victorian Britain also meant a concomitant increase in physical toil. In this respect Samuel's article reproduces on its novel terrain the familiar linear paleomarxist conception of capitalism's temporality. Samuel's claim that mechanization could increase toil is not so much wrong as one-sided; what it fails to recognize is that uneven development also created (and continues to create) significant pockets of privilege in the working class. The famous "golden age of the handloom weavers" is an early and obvious example. Weavers had high wages and enviable working conditions in the twenty years or so between the development of machine spinning and the general adoption of the power loom. The flood of cheap machine-spun yarns caused a sharp decline in finished cloth prices, which caused a prodigious expansion in the demand for cloth, which in turn caused a scarcity of the as yet irreplaceable labor of weavers. Their earnings consequently stayed high until the power loom destroyed their temporary advantage. The case of the handloom weavers has been recreated again and again in the history of capitalism, with infinite variations, from the mule-spinners of mid-nineteenth-century Lancashire, to the skilled engineers of the nineteenth-century machine industry, to the computer programmers of Silicon Valley. Such pockets of privilege are not permanent; they may last for a few years or for several decades, but the unpredictable lurches of capitalist development eventually wipe them out. However, the same lurches that destroy privileged job sectors may also create new ones. Capitalist development does not result, as Samuel's account seems to imply, in a relentless increase in toil. Instead, its effect on the labor force has been a widely varied, continually changing, kaleidoscopic mixture of exploitation and privilege.

The history of Marseille's dockworkers in the nineteenth century illustrates with particular clarity how the uneven development intrinsic to capitalism could create, and in time destroy, a privileged category of workers. From 1815 to the 1850s, booming maritime capitalism, combined with unchanging technical and organizational conditions on the docks, raised the dockworkers from obscurity to a position unique not only in Marseille but possibly in all of France. Then, in the course of a few years, a capitalist reorganization of waterfront work destroyed the dockworkers' niche, reducing them to little more than unskilled laborers. Although the position of Marseille's dockworkers was unusual, then, their story traces out a broad pattern that has been repeated over and over during the history of capital-

ism. But if the broad pattern is repeated over and over, each instance of the
pattern is unique, surprising, and unpredictable. The lurches of capitalist
development and the patterns of privilege and devastation they leave in
their wake must always be explained historically. That is to say, we must
use the tools of historical analysis to reconstruct the complex articulations
of trends, routines, and events—unique in each case we examine—that
sustain or undermine profitability, construct more or less durable ecological niches, advantage one sector of capital or labor over another, create
new opportunities for profitable investment, forge political protections for
certain forms of enterprise, or otherwise shape and reshape the field of
production and exchange. I find the concept of uneven development attractive precisely because it indicates that what I am calling the logics of
history—fatefulness, contingency, complexity, eventfulness, and causal
heterogeneity—are no less applicable to the history of labor, the economy,
or capitalism than to history of any other kind.

I have set two goals for this chapter: to explore the problem of social
reproduction in an environment of change and to develop an empirically
based critique of the reigning concepts of temporality in labor history. The
goals are intellectually distinct. But both depend on an analysis of the same
complex temporalities that are braided together in the dockworkers' history. The dockworkers' ability to sustain their privileged position is incomprehensible except as an outcome of the specific trends, events, and
routines that made their detailed control over work on the docks acceptable to Marseille's merchants and municipal authorities. But, from another
perspective, it is the same combination of trends, events, and routines that
made their relation to capitalist production and exchange divergent from
the norm, that constituted Marseille's waterfront as a site of unevenness in
the context of the French and European economy. If the two intellectual
goals of this chapter remain distinct, attaining either of them is possible
only by means of a close analysis of the contingent but patterned history
of work on Marseille's docks. It is to that analysis that we now turn.

THE DOCKWORKERS' GOLDEN AGE

Marseille's dockworkers (*portefaix*) were a sufficiently extraordinary case
that they were much remarked on by local authorities and other observers,
especially during their own "golden age" in the 1840s and 1850s.[7] It is there-

---

7. The dispute in the late 1850s and early 1860s that eventually destroyed the dockworkers'
privileged position generated tracts and police files now kept in the ADBdR. The dockworkers'

fore easier to write their history than those of most nineteenth-century working-class trades. Nevertheless, the documentation, however ample for some purposes, is extremely scarce for others. This chapter, like most "history from the bottom up," contains a good deal of hypothetical reconstruction based on scattered, diverse, and fragmentary evidence. It should be noted that at certain absolutely crucial points, the argument depends entirely on quantitative data derived from an extensive analysis of Marseille's marriage registers. The chapter therefore additionally illustrates the value of the quantitative techniques developed by social historians in the 1960s and 1970s and generally abandoned by more recent cultural history—even in an argument whose overall style is far more interpretive than positivist. Because the evidence is so incomplete, it seems best to begin with a portrait of the dockworkers in the 1840s and 1850s, which can be based on relatively complete documentation, and work backward into the earlier and more obscure decades.

Perhaps the most obvious indication of the dockworkers' privileged position at mid-century was their wage level. Estimates of dockworkers' earnings dating from the 1840s range from four to five-and-a-half francs a day. Dockworkers were actually paid on a piecework basis, so the earnings might in fact vary considerably around these sums. Because work on the docks was subject to periodic unemployment (when, for example, there were slumps in trade or the direction of the winds made it impossible for sailing ships to enter the port), these figures cannot simply be multiplied by the standard six-day week to derive an average weekly wage. But even taking unemployment into account, dockworkers were among the best-paid workers in the city. Their earnings were at least twice those of other

society was also studied in some detail during this period by two social investigators: Audiganne (1860, 2:265–68), and Laurent (1865, 2:547–52). For earlier decades, the evidence is sparser but still better than for most other trades. Particularly useful are the papers of the mayor's office from the Restoration period (1814–30), which are preserved in series I of the Archives de la Ville de Marseille (hereafter, AVM). The late Victor Nguyen's Diplôme d'Études Superieur (1961) is an excellent study of the dockworkers. Unfortunately, only the final portion of this diplôme, less interesting for my purposes than the earlier portions, has been published (Nguyen 1962). Although I differ with Nguyen on a number of points, I have learned a great deal from his work, as my footnotes in this article will testify. I also learned much about both the history of Marseille and the mysteries of its archives from many hours of conversation with him in 1967 and 1968 when I was carrying out my own dissertation research. More recent studies include Cornu (1974, 1999) and Claverie (1999). Particularly valuable is Gontier (1988), which systematically mines various "literary" sources on the dockworkers, carries out a painstaking analysis of the dockworkers' society's changing regulations, and carefully reconstructs the geography and organization of Marseille's port.

men engaged in heavy manual labor—for example, ditchdiggers or masons' laborers—and were well above those of most artisans, who usually received between three and three-and-a-half francs a day. In fact, dockworkers' wages were matched only by such highly skilled workers as glassblowers, shipwrights, machinists, watchmakers, and printers.[8] These high wages were maintained in part by strict limitations on entry into dockworking. It was very difficult to become a dockworker unless one's father already practiced the trade. Among dockworkers who were married in 1846 or 1851, no fewer than 70 percent were dockworkers' sons. This was by far the highest rate of inheritance of any occupation in the city, working-class or bourgeois; the next five occupations were fishermen with 58 percent, ropemakers with 47, tilemakers with 46, tanners with 43, and *négociants* or wholesale merchants (the top bourgeois occupation) with 42. The average rate for all occupations was only 23 percent.[9] These figures make it clear that the dockworkers' lucrative trade was a kind of hereditary possession for their families.

The dockworkers' high earnings and high level of occupational inheritance would have been impossible without a powerful labor organization. As I have already noted, the dockworkers were organized openly and unabashedly. Their "Society of Saint Peter and Saint Paul and of Our Lady of Mercy" was authorized by local officials in 1817, shortly after the defeat of Napoleon and the restoration of the Bourbon monarchy. Officially a mutual benefit society, it was actually a reconstitution of the dockworkers' guild from the Old Regime. The guild dated back at least to the end of the fourteenth century, but its statutes were first written down in 1704. These had been amended in 1789, just before the French Revolution; the statutes of 1814, in turn, were an amended version of those of 1789.[10] In 1814, members of the old guild and their sons could join the mutual aid society by paying a nominal fee of eight francs, while all other applicants had to pay eighty francs, a sum equivalent to better than a month's wages for most manual workers (AVM: 1 I 1/35, 1370). These entry fees were the same as

8. Wage figures for all these trades are available in *Travaux* (1837–73, 4:52–53; 5:346–47; 9:72–73), and in "Enquête sur le travail agricole et industriel," Archives Nationales: C 947.

9. These figures are based on a computer-aided analysis of Marseille's marriage registers from 1821–22, 1846, 1851, and 1869 (AVM, series 201 E). The marriage registers indicate the occupations of both bridegrooms and their fathers. For a thorough discussion of these data, see Sewell (1985b, esp. 317–19). This quantitative research was supported by a National Science Foundation Grant SOC 72-05249-AO 1.

10. The statutes of 1789 and 1817 are available in AVM: 1 I 1/35, 1370. See also Zanzi (1969, 4–7), and Laurent (1865, 2:458–59).

in the Old Regime corporation. In 1841, when the society's statutes were revised again, the entry fee charged for non-dockworkers' sons was increased to the impossible sum of a thousand francs.[11] Besides erecting these high financial barriers to admission, the dockworkers' society could simply refuse membership to men who attempted to enter, even if they could pay the fee.

Restrictions on entry into the dockworkers' society also meant restrictions on entry into the trade, for the society maintained a monopoly over the loading and unloading of ships in Marseille's harbor. Under the Old Regime, members of the guild had the exclusive privilege of carrying a special dockworkers' sack, and any man who worked on the docks without this mark of membership could be fined one hundred livres. This practice lost its legal standing after the Revolution, but it continued to be strictly observed. In fact, the 1817 statutes of the dockworkers' society included as one of its regulations that "only dockworkers admitted into the society have the right to carry the sack" (AVM: 1 I 1/35, 1370). Until the 1860s, it was impossible to work on the docks of Marseille without being a member of the dockworkers' society and carrying the identifying sack (Laurent 1865, 2:548–49).

The Society of Saint Peter and Saint Paul and of Our Lady of Mercy had a much more elaborate formal organization than most nineteenth-century mutual aid societies, more elaborate, in fact, than many eighteenth-century guilds. It had a Grand Conseil of sixty members that set general policy and a Petit Conseil of twelve that managed its day-to-day business. The Petit Conseil was responsible, for example, for organizing celebrations on the festival day of Saints Peter and Paul, with masses, processions, and acts of charity. The Petit Conseil was composed of six "visitors of the sick" and six "priors" (prieurs). The visitors of the sick were charged with administering the society's generous benefits, which amounted to six francs a week plus doctors' fees and medications in cases of sickness and five francs a week in retirement benefits for men who had worked on the docks for thirty years or more. To finance these benefits, the society required its members to pay 3 percent of their earnings as dues.[12] By 1852, the society had holdings of 232,666 francs, placed in various banks and in municipal bonds (Nguyen 1961, 14–15).

11. Laurent (1865, 2:549–50); Nguyen (1961, 15). A thousand francs amounted to an entire year's earnings for a skilled worker.

12. These are the provisions in the statutes of 1817. They were modified slightly in 1853. The 1853 statutes, which were printed together with a reproduction of the statutes of 1817, are available in ADBdR: XIV M 25/1.

The priors were responsible for all affairs of the society connected with work on the docks: mediating disputes between teams of dockworkers or between dockworkers and merchants, making sure that teams were not competing with one another so as to drive down wages, and above all ensuring that only members of the society were employed on the waterfront.[13] The priors also administered an institution known as "La Muse." Dockworkers who were not members of a regular team, or whose team had no job on a given day, would report to the Muse, where they were placed on a register in order of appearance, to be given daily work as it became available. Any job not being handled by a regular team had to be channeled through the Muse, and in certain categories of work, for example the unloading of grains, half the dockworkers hired for the job had to come from the Muse (Gontier 1988, 30). By means of the Muse, the dockworkers' society was able to apportion equitably the available work and to cushion its members against unemployment.[14] Finally, the priors were responsible for overseeing the nature and techniques of work. The society was resolutely opposed to any technical innovations, and in 1853 it adopted a regulation formally banning all wheeled vehicles from the docks, prescribing that all burdens be carried on the dockworkers' backs (ADBdR: XIV M 25/1). The society not only had a monopoly of work on the docks, it also determined how the work was to be done and, through its priors, enforced its own regulations. Its control of work was virtually absolute.

In the 1840s and 1850s, then, the dockworkers enjoyed an enviable position. Not only were they extremely well paid but they had unmatched job security, a workable pension plan, and an equitable system of allocating work during periods of unemployment. Their elaborately organized society was tolerated by the authorities, and by means of their society the dockworkers themselves controlled the organization and pace of their work, kept interlopers off the docks, and saw to it that good wages and working conditions were maintained. Moreover, dockworkers knew they could pass all these advantages on to their sons. By comparison with almost any other workers in Marseille, or in France for that matter, the dockworkers had a very comfortable situation.

---

13. AVM: 1 I 1/35, 1370; ADBdR: XIV M 25/I; Nguyen (1961, 14–15).

14. AVM: 1 I 1/35, 1370; ADBdR: XIV M 25/1; Gontier (1988, 30–33); Nguyen (1961, 16); Laurent (1865, 2:549).

ESTABLISHING AND REPRODUCING PRIVILEGE

The privileges of the dockworkers' society were firmly institutionalized—transformed into a network of reproducible routines—in the first years of the Restoration. But the reproduction of these privileges did not guarantee prosperity immediately; they became genuinely lucrative only when the long capitalist boom of the second quarter of the nineteenth century quickened the activity of Marseille's port. The dockworkers' "golden age," that is to say, resulted from the specific combination of a set of institutionalized routines with a long-term trend. And the initial institutionalization was the consequence of an event: the Bourbon Restoration. The dockworkers' society was established by a provisional decree of the Marquis d'Albertas, the prefect of the Bouches-du-Rhône, in 1814, only a few months after the restoration of the Bourbon monarchy. The statutes of the society were then officially approved in 1817 by the Marquis de Montgrand, mayor of Marseille. Unfortunately, the precise dynamics of this founding event remain obscure; existing documents do not make entirely clear the reasons for d'Albertas's and de Montgrand's support of the dockworkers. It was, of course, far from rare for officials of the Restoration to have sympathy for Old Regime guilds, which were viewed by many conservatives as a means of maintaining deference and discipline among the lower orders. But the Restoration's official policy was to maintain economically liberal Revolutionary and Napoleonic legislation, and no wholesale reestablishment of the guilds was undertaken. Indeed, no other trade in Marseille was treated even remotely like the dockworkers, and few, if any, were so treated elsewhere in France. From both a national and a local perspective, the dockworkers' society was an anomaly. Official sanction for its statutes would have been impossible to obtain had not the authorities regarded the dockworkers' and their association as somehow exceptional.

In fact, when de Montgrand proposed official approval of the dockworkers' statutes in 1817, the Comte de Villeneuve-Bargement, d'Albertas's successor as prefect, questioned their legality. De Montgrand, who was the dockworkers' principal patron from 1814 until he resigned from office after the July Revolution in 1830, managed to overcome the prefect's misgivings. In a letter of September 29, 1817, he claimed—implausibly, it must be said—that even under the Old Regime the dockworkers' association had not had "the character of a privileged corporation"; its statutes had been "purely the result of measures of public interest decreed . . . for the maintenance of an order necessary among the men of that profession." These reasons were as valid in 1817 as they had been before the French Revolution; the society's regulations would maintain "a discipline extremely favorable to tranquility, to public order, to the observation of principles of honesty and fidelity indispensable to the interests of commerce." Moreover, de Montgrand argued, regulations analogous to the proposed statutes of Marseille's dockworkers existed for work "on the quays and in the ports" of cities all over France. He even procured a copy of the recently enacted statutes of the dockworkers of Nantes to illustrate this argument. The Nantes statutes, however, were in fact far from comparable. They established no dockworkers' society with the power to limit entry into the occupation or to police the docks, and the mayor of Nantes prefaced the regulations governing dock work with this statement: "It is not possible, according to the principles of current laws, to accord to [the dockworkers] an exclusive privilege for the work in question." The Nantes statutes actually indicate how extraordinary the Marseille dockworkers' association was—although recent research seems to indicate that it was by no means rare for municipal governments in port cities to establish some sort of regulation of work on the docks.[15] Finally, de Montgrand argued that approving the statutes would have the additional benefit of assuring the dockworkers' loyalty to the new monarchical regime. "I will not speak, Monsieur le Comte, of the essential advantage there is for authority, from the political point of view, of keeping under a regular dependence, by its direct action on the heads of the association, a so numerous mass of men whose lapses or movements could in many circumstances be very disquieting" (AVM: 1 I 1/35).

But this political advantage was actually incidental to the central point. Dock work, de Montgrand implied, had a special public character that distinguished it from other trades, and it was therefore acceptable for the municipality to approve regulations that ensured its orderly performance. De Montgrand never spelled out exactly what made the dockworkers different from other workers. Perhaps it is that they worked outdoors, in a public

---

15. Barzman (1999, 59) indicates that the municipality of Le Havre in the 1820s maintained a list of three different categories of dockworkers, designated specific locations where they were to be hired, and saw to it that only those on the lists could work on the docks. These practices seem to have been suppressed with the coming of the more openly liberal July Monarchy in 1830. Pigenet (2004) speaks of the labor regime on the docks in French ports of the first half of the nineteenth century as characterized by a "veiled guild system" (258). His evidence, however, seems to come almost exclusively from Marseille and Le Havre. I have seen no evidence to date that other ports had dockworkers' organizations with anything approaching the elaborateness or power of Marseille's dockworkers' society.

space controlled by the municipality, rather than in enclosed, private spaces subject to the private discipline of the proprietor or entrepreneur. This might make it seem that the regulation of dock work was a simple exercise of the municipality's police authority.[16] But it was certainly extraordinary, in the nineteenth century, to delegate such police authority to the dock-workers' organization, making it—like the old regime guilds—a kind of semipublic institution. The dockworkers' society, under Old Regime and new, was expected to perform certain public functions for the municipality. It was required by its statutes, both in 1789 and in 1817, to constitute itself as an emergency fire brigade at the command of the municipality (ADBdR: XIV M 25/1; AVM: 1 I 1/35). During the eighteenth century, the dockworkers' corporation had frequently been called in by the municipality to help maintain order, for example, in 1777 during an official visit of Louis XVI's brother, in 1781 to guard the door of the cathedral during a mass celebrating the birth of the Dauphin, in 1784 during a balloon launching, and in 1789 after the pillaging of the house of a tax farmer (Zanzi 1969, 39–40).

In any case, the dockworkers' society was treated very differently from associations organized by other groups of workers, either in Marseille or elsewhere—whose attempts to limit entry into the trade, to control the nature and pace of work, or to maintain wage levels had to be carried on in secret. De Montgrand approved the charter of the dockworkers' society, defended it against the prefect, and was deeply involved in the day-to-day administration of its affairs—intervening in disputes about work, fines, and expulsions.[17] During his tenure, de Montgrand seems to have regarded the dockworkers' society almost as an auxiliary branch of the municipal government, one subject to his continual and benevolent oversight. There is little doubt that de Montgrand's actions, as the Comte de Villeneuve-Bargemont suspected, violated the spirit and the letter of the law, and in the end there is no way of knowing why de Montgrand showered such favor on the dockworkers. But the dockworkers certainly took full advantage of his patronage.

This persistent support of the municipality enabled the dockworkers' society to establish itself firmly—indeed, to all intents legally—on the waterfront. Institutionally, the dockworkers' society seems to have functioned as effectively in the 1820s as it later did during the dockworkers' golden age

---

16. Pigenet (1988, 258) implies that the authorities in Le Havre reasoned in this way.
17. See the mayor's correspondence in AVM: 1 I 1/36.

in the 1840s and 1850s. Although dockworkers seem to have been involved
in more disputes with other transport workers in the 1810s and 1820s than
in succeeding decades, they successfully maintained their monopoly against
all challenges. No satisfactory figures on wages are available for the early
decades, but what evidence there is indicates that the piece-rates paid to
dockworkers were essentially the same in the late 1810s as at mid-century.[18]
The marriage registers of the early 1820s show that the occupation of
dockworker had been passed from father to son at essentially the same
high rate in the 1820s as at mid-century. Dockworkers who were married
in 1821 or 1822 were sons of dockworkers in 73 percent of the cases—as at
mid-century, the highest rate of inheritance of any occupation in the city.
In all these respects, the dockworkers' control over their trade seems to
have been as solid in the 1820s as it was in the 1840s or 1850s.

Even with all these advantages, dockworkers seem to have been far less
prosperous in the late 1810s and the 1820s than they became in subsequent
decades. During the French Revolution and the Napoleonic period, dockworkers had been decimated by the effects of maritime war and blockade,
which had cut the traffic of the port to a trickle. Even after the revival of
maritime commerce in the 1820s, their situation was by no means splendid. It was only the long capitalist upswing of the French and European
economies during the second quarter of the nineteenth century that made
possible the prosperity of the 1840s and 1850s. Between 1821 and 1851, the
population of Marseille nearly doubled, and the traffic of the port more
than doubled, with the precise figure varying according to the method of
estimation.[19] This prodigious growth in port traffic is traced in figure 1.
The spectacular rise before the crisis of the late 1840s was a consequence
of several factors: an absence of general European wars, an expansion of
world trade, the development of industry in Marseille, in France, and in
the rest of Europe, and improvements in communications from Marseille
to the inland of France.[20]

18. Nguyen (1961, 28) found fragments of piece-rate schedules for various grains, which indicate that rates had risen by no more than 10 percent between 1818 and 1853.

19. The population of Marseille increased from 109,485 in 1821 to 195,135 in 1851 (Sewell
1985b, 147). The amount of customs duties paid in the port of Marseille rose by 178 percent from
1817–21 to 1847–51; the carrying capacity of ships entering the port rose by 121 percent from 1825–
29 (the first years for which these figures are available) to 1847–51. The choice of different starting and ending points for such comparisons would result in somewhat different figures, but
nearly all estimates indicate something between a doubling and tripling of maritime commerce
from the early 1820s to the late 1840s. The figures are derived from Julliany (1842, 1:145, 162),
Bousquet and Sapet (1857, 25–29), and *Travaux* (1837–73, 1:70; 19:92).

20. For a fuller discussion of the growth of maritime commerce, see Sewell (1985b, 18–23).

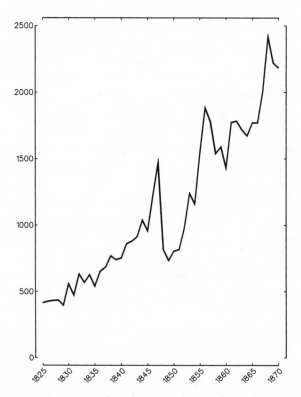

Figure 1. Carrying capacity of vessels entering the port of Marseille, 1825–70, in thousand tons. Adapted from William H. Sewell Jr., *Structure and Mobility: The Men and Women of Marseille, 1820–1870* (Cambridge: Cambridge University Press, 1985).

One would expect this rapid increase in the activity of the port to have brought about an equivalent rise in the number of dockworkers. But that was not the case. There are no really satisfactory figures for the number of dockworkers employed in the city before the middle of the nineteenth century, but a rough estimate of changes in the size of the labor force can be derived from figures for the number of dockworkers who married in a given year.[21] This figure averaged thirty-nine per year in 1821 and 1822, and

21. The normally relatively accurate "Enquête sur le travail agricole et industriel" estimates (Archives Nationales: C 947) put the number of dockworkers at mid-century at 2,500, whereas the far more accurate figures derived from a sample of every tenth household in the census of 1851 indicate only 1,530. This remarkable overestimate, which I suspect was supplied to the Chamber of Commerce's investigators by the dockworkers' society, should make one wary of accepting any contemporary estimates not based on solid figures of some kind. There are, unfortunately, no census figures giving occupation before 1851. Under these circumstances, figures from the marriage registers seem the best alternative. The number of men in a given occupation who were married

remained essentially unchanged, at an average of thirty-seven per year, in 1846 and 1851. Thus, in a period when the amount of labor to be done approximately doubled, the number of dockworkers available to do it seems to have remained essentially constant. These figures indicate an enormous change in the market for dockworkers' labor, one that, according to conventional economic theory, should have resulted in a steep rise in wage rates. Yet the evidence, which admittedly is thin, indicates no important rise in the piece-rates paid to dockworkers in this period. What the available evidence suggests is a quite different development but one no less favorable to the dockworkers.

By all reports, Marseille's dockworkers were able to handle the volume of goods that entered the port in the 1840s without relaxing either restrictions on entry into their society or control over work on the docks. This implies that there must have been a good deal of slack twenty or thirty years earlier, when the same number of men were handling only half as much work. If unemployment and underemployment were common in the 1820s and early 1830s, the main effect of the sustained commercial expansion on Marseille's dockworkers may not have been to increase wage rates but rather to increase the level of employment—by increasing either hours of labor, intensity of labor, or both. Since dockworkers were paid at fixed piece-rates, the result of any of these increases in employment should have been a proportional rise in their earnings. Evidence bearing on this question is both extremely scarce and indirect, but most of it is compatible with the hypothesis of a constant labor force whose level of employment rose substantially over time.

The first piece of evidence—hardly conclusive—is literary in nature. It derives from the memoirs of Victor Gelu, a writer and singer of Provençal songs, who was born in a popular quarter of Marseille in 1806. As a young man in the middle 1820s, Gelu spent much of his leisure time with young worker friends. Dockworkers were especially prominent among his drinking companions. When he was looking for entertainment, Gelu would stroll down to his neighborhood barbershop, which had a back room where young men gathered to talk, drink, and gamble. There he was always sure of finding plenty of dockworkers temporarily out of work; according to Gelu, this particular barbershop had so many dockworkers that it "had

depends on a number of factors besides the total number employed in the occupation, such as the age structure of the trade, changes in the age at marriage or the rate of marriage, and so on. Nevertheless, this statistic is probably accurate enough to provide a rough estimate of the magnitude of change in the size of an occupation over time.

become almost a branch office of the Muse" (Gelu 1971, 143). From Gelu's account, it would appear that days of unemployment were a normal experience of dockworkers, or at least of young dockworkers, in the 1820s.

The second piece of evidence—suggestive but not much more conclusive than the first—is the pattern of contestation on the docks. The period of the largest number of disputes seems to have been the late 1810s and the early 1820s, and, from what little we know of these disputes, they usually involved the problem of unemployment in some way. Thus, in 1819 and 1821, the dockworkers protested that sailors were being used to unload ships, thereby depriving them of work; in 1824, dockworkers who were registered at the Muse complained to the priors that some of the masters were bypassing the Muse and taking on new men of their own choice. Throughout the period, there were troubles between dockworkers and *robeirols*—laborers who waited around on street corners, ready to undertake assorted carrying tasks (Nguyen 1961, 19–22; AVM: 1 I 1/36). In principle, these robeirols were easily distinguishable from dockworkers by the baskets they wore on their backs for carrying their loads.[22] This pattern of frequent disputes involving issues of employment in the 1820s was followed by a virtual absence of disputes in the 1830s and 1840s fits the hypothesis of initially high levels of unemployment, followed by increasingly full employment in the 1830s and 1840s. One might have expected a rather different pattern had the rise in demand for dockworkers' labor been met mainly by changes in wage rates. In such circumstances, one might have expected relative quiescence in the early period, when high unemployment rates would have put workers in a weak bargaining position, and increasing contestation over wage levels as the workers took advantage of their increasing relative scarcity to force a rise in their rates.

The third piece of evidence—in my opinion, somewhat more conclusive than the other two—concerns changes in the number of workers employed in other heavy transportation trades. Although the number of dockworkers appearing on the marriage registers remained constant, the number of men identifying themselves as "carters" or "loaders" rose very sharply, from only fifteen per year in the early 1820s to fifty-three per year at mid-century. If these carters and loaders are added to the thirty-nine and then thirty-seven dockworkers, the rise in transportation workers as a whole was from fifty-four in the early 1820s to ninety at mid-century, not

22. This requirement that robeirols wear the *pallier* was written into the statutes of the dockworkers' society in 1817. ADBdR: XIV M 25/1.

Table 1. Number of Transport Workers Marrying

	1821–22	1846–51	1869	increase 1821–22 to 1846–51	increase 1846–51 to 1869
Dockworkers marrying per year	39	37	49	–6%	+32%
Other transport workers marrying per year	15	53	78	+253%	+47%
Total	54	90	127	+67%	+41%

as steep as the rise in the traffic of the port but not far behind (see table 1). These figures seem to indicate a major change in the division of labor between the privileged dockworkers and the distinctly unprivileged loaders and carters.[23]

I have been able to find no direct evidence about division of labor in the transportation trades. However, two hypotheses suggest themselves, one concerning changes in the work done by dockworkers and the other concerning changes in the work done by carters and loaders. According to the first hypothesis, in the 1820s, dockworkers may have been supplementing the earnings they gained from loading and unloading ships by engaging in assorted other carrying and hauling jobs that they picked up on a day-labor basis. Hence, as the traffic of the port rose in the 1830s and 1840s, they would have concentrated their efforts exclusively on the high-paying work of loading and unloading ships, leaving less lucrative carrying work to loaders and carters. The second hypothesis would suggest that dockworkers may not have engaged in other transportation labor even in the 1820s but that, as the volume of goods to be unloaded rose in the later 1830s and 1840s, they found ways to employ carters and loaders as auxiliary workers on the docks under the close supervision and control of the dockworkers' society, perhaps in moving goods to warehouses or to different locations on the docks or to warehouses elsewhere in the city once they had been unloaded from ships by dockworkers.[24] This arrangement would have

23. The dockworkers and the carters and loaders were from distinct social origins. Only 37 percent of the carters and loaders who married in Marseille in 1846 and 1851 had been born in Marseille, as against 89 percent of the dockworkers. Forty-one percent of the carters and loaders were sons of agriculturalists and 29 percent sons of unskilled workers.

24. This might explain a remark in the journal of the utopian socialist Flora Tristan, who briefly visited Marseille during her "tour de France" in 1844. She claimed that dockworkers who had contracted for a job would sometimes employ female Italian laborers, whom they could pay at exploitative rates, to do the actual carrying. Tristan denounced this profiteering as "white slavery" and as a prime example of "the exploitation of man by man" (Tristan 2001, 1:61; see also Cornu 1999, 173).

made it possible to utilize the cheap labor of carters and loaders without giving up the dockworkers' monopoly on cargo handling. The fact that the dockworkers' society was moved to ban the use of wheeled vehicles on the docks in 1853 suggests that some such experiments must have been going on. Either of these changes, or some combination of the two, would be consistent with the quantitative data. In any case, it seems clear that, as the traffic of the port increased, the dockworkers drew the practical boundary separating their work from that of other transportation laborers more tightly around the actual loading and unloading of ships.[25]

The available evidence suggests a marked improvement in the dockworkers' real conditions between the 1820s and mid-century, in spite of the continuity of institutions. The dockworkers' society was no less elaborate in the 1820s than it became by mid-century, its monopoly of work on the docks was no less enforceable, and men were every bit as capable of passing their occupations on to their sons. But these privileges (and privileges they were in the 1820s) were far less lucrative than they became by the 1840s. Unemployment and underemployment were endemic. Wages were good as long as work was available, but days without work were all too common. Hence dockworkers spent many daylight hours drinking and playing cards in the local bistros and cafes and may also have taken low-paying jobs doing assorted hauling and carrying to make ends meet. In a time when work on the docks was scarce, there were conflicts about its allocation among dockworkers, between dockworkers and sailors, or between dockworkers and robeirols. Dockworkers were by no means desperate or impoverished in the 1820s or early 1830s; their wages were good, and income could be supplemented by occasional day labor. But they were by no means so prosperous as they became by mid-century.

THE ECOLOGY OF DOCKWORKER PRIVILEGE

By the 1840s, some prominent Marseillais had begun to denounce the dockworkers' society for its restrictive practices. The most notable was Jules Julliany, *premier adjoint* to the mayor under the July Monarchy, and the author of a vast compendium on the commerce of the city. Writing in the early 1840s, he proposed that the city's merchants act to rid themselves of "this monopoly [that has] always weighed on the commerce of Marseille" by simply ignoring the regulations of the dockworkers' society and

---

25. This conclusion also seems consistent with Gontier's (1988) analysis of the changing division of labor on the docks.

hiring other workers of their choice. This action, Julliany implied, would probably be met by violent resistance from the dockworkers' society. But, if the merchants' chosen workers "were troubled or menaced, judicial authority, aided if necessary by military authority, would not fail to arrest and punish those who made themselves guilty of assaults or threats" (1842, 3:455). Julliany was certainly right that the state, if called in, would have backed the merchants and broken the dockworkers' monopoly by force: the restrictive practices of the dockworkers' society were a blatant violation of the criminal code and the Le Chapelier law. Moreover, dock work did not require a long period of training, and there were always plenty of badly paid and underemployed men in the city—particularly, Italian immigrants—who could have been recruited to load ships at rates far below those maintained by the dockworkers' society. Yet the merchants ignored Julliany's suggestions and continued uncomplainingly to accept the society's restrictive regulations and pay its high rates. Given the reputation of Marseille's merchants as astute businessmen, it is puzzling that they continued to submit to this apparently costly monopoly, especially after 1830, when the mayor who had been the dockworkers' patron had resigned, and the officials of the July Monarchy were loudly declaiming the virtues of laissez faire.

There are reasons to think that the merchants knew what they were doing, but explaining the merchants' toleration of the dockworkers' society requires a closer look at the organizational ecology and the daily routines of work on the docks. The loading of ships was carried out by teams of dockworkers, which might consist of ten to twenty men, headed by a master dockworker (see fig. 2). The masters were named not by the dockworkers' society but by the merchant whose goods were being handled.[26] A master was the merchant's representative on the docks. He recruited, organized, supervised, and paid his team of workers, and handled the sometimes complex formalities of customs clearance as well.[27] According to tradition, each dockworker, master included, was to get an equal share

26. On the relationship between the masters and the dockworkers who worked under them, see the excellent discussion of Gontier (1988, 27–30).

27. François Mazuy (1853, 206), an acute contemporary observer of Marseillais society, pointed out that under the protectionist tariff regime of the mid-nineteenth century, "to send a parcel, or a barrel, has become a difficult art," and that the master dockworker, "raised since his earliest childhood inside the customs labyrinth" and therefore able to deal with "these petty formalities," could "save the house that he represents on the docks from major difficulties."

Figure 2. A team of dockworkers unloading grain in the old port in 1876. The master is standing with crossed legs and smoking a pipe. Unloading of grains in the old port continued to be undertaken by traditionally organized teams of dockworkers even in the 1870s, after the general monopoly of the dockworkers' society had been broken. "Débarquement de blé sur le quai de Rive-Neuve," by Alfonse Moutte. Courtesy of the Musée du Vieux-Marseille.

of pay for the work accomplished. A master, however, could work for more than one merchant and could have more than one team working at a given time; he also probably benefited from various bonuses and gratuities from the merchant (Nguyen 1961, 38). A few master dockworkers actually became well-to-do; twenty of them (out of perhaps one hundred) met the substantial property qualifications required to become electors of the July Monarchy in 1844 (Nguyen 1961, 40). But the masters and simple workmen were equal in the eyes of the dockworkers' society: no privileges attached to the position, and dues, fees, obligations, and benefits of membership were the same for all. Masters were over-represented among officers of the society, but they never monopolized offices and there seem to have been very few complaints of prejudicial treatment by the ordinary workers. For whatever reasons—and the sources unfortunately are virtually silent on relations between masters and workers—teams of dockworkers seem generally to have worked together in harmony.

The master and his team of dockworkers were employed directly by the merchant whose goods were being handled. Marseille's merchants in the mid-nineteenth century carried on business much as they had in the eighteenth or seventeenth centuries. It was typical for each voyage of a ship to be financed by a different group of businessmen. The ship's captain, merchants whose goods were to be carried, and perhaps a banker or independent capitalist would become partners for a single voyage. When the ship returned, the profits or losses would be divided and the partnership dissolved, and a new partnership, normally including a different set of partners, would be established. A given merchant would be involved in several different ventures at once. He might have three or four ships coming in during a two-week period and then have none the next month.[28] A merchant's demand for labor was therefore extremely sporadic; he wanted to be able to hire a team of men when he needed them, and he wanted to be sure that they would do the work efficiently and honestly with a minimum of supervision. Rather than having to hire an assistant to supervise loading and unloading operations, merchants could count on the master dockworkers and their teams to take charge of the work when it needed doing. The dockworkers' society itself guaranteed responsible and orderly work on the docks, mediating whatever disputes might arise, providing extra workers from the Muse when they were required, and generally oversee-

---

28. See Carrière (1973, 2:875–984), for a lucid and detailed description of Marseille's mercantile capitalism in the eighteenth century.

ing loading and unloading of ships. From this perspective, the high wages paid to the dockworkers begin to seem a much better bargain. When a merchant hired a team of dockworkers, he was getting much more than willing muscles; he was also, in effect, putting-out or subcontracting the management of dock work to the masters and the dockworkers' society.

The high wages paid to dockworkers thus bought both physical labor and management services. But they also bought something else: security of the cargoes. The dockworkers' society ensured the honesty of the workers and effectively policed the docks. Pilferage is a chronic concern on the docks in all times and places, and the physical configuration of nineteenth-century Marseille posed particular difficulties for its prevention. Marseille's port basin was a rectangular inlet nestled between steep hills on the north and south. The old city of Marseille was built on the slope of the hill immediately to the north of the port, and, by the end of the seventeenth century, the city surrounded the port on all sides. The old city neighborhoods to the north of the port, which were crowded, labyrinthine, poor, and dangerous, reached right down to the quays (see fig. 3).[29] The narrow quays, never very ample even in the eighteenth century, became extraordinarily encumbered as a consequence of the explosive growth of maritime commerce in the nineteenth. In these circumstances, a dishonest dockworker could disappear into the old city in an instant with valuable cargoes.[30] This danger was multiplied by the fact that goods being held for transshipment had to be carried to warehouses scattered all over the city. The dockworkers' honesty, consequently, was a major financial consideration for merchants.

The dockworkers' society ensured the honesty of its members not only by its general tone of discipline and order but by specific regulations. The statutes of the dockworkers' society stated that dockworkers convicted of theft by the courts were to be banished from the society—and therefore from the docks. In addition, the society instituted its own proceedings against any dockworker denounced by the priors for having "permitted himself the baseness of embezzling, hiding, or holding back some portion

29. On the geography of poverty and crime in Marseille, see Sewell (1985b, 109–26, 228–32).

30. In this respect, Marseille differed from the other major French ports, for example, Bordeaux, Nantes, and Le Havre, which were all located along estuaries of major rivers, not on inlets in a mountainous shoreline surrounded by dense urban development. The quays in all three of these cities were wide enough to accommodate railroad tracks in the 1840s and 1850s; this would have been unthinkable in the old port of Marseille. See, e.g., Higounet (1980), Le Beuf (1857, 272), Aussel (2002, 170), and Corvisier (1983).

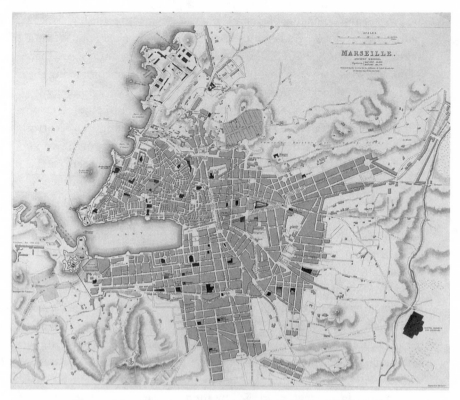

Figure 3. Marseille in 1837. Published by the Society for the Diffusion of Useful Knowledge.

of merchandise" or for "lacking trustworthiness in whatever way." If the case against the accused was judged by the society's general assembly to be proven, he was expelled from the society, and the outcome of the assembly's deliberation was sent to the Hotel de Ville "so that no one will remain ignorant" of the expulsion. By this means, the society guarded itself and the docks against dishonest dockworkers even if the merchant whose goods had been filched declined to press charges in the courts.[31] The merchants, sensibly enough, were willing to pay the high wages enforced by the dockworkers' society in order to gain this protection against potentially uncontrollable losses from pilfering.

31. The quotations are from the statutes of 1817. The 1853 statutes use somewhat different language and specify the procedures to be used in trying accused dockworkers in more detail, but essentially they follow the 1817 provisions, which in turn follow those of 1789 (ADBdR: XIV M 25/1; AVM: 1 I 1/35).

The dockworkers' society, then, was an integral part of the maritime economy of mid-nineteenth-century Marseille. The society had grown in tandem with Marseille's merchant community, and the relations they had established constituted a mutually beneficial ecology as long as no major changes took place in the overall organization of commerce. Even the huge rise in demand for dockworkers' labor that resulted from the commercial boom of the 1820s, 1830s, and 1840s failed to upset existing relations between dockworkers and merchants. Because the rising demand for labor was met by eliminating the dockworkers' irregularity of employment and by leaving other loading and carrying jobs to unskilled carters, loaders, and robeirols, it resulted in no upward pressure on the dockworkers' piece-rate wages. Dockworkers' earnings rose substantially, yet the costs faced by a merchant hiring a team of dockworkers for a day in the 1840s or 1850s was virtually the same as it had been in the 1820s. For this reason, the dockworkers were able to gain an enormous advantage from the maritime boom without adversely affecting the profits of their employers, the merchants. Until the great transformation of the docks and the maritime economy that began to take shape toward the end of the 1850s, neither the merchants nor the municipality had any reason to challenge the power of the dockworkers' society. The society relieved the merchants of responsibility for supervising loading and unloading operations, it protected them against the danger of potentially rampant waterfront theft, and its members' growing prosperity in the 1830s and 1840s did not increase the merchants' costs. Consequently, the dockworkers were secure and prosperous, for the time being, in a protected ecological niche.

THE DOCKS TRANSFORMED

If the expansion of commerce posed no immediate challenge to the customary organization of dockwork in Marseille, it soon began to strain the physical capacity of the old port. The port was already overcrowded by the 1820s, and by the middle 1830s the situation became critical. Several stop-gap measures were undertaken, such as the razing of buildings along the northern edge of the port to expand the surface of the docks and dredging the port's southeastern corner to make room for another twenty to thirty ships. But, even after improvements, the docks measured only 3,200 meters for an annual traffic of 7,000 to 8,000 ships in the late 1840s. By contrast, Le Havre, Marseille's chief French competitor, had 5,920 meters of docks for fewer than 5,000 ships (Masson 1922, 429–33, 437). Minor improvements were insufficient to alleviate the problem; the traffic of the port grew far faster than the available space. Crowding was further exacerbated in the 1830s by the appearance of steamships, which were much larger than sailing vessels and difficult to accommodate in the confines of the old port.

The increasing inadequacy of the port was obviously a problem for Marseille, but it was also a problem that transcended Marseille. Marseille was the busiest port in France and was therefore a key site of the capitalist economy on a national and world scale. A slowdown in the growth of Marseille's maritime traffic, which would adversely affect trade and industry in much of France, was unthinkable for capitalists and the state alike. At this point, the temporalities of world capitalist development clearly weighed directly on the docks of Marseille. It was evident that a new basin at least as big as the old port was urgently required. But given the geography of Marseille, this meant a gigantic program of construction — what David Harvey (1982) has dubbed a "spatial fix" — that would require an investment of fixed capital far beyond the resources of either Marseille's municipality or its merchant community. The old port is the only part of the coastline of Marseille with natural shelter against storms, good access to the shore, and sufficient depth of water, all of which are required for a good port. The immediately adjacent coastline both to the north and to the southwest of the old port was so jagged, steep, and rocky as to make the difficulty and cost of construction formidable (see fig. 3).

Construction of the new port basins required complex cooperation of both public and private entities. In 1835 Marseille's Chamber of Commerce, the organ of the merchant community, began the consideration of port expansion by commissioning a range of different proposals. The following year, the local director of the state civil engineering bureau, the Corps des Ponts-et-Chaussées, officially took the task in hand. It was not until 1844 that the Paris-based Council of the Ponts-et-Chaussées officially approved a plan for construction of a new port basin immediately to the north of the old port. The Chamber of Deputies immediately passed a law providing the funding, and work on the project began later that year. The new basin was already usable in 1847, when it was crowded by vessels carrying wheat to provision France's granaries, which had been depleted by the crop failures of that year, but it was not fully completed until 1853. As early as 1848, however, the local director of the Corps des Ponts et Chaussées had decided that a further northward extension was necessary (Masson 1922, 441–47). The Revolution of 1848, and the financial insolvency and reduction in port traffic that it brought in its wake, interrupted

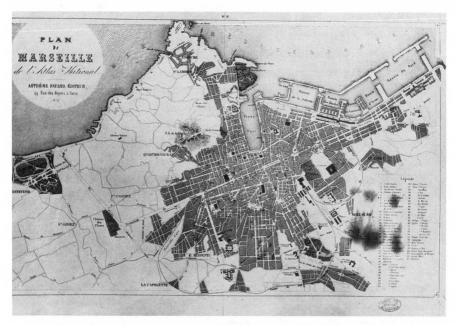

Figure 4. Marseille in 1874. Courtesy of the Archives de la Chambre de Commerce et d'Industrie de Marseille.

plans for extension. But by 1852, maritime commerce began to grow at its pre-1848 pace once again, and the expansion continued through the 1850s and 1860s (see fig. 1). In 1856, work began on a series of three new port basins stretching northward along the coast. (The old and new port basins can be seen clearly in fig. 4, a plan of Marseille in 1874.) These new basins were a much more ambitious project, and their financing was undertaken by combined public and private means. The French state undertook the building of the necessary jetty and breakwater on its own account. But to finance the docks themselves, the state ceded the land in question to the city, which in turn sold it to two joint stock companies, the Compagnie des Docks et Entrepôts de Marseille and the Société des Ports de Marseille, formed by two major Parisian bankers.[32] It was these joint stock companies that undertook the building of the docks, the necessary rail links, the warehouses to store goods awaiting shipment, and the offices from which

32. Joint stock companies (sociétés anonymes) were a rather new form of enterprise in France in this period, and were much favored by the Second Empire state for carrying out major infrastructure projects (see Girard 1952).

the new complex would be managed, as well as developing and selling off the adjoining real estate (Masson 1922, 452–53; Girard 1961).

The basin completed in 1853 had no significant effect on the organization of dock work. The system that had been used in the old port was simply extended to the new. But the basins begun in 1856 were a very different matter. The Compagnie des Docks et Entrepôts de Marseille, which built and managed the docks, revolutionized methods of handling cargoes (Masson 1922, 9: 450–52; Girard 1961; Nguyen 1961, 79; Gontier 1988). First, the new dock was what was called a *dock à l'anglais*—that is, it introduced labor-saving equipment of the sort used on English docks, of which steam-driven hydraulic cranes and lifts were the most important. Second, the quays were physically set off from the working-class neighborhoods of the old city. Third, all goods in transshipment were to be concentrated in warehouses in the new basins rather than being scattered through the city. Fourth, dockworkers were no longer to work in teams for the merchants whose goods were being unloaded: they had to become employees of the Compagnie des Docks. Work was to be organized and policed not by the masters and the dockworkers' society but by employees of the company. It should be clear that this spatial and organizational rearrangement of dockwork would entirely undermine both the ecological and the institutional conditions that had enabled the dockworkers' society to perpetuate its privileges.

The dockworkers quickly recognized that their position was gravely threatened. In 1858, they learned that all steamships would be required to use the as-yet-uncompleted docks as soon as provisional operations began. The dockworkers' society sent delegations to the company, the mayor, and the prefect to protest this regulation, which would effectively put the rapidly growing steamship trade beyond the society's reach. In January 1859, the dockworkers' society even obtained an audience with Emperor Napoleon III, who answered their plea with vague, and in the end empty, promises of help: "Messieurs, you have done very well to count on me. I will do for your interests everything that may be in my power" (ADBdR: XIV M 25/1). When the docks began provisional operations in the summer of 1859, a number of dockworkers went to work for the company. The society forbade its members to do so and expelled all who did. In other words, it threatened to withhold labor from the company, demanding that dockworkers be allowed to handle work for their merchants as before, without becoming the company's employees. The company, as yet in a weak economic position, negotiated a compromise that allowed society members to handle some kinds of work without becoming employees (Nguyen 1961, 81). But both sides knew that this was only a truce in a long battle, and that the real showdown would come in 1864, when the new docks were scheduled to go into full operation.

During its long struggle with the company, the dockworkers' society did its best to cultivate public opinion. It obtained the signatures of 850 merchants on a petition addressed to the ministry of industry and commerce and won the support of the Chamber of Commerce, the bastion of Marseille's merchant community (Nguyen 1961, 83). That it succeeded in gaining the support of the merchant community is impressive, since the Compagnie des Docks was able to offer considerably lower prices than the dockworkers' society. In part, this support is a measure of the long-standing ties between the merchants and the dockworkers, especially the master dockworkers. The dockworkers' society, in a memorandum addressed to Marseille's merchants in 1859, for example, made much of the paternal relations of "confidence" and "devotion" that existed between merchants and "their" dockworkers (ADBdR: XIV M 25/1). But the merchants also had grievances of their own. In the 1850s and 1860s, Marseille's maritime commerce was completely restructured (Sewell 1985b, 38–43; Cornu 1974, 1999). One important development was the rise of steam navigation and joint-stock steamship companies. Steamships, which accounted for only 10 percent of the cargoes entering the port of Marseille in 1840, accounted for 14 percent by 1850, 32 percent by 1860, and 44 percent by 1870 (Masson 1922, 56, 74). The early steamships were often owned by individuals or simple partnerships, but these small operators were soon pushed aside by large joint-stock steamship companies. Between 1852 and 1865, four companies — the Messageries Impériales, the Société Générale de Transports Maritimes à Vapeur, the Compagnie Marseillaise de Navigation à Vapeur, and the Compagnie de Navigation Mixte — came to dominate steam shipping in Marseille, accounting for almost 90 percent of the city's steamer tonnage by 1869. Only one of these companies, the Compagnie Marseillaise, was controlled by local capital; the majority of the capital in the other three was from Paris or Lyon (Masson 1922, 67–76). The rise of these steamship companies disrupted the traditional organization of commerce. Rather than forming a series of short-term partnerships for single voyages, merchants increasingly found themselves dealing with large bureaucratic shipping lines. Moreover, the steamship companies, together with the Compagnie des Docks, rivaled the power of the traditional merchant community and its organ, the Chamber of Commerce. Marseille's merchants, long the dominant force in the political and economic life of the city, were rapidly being displaced by "foreign" capital. "Marseille," as the scion of an old mercantile family remarked in 1863, "no longer seems to belong to herself" (Guiral 1957, 174). Under these circumstances, the dockworkers' struggle against the Compagnie des Docks could be seen as a battle against foreign domination. As such, it won the support of the merchants and the Chamber of Commerce.

If the battle against the company strengthened the bonds between merchants and dockworkers, it gradually opened a rift between masters and ordinary dockworkers. It was the masters whose position was threatened most drastically by the new dock. Ordinary dockworkers stood to lose their collective self-governance and to suffer a decline in earnings. But the master dockworkers risked the annihilation of their peculiar function and status. The masters were therefore willing to make dramatic gestures to gain the support of the merchants. In 1859, they offered a 10 percent reduction in piece-rates that would come entirely from their own profits, without reducing the rates to be paid to the workers (ADBdR: XIV M 25/1). But, as early as 1859, some of the ordinary dockworkers regarded the victory of the company as inevitable and wished to negotiate with the company rather than refusing to work at the dock altogether. In this respect, it is interesting that the first thirty-seven dockworkers to sign up for work at the dock in August 1859 had previously been employed not by merchants but by the Messageries Impériales steamship company; they had, in other words, already made their peace with the new bureaucratic capitalist order. Another 290 workers came to sign up with the dock shortly after; all of these were expelled from the dockworkers' society (ADBdR: XIV M 25/1). Throughout the struggle, it was always the masters who insisted on total noncooperation, whereas at least some of the workers were willing to accept work at the dock if the terms were sufficiently favorable.

In the summer of 1864, the dock began full-scale operation. Once again, the Compagnie des Docks insisted that anyone engaged in loading and unloading of ships be an employee of the dock, and once again the dockworkers' society responded by refusing to work under the company's conditions. This time, the company was prepared; it simply staffed the docks with unskilled laborers, mostly Italian immigrants, and offered merchants lower rates than the dockworkers' society could match. Once again, a number of dockworkers took work with the company in defiance of the society and were duly expelled. They brought suit, charging that the society had no right to exclude them for exercising their liberty to work where they wished. The court, as Julliany had predicted some twenty years earlier, ruled on behalf of the expelled men, striking a mortal blow to the society's powers. Not long after this decision, the emperor passed through Marseille and was greeted by a demonstration of some 5,000 dockworkers and supporters. One of the society's priors addressed the emperor, reminding him of the promises he had made in 1859, and ended his speech with a cry of "Vive l'Empereur!" Louis Napoleon once again promised to look into the affair, and a few months later the same prior went to Paris to negotiate a solution. But the proposal he brought back to Marseille proved to be unacceptable to the society, and the effort ended in mutual recrimination (Nguyen 1961, 363–69).

The dockworkers' struggle ended in victory for the Compagnie des Docks. Most of the society's members eventually went to work for the company, and the society, stripped of its monopoly, faded into an ordinary mutual aid society that administered sickness and retirement benefits. The merchants, in spite of their preference for the dockworkers' society, soon made their peace with the company as well. The company, after all, was able to offer them virtually everything the society had offered in the past. It provided workers, organized and supervised dock work, maintained secure and efficient warehouses, and protected the merchants' goods against losses from theft—a task made vastly easier, of course, by the physical separation of the new docks from the neighborhoods of the old city. Moreover, it could offer all this at a lower rate than the dockworkers' old price schedule. The merchants lost the personal satisfaction of paternal relations with trusted master dockworkers and had to accustom themselves to the bureaucracy of the new company. But, unlike that of the dockworkers, their own privileged and lucrative position in maritime trade was not genuinely damaged. A new level of capitalist organization had come to Marseille's docks; to the merchants, it meant a change in the tone and character of their work and the loss of their once unchallenged supremacy in the city's maritime economy. To the dockworkers, it meant much more: the destruction of the cherished privileges of their society and the reduction of its members to ordinary proletarian wage laborers.

The uneven capitalist development that had enabled the dockworkers to construct and defend a privileged ecological niche in the first half of the nineteenth century destroyed it in the 1860s. The general development of French, European, and world capitalism caused a massive expansion in Marseille's maritime trade in the nineteenth century. For some decades, this advance in capitalist development did not cause a corresponding ad-

vance in the methods of dock work. On the contrary, it actually strengthened an archaic form of labor organization on the docks: the dockworkers'
society, which was in fact a carryover from the guild system of the Old
Regime. In this case, the unevenness that characterized all capitalist development also gave rise to combined development: the strengthening of
archaic forms in symbiosis with an advanced sector. But, in the end, the exigencies of continuing capitalist development, that is, the need for more
space in the port, shattered archaic forms and obliterated the temporarily
privileged position of the dockworkers. Marseille's dockworkers were a
particular case but a case that fits a very general pattern. The intrinsic and
inescapable unevenness of capitalist development promiscuously creates
privileged niches for workers who are advantageously placed in a particular phase of development. But it also, no less promiscuously, destroys the
same privileged niches it had created in earlier phases.

THE DOCKWORKERS' POLITICS

At first glance, it would seem that the dockworkers' economic vicissitudes
had a direct effect on their politics. The role of dockworkers in the three
great revolutionary crises of the nineteenth century (1830–34, 1848–51, and
1870–71) appears to correspond admirably to the evolution of their economic circumstances. The dockworkers seem to have been radical, or at
least politically restive, in the first crisis, before their rise to the high prosperity of mid-century; to have been notoriously reactionary at mid-century,
when their privileges were at their height; and to have been ardent revolutionaries at the time of the Commune, when their society had been crushed
and they had been definitively reduced to proletarian status.

During the crisis that extended from the July Revolution of 1830 to the
suppression of the Lyonnais and Parisian workers' rebellions of April 1834,
Marseille was not the center of a major radical movement. In fact, the local
authorities of the new July Monarchy were at first much more concerned
about the possibility of a popular uprising in favor of the ousted Bourbon
monarchical regime than about republican agitation. By 1833, however, a
chapter of the revolutionary Society of the Rights of Man had been
founded, and the police responded by infiltrating it with an informer. In
April 1834, at the time of the Lyonnais and Parisian insurrections, Marseille's society deliberated about launching a revolt of its own. According to
the informer's report, among the most ardent advocates of violent action
were three dockworkers, who claimed to be able "to direct at their will at
least 200 of their colleagues" in the event of a revolt. This claim may have

been wildly exaggerated; we will never know, because the Society of the Rights of Man finally decided against an insurrection. But it suggests that a sizable minority of the dockworkers had been touched by the radical agitations of the period (ADBdR: M6/334).

The dockworkers' growing prosperity during the following decade and a half seems to have wiped out any remnants of radicalism. By February 1848, when the July Monarchy was overthrown and replaced by a republic, any claim that dockworkers would join a radical insurrection would have been dismissed as ridiculous; all political factions assumed that dockworkers were unshakably conservative. This assumption explains the way they were treated by the mayor of the fallen regime during his final days in power. The news of the Parisian insurrection reached Marseille on February 24, but it was not until March 1 that the commissioner sent from Paris by the provisional government arrived to establish republican power in the city. During this interval, the mayor did what he could to strengthen the hand of conservatives. Most importantly, he called in supporters of the fallen regime, set them up as companies in the national guard, and distributed to them all the city's available rifles. Nearly all the companies created by this maneuver were composed of merchants, professional men, shopkeepers, and clerks, but the dockworkers were armed to a man and allowed to form a special company of their own. This was in the sharpest contrast to the treatment received by other workers. When they came to the city hall to join the national guard, they were told that no arms were available. As one republican militant wrote, "If the dockworkers were admitted, it was in the thought, which [the authorities] did not even attempt to dissimulate, that these men of the people, feudatories of their patrons the merchants, would serve to combat that other people, the workers, whose very name brought on the shivers" (Dubosc 1848, 5).[33] In 1848, conservatives and revolutionaries agreed that the dockworkers could be relied on to act as a counterrevolutionary force.

But the dockworkers' conservatism did not withstand the disasters of the 1860s. Their reduction from a privileged elite to ordinary proletarians made them notoriously hostile to the Imperial regime that had succeeded the Second Republic, all the more so because the emperor himself had twice deceived them during their struggle with the Compagnie des Docks

---

33. This highly irregular, last-minute formation of a conservative national guard was documented in a detailed report by the revolutionary municipal commission's committee on the national guard (AVM: I D 73, session of June 10, 1848).

by giving vague but empty promises of help. It is therefore hardly surprising that dockworkers figured prominently in a republican demonstration
in Marseille during July 1870, two months before the overthrow of the Empire and the establishment of the Third Republic, or that several dockworkers were active in Marseille's Commune in 1871. One of these, Étienne
père, was the Commune's second in command and was condemned to
death after the suppression of the Commune, although his sentence was
subsequently commuted (Nguyen 1962, 376–80).[34] The correlation with
politics therefore appears straightforward: if the rise of the dockworkers
to prosperity made them conservative by 1848, their fall from prosperity
led them to political radicalism at the time of the Commune.

On closer observation, however, this intimate association between economic trends and political behavior turns out to be seriously flawed. It is
true that the dockworkers were staunch conservatives in February 1848
and exemplary revolutionaries in 1871. But it appears that their shift to the
left began during the period of the Second Republic, several years before
the demise of their economic fortunes. The evidence for this shift is scattered, incomplete, and not entirely conclusive, but it all seems to point toward a general drift to the left, beginning hesitantly in the spring of 1848,
accelerating in 1849, and sustained up to and beyond Louis Napoleon's
coup d'état in 1851. The first sign of such a drift occurred in June 1848,
when radical workers in Marseille revolted at the time of the far more famous Parisian June Days. The dockworkers' national guard company—
originally formed, as we have seen, as a bastion of reaction—refused to
respond to orders on discovering that it might be asked to fire on fellow
workers (Dubosc 1848, 48). A year later, there was a sign that the dockworkers were moving toward a more insurgent position. In June 1849,
some 500 dockworkers held a banquet in honor of Louis Astouin, a dockworker who had written a widely acclaimed book of poetry and who had
just been defeated in a bid for reelection to the National Assembly on the
democratic ticket. The banquet ended with the entire crowd shouting
"Vive la République démocratique et sociale!" and some 114 francs were
collected for the families of the insurrectionaries of the prior June who remained in custody.[35] Neither of these actions would have been thinkable
in the early days of the Second Republic.

34. Antoine Olivesi (1950, 76), in his history of Marseille's Commune, describes Étienne as
"a pure revolutionary with the soul of an apostle."

35. There is an account of the banquet in the republican newspaper *La Voix du peuple*, June 8,
1849.

Table 2. Participation of Dockworkers in Radical Politics

	1 dockworker participants/all participants	2 dockworkers as percent of participants	3 dockworkers as percent of work force	4 dockworker participation 2/3
Insurrection, 1848	3/270	1.1	2.9	0.4
Coup d'etat, 1851	6/297	2.0	2.9	0.7
"Dangerous individuals," 1853–59	18/346	5.2	2.9	1.8
Miscellaneous political offences,				
1848–49	0/20	0.0	2.9	0.0
1850–51	2/51	3.9	2.9	1.3
1852–59	8/85	9.4	2.9	3.2

Sparse but intriguing quantitative figures on dockworkers' participation in revolutionary activities in the decade following the Revolution of 1848 seem to indicate that the drift to the left that began in 1848 and 1849 was not slowed by the mounting repression of the final years of the Second Republic or even by the establishment of Louis Napoleon's embryonic police state (see table 2). Only three of the 270 men who were convicted of participating in Marseille's June 1848 insurrection were dockworkers. Dockworkers thus made up 1.1 percent of the insurrectionaries, as against 2.9 percent of the adult male population. Dockworkers may have been reluctant to fire on other workers, but few were ready to join in an armed insurrectionary movement. Among the 297 radicals rounded up after Louis Napolean's coup d'etat in 1851 were six dockworkers. This was 2 percent, still below the dockworkers' percentage of the population but double the 1848 percentage. When the police drew up lists in 1853, 1855, and 1858, composed of "dangerous individuals" who were to be rounded up if an insurrection should take place, dockworkers made up eighteen of 346 names, which is 5.2 percent, or well above their proportion in the population. The same development, but even more pronounced, can be seen in the identities of men convicted of assorted political offenses over the same years. The offenses included were quite diverse, the most common being politically motivated acts of violence against police or other authorities, membership in secret revolutionary societies, or singing subversive songs or uttering "seditious cries" in the streets. No dockworker was among the twenty convicted of such offenses in 1848 and 1849. In 1850 and 1851, there were two dockworkers among the fifty-one men convicted, a number somewhat above their proportion in the population. In the first eight years of the Second Empire, dockworkers made up eight of the eighty-five men convicted of political offenses, about triple their proportion in the population. These figures are obviously insufficient as measures of the overall political opinions and behavior of the dockworkers, but they would seem to confirm that dockworkers were moving toward the left in the years following 1848.

There is one final indication — once again, hardly conclusive in itself — of the dockworkers' shift to the left between 1848 and the early 1850s. This is a remark made by Armand Audiganne, a prominent Parisian social investigator, in 1855, in his monumental *Les populations ouvrières et les industries de la France*. He reported that the revolutionary movement of 1848 in Marseille "received support above all from the corporation of the dockworkers, justly famous for their riotous temperament" (Audiganne 1860, 2:154). This manifestly false statement would seem to be explained by the fact that he visited Marseille in 1852 or 1853 and projected the then-evident radicalism of the dockworkers backward in time to an era when, in fact, they were regarded by democrats and reactionaries alike as staunch supporters of the existing social and political order.

All the evidence points to a significant radicalization of dockworkers' political opinions and behavior between 1848 and the mid-1850s, a decade before the drastic restructuring of work reduced the dockworkers to proletarians. It therefore appears that changes in dockworker politics cannot be explained as a simple reflex of proletarianization. Instead, the seemingly paradoxical rise of dockworker radicalism over the decade following the Revolution of 1848 requires a complex explanation, one that recognizes the simultaneous autonomy and interrelationship of economic and political temporalities.

Let us begin with economics. Although the dockworkers' favorable structural position in the maritime economy was not challenged in the late 1840s and 1850s, their economic well-being was sharply affected by short-term flucuations. The traffic of Marseille's port fell precipitously in 1848 and remained low for the following three years (see fig. 1). The revolutionary upheavals of 1848 in France and Europe caused a general panic among the possessing classes; credit dried up and investment fell, causing a depression in industry and trade. It was not until 1852, after Louis Napoleon's coup d'état had ended the fear of political instability, that the traffic of the port rebounded to the level of the middle 1840s (Guiral 1956, 200–25). The long commercial depression surely increased unemployment and sharply cut incomes on the docks, reducing the dockworkers to economic circumstances more or less comparable to those of the early 1830s, when, as we have seen, they were also involved in revolutionary agitation. The dockworkers were not thrown into desperate poverty by the depression, and the Muse operated to distribute available employment equitably. Indeed, the Muse probably made the impact of the depression less severe for the dockworkers than for most of the city's workers. Nevertheless, lower incomes and high levels of unemployment sustained for four years must have made dockworkers more receptive to the republican and socialist agitation of the era than would have been the case had employment remained high. This economically induced receptivity undoubtedly helps to explain the dockworkers' initial drift to the left from 1848 to 1851.

These economic changes were paralleled by (and in part caused by) autonomous shifts in the French political system. Literature on the autonomy, or relative autonomy, of politics has focused on the autonomy of the state. States, this literature argues, have their own interests, structures, and developmental tendencies that cannot be reduced to the interests of the dominant class, classes, or groups. Explaining historical change therefore requires attention not only to the changing conditions of the classes and class fractions that make up a society but also to the changing form and functioning of states (e.g., Skocpol 1979; Evans, Rueschemeyer, and Skocpol 1985). The importance of changes in political structures is clear in revolutionary upheavals. The Revolution of 1848 drastically altered the structure of the French state. The sudden victory of the February 1848 insurrection overthrew a monarch, dissolved a legislative body, and threw existing state institutions into disarray. It created a new but insecure provisional government, which instituted universal male suffrage and abolished censorship and restrictions on the formation of political associations and trade unions. Under pressure from Parisian workers, it also declared a new fundamental right, the right to work, and established the Luxembourg Commission, headed by socialist Louis Blanc, which was to prepare a new "organization of labor" for the country. The new and rather chaotic structure of the French state in the immediate aftermath of the February Revolution enormously expanded the possibilities for political action by workers. Granted the vote, allowed to organize in political clubs and trade associations, and promised a fundamental reorganization of the economy, workers in cities throughout France responded with a frenetic burst of political activity. A fundamental cause of the radicalization of French workers in general, this change in the structure of the state certainly affected Marseille's dockworkers.

The February Revolution also brought about another closely related kind of change in the nature of politics: a transformation of political discourse.[36] If the hard economic times of the Second Republic made dockworkers more receptive to messages critical of the status quo, revolutionary politics changed the character and increased the volume of such messages.[37] The Revolution of 1848 made "worker" (*ouvrier* or *travailleur*) a politically potent term and made the fact that one belonged to the socioeconomic category of manual workers politically relevant in a way it had not been before. In Marseille, as elsewhere in France in the spring of 1848, not only socialists but public officials, moderates, and even the most reactionary monarchists addressed a blizzard of pamphlets, newspaper articles, speeches, handbills, and proclamations "to the workers." In Louis Althusser's terminology (1971), one could say that after February 1848 the utterance "worker" insistently interpellated or hailed workers as ideologically defined political subjects. Bombarded by this outpouring of ideological discourse, even the dockworkers, who had been monarchist or apolitical before 1848, surely were aware that the revolution was promising to raise manual labor to a new dignity in the state and must have pondered what their unquestioned status as workers implied for their own role in politics.

Much of the discourse directed specifically at Marseille's dockworkers in the spring of 1848 came from conservative quarters and praised them for their "moderation." For example, on February 26, the day the dockworkers were incorporated into the national guard, the conservative newspaper *Le Nouvelliste* remarked that the dockworkers' firm repudiation of the "tumultuous demonstrations that have alarmed this city" had "honored in the highest degree the working population [*population ouvrière*] of our city":

> This evening more than 2,000 of these estimable workers [*ouvriers*], armed and incorporated into the national guard, will efficaciously stand guard to assure due respect to persons and property. . . . We do not doubt that the noble example of the dockworkers' corporation will be followed by the entire working population [*population ouvrière*] of Marseille, because nowhere else, and we say this with a just pride, do the laboring classes [*classes laborieuses*] offer, to the same extent as ours, such guaranties of morality and devotion to the sacred bonds of the family, from which flow essentially all instincts of order and legality. (*Le Nouvelliste*, February 26, 1848)

36. For an exchange on these issues concerning the French Revolution, see Sewell (1985a) and Skocpol (1985).

37. I have argued this at some length in Sewell (1980, chap. 11).

This editorial not only attempts to reinforce the dockworkers' conservatism but holds up the dockworkers as a model for all of Marseille's workers, who, interestingly, are praised not so much for their political conservatism as for their apolitical attachment to family bonds, which is assumed to be a guarantee of good political behavior. Yet even this text paradoxically contributes to the dockworkers' identity as workers and, in spite of its reactionary intent, makes this identity politically potent.

From the very beginning of the revolution, Marseille's conservatives, by ostentatiously adopting the dockworkers as the apotheosis of the apolitical *sage ouvrier* [good worker], unwittingly contributed to their politicization. Once dockworkers had been encouraged to think of themselves as somehow exemplary of workers in general, they could not be prevented from recognizing that republicans and socialists were hailing all workers as constituents of a new and better state and society, a "democratic and social republic" in which labor would be properly "organized" and duly rewarded as the basis of all wealth. By June 1848, the republicans and socialists had not succeeded in constituting dockworkers as revolutionaries. But the fact that the dockworkers' unit of the national guard refused to report for duty at the time of the June insurrection because they were unwilling to fire on "fellow workers" indicates that they had begun to accept "worker" as a political identity and to act on that identity even against an express command of the forces of "order and legality."

The shift in state structure and political discourse that took place in the spring of 1848, together with the sharp rise of unemployment, appears to have moved the dockworkers beyond the reactionary docility attributed to them by both monarchists and republicans in February. But it was not until 1849 or later that dockworkers began to appear with some frequency in the ranks of Marseille's militant republicans and socialists. This delayed conversion of dockworkers to the radical movement was in fact unique in Marseille. The great era of political radicalization of workers was the turbulent spring of 1848, not the increasingly repressive years that followed. The figures on participation in Marseille's revolutionary movement show that, with the exception of the dockworkers, trades that were radical in 1851 or the middle 1850s had already been radical at the time of the June 1848 rebellion. The dockworkers were the only significant working-class trade that had been conservative in June 1848 but turned radical later. Hence the factors that explain the general radicalization of workers in 1848 cannot fully account for the particular case of the dockworkers.

Explaining the changing politics of dockworkers requires that we recognize the autonomy of politics in yet another sense: that in addition to considering changes in state structures and political discourses, we must also consider the unique details of their political history—the political "structure of the conjuncture." From 1849 to 1851, the political history of the dockworkers was closely tied to the surprising career of Louis Astouin, the dockworker poet-politician. Astouin was initially named to the monarchist slate of candidates in the legislative elections of April 1848. The monarchists chose him because of his prominence and popularity as a worker-poet, assuming that his apparent lack of pronounced political views indicated the docile conservatism for which his fellow dockworkers were famous. But in the National Assembly he turned out to be a sincere, if moderate, republican. He was therefore dropped from the monarchist list for the elections of 1849 and replaced by another dockworker of known reactionary opinions. The democrats, however, named Astouin to their list, and he responded by moving considerably to the left and espousing the cause of social democracy. Astouin became a tireless campaigner. Although narrowly defeated in the 1849 election, he continued to work for the democratic and social republic, until Louis Napoleon's coup d'état in December 1851. Astouin's towering prestige among the dockworkers, together with his diligent and incessant proselytising, was surely a major source of the new political insurgency that characterized the dockworkers after 1849.[38]

Three different temporal processes, then, must be taken into account to explain the radicalization of Marseille's dockworkers in the years following 1848. First, the change was made possible by an event of the first order: a revolutionary transformation of the state and a consequent upsurge in radical discourse that established "the worker" as a constituent of a new "democratic and social republic." This new vision of work and politics so dominated the discourse of the spring of 1848 that even conservative workers such as the dockworkers could not escape a new politicized working-class identity. Second, the cyclical maritime depression of the Second Republic doubtless made dockworkers more receptive to the radical message than they would have been in a period of full employment. Finally, the particular political career of Louis Astouin meant that the gospel of the "democratic and social republic" reached the dockworkers with special au-

38. Astouin's career can be traced from the spring of 1849 to the fall of 1851 by occasional items in the police files in the ADBdR and by articles in the radical newspaper *La Voix du peuple* and its successor, *Le Peuple*.

thority and intensity between 1849 and 1851. The confluence of these temporal processes had the effect of transforming dockworkers from notorious reactionaries to active republicans by the end of the Second Republic.

None of these factors, however, can satisfactorily explain the increasing prominence of dockworker militants in the underground republican movement that followed Louis Napoleon's coup d'état and the establishment of the Second Empire. The maritime economy, after four years of depression, turned sharply upward in 1852 and remained relatively buoyant to the end of the decade. After 1851, republican and socialist discourse was choked off by the tight censorship and oppressive police of the Imperial state. And Louis Astouin was arrested after the coup d'état in 1851, placed in internment in Valence and then in Besançon, and kept under close police surveillance when he returned to Marseille in 1853; he was no longer able to participate actively in the now illegal republican movement.[39] Yet the dockworkers did not relapse into the deferential conservatism of the 1840s. To judge from evidence in the archives of repression, summarized in table 2, dockworkers were among the most active trades in the underground republican movement that took shape in Marseille in the 1850s; their participation in radical politics became more prominent as repression got more severe. The most likely explanation for this increasing prominence is the dockworkers' superior organizational experience. One suspects that they were able to transpose the many of the skills, schemas, and routines developed in the daily life of the dockworkers' society onto the rather different organizational terrain of the political underground. The dockworkers' initial conversion to radical politics may have been slow, but, once they were committed to the democratic and social republic, their superior command of social resources and institutional routines moved them to the center of the political struggle. The dockworkers' politics, then, was hardly a reflex of their relation to the means of production. Socioeconomic conditions were far from irrelevant, but the evolution of dockworker politics cannot be explained without reference both to transformations in state structure and political discourse and to the details of politics and personalities in Marseille.

This recognition of the autonomous temporalities of politics is, one might say, consonant with the "revival of narrative" hailed some time ago

---

39. Astouin died in 1855 at the age of thirty-three. His death was attributed to an illness he contracted in 1853, not long after his return to Marseille, when he threw himself into the cold waters of the harbor to save a drowning child (Masson 1913, 27).

by Lawrence Stone (1979; see also Hobsbawm 1980; Abrams 1980). It is one of the themes of this book that any attempt to explain historical change in a nonreductionist fashion implies a "narrative" concern for sequence, contingency, and agency. But the autonomy of politics should not be used as a license for historians to revel atheoretically in the particularity of each case's sequence of events or to resurrect (as it might seem I have done with Louis Astouin) the "great man" theory of history. The account of dockworker radicalization that I have sketched out here is not a return to old-fashioned narrative history but rather a theoretically motivated response to the crisis of labor history's explanatory strategy. If capitalist development is uneven in the sense I have been arguing in this essay—that is, if it produces not an increasingly solid and uniform proletarian continent but a continually changing archipelago of variegated working-class categories—then the appropriate explanatory strategy for labor historians is not to look for evidence of proletarianization behind every surge of working-class political radicalism but to ask how and why workers with widely varying economic trajectories and workplace experiences could successfully be constituted as political insurgents. For some trades, in some historical instances, for example, Christopher Johnson's French tailors in the 1830s and 1840s, proletarianization may well be the most important single answer. But we would be wrong to think that the tailors epitomized nineteenth-century working-class experience.

This study of Marseille's dockworkers indicates that even highly privileged workers could, under certain conditions, be induced to identify themselves with less fortunate workers and struggle for a radical transformation of the social order. If historians are to understand those occasions when a wide variety of workers joined radical revolts, such as the French workers' insurgencies of 1833–34, 1848–51, and 1870–71, the widespread English workers' agitation on the eve of the Reform Bill or during the Chartist movement, the New York labor uprising of 1850, or the Russian revolutions of 1905 and 1917, we must ask how a conjunction of new or preexisting social routines, economic changes, transformations of state structures and political discourse, and purposive actions by prominent or strategically placed persons or groups made possible the construction— at least for a time—of a common working-class political identity and program. Such a strategy should also help us explain why, in a capitalist economy that supposedly produces an increasingly uniform proletariat, these triumphs of class unity have repeatedly proved ephemeral. The case of Marseille's dockworkers should help us to see that socialism and class consciousness were contingent and fragile achievements of political struggle, not necessary and automatic products of nineteenth-century capitalist development.

Marseille's dockworkers, to be sure, are only a single case. But a single case, if well chosen and adequately analyzed, can be enormously informative. The dockworkers' history, properly understood, sheds light on the dynamics of social reproduction in times of change, on the significance of uneven temporalities in capitalist development, on the importance of organizational ecology in explaining institutional persistence, on the autonomy of working-class politics from the bare facts of exploitation and privilege, and on the power of well-placed individuals to promote political and cultural change. The development of an adequate explanatory vocabulary for historical social science depends crucially on such theoretically motivated explorations of particular cases.

⫷10⫸

REFIGURING THE "SOCIAL" IN SOCIAL SCIENCE
An Interpretivist Manifesto

We understood perfectly well that *social*, in particular, is one of those adjectives that has been made to say so many things, in the course of time, that in the end it means almost nothing at all. . . . We were in agreement in thinking that, precisely, a word as vague as this seemed to have been created . . . by a special decree of historical providence to serve as the insignia of a review that wished not to close itself off behind walls, but to radiate, widely, freely, even indiscriminately, into all gardens in its vicinity, a spirit, its spirit; I mean to say a spirit of untrammeled critique and of initiative in all directions. . . .

Nous savions bien que social en particulier, est un de ces adjectives à qui on a fait dire tant de choses, dans le cours du temps, qu'il ne veut finalement à peu près plus rien dire. . . . Nous étions d'accord pour penser que, précisément, un mot aussi vague semblait avoir été créé . . . par un décret nominatif de la providence historique pour servir d'enseigne à une revue qui prétendait ne pas s'entourer de murailles, mais faire rayonner largement, librement, indiscrètement même, sur tous les jardins du voisinage, un esprit, son esprit; je veux dire un esprit de libre critique et d'initiative en tous sens. . . .

—Lucien Febvre (1953, 19–20) speaking about his and Marc Bloch's
choice of *Annales d'histoire économique et sociale* as the name
of their new journal in 1929

What do we mean by the "social" in "social science"? This apparently innocuous question turns out to be disconcertingly difficult to answer. Most social scientists appear not to have given it much thought. Some have little investment in the concept of the social: many economists, for example, would probably prefer to have their discipline thought of as

This chapter incorporates some passages from "Whatever Happened to the 'Social' in Social History," which appeared in *Schools of Thought: Twenty-five Years of Interpretive Social Science*, ed. Joan W. Scott and Deborah Keates. Copyright © 2001 by Princeton University Press; reprinted with the permission of Princeton University Press. I have received useful comments on earlier versions of this essay from Keith Baker and Jan Goldstein.

one of the mathematical sciences, and many psychologists would probably rather be classified as biologists. The remaining core social sciences—anthropology, geography, political science, and sociology—certainly take the notion of the social seriously, but they show little interest in defining it. Geographers, anthropologists, and political scientists make use of the terms "social" or "society" constantly, but their high-stakes terminological squabbles are centered on the specific keywords of their own disciplines: "space" versus "place" in geography, "culture" in anthropology, and "politics" and "rationality" in political science. Even in sociology, whose very name (socio-logy) tells us that it is "the science of the social," the terms "social" and "society" are generally taken for granted. According to my own extensive participant observation in the discipline, when you ask a sociologist to define the social, you usually get a tautology, with the terms "social structure" or "social relations" appearing somewhere in the definition. Sociologists certainly do think of their discipline as the science of society, but they are vastly more articulate about the science half of this lexical couple than about the society half. So long as they can convince themselves and their colleagues that what they are doing is science, sociologists generally seem satisfied to let the "social" in social science take care of itself.

Paradoxically, more discussion about the social has been generated in recent years in the amphibious half-social-science half-humanities discipline of history than in the "core" social science disciplines. Although I complained in chapter 2 that the widespread turn from social to cultural history was accepted rather too easily in the historical profession during the past two decades, it nevertheless did lead, in the 1980s and 1990s, to debates that put status of "the social" explicitly in question. A few historians have even raised the bracing question as to whether "the social" remains a useful category for historical analysis at all (Joyce 1995; Cabrera 2004). Moreover, cultural historians have made us keenly aware that concepts like "the social" are historically constituted—that they arise and are transformed in meaning over the course of historical time.[1] My reflections about the social in this chapter take the historians' debates as their starting point. But I proceed on the assumption that how we define the social matters for the other social sciences as well.

The question of the social is an ontological question, a question about the nature of the world. Social scientists tend to be rather shy about making explicitly ontological statements. What I have said about sociologists

1. On the changing meaning of "social," see the essays in Joyce (2002).

above is true of most social scientists: they are much more comfortable theorizing about "science"—that is, how we may gain knowledge of the world—than about the social. Or, to put the same point in different words, the social sciences have far more highly developed methodologies than ontologies. But methodologies in fact always imply ontologies, whether stated or assumed. "Methodological individualism," for example, may be a methodological position, but it assumes an individualist ontology—a world in which any "social" reality is reducible to individuals and their willed actions. Adopting this or any other methodological stance—whether multivariate positivism, rational choice, social network analysis, post-structuralism, or hermeneutics—implies a conceptualization of the nature of the social world. What we are able to study in social science and how we are able to study it are inseparable from our social ontologies. This chapter is based on the premise that it is better for social scientists to conceptualize the social explicitly than to let our conceptualizations be unstated and unexamined corollaries of our methodological positions.

Readers of the previous chapters of this book should be aware by now that I have strong methodological preferences of my own. I freely affirm my commitment to accounts of social life that are at once interpretive or hermeneutic and historical. In such accounts the central questions about any social action, institution, or event are, first, its meaning to those who experience it and, second, its place in the changing frameworks that make meanings decipherable both to those whom we study and to ourselves. The central challenge for researchers is to reconstruct those meanings and experiences in a form simultaneously true to the ever-changing world being studied and graspable by the researcher's audience. My goal in this chapter is to refigure the social by developing a social ontology adequate to an interpretive conception of the social sciences. But, as the reader will discover toward the end of this essay, I shall argue that a fully worked out interpretivist ontology of the social implies embracing methods not usually considered part of the hermeneutic armory.

Throughout most of this book, I have leaned rather heavily on the concept of structure in my thinking about history and the social sciences, although always in full awareness of the concept's essentially metaphorical character. In this chapter I suggest a rather different metaphorization of social life. I begin by considering the notion that the social may be thought of as a "language game" and end by suggesting that it must also—simultaneously and dialectically—be thought of as a "built environment." One reader of a previous version of this chapter felt that by moving from a no-

tion of structure to one of language game, I was watering down the
strongly sociological emphasis of the previous chapters. I hope this is not
the case. I am attempting to set forth in fresh terms a social ontology that
seems to me compatible with the "structural" approach to history and the
social sciences that I have elaborated—both theoretically and empirically—in the previous chapters. While it is certainly true that neither "language game" nor "built environment" has the incantatory rhetorical force
of the "structure" metaphor, this may sometimes be an advantage: the heavy
semantic load of "structure" can occasionally short-circuit our analysis and
make it appear that something has been explained when it has simply been
covered by a language that implies explanatory closure. I see the theorization worked out in this chapter as perfectly compatible with the arguments
about structure that I initially elaborate in chapter 4 and utilize extensively
in other chapters. Whether my perception of compatibility is accurate or
even plausible must, in the end, be decided by my readers.

HISTORY AND USAGE OF "SOCIAL" AND "SOCIETY"

"Social" and its cognate "society" are notoriously vague terms; they are concepts that, paradoxically, have proven as amorphous as they are indispensable. A brief glance at the history of the terms "social" and "society," and at
the usage of these terms in ordinary academic language, might at least clarify the nature of our shared confusion. "Social" and "society" are originally
derived from the Latin *socius*, meaning friend or companion. Early usages
of "society" tend to imply active companionship (as in "they sought out one
another's society"). It also came to signify "persons associated together by
some common interest or purpose," in other words, a corporate collectivity formed by a voluntary act of association (as in "the Society of Jesus"
or "the Society of Surgeons"). Both of these meanings retained an active
sense of willful association among persons. A more passive, abstract, general, and reified usage—closer to our predominant contemporary meaning—became increasingly common in English from the seventeenth century onward. Society in this sense signified "the aggregate of persons living
in a more or less ordered community" or "under the same organization or
government" (OED), as in "a due reverence . . . towards Society wherein we
live" or "to the benefit of society" (Williams 1983, 291–94). The most widespread philosophical theorization of society in the later seventeenth and
eighteenth centuries, the "social contract" theory, actually combined these
latter two meanings. According to social contract theory, society in the
passive, abstract, and general sense was a product of a formal act of associ-

ation, and the rights, duties, and limits of citizens and governments derived from this initial act. The ubiquity of the social contract theory in the
eighteenth century indicates the continuing grip of the active and unreified
sense of the term.

In the nineteenth century, the more abstract meanings came to predominate. Society, in the nineteenth century, had what might be called both a
limited and an expansive meaning. The limited meaning, which derived
from eighteenth-century anti-absolutist political theory, defined society as
a sphere of human activity distinct from the state and in principle exterior
to it. This meaning, both in the eighteenth century and in the nineteenth,
was often designated by adding the term "civil" to "society" (Cohen 1998,
369–72). Although this usage defined civil society as distinct from the state,
it also commonly had an expansive implication: eighteenth-century social
contract theory, where the usage first developed, argued that civil society
was prior to the state and that the state should therefore be subordinated
to its requirements. Nineteenth-century liberals, although they generally
abandoned the notion of a primordial social contract, continued to argue
that the state existed at the behest of and should be subordinated to civil
society. Over the course of the nineteenth century, however, an even more
expansive abstract and general meaning of "society" became common. The
early advocates of "social science," such as Saint Simon, began to conceptualize society as having "social laws" that were impersonal, anonymous, and
independent of the conscious intentions of the individuals of whom it was
composed, but that were, like the laws of nature, amenable to scientific
study (Baker 1964). It was this sense that was taken up by Comte, who
coined the term "sociology" to signify the scientific study of society. This
process of reification of the social reached its apogee in Durkheim's notion
of society as a "sui generis" collective reality that acts upon individuals as an
external constraining force (Durkheim [1912] 1965, 29).

This sense of society as a reified totality is surely the predominant
contemporary usage of the term in both academic and ordinary language;
other meanings of society have become decidedly secondary.[2] The term
can still be used to designate formal associations (as in "Society for French
Historical Studies" or the French bank "Société Générale"), but society in

2. The term "civil society" has been revived in the late twentieth century in discussions of
would-be totalitarian political orders, essentially to designate forms of association that remain
independent of the long tentacles of the state. But such discussions always use the adjective
"civil" to modify society, because the unmodified usage would imply a totality that included both
the state and non-state institutions. See Cohen (1998).

the sense of companionship is now distinctly archaic. The generalization and standardization of the abstract usage of the term has undoubtedly been furthered by the usually implicit identification of "society" with "nation" or "nation state" (as in "French society" or "Jordanian society"). It is, however, my sense that in recent years, at least in academic usage, this implicit identification of society with the nation state has put the term under a certain semantic pressure. Because the processes of "globalization" have made it increasingly difficult to think of the nation-state as enclosing a bounded social order, I find myself using the term "society" considerably less frequently and more hesitantly than I would have two or three decades ago.[3]

The meanings of "social" have remained rather more ambiguous in contemporary usage than those of " society." "Social" may refer to society as a reified totality (as in "social law" or "social norms"), but the sense of companionship or conviviality remains current (as in "social gathering" or "he has a rich social life"). Even in academic usage, "social" does not necessarily signify something that pertains to the society as a whole. The term is also used for things that pertain to the relations among particular persons or groups (as in "social networks" or "the social world of the New York artist"). This ambiguity of the term "social" has led to the invention of the term "societal," which many social scientists now use when referring to characteristics of society as a whole. In this usage, a "societal norm" would be one recognized universally in a society, whereas a "social norm" would be a norm recognized only by some "sub-societal" group. The universalization of this usage might somewhat attenuate this particular ambiguity of the term "social," but thus far the societal/social distinction is a distinctly minority usage, and in any case this is just one ambiguity among many. The meaning of "social" is rendered yet more ambiguous by another nineteenth-century development—a contrast between "social" and "individual." This distinction arose largely out of critiques of liberal economic ideas and practices, which were branded by their opponents as egoist or individualist, and contrasted with properly "social" considerations—of

3. The conventional equation of "society" with "nation state" has been sharply challenged by Immanuel Wallerstein and his many acolytes in the "world-system" school of social science, who argue that what we commonly regard as distinct and autonomous "societies" are in fact only sub-units of a larger global social totality (Wallerstein 1974a, 1974b). Without accepting Wallerstein's hypostatization of the "world-system" as a global "society," Arjun Appadurai (1996) has argued that—thanks to increased migration and the development of new technologies of transportation and communication that enable immense transnational cultural flows—the world is increasingly made up of not of distinct and bounded societies, but of overlapping transnational ethnic communities that he dubs "global ethnoscapes."

solidarity, of concern for the fate of the poor, of fellow feeling. "Social" in
this sense had a strong moral charge. It was used in such terms as "the social question," quickly found its way into the new term "socialism," and is
still very much with us in terms like "social activist." Socialism was, of
course, largely a masculine affair, but social in the morally charged sense
also gained a distinctly feminine inflection in bourgeois discourses of social reform, which both focused on the domestic failings of working-class
families, rather than the inadequacy of workers' wages, and identified female middle-class philanthropic workers as the chosen agents of reform
(Riley 1988). This feminized meliorist conception of the social has continuing echoes in the contemporary academic discipline of "social work."

    "The social," in short, is an exceptionally complex or polysemic concept.
As used by most academics, "social" actually calls up a combination of these
various meanings. Thus, the term "social history" tends to imply simultaneously the history of everyday bonds of friendship and association, the
history of relations between persons or between groups of persons, the
history of the totality of such relations in a given society or aggregate of societies, and the history of the struggles and sufferings of the poor and oppressed. But the difficulty of the term "social" goes beyond its ambiguity
or polysemy. Virtually all of the central analytic concepts of social science
are polysemous—think of such terms as rationality, symbol, structure,
charisma, cost, cause, or exploitation, to take a few examples more or less
at random.[4] In addition to being ambiguous or polysemous, "social" is beset by a peculiar vagueness, even mysteriousness, that most of these other
terms lack.

    I think we can appreciate the vagueness of the term "social" by examin-
ing the standard academic division of labor in the social sciences and
humanities, which is based on a distinction between the adjectives "social,"
"economic," "political," and "cultural" or the corresponding nouns "society,"
"economics," "politics," and "culture." These terms, which took on their
modern meanings in the late eighteenth and early nineteenth centuries,
distinguish different spheres of life or activity that, by the end of the nineteenth century, were studied by different academic specialties: sociology,

4. Indeed, I would maintain that the polysemy of these concepts is actually linked to their
centrality because their centrality is enhanced by their ability to call up simultaneously a number of interrelated meanings. Moreover, their centrality enhances their polysemy, since speakers
and writers are likely to attempt to harness the terms' power by stretching their meaning to cover
the arguments currently being made. On the relationship between the power and polysemous
character of symbols in the context of ritual, see Turner (1967, 50–51).

economics, political science, and, in the complex case of culture, either anthropology or the various "humanist" disciplines of literature, classics, art
history, musicology, and philosophy. But on closer inspection, the four
seemingly parallel terms are in fact asymmetrical. "Economic," "political,"
and "cultural" are usually understood as referring to particular sorts of activities carried on in particular sorts of institutions. But "social" refers to
no particular institutional location; it is characteristic of all institutional
spheres and types of activities. As this difference implies, there is also an
asymmetry in the subject matter studied by the different academic disciplines: economics, literature, and political science have usually been seen
as studies of restricted and namable domains, whereas sociology may
study any and all domains—any activity that falls under the rubric of
"society" as a whole.[5] As this difference implies, the "social" is understood
as in some sense containing or subsuming the other three supposedly parallel categories. A claim that economics, politics, and culture are all subsets
of society seems unexceptionable, whereas a claim that, say, economics, society, and culture are subsets of politics is distinctly counter-intuitive and
contentious. Another way of getting at this asymmetry is to note that in
the set of distinctions "economic/social," "political/social," and "cultural/
social," it turns out that the first of the terms in these pairs is always a
marked term and the second unmarked. The social is defined in each distinction purely by its contrast to some other specific and (more) definable
sphere but lacks a specific definition of its own. In each contrast, the social
refers to a rather vague but nevertheless significant residual category indicating that there are other forces, structures, and relations that determine
human conduct than those named in the first of the contrasting terms.

The fact that the term "social" is peculiarly vague does not mean that it
is vacuous. Quite the contrary, the term is vague because it is oversaturated
with meaning. This has been true since the Enlightenment, when, as the
cultural historian Keith Baker has argued, the concept of society replaced
religion "as the ultimate ground of order" (1994, 113). In the disenchanted
world that the Enlightenment invented and that the social sciences have

5. It is interesting to note that in the past couple of decades, the domain covered by literary
studies has expanded extraordinarily, so that scholars in departments of English or German now
regularly study not only film, popular culture, art, architecture, and music, but also the discourses of history, the social sciences, biology, journalism, physical science, and technology. This
remarkable expansion in the subject matter of literary studies has been accompanied and enabled by an equally remarkable inflation in the meanings of the terms culture and language,
which, in the last third of the twentieth century, came to challenge "social" and "society" as foundational concepts in the human sciences.

taken up as their object of study, "society" and "the social" came to signify
the complex and ultimately unknowable reality of human existence, a reality previously represented by such religious concepts as Divine Will or
Providence. "The social" inherited the mysterious ontological referent of
the divine, but "the social" represents this ultimate reality very differently —
not as an inscrutable anthropomorphic will but as constituted by a complex "interdependence in human relations" (1994, 114). Diderot's and
d'Alembert's *Encyclopédie* said of the "philosophe" that "civil society is, so to
speak, a divinity on earth for him." As Baker points out, this holds for the
contemporary scholar as well. "Society," he remarks, "is our God, the ontological frame of our human existence. The social (as anyone who presumes
to question its priority is reminded) is our name for the 'really real.' It se-
cures the existential ground beneath our feet, presenting a bedrock of reality beneath the shifting sands of discourse" (1994, 95–96).[6] Baker (who
has indeed been chided by social historians for questioning the priority of
"the social") here gets to the historical origins of our contemporary inability to define "social" and "society." The concept of "the social" is vague and
mysterious because it still carries a whiff of the divine. An underlying generalized ontological signification — of the totality of complex interrelatedness that we understand as constituting the basic reality of human existence — continues to adhere to its varied uses.

Baker's historical exegesis of the eighteenth century meanings of "society" and "social" exemplifies contemporary cultural history at its best. His
research throws important light on the conceptual terrain of the eighteenth
century, but it also clarifies current theoretical conundrums. It performs
the essential and edifying "postmodern" task of making us aware that what
we have commonly taken as a solid and indubitable intellectual foundation
is in fact a contingent historical construct and therefore mutable and open
to question. "The social" is not "the really real" but only a sign conventionally understood as signifying "the really real." "The social," Baker reminds
us, is a historically constituted fact of discourse, not a self-evident and
permanently valid category of the real world. But understanding that "the
social" is a discursive fact does not dissolve the problem that its novel
eighteenth-century usages attempted to solve — providing an ontological
grounding of human life. Because contemporary scholars in the social sciences and humanities still occupy the secular disenchanted world created

6. I have translated the passage from the *Encyclopédie*, which Baker quotes in French.

by the Enlightenment, they cannot avoid the ontological questions and anxieties that such a world poses.

In this respect, it is important to recognize that "the social" and "society" are by no means the only terms that serve as generalized signifiers for "the really real." In fact "history" itself is precisely such a term. The oldest meanings of "history" derive more or less directly from the root meaning "story" and refer to history as a narrative or representation of the past. These include (1) "a narrative, tale, or story"; (2) "a written narrative constituting a continuous methodical record, in order of time, of important or public events"; and (3) "that branch of knowledge that deals with past events" (OED). In the seventeenth and eighteenth centuries, "history" also began to be used to refer to the sequence of happenings about which a history might be narrated: "the whole train of events connected with a particular country, society, person, thing, etc." In the eighteenth and nineteenth centuries, history also came to be used in a more abstract sense as "the aggregate of past events in general." Raymond Williams points out in *Keywords* that "history," in this usage, is viewed as "human self-development" and that "past events are seen not as specific *histories* but as a continuous and connected process." He attributes this usage to the new "universal histories" of the sort written by Vico or the Scottish Enlightenment authors (Williams 1983, 146). "History" in this sense is in many respects parallel to the generalized meaning of "society" that emerged in the same era. History is the entire human past and is thought of as determining or shaping the human present and future. Just as "society" was conceived of as governed by "social laws" and "social forces," so history was thought to be governed by "historical laws" and "historical forces." If society is our God, then history is the *same* God, viewed as acting through time. Properly understood, the term "history" is hardly less difficult, mysterious, and abstract than "social" or "society." "Society" and "history" are but two aspects of the Enlightenment idea of a self-created secular human existence that moderns and postmoderns alike posit as the ultimate ontological ground.

Nor can the difficulty of the generalized ontological meaning of "the social" be avoided by abandoning the term "social" and switching to "cultural"—as in "cultural history." As the term culture has become ever more widely used, it has also come to carry much of the same ontological baggage as "social" and "history." Moreover, the usage of the term "culture" actually has a history quite parallel to those of "society" and "history." Prior to the eighteenth century the active sense of cultivation was primary, but

in the course of the eighteenth and nineteenth centuries a more abstract
meaning emerged—the way of life or the aesthetic and intellectual forms
that a people or a society develop over the course of its history by means
of such cultivation. Eventually, in the late nineteenth and twentieth centuries,"culture" also came to stand for the symbolically constituted ground
of human existence in general (Williams 1983, 87–93)—to use Max Weber's metaphor, the self-spun web of meaning in which humankind is suspended. This generalized usage of culture was particularly characteristic
of the discipline of anthropology, in which distinct peoples—the Bororo,
the Ndembu, or the Balinese—were commonly characterized as"cultures"
or "societies" more or less interchangeably."Culture," no less than "society"
or"history," refers to a generalized, secular, and humanly created reality—
it just specifies that reality in a somewhat different way."Language" and
"discourse" have also—although rather more recently—become generalized signifiers of the secular ontological ground of human life. Replacing
the"social" in social history by the term"cultural" or"discursive" does not,
then, nullify the ontological problem that Baker has found lurking in the
terms"social" and"society." I believe that any attempt to remedy the vagueness of the social by this means will, over the long run, simply transfer the
same foundational vagueness—and rhetorical power—to the would-be
substitute term: culture, or language, or discourse.

IS ALL THE WORLD A TEXT?

How, then, do we lift ourselves from this epistemic murk? I think we are
stuck with the term"social," in part because both"social" and"society" are
constantly used in this highly generalized foundational way in ordinary
speech. Attempting to ban this usage of "social" from our academic vocabularies or to replace it with some other term would almost certainly be futile. Besides, the very generality of the concept"social" also makes it a particularly capacious container. Better than any substitute, I believe, it can
signify the totality of "interdependence in human relations" (to use Baker's
phrase) that since the Enlightenment we have come to understand as the
ultimate ontological ground of human life. I believe we must confront the
conundrum that Baker has discovered in the social and wrestle with it; that
we must at once acknowledge the existence of a certain irreducible vagueness or mystery surrounding this ultimate foundational concept and at the
same time clarify it as much as possible by conceptualizing it more explicitly. I propose, therefore, that we should continue to accept"social" as our

foundational term and to understand such terms as "culture" and "language" as contained within the social.

On the other hand, it is crucial to give the conceptual container signified by the social some sort of internal structure and content so that it can be used to sort out, clarify, and explain the nature and dynamics of interdependence in human relations. I suggest that we begin this task by looking back at the original meaning of the term. Initially "social" signified friendship or companionship, what sociologists might call a face-to-face relationship. All the subsequent meanings of the term, I would suggest, are metaphorical extensions of this original meaning. Thus, in addition to the original meaning of unmediated, face-to face-relationship, "social" and "society" came to signify the various *mediated* forms of human interrelationship—for example, willfully formed associations, the aggregate of persons living in an ordered community of some sort, and eventually the reified totality "society" whose social laws could be discerned by the social sciences. I suggest that a useful way to get a conceptual handle on the social is to think of it in terms of the various *mediations* that place people into "social" relations with one another—mediations that may not make them companions but that, in one way or another, make them interdependent members of each other's worlds.

It should be noted at the outset that this approach departs sharply from conventional or common-sense conceptualizations of the social, which tend to begin not with forms of mediation but with the various social units formed *by* mediations. The common-sense view understands social science as the study of "societies," which are seen as composed of a multitude of groups, classes, social categories, or institutions, which are in turn composed of individual persons. The social would then be the relationships between these groups and between the groups and the individuals that make them up. This is what might be called the building-block view of social structure. It is based on the implicit identification of the "society" with the bounded nation state, and it assumes that the social units and individuals that make up the society are themselves bounded units that are assembled into a structured whole. In my opinion, this common-sense view has several important flaws. First, it implies that boundedness of groups and of societies is a natural condition rather than an (at best incomplete) achievement that, when present, needs to be explained. Second, it privileges stasis over process, implying that historical change, when it occurs, must be a consequence of strains, conflicts, or contradictions between already constituted groups, rather than an ever-present process out of which groups are themselves precipitated, re-shaped, or dissolved. Third, it implies that individuals, as the fundamental building blocks of all social structures, are autonomous and given, rather than ever-changing products of the social processes in which they are implicated. Fourth, it assumes that developments taking place within "societies" are autochthonous, an outcome of relationships between units of the bounded society. This makes it conceptually difficult to take into account the effects of the many and important processes, loyalties, or forces that transcend the assumed boundaries of a given society.

I do not wish to deny the importance of the phenomena that the building-block model of the social highlights. Groups, institutions, classes, ethnicities, professions, and the like do frequently manage to establish relatively clear boundaries and to police them effectively. Historical changes often do result from conflicts or strains between well-bounded groups or institutions. Individuals do frequently establish solid identities that endure for long periods. Many crucial developments in modern nations result to a significant extent from forces and relations internal to the boundaries of the nation. But all of these phenomena seem to me contingent historical outcomes of more basic social processes, not fundamental building blocks of social order in general. What I take as basic are streams or sequences of mediated human actions and the humanly created and therefore changeable forms that mediate them. I certainly would not deny that institutions, bounded groups, or national boundaries sometimes figure among the humanly created forms that mediate streams of human action. But they are members of a much broader set of phenomena, whose natures and spatial geometries—sometimes weakly bounded, sometimes extremely far-flung, sometimes mutually interpenetrating or entwined—are often very different from the building blocks assumed by the common-sense model of the social.

The building-block model is of course a metaphor, one likening "social structure" to the structure of a building. This architectural notion of structure is a very old and deeply entrenched epistemic metaphor in all of the sciences, physical and biological as well as social or human. The more interpretivist account of the social I am developing here is based on a much more recent but also very widespread epistemic metaphor: the claim that society or the social is like language. It is this metaphor that underlies the by now much celebrated "linguistic turn" that swept through the human sciences in the final third of the twentieth century. The language metaphor for society or the social order has been with us for a half-century now; one might reasonably date it from the publication Claude Lévi-Strauss's *Structures élémentaires de la parenté* in 1949 and, in a quite different Anglo-American version, from the publication of Ludwig Wittgenstein's *Philosophical Investigations* in 1953.[7] The history of the spread and mutations of the linguistic metaphor in the human sciences since that time is rich, complex, and still mostly unwritten, but it is clear that the "linguistic turn" has been one of the great intellectual movements of the second half of the twentieth century.[8] This can be indicated clearly by invoking the names of some of the major thinkers who have worked in this complex and evolving tradition. Here is a sampling: Louis Althusser (1969), J. L. Austin (1962), Roland Barthes ([1957] 1972), Michel de Certeau (1984), Natalie Zemon Davis (1975), Jacques Derrida (1976), Michel Foucault (1971), François Furet (1981), Clifford Geertz (1973a), Jürgen Habermas (1984), Julia Kristeva (1980), Thomas Kuhn (1962), Jacques Lacan (1977), J. G. A. Pocock (1975), Paul Ricoeur (1974), Marshall Sahlins (1976), Quentin Skinner (1978), Victor Turner (1967), and Raymond Williams (1983).

I believe that language has worked so effectively as a metaphor for the social because, to use an Enlightenment conceit, it is founded on the nature of things: human social action can be understood as linguistic because humans are symbol-using animals. Much of what humans accomplish depends on the use of language in the most literal sense — we coordinate activities, make plans, communicate emotional states, and fix the meanings of our experiences by means of speech or writing. But what makes language so powerful as a *metaphor* is that when humans assign meaning to things and communicate those meanings to others by means that are, strictly speaking, nonlinguistic — for example, by gesture, image, or the fashioning of objects — those assignments of meaning operate in ways strongly analogous to language. Image, gesture, or other practices can be thought of as having something like a semantics (a system of meaningful symbols) and a syntax (a set of rules for combining them). Likewise, image or gesture can be seen as having what the great structural linguist Fer-

---

7. Lévi-Strauss's work was not well known in the English-speaking world until the 1960s (1961, 1963a, 1963b, 1966, 1969). It should be noted that Lévi-Strauss's work was modeled upon the so-called structural school of linguistics, which had already appropriated and of course significantly transformed the much older and scientifically prestigious architectural metaphor of structure. In fact, the French version of the school of social research based on the language metaphor was generally known as "structuralism."

8. Histories of aspects of the linguistic turn are Dosse (1997) and Megill (1985).

dinand de Saussure (1966) designated as a *langue* and a *parole* aspect—that is, as having a known set of rules that must be grasped synchronically (langue) and a flow of practice (parole) that must be grasped diachronically. Langue, as a structure or system, simultaneously enables and constrains parole—that is, it gives the speaker (or image maker or gesturer) tools with which to say something and thereby limits what can be said. And parole both reproduces langue by instantiating its structures and effects change in langue by stretching, bending or elaborating the rules— partly for the sheer fun of it, partly to find adequate means of making sense of an unpredictable world. It is precisely because nonlinguistic meaningful actions have these quasi-linguistic qualities that language is a fruitful metaphor for the social.

The language metaphor also entails a specific, linguistically inflected methodological program: what I would call *paradigmatic explanation*. This form of explanation accounts for patterns of human action by specifying the paradigms or codes that enable human actors to produce them—for example, the implicit rules of phonics, semantics, and syntax that enable the speaker of a language to enunciate a comprehensible sentence, or the vocabularies, rhetorics, stylistic conventions, and so on that mark linguistic utterances as belonging to specific discourses. A particular instance of performance is explained, in other words, as an instantiation of the (usually implicit) preexisting code. This explanatory form was developed most influentially by such pioneering linguists as Ferdinand de Saussure (1966) and Roman Jakobson (1970), who delineated the binary logics of various linguistic forms. Paradigmatic explanation, in one or another of its forms, is the fundamental tool of what are generally called "interpretive" methods. Interpretive scholars proceed by "reading" texts, rituals, images, sequences of action, or other repositories of meaning and then attempting to reconstruct the codes—phonological, iconographic, technical, semantic, rhetorical, architectural, gestural, or what have you—that the texts or text analogues instantiate and upon which their authors can be presumed to have drawn in carrying out their actions.

This broadly linguistic conception of the social has been influential across almost the entire range of the human sciences—with the exception, as far as I can tell, of economics. Apart from the field of literary studies, which has, of course, always studied linguistic meaning, the language metaphor has probably been most influential in anthropology and history. The large and thriving subfields of cultural anthropology and cultural history are both based on the linguistic model of the social. My strategy in this essay will be to focus on the ontological assumptions underlying contemporary cultural history, but I believe that my arguments will be broadly valid for interpretive social science across a wide range of disciplines. I shall begin by considering the views of Keith Baker, a leading contemporary cultural historian who has been introduced earlier in this essay. Because he has argued with particular cogency for an uncompromisingly linguistic approach to history, his views make a good starting place for my own argument.[9]

In the introduction to his path-breaking book *Inventing the French Revolution*, Baker begins by offering what he calls a "linguistic" definition of politics and political culture, but soon moves on to argue that the social is also purely linguistic. Politics, he says, is

> the activity through which individuals and groups in any society articulate, negotiate, implement, and enforce the competing claims they make upon one another and upon the whole. Political culture is, in this sense, the set of discourses or symbolic practices by which these claims are made. . . . Political authority is, in this view, essentially a matter of linguistic authority: first, in the sense that political functions are defined and allocated within the framework of a given political discourse; and second, in the sense that their exercise takes the form of upholding authoritative definitions of the terms within that discourse.

Having defined politics as a linguistic phenomenon, he proceeds to answer the anticipated objection: that such a definition "denies the relevance of social interests to political practice." His response to this is formulated on a distinctly ontological terrain. He denies categorically the existence of "social realities independent of symbolic meanings."

> All social activity has a symbolic dimension that gives it meaning, just as all symbolic activity has a social dimension that gives it point. This is to argue that claims to delimit the field of discourse in relation to nondiscursive social realities that lie beyond it invariably point to a domain of action that is itself discursively constituted. They distinguish, in effect, between different discursive practices — different language games — rather than between discursive and nondiscursive phenomena. (Baker 1990, 4–5)

Baker begins this passage by asserting that human activities have two parallel and apparently equal dimensions: the "social" and the "symbolic."

---

9. It should probably be pointed out that a position quite similar to Baker's has been elaborated quite independently by Gareth Stedman Jones (1996).

Baker's language of dimensions implies that all domains of social action are constituted simultaneously by both "social" and "symbolic" considerations—that the shaping of the social by the symbolic and the symbolic by the social is mutual and fully reciprocal. But after setting up this apparent parallel, Baker effectively denies it by asserting that so-called "social realities" are themselves "discursively constituted." The implication of his argument would seem to be that "the social" is an illusion and that invoking it is an analytical error: what appear to be "social" influences on discourse are in reality just links between different language games. Or, alternatively, we might say that Baker is redefining the social (understood, still, as "interdependence in human relationships") as entirely a matter of *intertextuality*. The interrelationship of humans takes place, Baker seems to be saying, purely through the *medium* of language. As far as I can tell, Baker is here using language not as a metaphor, but literally; for him, apparently, the social really *is* language. History, or society, on this view, must be understood as a complex, multilevel text that we humans, ourselves constituted by the text, are nevertheless continually writing and revising.

But precisely what sort of text is the world? Baker is an expert on what one might call "high" political culture—political theory and formal political argument. It is certainly true that the world of formal political argument is profoundly textual. But although Baker asserts that *all* human practices are discursively constituted, he actually has had little to say in his empirical historical studies about the sorts of practices that are usually evoked by the term "social"—such matters as work relations, consumption, modes of sociability, kinship, institutional dynamics, status hierarchies, or material culture. We must, therefore, take on faith his claim that such arenas of practice are best understood as "language games" and can therefore be analyzed adequately by means of linguistic methods. Roger Chartier, another leading cultural historian of early modern France, has sharply challenged Baker's assertion that all such spheres of human practice are linguistic or textual (Baker and Chartier 1994; Chartier 1997). He insists that even within the realm of cultural practices, the textual model is of strictly limited applicability. "Experience," he warns, "is not reducible to discourse" and historians therefore "must guard against unconstrained use of the category of the 'text'—a term too often inappropriately applied to practices . . . whose tactics and procedures bear no resemblance to discursive strategies" (Chartier 1997, 18–19, 20). For Chartier, maintaining the distinction between discursive and nondiscursive practices is essential. There is, he argues, "a radical difference between the lettered, logocentric, and hermeneutic rationality that organizes the production of discourses and the rationality informing all other realms of practice" (Chartier 1997, 77).

Yet on closer inspection many of the analyses of "nondiscursive practices" that Chartier singles out as exemplary have a surprisingly "textual" quality—for example, Louis Marin's work (1988, 1993) on the logic of images, Michel de Certeau's (1984) on practices of daily life, and Michel Foucault's (1977) on the microtechnologies of discipline. It is true that these works focus on practices whose logics are not strictly speaking linguistic—iconic representation, urban strolling, or meticulous bodily training. But practices of this kind are "textual" in a more extended or metaphorical sense—that is, to use Chartier's own definition of textuality, they are "based on signs whose meaning is fixed by convention" and "constitute semiotic systems open to interpretation."[10] Although Chartier sharply criticizes what he calls "the American 'linguistic turn,'" he does not deny that all social life is symbolically constituted. He merely insists that the symbolic practices that constitute social life cannot be reduced to forms of *discourse*. Chartier reminds us that many, perhaps most, of the practices studied by cultural history are not governed by the specific semiotic mechanisms of language, but by a great variety of other quite distinct semiotic practices—iconic, ludic, spatial, technical, gestural, ritual, disciplinary, and the like.

By semiotic practices, I mean any practices that communicate information by means of some sort of signs and are therefore open to interpretation. I agree with Chartier that use of the linguistic term "discourse" as the general signifier for semiotic practices is misleading and that it threatens to turn our attention away from practices that operate by rules of a nonlinguistic kind. But in my opinion Chartier's observations do not so much refute Baker's point about the "discursive" constitution of all human practices as they complicate and enrich it, pointing out that the world of meaning is much wider than the world of speech and writing.[11] We might say that Chartier reminds us that the notion that the world is a text is, after all, a metaphor, and that our metaphorical "inscriptions" of meaning—our semiotic practices—are fixed in many media besides language. Take the example of kinship. Kinship is certainly in part a genuinely linguistic phenomenon: there is a structured set of terms for kin relations, and there are

10. Chartier himself (1997, 81) defines texts in this way in his discussion of D. F. McKensie. For a comparable extension of the notion of text, see Ricoeur (1971).

11. For a more extensive critical evaluation of Chartier's position, see Sewell (1998).

many discourses prescribing the appropriate forms of feeling and behavior among kin. But kinship as a meaning system is also "inscribed" or fixed in sex, in procreation, in exchanges of money or material goods, and in feelings of security, rage, or loyalty.[12] Kinship is "written" in the scripts of the body and material possessions, not only in texts or utterances.

I believe that one useful way of grasping the nature of the world's metaphorical "textuality" is to consider further Baker's Wittgensteinian reference to "language games." Baker's usage of the language game metaphor seems to suggest that the key to understanding various practices that we think of as "social" is to show how they are constituted by linguistic practices. But it seems to me that the implication of the term "language games" in Wittgenstein's usage actually points as much in the opposite direction — the metaphor indicates that in order to know what words mean, we have to understand the system of structured and purposive activities, the "game," within which they are used. It is true that words are part and parcel of the activity in question — these are *language* games. But the meanings of words are not intrinsic; they are given by their place in the activity being carried out. As Wittgenstein puts it, "the term 'language-*game*' is meant to bring into prominence the fact that the *speaking* of language is part of an activity, or of a form of life" (Wittgenstein 1958, 11). The implication is that although a given activity involves specific linguistic usages and although language is constitutive of the activity in question, the activities — that is, the "language games" or "forms of life" — are not *reducible* to language. Although they are in important respects made up of language, they are also made up of something more than language.

This is obvious in the case of the language that Wittgenstein posits at the very inception of the *Philosophical Investigations*. There we are asked to imagine a language used for communication between a builder and an assistant, a language with only four words: "block," "pillar," "slab," and "beam." In this language game, the builder calls out a word — e.g., "slab" — and the assistant brings it to him. In this instance, which Wittgenstein characterizes as "a complete primitive language," it is clear that the four-word language only makes sense within the activity or language game of building, in which the various building materials are brought to the builder who uses them to erect a house, a temple, or a barn (3). Simply knowing the words that constitute the language would tell us nothing unless we understood what building was, why building materials had to be brought to the

12. Schneider (1968) famously argued that the central symbol of American kinship is coitus.

builder, and how they might be assembled to make a structure. To be sure, Wittgenstein was a philosopher of language and he in fact paid little systematic attention to the nonlinguistic aspects of language games or forms of life in the *Philosophical Investigations*. But if we are to make serious use of his concepts in analyzing historical processes, I maintain that we need to think as seriously about the "games" aspect of Wittgenstein's metaphor as about the "language" aspect.[13]

Here it might be useful to think about the many far from "primitive" games — most obviously competitive athletic games — in which the role of linguistic utterance per se is distinctly secondary. There are, of course, linguistic terms for the various moves and meaningful objects in, for example, the game of basketball: "free throw," "pass," "rebound," "foul line," "backboard," "point guard," "three-point line," "post-up," "jump shot," "pick and roll," "power forward," "pump fake," "fast break," "the paint," "hard foul," "press," and so on. Language figures in basketball in many ways. There are written rules; infractions of rules may be explained verbally by the referees; strategies can be developed and explained in language; coaches instruct players partly by telling them what they are doing wrong and right; teams play in leagues that represent cities or educational institutions, and the identities between the teams and the cities or schools are sustained by endless talk and writing. In all these senses, the game of basketball is constituted by language. But most of the knowledge and strategy that makes a basketball game work and that distinguishes a skillful player or team from a mediocre one is not constituted primarily by language — it is above all bodily or kinesthetic. The jump shot or the dunk is communicated from one player to another visually rather than linguistically and it is mastered by physical emulation and repetition. The role of language in teaching basketball skills is itself keyed to the kinesthetic register — "make sure you're at the top of the jump before you release the shot," "put a little more arc on the ball," or "extend your follow-through." It may be argued that this kinesthetic knowledge itself constitutes a semiotic system. Players with kinesthetic competence give off and respond to each others' bodily cues and are capable of making meaningful kinesthetic innovations that lead to responding innovations by teammates and opponents. These cues and responses are also interpreted and appreciated by knowledgeable spectators. One indication that kinesthetic basketball competency is semiotic is that strategies are often based on bodily deception — like the pump fake, which

13. Here I am following up a suggestion made in conversation by Stuart Hall.

mimics the beginning of a jump shot, thereby making the defender leave his or her feet to disrupt the expected shot, after which the shooter can go up for an unhindered jump shot while the defender is on the way down. But I am deeply skeptical about any claim that this system can be said to work by genuinely linguistic rules. It might be possible to analyze the kinesthetic dimension of basketball as having a syntax and semantics, or as system of signs whose meanings are determined by their relations of contrast with other signs. But I suspect that efforts to apply a fully discursive or linguistic model would probably result in fundamentally misconstruing the dynamics of the game and missing the distinctive logics that actually characterize basketball—and probably kinesthetic systems of knowledge in general.[14]

Thinking about games like basketball reinforces and radicalizes Chartier's argument against the linguistic reductionism implicit in much current cultural history and revalues the significance of Baker's invocation of language games. The diverse and interconnected domains of practice—or language games—that make up the object of historical study are by no means reducible to what usually goes by the name of discourse. But, as I think the example of basketball demonstrates, they are complex systems of meaningful action. In this sense they are semiotic systems, or, since they connect discourses with nondiscursive semiotic practices, we might say they are semiotic complexes. They therefore can be subjected to the general family of methods that are usually associated with the study of linguistic phenomena, in which the character of observed practices are explained by specifying the paradigms or codes that enable human actors to produce them. One means of correcting what I have called in chapter 2 the "thinning of the social" in cultural history would be to extend radically the range and ambition of cultural history. We could do this by shifting our focus from discourses in the strict sense—that is, linguistic performances—toward attempts at specifying the codes or paradigms underlying meaningful practices that seem resistant to linguistic analysis and that might conventionally be thought of precisely as the sort of "nondiscursive social realities" that causally limit or shape discourses. Important examples of such efforts already exist, such as Richard Biernacki's study of how largely implicit and practical conceptions of wage labor structured work experience in nineteenth-century British and German factories (1995), Loïc Wacquant's studies of the bodily practices of boxers (1995, 2004), Peter

---

14. For a very different kinesthetic semiotic practice, see Wacquant (1995, 2004).

REFIGURING THE "SOCIAL" IN SOCIAL SCIENCE

Galison's studies of the "languages" of the mechanical apparatus of physics (1997), or Anthony Wallace's brief but brilliant excursus on the semiotics of mechanical thinking in nineteenth-century America (1978, 237–79).

Such a program for historical research would remain within the territory staked out by Baker, when he claims that invocations of social causality are references to domains of action that are themselves discursively constituted. Or, rather, it would remain within the territory staked out by the expanded or metaphorized version of this claim: that such invocations refer to domains of action constituted by some sort of *semiotic* practices. But it would significantly alter the claim by pointing out that the paradigms or codes uncovered in such research are often likely to be governed by semiotic logics very different in form and in medium from linguistic codes. Rather than making it appear that we can easily make sense of the relationships between different "language games" by already available discursive methods—for example, those of literary criticism or "Cambridge school" intellectual history—this radicalization of cultural history would imply the search for a much wider variety of semiotic methods.[15] And it would also imply close attention to the question of how semiotic practices carried out in such different media and according to such different logics are *articulated* to one another.

THE PROBLEM OF ARTICULATION

By "articulation" I mean, in the words of the *Oxford English Dictionary*, "the action or process of jointing; the state of being jointed; or the mode of jointing or junction." In the case of discourses, articulation implies the attachment or "jointing" of distinct discourses to one another. In poststructuralist language, the operation of joining together distinct discourses is often called "suturing." Whereas "articulation" might be taken to imply that the discourses joined together fit together naturally—as the vertebra are articulated in a human body—the term "suture" implies the active intervention of a surgeon who sews together tissues previously not joined. The question of the articulation or suturing of discourses is the bread and butter of cultural history. For example, Lenore Davidoff and Catherine Hall have shown how, in nineteenth-century Britain, a discourse of femininity was attached to a discourse about the middle-class

---

15. I should avow that my citing of Cambridge school intellectual history is not entirely innocent. Baker's style of cultural history is very much in the Cambridge school tradition, and Gareth Stedman Jones (1996, 34) specifically cites Cambridge school historians as exemplars for developing the sort of truly linguistic approach to history that he advocates.

home to form an ideology of domesticity (1987). Similarly, I have shown how, in the years following the July Revolution of 1830 in France, militant workers joined together a liberal discourse about individual freedom with their corporate discourse about trade solidarity to create a proto-socialist form of class consciousness around the key term "association" (1980, 194–218; 1981). In such cases, cultural historians show how particular motivated acts of linguistic invention fuse or bind together previously distinct discursive fields, permanently affecting the semantics and syntax of both of the now articulated fields.

But the realization that these discourses are themselves embedded in "language games" immediately makes the problem of articulation more complex. If we follow the interpretation I have elaborated above, language games *in general* are constituted of something more than language. Any discussion of a discourse conceived as a language game must take into account the articulations of linguistic practices to other forms of semiotic practice, which, conjointly, constitute a language game. Again, cultural historians have certainly addressed this problem implicitly in their work. Thus, when Davidoff and Hall discuss the discourse of the middle-class home, they not only quote poems and manuals but indicate how these discourses were articulated to new architectural forms and practices of gardening, which gave the discourse a particular and highly reinforcing material instantiation in such neighborhoods as Birmingham's Edgebaston (1987, 357–96). Or when I discuss the corporate language of the artisan trades in early nineteenth-century France, I show how these were articulated to specific forms of artisanal organization and to artisans' methods of controlling production in the workplace (Sewell 1980, 1981). Likewise, the game of basketball, to return to my earlier example, involves articulations between a number of different types of semiotic practices. The various kinesthetic moves and strategies of basketball are articulated simultaneously to what one might call the technical discourses of coaches and players, to the physical codes of honor of young urban African-American men, to the media discourses of basketball connoisseurship, to the legal structures that regulate the flow of play on the floor, to the advertising discourse of sports celebrity, to the financial strategies that, in combination with the supply of talent, determine the economic remuneration of the players, and to plenty of others. To do cultural analysis at all, I maintain, brings one face-to-face with the problem of articulations between diverse semiotic modalities.

The connections between different modalities of language games can be expected, normally, to result in a more or less stable alignment, such that, for example, the kinesthetic strategies of basketball and the rules that govern the flow of the game are mutually sustaining. It is the mutual attuning of language and other semiotic practices that constitutes a language game in the first place.[16] But the fit may be considerably less than perfect. Imperfections or slippages in the articulations between different modalities of semiotic practices seem to me important sources of changes in the overall shape of the games in question—which is to say, of social life. To continue with the basketball example, one of the major forms of kinesthetic strategy is to devise new techniques that are legally consonant with the rules but that change the odds in favor of the team that employs them. This then gives rise to compensating changes in rules, which lead to other innovations, which lead to yet other changes in rules. The consequence is that the rules, the kinesthetic moves, and the overall shape of the game change remarkably over time. An early basketball innovation was to recruit an exceptionally tall player who could park himself under the basket on defense and simply leap up and intercept the path of the ball when it was headed for the basket. The result was that the teams adopting the strategy tended to dominate all other teams. This led the sport's rule-making body to introduce the infraction known as "goal tending," which forbade a defensive player from touching the ball when an opponent's shot was on the downward portion of its arc.[17] One of the major dynamics of the sport ever since has been for the kinesthetic strategists to figure out new ways of taking advantage of exceptional height and for the rule-makers to respond by attempting to counteract height's advantages. The responses by the rule-makers include the introduction of the "three-second violation," which kept very tall players from parking under the basket on offense; the widening of the free-throw lane, which extended the area to which the three-second violation applied; and the introduction of the three-point line, which made shots from long distance worth three points rather than two, thereby advantaging the smaller players who could shoot accurately from long range. The result has been a continuing co-evolution of the kinesthetic and legal semiotic practices that are articulated with each other to make up the game of basketball.

The generative quality of slippages between semiotic practices in differ-

16. This is one place where my discussion of language games seems to me quite parallel to my discussion of structure in chapter 4.

17. The National Collegiate Athletic Association introduced the infraction of goal tending in 1944 to limit the advantage of such tall players as Bob Kurland (seven feet) of Oklahoma A&M and Bob Mikan (six feet ten inches) of DePaul (Hollander 1973, 39, 127).

ent modalities is hardly limited to the bundle of semiotic practices known as basketball. Slippage figures importantly, for example, in William Reddy's recent work on the history of emotions. Reddy argues that discursive vocabularies of emotion are articulated to variations in feeling, encouraging some feeling states and discouraging others and consequently giving rise to distinctive emotional cultures in particular times and places. But these emotional cultures can never be fixed, Reddy argues, because even though the dynamics of feelings are profoundly shaped by emotion discourses, the emotions and discourses are so different in their nature and logics that they can never be matched up flawlessly (2001). This problem of slippages in articulations can also be illustrated in my own work in chapter 8 of this book on the taking of the Bastille during the French Revolution. I have shown how in the days following July 14, 1789, deputies in the National Assembly came to represent this urban revolt as a legitimate rising of the sovereign people, thereby articulating the modality of urban violence to the political discourse of popular sovereignty in the new and fateful category of revolution. The articulation between the semiotics of urban crowd behavior and the semiotics of the theory of popular sovereignty changed the meanings and potentialities of both, reinforcing at once the power of the crowd and the ideology of popular sovereignty. This articulation, which created the new political category "revolution," turned out to be irreversible. The genie of revolution, once released, could not be put back into the bottle. But at the same time the language game of revolution was dynamic and unstable, with new outbreaks of crowd violence resulting in constant readjustments in the political theory, and with discursive innovations in the theory giving rise to new possibilities of "revolutionary" violence. Slippages in articulations between different types of semiotic practices are a potent source of historical change.

But slippages of this sort are not the only form of articulatory misfit between different semiotic practices. Equally important is the problem of misfits between the scopes, scales, or locations of the practices being articulated. Again, examples should help to make the point. I mentioned earlier that the kinesthetic strategies of basketball are articulated to the physical codes of honor of young African-American males. Because the colleges recruit so many of their best basketball players from working-class urban African-American neighborhoods, the coaches, referees, and white players find that the game must both accommodate and keep under control certain African-American working-class norms regulating the assertion of and resistance to physical intimidation. The result of this spatial or locational misfit between distinct but articulated semiotic practices (codes of honor located in working-class African-American neighborhoods, kinesthetic practices located in college gymnasiums) has been distinctive changes in the kinesthetic moves and emotional attitudes even of college basketball players who themselves grew up in affluent white suburbs.

There are even cases in which connected semiotic practices operate at such different spatial scales that their articulation appears to take the form of dumb compulsion rather than the intersubjective understanding assumed by linguistic or hermeneutic models. Take the language game of middle-class financial prudence, which in Buenos Aires, Osaka, Oslo, Taipei, or Atlanta features putting aside savings for future needs. This language game obviously involves complexly articulated and usually mutually reinforcing semiotic practices—discourses of thrift, practices of maintaining savings accounts, certain strategies of deferred consumption, etc. But all of these practices are also articulated indirectly to a world-wide futures market in currencies, whose fluctuations can inflate or wipe out a middle-class saver's bank accounts almost overnight. A moment's reflection makes it clear that the currency futures market is also a language game in the sense I have been using in this essay. From the point of view of currency traders, Argentine pesos or Japanese yen are counters in a high stakes game—a largely self-contained semiotic system with its own rules, strategies, categorical distinctions, vocabulary, signals, rewards, and motivations. But the effects of moves in the currency-trading game can be devastating for players in the other games to which it is connected. Witness the tragic events of 2001 in Argentina, when systematic short-selling of the peso by traders had a devastating effect on Argentine savers, whose accounts fell to a fraction of their previous value. In the process, the Argentine language game of middle-class financial prudence itself came apart, violently disarticulated by the shock. Its players were despoiled, discourses of thrift devalued, practices of saving abandoned, and major purchases deferred not to a calculable future, but indefinitely.

Looked at from the point of view of bourgeois savers in Buenos Aires, the Argentine peso crisis might seem a sort of limiting case—one in which the articulations of semiotic practices are characterized by such violence and inscrutability that linguistic models seem overwhelmed. At junctures like this we tend to throw up our hands and talk of systemic forces or the inherent dynamics of capitalism. Yet if we are to understand social tragedies of this sort, when local actors are devastated by forces utterly beyond their control, we are likely to gain more analytical purchase by attempting to re-

construct the concrete semiotic practices and their articulations than by
alluding to "systems" or "dynamics." Indeed, such "macro" concepts only
become useful if they can be specified concretely—by showing how the
systems or dynamics are composed of interrelated language games. We too
often tend to think of micro and macro processes as going on or at least as
being decipherable at different "levels of abstraction." But the semiotic
practices of currency traders are in fact just as concrete as those of middle-
class savers (and just as abstract—both are manipulating highly abstract
signs of value). What makes the currency traders different is that the technologies they work with enable them to operate on a vastly greater spatial
scale and that their activities happen to involve resources—they may
trade hundreds of billions of dollars a day—that are beyond the imagination of even the most avid middle-class Argentine saver.

Much of what we think of as macro relations are simply articulated
semiotic practices of unusually great power and scope. Nor are capitalist
relations unique in this respect. Such social tragedies as a rural Afghan
wedding party blown to bits by a missile from a drone aircraft or a Syrian
immigrant worker separated from his family and deported from the United
States for a minor crime committed twenty years ago are explicable in
analogous ways. As these two examples suggest, the state, in both its
military and civil guises, is a network of semiotic practices whose scope is
very wide and whose power is very great. In this respect it resembles the
collection of language games we call capitalism. The articulations of the
state's language games with the lives of ordinary people can also seem utterly arbitrary and violent. But we are unlikely to gain any real understanding this kind of arbitrariness and violence unless we pay close attention to the specific articulations between concrete semiotic practices
carried on at very different scopes or scales. Provisionally, at least, it seems
worth positing that the difference between micro and macro relations is
better understood as a difference in the scope or scale of semiotic practices
rather than a difference in levels of abstraction.

Before leaving the question of articulation, I wish to make one additional comment on the analytical value of recognizing that semiotic practices come in a variety of modalities, and that language games always
include articulations between linguistic and nonlinguistic semiotic modalities. Making this distinction seems to me much preferable to stretching
the notion of language to cover all semiotic practices. It is better, in part,
because it enables us to recognize some very consequential qualities of language that are either absent or not present to such a heightened degree in

the other semiotic practices to which it is articulated in the bundles of practices I am calling language games. I am thinking, above all, of the reflexive capacity of language. Language is capable of reflecting upon itself, or, to put this in a less reified fashion, a user of language is capable of reflecting in language upon the language—or iconography, or kinesthetic practice—that she and her fellows use. Indeed, she may even reflect upon these reflections, pondering about whether the language she uses to make such reflections is actually adequate to her purposes, or whether, for example, she needs to supplement her usual Marxist evaluative discourse with arguments cast in Freudian language.

There is no doubt that some degree of reflexivity is possible in other semiotic modalities. Art historians point out that painters comment on the existing traditions of artistic representation by, for example, making satirical use of the stylistic conventions for painting nudes, or by developing styles that draw attention to the way the medium of paint is being used. Or a basketball player can spoof another player's kinesthetic moves by imitating them in an exaggerated way. But the specific qualities of language as a semiotic practice—for example, its extraordinary plasticity and complexity or its ability to mark temporality in the tenses of verbs or to distinguish indicative, subjunctive, and conditional moods—make it a particularly suitable medium for carrying out reflection and evaluation. My story about the dialectical relationship between kinesthetic innovations and responding innovations in the rules of basketball can be used to illustrate the specific value of language as a medium of reflection. The kinesthetic innovation of placing an exceptionally tall defensive player under the basket to bat away the shots of the opposition produced a crisis in the game, threatening to reduce scoring drastically and make the game much less enjoyable to watch. But the solution to this kinesthetically generated problem was worked out in language—in deliberations by the sport's rule-making body that eventuated in changes in the written rules. It was only in language that the question of changing rules to protect the integrity of the game could be deliberated about and resolved. Here, as usual, basketball serves as an allegory for social life in general, where reflection, deliberation, and argumentation in language plays a disproportionate role in governing semiotic practices of all kinds. I am happy to affirm, in other words, that language may properly be singled out as a particularly important form of semiotic practice—important because its reflexive capacity enables it to govern semiotic practices of all kinds and therefore to have particularly powerful effects on their development. But it is only if we are willing to restrict the notion of language to its proper scope, rather than claiming that all human action is linguistic, that we can properly recognize language's specific powers.

BEYOND THE SEMIOTIC MODEL?

What point have we reached in the effort to refigure the social? I began by considering the ontological position posited by the linguistic turn—the claim that interdependence in human relations (in other words, "the social") is established and maintained in the medium of *language*. I have, however, suggested that we need to push the claim that the social is "linguistic" beyond the realm of language or discourse proper to encompass other kinds of semiotic practices, practices that presumably belong in the same family as language because we can effectively explain or explicate them by comparable methodological procedures. The social, in this rendering, should be conceptualized as constituted not only by linguistic mediation, but by a whole variety of types of semiotic mediations (for example, kinesthetic, iconographic, architectural, emotional, and so on) that create and sustain interdependence in human relations. I have further argued that we need to pay especially close attention to the *articulations* between diverse semiotic practices, since the "language games" that form the basic units of the social are themselves composites of semiotic practices in more than one medium. I have argued in particular that the joints or articulations between different semiotic practices are important sources of strain and transformation in social life because of inevitable misfits between the practices being joined together. One reason for misfits is that different semiotic practices are embodied in different media with different logics (bodily movement, speech, buildings, images, prices, and so on). Another is that the various semiotic practices that constitute a language game often are not congruent in scope. This means that semiotic practices articulated in a given language game are also likely to be articulated into other language games where they are connected to yet other semiotic practices, with quite other logics, that can feed back through the initial point of articulation into the original language game. (Think of the case of basketball and urban African-American male honor codes.) The semiotic model I have been elaborating implies that the social is a complex network, in which language games are nodes of articulation between various overlapping but differently shaped semiotic practices. All of this surely takes us well beyond the initial definition of the social as constituted by language. I also believe that it thickens the social in salutary ways and that it does so without straying off the broad terrain defined by the linguistic turn.

But is this semiotic conception of the social really adequate? Even if language is a major, or *the* major, way that interdependence in human relationships is mediated, are there consequential forms of social mediation that cannot be grasped adequately by means of semiotic methods? Given that quantitative methods and positivist epistemology have long been dominant in American social science, most social scientists (or at least most social scientists outside of history and anthropology) surely would answer that semiotic methods are far from sufficient for making sense of the social world. Interpretive methods, often known as "qualitiative" methods, are generally marginalized and very much on the defensive in the so-called "hard" social sciences. By contrast with the interpretivists' paradigmatic explanation, most social scientists employ a very different form of explanation, which I would call mechanistic. Mechanistic explanation specifies not paradigm and performance but cause and effect. Unlike semiotic explanation, which can be applied only to humans, the mechanistic form of explanation applies most obviously to physical nature. Its analogical extension to human relations has traditionally been the prime goal of the social sciences. In the simplest form of mechanistic explanation, the presence of some phenomenon (a cause) determines the appearance of another phenomenon (an effect). Thus the application of heat sufficient to raise the temperature of water to one hundred degrees Celsius causes the latter to turn to steam. Of course, the laws posited as governing social phenomena always take a probabilistic form, thanks to the extraordinary complexity of the determinants of human behavior. Generally speaking, social scientists engage in the mechanistic form of explanation tend to model themselves on the natural sciences, espousing positivist or objectivist epistemologies and using formal quantitative methods—assembling databases, plotting graphs, calculating rates and proportions, and performing statistical tests. Researchers who espouse quantification generally conceive of the social as made up of stable entities with measurable attributes or variables and a set of causal connections between the variables that can be stated in law-like form (Abbott 1988). Although there are exceptions, such scholars tend to be dismissive of interpretive research as "literary" or "unscientific," as unworthy of the name of social science.

I have assembled my share of databases and have plotted my share of graphs, but my sympathies in the epistemological struggles between interpretivists and positivists are firmly in the interpretivist camp. Nevertheless, I think it would be rash and naïve to reject quantitative methods and mechanistic forms of explanation out of hand. Above all, I think we need to take notice of the elephant in interpretive social science's parlor:

the constant presence of powerful economic constraints and pressures on semiotic practices of all kinds — not only in the present, but at least since the beginning of the capitalist era, some half a millennium ago. Economists, who have managed to establish themselves as the preeminent interpreters of such constraints and pressures, claim that they must be understood mechanistically and studied quantitatively. This claim is certainly hard to reject out of hand because such approaches do seem to have afforded economists a significant grasp of economic relations. I would argue that quantification is necessary for the study of the economy, but only because of the particular semiotic qualities of capitalist social relations. As Karl Marx argued famously in chapter 1 of *Capital*, the generalization of the commodity form has tended to transform all kinds of qualitative relations into quantitative relations of economic value (1977). From my perspective, the commodity form must itself be understood as a cultural construction. Money is an abstract symbolic system that establishes a quantitative equivalence between otherwise apparently unrelated things — the skills of weavers in Bangladesh, the production of wheat in Kansas, and the means of providing credit in Sao Paolo. But this quantitative symbolic form is what some Marxist scholars have called a "real abstraction," one that informs the very textures of our social world (Postone 1993). What the ubiquity of the commodity form implies, one might say, is that all kinds of distinct semiotic practices are articulated into a particularly powerful family of language games — capitalist production and exchange — that is itself fundamentally quantitative in form and is therefore intrinsically susceptible to mathematical analysis.

The semiotic practices that make up social life are maintained or transformed by interpretations and manipulations of the codes that govern their practice. Normally the various actors engaged in semiotic practices have an intersubjective understanding of what the various interpretations or manipulations of the codes mean. The peculiarity of capitalist language games is that because every commodity is articulated to every other commodity through the universal, worldwide symbolic medium of money, actors in these games are continually buffeted by actions that lie far beyond their semiotic reach. Thus, for example, producers of cotton textiles not only have to worry about changes in language games to which they are obviously articulated, such as the fashion industry or the production of rival fibers like wool and synthetics, but about matters that are completely beyond their ken as cotton producers and that affect them as brute quantitative constraints — for example, fluctuations in the stock market, the cost of

borrowing money, or exchange rates between currencies. Crucially important aspects of the social reality faced by participants in the language
games of capitalism present themselves phenomenally as a complex of
quantitative fluctuations in prices that act upon participants by what appears to be a mute mechanical causality, not by an intersubjective adjust-
ment of semiotic codes. If this is so, if players in the most powerful and
widespread complex of language games shaping our own lives experience
significant aspects of their interrelationships in a quantitative and mechanical form, then even a conception of the social based on a purely
semiotic model must take into account quantitative methods. Hence, as a
convinced interpretivist, I must endorse the methodological necessity of
embracing quantitative reasoning.

However, I emphatically do not endorse the dominant ideology of
quantitative social science. This ideology, as I see it, makes the error of on-
tologizing the quantifiable features of the social world, of assuming that
the world is naturally and necessarily composed of quantifiable units and
that these units are its essence. This, I would argue, has perverse and ultimately crippling effects. It blocks from view the semiotic quality of the
myriad capitalist language games that actually produce quantifiable forms
of social relations; it tends to cancel out the ways that capitalist language
games themselves are shaped by their articulations with a range of other
unquantifiable semiotic practices; and it hides the fact that our fascination
with quantification itself arises out of the generalized commodification of
our social life. For a quick and dirty illustration of this last point—our cultural fascination with quantification—one need only turn (in keeping with
the recurring sub-theme of this chapter) to the sports page of the newspaper, where the reader is regaled with all kinds of statistics: batting aver-
ages and slugging percentages of baseball players; numerical rankings of
basketball players by scoring, rebounding, steals, and free-throw percentage; composite quarterback ratings and computer rankings of football
teams. It is a trivial but very telling fact about contemporary culture that
to be a sports fan is also to be an avid consumer of statistics.

Thus, as I see it, mainstream social science is wrong to mistake as natural the quantifiable characteristics of social life that have in fact been produced historically by the rise and metastatic spread of the quantitatively
shaped language games of capitalism. However, I do not use this argument
to debunk quantitative reasoning. Quantitative reasoning is crucial, as I
have stated above, for understanding the very real and very powerful
modalities of interdependence in human relations that capitalist language

games put into play. But I would also argue, additionally, that it makes us aware of, and gives us intellectual means of analyzing, quantifiable features of even noncapitalist or precapitalist social relations. Here the argument may seem paradoxical. If we assume, as I do, that all social relations are semiotically generated, why should quantitative reasoning or a mechanical model of causation enable us to see features of the social world that are not readily accessible to semiotic analysis itself?

I think the question of the utility of quantitative reasoning should be considered separately from that of the utility of mechanical models of causation. Quantitative reasoning works because semiotic practices of all sorts (precisely because they are generated by more or less stable codes or paradigms) produce regularities in human action. Once the generalization of the commodity form has made it possible to conceive the possibility of coding all aspects of life quantitatively, semiotically produced regularities can be manipulated and interpreted by mathematical means. Hence, regularities of language games that are not readily grasped from a semiotic perspective can sometimes be captured and stated elegantly with the powerful abstracting, abbreviating, and summarizing techniques of quantitative reason. The example of the batting average informs us that statistics can actually teach us something about the game of baseball, which, although played in a capitalist society, is hardly capitalist in its fundamental semiotic forms. The batting average certainly flattens Tony Gwynn's semiotic artistry at the plate, but it tells us something very real about the likelihood he will get a hit the next time he bats. And it is not only fans who pay attention to such statistics. The baseball teams themselves keep a complex array of statistics, so that the manager not only will be aware of a given player's batting average, but will know how his batting average with men on base compares with his batting average when the bases are empty, what his batting average is when facing left-handed vs. right-handed pitchers or when facing the pitcher currently on the mound. Such statistics have practical value for managers when they must make strategic decisions, such as whether to use a pinch hitter or when to call in a left-handed relief pitcher.

It is, then, possible to argue for the utility of quantification on entirely pragmatic grounds. The pragmatic reasons for using quantification are various. There are cases, nicely represented by the batting average, in which the ability of mathematics to summarize and manipulate information enables us to pin down phenomena that would remain difficult to specify clearly using purely interpretive methods. Thus, intellectual historians use vast linguistic databases to date the emergence of new usages of words, and social historians plot occurrences of different forms of protest over time to discern when food riots and tax rebellions gave way to strikes, demonstrations, and political meetings.[18] On other occasions, quantification is used as a kind of proxy because full information on the semiotic practices at issue is impossible to find. This is particularly common among historians, whose long-dead subjects can hardly be observed directly, let alone interviewed. Thus historians may get at changes in popular religious practices by tracking the frequency of requests for masses for the deceased in wills, or discern the social standing of nineteenth-century occupational groups by calculating the proportion of merchants, lawyers, and doctors who appeared as witnesses at their weddings (Vovelle 1973; Sewell 1985b). But pragmatic abbreviation of this sort might also be necessary (or, at least, advisable) even when adequate semiotic evidence is in principle available.

Given that semiotic practices are articulated to numerous other semiotic practices, which vary enormously in scope, even a very localized study could soon spiral out of control without some means of abbreviation. For example, a study of contemporary practices of bourgeois respectability in Buenos Aires could hardly avoid consideration of the brutal devaluation of the peso in 2001, a devaluation brought about, as I have pointed out above, by speculation on the world market in currency futures. But even though it is possible to do detailed research on the semiotic practices of currency futures traders in New York, Singapore, or London (Salzinger 2003), a researcher might well conclude that doing so would be a distracting detour from the study of the middle class of Buenos Aires. Such a researcher would surely be justified in relying instead on a quantitative summary of the plunging value of the peso against the dollar. In the case of the historian who lacks sufficient evidence of past rituals and discourses, or the ethnographer who can not do a detailed study of all the semiotic practices that are articulated in her topic of research, it is both possible and justifiable to use quantitative techniques without for a moment abandoning the notion that all social relations are constituted by semiotic practice.

THE PROBLEM OF UNINTENDED CONSEQUENCES

The issue of mechanical causality also appears to raise difficult ontological questions. Why, if all human action is semiotically generated, should we

18. Daniel Gordon (1994) uses the ARTFL (American Research on the Treasury of the French Language) data base to show the explosion in uses of the terms société, social, sociable, and sociabilité in the late seventeenth and eighteenth century. Charles Tilly (1986, 1995) counts changes in the incidence of different forms of protest.

ever need to resort to forms of explanation whose logics are mechanical rather than semiotic? Ontologically speaking, mechanical causality seems fundamentally incompatible with a semiotic conception of social life. Nevertheless, there is a ubiquitous problem of human social action that I believe makes mechanical causation seem plausible: the problem of unintended consequences of action. I touched on this problem in passing in my analysis of capitalist language games, where I argued that players are regularly subject to price fluctuations that occur for reasons that are beyond their semiotic reach. But unintended consequences are by no means limited to the sphere of economic action. Human action constantly puts into play symbols that are ambiguous or polysemous and that therefore can be interpreted or used to different ends by other participants even within the same language game, thereby deflecting the consequences of action from the intent of any single actor. Actors can never be certain how others will act in response to an event or to a piece of information, and the effects of the combined actions of all actors may frustrate the intentions of each of the individual actors. Because different language games are interarticulated, action undertaken in one game may be subjected to interpretations and responses in other language games of which the initial players are at best dimly aware. Moreover, actors are never fully aware of the conditions that make their actions possible, and these conditions may change without actors' knowledge, thereby deflecting actions from their intended goals. Or these conditions may systematically bias the effects of actions, leading to cumulative consequences that are not only unintended but even hard to discern, at least initially.

Both as analysts of social life and as participants in it, we frequently come up against what we think of as barriers to action or to the effectiveness of action. "Blind forces" or "dumb coercions" seem to be at work in our life-worlds and in those of people we study. These forces or coercions may enhance or minimize the effects of semiotic practices of all kinds, force people to do things they do not wish to do, enable them to do things they never expected to be able to do, or cause actions to have very real effects quite other than those their initiators imagined. We continually experience the inadequacy of our semiotic knowledge, our inability to control the consequences or recognize the conditions of our action. This makes the interdependence of human relations which we call the social seem impossibly vast and unmasterable, constantly reinstating its mysteriousness as the ultimate ground of our being. It is, I believe, the experience of the unmasterability of the social that makes mechanical causation seem plausible as a way of analyzing social life, that makes it appear reasonable to think of "the social" as a sphere in which anonymous causal forces or experience-remote regularities govern our lives behind our backs.

The problem of unintended consequences has, of course, long been a major concern of the field of economics—indeed, one might argue it has been economics' defining concern. Adam Smith, the founding figure of economics, made the paradoxical but powerful claim that under a regime of free markets, behavior undertaken selfishly, with no thought of its consequences for the public, nevertheless serves the common good. Ever since, economists have been trying to explain how, in a system of anonymous exchange mediated by money and motivated by material gain, markets have logics that continually escape the narrow purposes of economic actors of all sorts, sometimes in beneficial and sometimes in detrimental ways. In a very real sense, economics is a science of unintended consequences. Economics would therefore seem to be a truly dismal science, one that demonstrates over and over, with increasingly sophisticated mathematical means, the weakness of human intelligence in the face of the complexity of social life. Yet the moral thrust of the discipline is exactly the contrary: economics is, in fact, generally a rather upbeat discipline. Although economists may think of their discipline as a quasi-deductive mathematical science analogous to physics, it is also a practical mathematical hermeneutic whose goal is to decipher the mysteries of economic fluctuations in order to give us mastery over them. Each discovery of a barrier standing between economic actors and the realization of their goals simultaneously provides us with, or at least points us toward, an understanding of how to circumvent or neutralize the barrier. Although economics develops mathematical models of causal mechanisms that operate behind the backs of economic actors, its intended practical effect is to render the mechanisms visible and to develop semiotic protocols that will bring economic processes under the control of human purposes—that is, one might say, to render them no longer genuinely mechanical.

The real-world power of this practical mathematical hermeneutic is attested by its explicit use in capitalism's language games. Economists hold high positions and make enormously important decisions in governments all around the world and in powerful quasi-governmental bodies like the World Bank and the International Monetary Fund. How effective they have been at the task of managing national economies and the world economy is of course a matter of debate. There is an old joke to the effect that economics is a genuinely counter-cyclical industry because economists are most in demand at times of general economic crisis, exactly when they have demonstrated most clearly their inability to understand or manage the economy. But it is important to note that over the past few decades, economists have been increasingly in demand outside the public sector. Formal economics is an ever more important semiotic practice in the language games of capitalism itself, most particularly at the top of the capitalist food chain. It is part and parcel of the burgeoning financial services industry, one of whose specialties is using the techniques of mathematical economics to maximize profits in financial transactions. We academics experience this development above all in the growing enrollments of business schools and the soaring salaries of their faculties. Perhaps the most spectacular example of the contemporary fusing of professional economics and for-profit business was Long-Term Capital Management, two of whose founders—Robert C. Merton and Myron S. Scholes—were winners of the Nobel Prize in economics. Before its collapse in 1998, this investment fund had assets with a notional value greater than the budget of the United States government. The fact that Long-Term Capital Management collapsed, and that its fall came close to bringing down the entire world financial system, is a salutary reminder of the incompleteness of the mastery supplied by the economists' practical mathematical hermeneutic. But mathematical techniques developed by economists continue to guide much of the financial industry—the controlling nerve center of contemporary capitalism. Economics is at least believed by important players in capitalism's language games to provide an element of mastery over the mysterious gyrations of markets.

I discuss economics at such length not because I think other social scientists should model themselves on the economists. Indeed, I strongly believe that while economics' use of mathematics has increased its intellectual powers in important ways, its mathematical obsession has also dangerously narrowed its vision, defining as out of bounds the myriad crucial economic problems that do not readily yield up their secrets to mathematical methods. An economics without a serious program of interpretive research is, in my opinion, crippled as a practical hermeneutic. But what is notable about economics from the point of view of my argument is that this most mechanistic of social sciences actually has an antimechanistic practical thrust, that its immanent goal is to develop semiotic protocols, both mathematical and nonmathematical, that subject blind mechanical economic forces to explicit semiotic control—to policies imposing various forms of regulation on the semiotic practices of diverse capitalist language games.[19]

Something like this same immanent goal seems equally present in discussions of apparently mechanical causality in other social sciences as well. When social scientists invoke mechanical constraints—showing how high social-class origin enables people to succeed financially or occupationally beyond any advantages they may have in intelligence and education, or how the "glass ceiling" limits women's access to the higher reaches of corporate power—the effect of their work is to make visible complex processes of which we had previously not been aware, and hence to make intelligent interventions possible (Morrison, White, and Van Velsor 1987). The "glass ceiling" is a particularly revealing metaphor in this context. A glass ceiling is an invisible but in some sense very real barrier to women's upward mobility in the corporate world. The social analyst, by making us conscious of the existence of this seemingly mechanical barrier, is in effect urging us to figure out what semiotic practices in what language games created it and hence how these practices would have to be changed to eliminate it. This thrust is present even in disciplines like history or anthropology that generally are not explicitly concerned with questions of policy. Thus historians, by showing that unintended and unrecognized social processes are in fact constructed over time by complexly articulated semiotic practices, demonstrate that these constructions can be and historically have been rehabilitated, torn down, reconstructed, abandoned, or put to different uses by changes in semiotic practices.

In short, social scientists' resort to mechanical explanation, like their resort to quantitative reason, might be justified as a purely pragmatic move, as a means of abstracting, abbreviating, and summarizing aspects of what we recognize as a reality ultimately made up of complexly articulated semiotic practices. Under this interpretation, language of mechanical causation should be seen as a way-station to a fuller interpretive account of the human practices that construct the phenomenon in question, an account that, unlike the purely mechanical account, will also, at least in principle, contain indications of how the phenomenon might be de- or re-constructed. The problem is not that social scientists engage in arguments of the mechanical type, but that they often reify such arguments, imagining that the so-

---

19. It should perhaps be pointed out here that so-called "de-regulation" of an economic practice is actually a change in the forms of its regulation.

cial world actually *is* constituted by a complex mechanism. The proper
procedure, as I see it, is not to reify mechanisms, but to use mechanistic
arguments as means toward the proper goal of the social sciences: de-
reifying what appear to be mechanical causes, identifying the articulated
semiotic practices that actually construct the unintended consequences
and unrecognized conditions of human social action.[20]

THE SIGNIFICANCE OF "SOCIAL CONSTRUCTION"

It should be noted that the metaphor of "social construction" has appeared
repeatedly in the past few paragraphs, partially displacing the language
metaphor with which this essay began. On the face of it, the construction
metaphor seems rather out of place on the terrain marked out by the linguistic turn. It would seem instead to be firmly in the metaphorical territory of the "building-block" conception of social structure against which
interpretive social science is arguing. Nevertheless, the metaphor—and
the concept—of "social construction" has become very prominent in the
work of interpretivist social scientists in recent years. The term "social construction" seems to have been introduced by Peter Berger and Thomas
Luckmann in their well-known book *The Social Construction of Reality*, published in 1966. A quick check of the Princeton University on-line library
catalog indicates that the term social construction was used in the titles of
books held in that library only twice in the next decade, but was used nineteen times in the decade between 1977 and 1986, and has been used no fewer
than eighty-eight times in the seventeen years since then. This count does
not include dozens of additional titles published since the mid-1980s that
use cultural, or linguistic, or historical construction, or that use terms like
the construction of scientific truth or madness, or gender, or homosexual-
ity. Nor, of course, does it include the many books and articles that use the
social construction metaphor somewhere besides the title. These empirical data on titles imply that the metaphor of social construction initially
caught on in the later 1970s and has become extremely common since the
late 1980s. This temporal rhythm corresponds almost perfectly with the
timing of the so-called "cultural turn" in the American human sciences,

20. It should be noted that not all uses of the mechanical metaphor imply reification. For example, I might speak of the "mechanisms" linking one semiotic practice with another and merely
mean that I want to spell out the connections in detail—as if I were explaining how stepping on
the accelerator results in increasing the speed of an automobile by detailing the connection of
each part to the next in a chain of mechanical action. Indeed, my key metaphor of "articulation"
is itself a quasi-mechanical metaphor.

and, in the history profession, with the rise of cultural history and its triumph over social history as the cutting edge of historical research.

The social construction metaphor is typically used to signify that some notion or social form that is regarded as natural or necessary—ethnicity, the nation, mental illness, race, or gender roles, for example—is in fact a historically contingent social product, the result of some particular complex series of human actions. The main political thrust of the metaphor of construction is to imply that, for example, gender roles could in fact be arranged in some utterly different fashion, or that nations might, in the future, entirely disappear from the political landscape. Its main analytical thrust is to provide an historical account of how some notion was so widely institutionalized, so thoroughly engrained in habit, so built into the assumptions, vocabularies, and landscapes of the social world that it came to be regarded as natural. The social construction metaphor emphasizes the historical or cumulative character of the social constraints and mechanisms that so frequently bend our actions to ends that we do not seek. It suggests that one reason we lack discursive control over the shapes of our lives is that actions are constantly subjected to habitual or ingrained biases whose semiotic origins we no longer fully comprehend.

It is interesting to note that elements of a language of construction have been present from the very beginning of the linguistic turn. After all, as I have mentioned earlier in this essay, Claude Lévi-Strauss, who inaugurated the French version of the linguistic turn, entitled his great first book *The Elementary Structures of Kinship*. And Wittgenstein's *Philosophical Investigations*, which is usually regarded as the beginning of the English version of the linguistic turn, introduced the notion of "language games" by discussing an imaginary four-word language that is part of a "game" of building. But the language of construction had a quite different significance in this period than it came to have from the mid-1970s forward. Lévi-Strauss's use of "structure" in his title was almost certainly intended to signal his high scientific ambitions—the term structure was already a common epistemic metaphor in the natural sciences. Moreover, Lévi-Strauss's argument is specifically anticonstructivist. He treats structures as essentially given, as the invariant source of the surface variations in human cultural forms, as the underlying reality to be unearthed by the social scientist. Indeed, in *The Savage Mind* (1966) he implies that the mental structures he discovers in his research—and whose operations are likened, in another building metaphor, to *bricolage*—are ultimately lodged in the biological structures of the brain. Lévi-Strauss's structures, like those of the physicists, were not so-

cially constructed but permanent and natural. And his structural anthropology was resolutely synchronic—by contrast with the nineteenth-
century evolutionist style of social science, which was still alive and well in
the 1950s and 1960s in France in the form of Marxism and modernization
theory.

Wittgenstein's theoretical stance is surely more compatible with a social
constructionist position than is that of Lévi-Strauss. Yet Wittgenstein
never used his building example to explore the question of what language
games build. Indeed, after the first twenty pages of the text, language
games of building never recur. They are replaced with examples concerning chess, other board games, grammatical rules, mathematics, facial ex-
pressions, and so on. And it is clear that Wittgenstein's investigations of
language are aimed above all at casting light on propositions in existing
philosophy of language—about, for example, intention, naming, mea-
surement, description, memory, definition, and the like. My hunch is that
Wittgenstein chose his building example because the everyday material
aura of building was useful in deflating the preciousness and abstraction of
contemporary philosophical discourse. But Wittgenstein's theoretical approach, like Lévi-Strauss's, was essentially synchronic—he was interested
in how language was implicated in forms of life rather than in how various
language games came into being, endured, and were transformed over
time.

In short, language of construction has been present from the very beginning of the linguistic turn. But as long as those working in this tradition maintained a purely synchronic outlook, the processual potential of
the construction metaphor lay completely dormant. Structures were assumed to be given both to the analyst and to social actors; the question of
how the structures were built remained unasked. The emergence of the diachronic metaphor of social construction is a sign of what might be called
a historical turn within the linguistic turn, a new interest in the diachronic
aspect of social life that emerged in the 1970s and thrived in the 1980s and
1990s (see McDonald 1996). Here one might think of the work of Anthony Giddens, who by the late 1970s was arguing that sociologists needed
to move from the problematic of structure, synchronically understood, to
that of the diachronic process of what he calls "structuration" (1976, 1979),
or of anthropologists such as Bernard Cohn (1987), Marshall Sahlins
(1981), and Renato Rosaldo (1980), who in the same period were posing
questions about the historical transformations of cultures.

It was a historical turn within the linguistic turn that made the problem of sedimented consequences of action loom so large, and that has given rise to the broad currency of the notion of the social construction of reality in interpretive social science since the early 1980s. For all its powers, the language metaphor seems insufficient for such problems. What the language metaphor is particularly useful for is explaining why actions take the forms they do. It does this by referring actions back to the codes—the skills, knowledge, protocols, or habits that enable actors to perform specific sorts of actions. This is, of course, a synchronic procedure. But the language metaphor is less useful for explaining why the semiotic codes take the form they do or how they come into existence, persist, and get transformed. To get at this problem, interpretivist scholars have gravitated to the construction metaphor—a metaphor that serves as a kind of external but necessary supplement to the language metaphor. I would argue that we need to recognize more explicitly both the importance of the construction metaphor in the contemporary practice of interpretive social science and its uneasy relationship to the linguistic metaphor.

The construction metaphor diverges from the language metaphor in two respects. First, it differs in temporality. The Saussurian revolution in linguistics was based on a privileging of the synchronic dimension of language over the diachronic—of *langue* over *parole*. For Saussure and his followers, it was langue that embodied the systemic properties of language, and it was only by suspending the problem of variation or change in linguistic usage that the systematic rules, codes, or paradigms of language could be discovered and specified. While recognizing in principle that these codes can change over time, Saussurian linguistics bracketed such changes, treating *langue* as if it were invariant. It abstracted the question of change over time out of the analysis. It was also language's systemic properties that carried explanatory weight in the Saussurian system. Instances of *parole*—particular, varied, fleeting linguistic performances—were to be explained by referring them back to the systemic codes that made up *langue*. I have argued throughout this essay that this basic synchronic procedure—what I have called paradigmatic explanation—lies behind applications of the language metaphor to social life. This synchronic mode of paradigmatic explanation can in fact be used to illuminate questions of change in semiotic figures, but only in a very particular way. It can show how new figures arise *formally*, by showing how the new figure results from, for example, the inversion of an element of the existing code, or from the splicing of an element from one existing figure into another existing figure to form a new figure different from either of its predecessors. In other words, the linguistic mode of explanation can specify the formal nature of transformations, but can do so only atemporally, by representing them as essentially reversible logical rearticulations of existing elements of semiotic systems. What this mode of explanation cannot grasp adequately is the temporal rhythms and durations of transformations in semiotic practices.

The construction metaphor implies a very different, thoroughly diachronic, temporality. Construction is a noun formed from a verb; it signifies a *process* of building, carried out by human actors and stretched out over time. (Rome, as the proverb puts it, was not built in a day.) The social or cultural construction of meaning is also, by implication, a temporally extended process that requires the sustained labor of human actors. Social construction also implies that when a meaning has been built it has a strong tendency to remain in place: socially constructed gender relations or scientific truths often become naturalized, accepted, and enduring features of the world, just as buildings, once built, continue to remain as an enduring feature of the physical environment. But whether signifying the *process* of building or the *endurance* of that which has been built, the implied temporality of the construction metaphor is always diachronic. In either case, that which is socially constructed is conceptualized as existing in and through time.

It is hardly surprising that historians and social scientists attempting to make sense of historical change by applying linguistic procedures to the social might find themselves forced to elaborate a diachronic perspective such as that implied by the metaphor of social construction. The linguistic approach could effectively delineate the conceptual resources available to historical actors and could provide satisfying formal analyses of how these resources were creatively used in innovative actions. But the linguistic approach in itself provided no means of conceptualizing the temporally enduring consequences of those actions. Which innovations had important consequences and which were fruitless? How, why, and to what extent did the consequences of innovations escape from the intentions of their authors? Why were some innovations quickly transformed into common sense, whereas others remained embattled or controversial, or were soon forgotten? None of these questions could be answered, or even coherently addressed, from a purely linguistic perspective; all of them required researchers to look at the question of how linguistic innovations were built into the world. The construction metaphor emerged over time as a means of addressing precisely this question.

This leads to the second major difference between the language metaphor and the construction metaphor. By implication, at least, the construction metaphor emphasizes something that the language metaphor relegates to the background: the materiality of human social life.[21] Language is perhaps the most immaterial of human activities, requiring no physical media beyond the human body, while construction, the building of physical objects, is expressly and fundamentally material.[22] As I have noted, formal semiotic innovations are in themselves fleeting and logically reversible; they only have the power to impose lasting transformations on preexisting semiotic codes when they are somehow built into the world, when they have continuing worldly effects that matter to actors. Take the jump shot in basketball, which initially must have seemed a terribly ungainly kinesthetic innovation. The jump shot was a successful innovation—in the end entirely driving the set shot from players' repertoires—because players who incorporated the jump shot into their set of bodily skills scored more points and won more games. Its advantages were material and were demonstrable: it was much harder for a defensive player to block, it could be taken while a player was running at full speed, and it enabled a player to maneuver with his back to the basket and then suddenly shoot facing the basket. Similarly, the articulation of urban uprising to popular sovereignty in the new semiotic figure of revolution succeeded in the months and years following the summer of 1789 not because of the formal elegance of the new semiotic figure, but because it harnessed the physical and emotional energies of hundreds of thousands of French men and women, in Paris and in the provinces, to the projects of the National Assembly. Its worldly powers were both demonstrated and greatly extended on the night of August 4, 1789. On that occasion, the National Assembly employed the powers bestowed on it by the new semiotic figure of revolution to thoroughly transform the fundamental institutional structures of French state and society—for example, by abolishing seigneurial dues in the countryside, by abolishing a wide range of monetary and honorary privileges, and by confiscating the landed holdings of the church and using the "national properties" (biens nationaux) thereby created to finance the new revolutionary state. Here, indeed, was a thoroughgoing program of

21. I say "by implication" because some who use the construction metaphor seem to imagine that social or cultural construction of the world takes place solely in language.

22. This is true, of course, of spoken language, but not of written language, which requires some sort of physical media for its fixation—paper and brush, clay and stylus, or transistors and cathode ray tubes.

social (and cultural and political) construction. By installing a new administrative and institutional order, new forms of property rights, and a new financial basis for the state, the National Assembly built the revolution deeply into the daily lives and strategic calculations of citizens. This made the revolution a complex "fact on the ground" that would prove impossible to reverse—even twenty-five years later, when the defeat of Napoleon led to the restoration of the Bourbon monarchy. What was true of the jump shot and of the new political category of revolution is, I believe, true generally. Significant and enduring changes in semiotic practices—that is to say, in social life—can only be explained by tracing out the temporally extended effects of semiotic innovations in the material world, by showing how they lead to the construction of facts on the ground whose presence and perpetuation reinforces (but may also inflect) the initial semiotic innovations.

THE BUILT ENVIRONMENT

The materially instantiated and temporally enduring processes that the social construction metaphor illuminates seem to me absolutely crucial for understanding the problem of unintended consequences. I believe, however, that the term social construction, however revealing, is not really sufficient as a label for the phenomenon. It has usually been employed to point out that some single feature of the social world has in fact been constructed—gender roles, or the nation, or racial difference, or science. Moreover, works employing the term often emphasize changes in linguistic meanings without sufficiently investigating the worldly material transformations that are the condition for the linguistic changes. I think we need a term that emphasizes both the constructed quality of the entire social world and the importance of material instantiation—that sees any given social construction as but one element of a universally constructed (and continually reconstructed) material social fabric. The term "built environment," which I borrow from human geography, seems to me much more adequate for this purpose, and I will devote the remainder of this chapter to arguing for its value as an epistemic metaphor. Of course, no term taken from ordinary language, even the ordinary language of academic social science, is likely to be without awkward connotations. The chief difficulty with "built environment" is that it, too, has had an essentially synchronic past. In the 1950s and 1960s, geographers tended to treat the word "built" in built environment all too literally as a past participle, as indicating that the accumulation of housing, roads, waterways, mines, fields, ports, and so on that humans had built into the earth's surface was to be taken as a given, as a set of structural constraints that would determine plant location, patterns of population circulation, and the like. It was in the 1970s and 1980s that a new generation of geographers, in a move that by now should be familiar to readers of this essay, took up the processual implications of the term to argue that the built environment is continually rebuilt, through selective exploitation, demolition, construction, and reuse of existing physical structures and landscapes and by refiguring the meanings and uses of preexisting places, spaces, and physical structures (see, e.g., Harvey 1985). It is this more recent and more processual meaning that I wish to invoke here.

I am treating the term built environment as an epistemic metaphor, as a means of thinking not simply about roads, sewers, airports, factories, and housing stock but about the social world in general. Like the language metaphor, the built-environment metaphor has the advantage of being founded on the nature of things. Humans are, after all, environment-transforming animals. Human action takes place in a physical world, but it profoundly changes the nature of that world to suit human purposes. It does so by rearranging the world's elements — through, for example, agriculture, industry, and the construction of buildings and transportation facilities. In this sense, humans literally build and continually rebuild their physical environments. The built environment, like language, constrains and enables. We are born into a built environment just as we are born into a language. The built environment powerfully mediates our social existence. Our daily routines, whom we will interact with, how we can earn our living, our sense of the limits of the manipulable world, the means of bringing people together for coordinated action — these are constantly mediated, in ways that are simultaneously enabling and constraining, by the built environment. But, reciprocally, human activities also transform the built environment. The world we inhabit is constantly reworked by human activity, but in ways that are shaped by the built environment's already existing constraints and possibilities. Existing stocks of spatially fixed resources will therefore have continuing effects on the social world well into the future.

These features of the built environment may also be stretched metaphorically to characterize human life in general. We are born into settled routines, institutional environments, habits of judgment, and techniques of production, and these mediate our human interrelationships. But by acting within these specific and given forms of life we reproduce but also alter routines, replace or reform institutions, learn to judge differently, and devise new productive techniques. Our passage through life not only leaves behind a physical fabric transformed by our collective activities and bequeathed to our survivors, but a complex social fabric into which our activities have interwoven new patterns, new distributions of resources, and new protocols for semiotic practice, that will structure the activities of our successors. But it is also true that existing forms of life tend to have a certain inertia. They have a powerful tendency to endure through time, often surviving even in episodes of pervasive social transformation. All aspects of this metaphorically stretched notion of the built environment could be illustrated by the case of Marseille's dockworkers, where the timely action of the Restoration mayor, the physical form of the city and the harbor; the sedimented relations between dockworkers, merchants, and municipality; the institutional entrenchment of the dockworkers' society; the daily operations of the "muse"; the practice of occupational inheritance; the structured but changing relations between dockworkers and carters and loaders; and the many other features of life on the waterfront analyzed in chapter 9 formed a durable yet flexible social and material complex—one that, for several decades, made it possible for the dockworkers to exercise an unparalleled control over their social and economic fates.

It should be apparent that the notion of social construction fits more comfortably within a complex defined metaphorically by the built environment than within the metaphorical ambit of language. Social constructs are built, inherited, and rebuilt over time by located social actors. They come to form the common-sense shape—the landscape, as we sometimes put it—of their lives. They accumulate over time and are instantiated in the physical world. Gender differences, for example, are built into housing, whether in the form of the dark and moist feminine versus light and dry masculine regions of the Kabyle house analyzed by Pierre Bourdieu (1977) or the twentieth-century suburban American kitchens analyzed by Dolores Hayden (1984). They are also physically instantiated in bodies. Gender is expressed and experienced in our bodily movements and gestures, the modulations of our voices, the very emotions we feel (Young 1990a, 1990b). The social construct of race is elided with the physical pigmentation of skin and consequently experienced as a bodily fact. It is also built into the segregated neighborhoods and public spaces of American cities. Situating existing thinking about social construction in the larger metaphorical framework of the built environment might enable us to consolidate its achievements and to think more clearly and powerfully about the historically sedimented and physically instantiated character of the forces and constraints that mediate human interrelationships. Within the discipline of history, attaching the idea of social construction to the epistemic metaphor of the built environment could help to "thicken" cultural history by effectively linking it in a new way with some classical social-historical questions and problematics that were largely abandoned during history's cultural turn—for example, questions about geographical location, population dynamics, means and relations of production, class structures, or institutional frameworks.

The built environment and language metaphors tend to authorize different styles of social research. Yet it is crucial that the metaphors not be seen as existing in a relationship of rivalry or opposition. The fact that the social construction metaphor has developed and become an absolutely indispensable feature of the terrain opened up by the linguistic turn would seem to indicate that the language and built-environment metaphors should be seen as complementary rather than opposed. They should, in my opinion, be understood as two aspects of or perspectives upon a single whole: the complex interdependence of human interrelationships that we call the social. Here it is worth noting that the two aspects of human nature on which these complementary metaphors are built—we might call them *homo sapiens* and *homo faber*—are also inextricably intertwined, both existentially and phylogenetically. They are intertwined existentially in that humans can transform their environments in such radical ways only because they are symbol users who are capable of making, manipulating, and communicating plans. They are tightly intertwined phylogentically in that erect posture and the transposable thumb, which make possible homo faber, evolved in tandem with the use of symbols, the essential characteristic of homo sapiens.[23]

I believe that the relationship between language and built environment should be understood as dialectical. The dialectic might be thought of as tracing out the reciprocal constitution of semiotic form and material embodiment. Such a dialectic has been worked out most elegantly, perhaps, by Marshall Sahlins in his reflections on Hawaiian history (1981, 1985), which I have discussed at length in chapter 7 of this book. Appropriately enough for an anthropologist undertaking a historical turn in the early 1980s, Sahlins used a vocabulary based on Lévi-Straussian structuralism. Sahlins argued that semiotic acts, which can be seen from one perspective

23. See the pellucid discussion in Geertz (1973c). See also chap. 6, above.

as applications of a cultural schema or paradigm, are at the same time acts of reference in the world, since they imply that really existing objects (for example Captain Cook) are instances of cultural categories (in this case gods). When the objects referred to do not act in the expected way—because their actions are governed by quite other paradigms, or because they are subject to natural processes that cannot be controlled by the act of reference, or for whatever reason—the categories, and therefore the organized set of categories that make up the initial paradigm, are subject to redefinition. When the anomalous acts of reference are made frequently enough, or in sufficiently unsettled junctures, or by sufficiently powerful actors, the paradigms may shift permanently, generating different performances than had previously been the case. Sahlins has taken what was originally a synchronic Lévi-Straussian model and has made it both diachronic and dialectical—dialectical because acts initially undertaken from within a given paradigm act back upon the initial paradigm to transform it.

But what does the Hawaiian case have to do with the built environment, either literally or metaphorically? Isn't reference, the key to the transformation in Sahlins's account, an action undertaken purely within language? But reference is always a reference to some feature of the world. As Sahlins puts it, "in action in the world . . . the cultural categories acquire new functional values. Burdened with the world, the cultural meanings are thus altered" (1985, 138). Because we are worldly beings, our paradigmatically generated actions continuously burden our cultural categories with their worldly instantiations. And, reciprocally, our cultural categories continuously burden the world, marking English ship captains as gods, or Western ships and guns as mana. The murdered Captain Cook, whose carefully preserved bones became treasured possessions of the Hawaiian king, became a fundamental feature of the Hawaiian built environment, an important source of power that endowed the king with a British mana and made trade goods coming from the West possessions of the king and his loyal nobles—including the guns and ships that he used to conquer the other islands and unite them in a single kingdom for the first time in history. It was by means of their material instantiations that shifts in semiotic reference could reach back and transform the paradigms that had made the initial reference possible. It seems to me that the burdening of the world by language and of language by the world might properly be rendered as a dialectical interrelationship between language and the built environment.

Sahlins's story is exotic, but the dialectic he outlines is general. Semiot-

REFIGURING THE "SOCIAL" IN SOCIAL SCIENCE

ically generated practices necessarily give rise to social mediations based on the built environment. Semiotic practices are carried out by embodied persons in and by means of physical media—their bodies; ink and paper; wood, stone, metal, and fabric; soil, water, animals, and plants; silicon chips, copper wiring, laser beams, cathode ray tubes, and fiber-optic cables. The carrying out of our semiotic practices arranges, combines, accumulates, and segregates these physical media in specific locations on the earth's surface. The enacting and creative transformation of semiotic codes is realized through exploiting the characteristics of physical media, but these media, because they are subject to other determinations than the semiotic, also constrain, thereby acting back upon the codes that exploit them— bodies require food, desire sex, change with age, and eventually die; paper and ink are durable but need protection from the elements; the soil's minerals and organic matter must be replenished if it is to remain fertile; messages can be sent instantaneously over fiber-optic cables; meat and grain spoil, but at different rates; buildings are costly to erect and to dismantle. The physical media of human action (including, let us remember, the human body itself) are in constant interplay with semiotic practices, giving rise to scarcities and abundances, inflecting the meanings of the practices, limiting the spread of discourses or making them available far beyond their places of origin, enabling the displacement of one semiotic practice by another, resulting in definite correlations between some practices (wheat growing or Internet development) and certain geographical locations (Ukraine or San Francisco). In these and other ways, the social as built environment and as language are constantly and necessarily intertwined.

That the dialectical intertwining of semiotic and constructed elements of the social is characteristic of places much less exotic than eighteenth-century Hawaii can be illustrated by the work of the American sociologists William Julius Wilson (1987, 1996) and Douglas Massey and Nancy Denton (1993) on the effects of racial segregation in American cities. These works show that semiotic processes have extensive built-environment effects, that they create processes, forces, or structures whose shapes and dynamics surpass the discourses that created them. The stigmatization of dark skin has long been a deeply entrenched semiotic fact in American life. One widespread effect of this semiotic fact is massive housing discrimination against African-Americans. But housing discrimination, while semiotically generated, also has powerful built-environment effects—for example, it physically restricts African-Americans to certain urban neighborhoods in the cities of the industrial North. In the 1970s, 1980s, and

1990s, this geographical constraint has had powerfully negative effects on African-American well-being over and above the continuing direct effects of the racial stigmatization that restricted blacks to urban ghettos in the first place. Thus, when job opportunities moved outwards into the sub-urbs, African-Americans found themselves physically removed from po-tential sources of employment and unable to follow them. This resulted in an intensification of certain problems of life in working-class African-American neighborhoods: higher rates of unemployment, lower incomes, deteriorating housing stock, boarded up storefronts, increasing attractive-ness of criminal careers, widespread abuse of alcohol and drugs, and a rise in single-parent households. In this case, a semiotic fact had enduring spa-tial or geographical effects that were sedimented into the urban physical landscape and that operated with some autonomy from, but also reacted back upon, the initial semiotic fact of the stigmatization of dark skin. The point I mean to illustrate with this brief example is general: I claim that discursive or semiotic processes (that is to say, meaningful human actions) are conditioned by and give rise to structures or forces governed by built-environment logics (logics of spatial fixing, material instantiation, accre-tion, and duration) and that such built-environment logics condition semiotic processes (by stabilizing them, undermining them, or by subject-ing them to transformative pressure). An adequate conceptualization of the social must recognize both the semiotic and the built-environment logics and trace out their dialectical interrelationships.

A final remark about built environments: just as semiotic practices or language games differ vastly in their scopes or scales, so likewise do built environments, both literal and metaphorical. The language games of con-temporary international currency trading both presume and build up a complex worldwide network of computers interlinked by satellites and fiber-optic cables—a built environment in the most literal sense—but also an evolving internationally shared set of business institutions, laws, and norms, and a common lingua franca (English), that enable traders to carry on their semiotic practices in confidence that an action taken by a trader in Singapore will be understood immediately in Frankfurt or Sao Paolo. The semiotic practices that constituted the nineteenth-century British Empire entailed the building of a chain of naval bases and coaling stations spanning the world and establishing and elaborating rituals of colonial distinction that made the colonial civil service immediately recog-nizable in Delhi, Kampala, Rangoon, or Nairobi (see, e.g., Ranger 1983; Cohn 1983). Just as in the case of semiotic practices, the question of articulations between built environments of different scales—between, for example, the contemporary network of global finance and various neighborhood practices in the "world cities" where the trading is based, or the norms of the British colonial civil service and the customs of Ugandan villagers—mark some of the most important frontiers of current social scientific and historical inquiry.

*   *   *

So, then: What *is* "the social" in social science? I shall conclude with an answer to my initial question. The social is the complex and inescapable ontological ground of our common life as humans. It is best understood as, first, an articulated, evolving web of semiotic practices (this is the language metaphor) that, second, builds up and transforms a range of physical frameworks that both provide matrices for these practices and constrain their consequences (this is the built environment metaphor). The fundamental method for analyzing the social, so understood, is interpretive— that is, explicating performances by reconstructing the semiotic codes that enable their production. But this interpretive method must be expanded to encompass the built-environment effects of performances—the social construction and historical duration of the material matrices of human interrelations. The methods used to get at built-environment effects may well include quantification, mathematical manipulation, and the sketching out of seemingly mechanical relations of causality—indeed, in studying modern, capitalist, society, some pragmatic resort to such methods is probably unavoidable. But such methods must be employed critically, resisting mainstream social science's powerful tendency toward reification of quantity and mechanism. Our goal must be understood as the de-reification of social life—revealing how apparently blind social forces and dumb social coercions are actually intelligible as products of semiotically generated action.

CODA: HERMENEUTICAL QUANTIFICATION

This conceptualization of the social and of the de-reifying program of research it entails has important implications for how we should think about quantitative methods. It has long seemed to me that the accounts typically given of quantitative and interpretive methodologies exaggerate the real differences between them. Advocates of quantitative methodologies typically adopt the assumptions and techniques of formal statistical inference and the language of positivist philosophy of science. "Interpretivists," by contrast, tend to invoke literary theory and Geertzian "thick description."

If we were to judge on the basis of methodological manifestos, the work of scholars in the two traditions would seem to be divided by an unbridgeable epistemic gap. This impression seems confirmed by the informal attitudes of the researchers in question: quantifiers generally regard the interpretivists as hopelessly fuzzy-minded and unscientific, and the interpretivists tend to dismiss the quantifiers as thick-headed and unsubtle. Yet this assumption that quantitative and interpretive methods belong to incompatible epistemic universes is both theoretically troubling and practically doubtful. Such an epistemological dualism is theoretically troubling because discursive and quantitative forms of evidence are produced in very similar ways: by human actors who, relying on symbolic systems of communication, fix their observations in texts of some sort. Indeed, the same text, resulting from the same act of symbolic fixation, can sometimes be used by both quantifiers and interpretivists. Thus, wills can be read interpretively to determine attitudes toward family relations, death, and the hereafter or analyzed statistically to determine the testators' occupations, experiences of occupational mobility, types of material possessions, or networks of kinship. Any methodological discourse implying that the results of these two types of intellectual operations occupy distinct and noncommunicating epistemological spaces seems to me suspect on its face.

This leads to the practical difficulty of epistemological dualism. Anyone who has read much quantitative social history will notice that it is often extremely difficult to determine in these works where the "interpretive" epistemic space ends and the "quantitative" epistemic space begins. Discursive texts are used to interpret quantitative findings and even to establish the categories upon which calculations are built. Discursive statements are interpreted in light of quantitative findings — for example, as reflecting the demographic experience of a particular generation or the economic perspective of a particular occupational grouping. Social historians typically move back and forth between quantitative and discursive sources and methods in building their historical arguments. My analysis of the history of Marseille's dockworkers in chapter 9 of this book is a fairly typical example of this relatively seamless interweaving of quantitative and semiotic evidence. Moreover, some quantitative measurements are actually assessments of the discursive characteristics of texts. Thus Michel Vovelle made a famous statistical study of meaningful variations in the language of wills to trace the process of "dechristianization" in eighteenth-century Provence, examining quantitative differences in such language not only over time but by social category, gender, and geograph-

REFIGURING THE "SOCIAL" IN SOCIAL SCIENCE

ical location as well (Vovelle 1973). Any presumption of a necessary epistemic gap between discursive and quantitative methods seems refuted in practice by the existence of histories such as Vovelle's. Rather, the work of social historians in general would seem to argue for epistemic continuity between discursive and quantitative analysis, implying that discursive and quantitative methods are nothing more than two different perspectives on the same social world.

Vovelle's example should also make us realize that not all discursive analysis fits the usual model of interpretive method. The actual techniques used in such analyses vary enormously — from relatively intuitive to highly formalist. Structuralists of the Lévi-Straussian stripe are sometimes every bit as objectivist as quantitative sociologists, and quantitative analyses of the use of lexemes is a common practice among historical lexicographers. Quantitative research has, by its very nature, a formalist character. But there is also a hermeneutical element in much quantitative research that is rarely acknowledged, let alone highlighted or theorized. Scholars who have worked with complex quantitative data sets know that part of the process is something often expressed as "getting to know your data." Rather than simply deciding a priori on the categories into which cases will be placed and the kinds of analytic techniques that will be used, quantifiers usually engage in a good deal of preliminary probing that — except for the fact that what one "reads" is statistical tables, graphs, or indices — seems quite similar to the "hermeneutic circle," as described, for example, by Paul Ricoeur (1971). The investigator formulates guesses or hypotheses about the categories appropriate to the data set, produces a set of statistical measures based on them, finds anomalies in the results, refines or alters the hypotheses, uses these altered hypotheses to interrogate the data set again and so on until she is satisfied that the categories used in the analysis are true to the data set's internal structure. In the course of this hermeneutical interrogation of the data set, the investigator may also turn to nonquantitative sources of information — attempting, for example, to learn from apprenticeship contracts whether plumbers should be classified with other builders or other metal workers. Virtually none of this "hermeneutical quantification" ever finds its way into print in books or articles. I think positivist social scientists fear that if they admitted that they worked this way, they would be accused of "cooking their data" — when, in fact, they are simply gaining enough sense of the inherent structures of their quantitative "texts" to be able to "read" them effectively, to plumb their depths. I think that quantifiers need to reflect more on the epistemic implications of their hermeneutic interrogation of their data bases. In my opinion, the real point of quantitative social research is actually a sensitive and probing examination of the structures of present and past lifeworlds—not the ever-receding phantom of statistically verifiable generalizations of the "covering law" type. My own experience as a former quantitative historian who has more recently taken the cultural turn is that the real procedures of quantitative researchers have far more in common with interpretive methods than the official methodologists would ever suspect.

REFERENCES

Abbott, Andrew. 1988. "Transcending General Linear Reality." *Sociological Theory* 6:169–86.

———. 1991. "History and Sociology: The Lost Synthesis." *Social Science History* 15:201–38.

———. 1992. "From Causes to Events." *Sociological Methods and Research* 20:428–55.

———. 1999. *Department and Discipline: Chicago Sociology at One Hundred.* Chicago: University of Chicago Press.

———. 2001. *Time Matters: On Theory and Method.* Chicago: University of Chicago Press.

Abrams, Philip. 1980. "History, Sociology, Historical Sociology." *Past and Present,* no. 87:3–16.

———. 1982. *Historical Sociology.* Ithaca: Cornell University Press.

Abu-Lughod, Lila. 1986. *Veiled Sentiments: Honor and Poetry in a Bedouin Society.* Berkeley and Los Angeles: University of California Press.

———. 1991. "Writing Against Culture." In *Recapturing Anthropology: Working in the Present,* ed. Richard G. Fox, 137–62. Santa Fe: School of American Research.

Aglietta, Michel. 1979. *A Theory of Capitalist Regulation: The US Experience.* London: New Left Books.

Agulhon, Maurice. 1968. *Pénitants et Francs-Maçons de l'ancienne Provence.* Paris: Fayard.

———. 1970a. *La vie sociale en Provence intérieure au lendemain de la revolution.* Paris: Société d'Études Robespierristes.

———. 1970b. *Une ville ouvrière au temps du socialisme utopique: Toulon de 1800 à 1851.* Paris: Mouton.

———. 1970c. *La République au village.* Paris: Plon.

———. 1979. *Marianne au combat: L'imagerie et la symbolique républicaines de 1789 à 1880.* Paris: Flammarion.

———. 1987. "Vu des coulisses." In *Essais d'égo-histoire,* ed. Pierre Nora, 11–59. Paris: Gallimard.

Althusser, Louis. 1969. *For Marx.* Translated by Ben Brewster. New York: Pantheon Books.

———. 1971. "Ideology and Ideological State Apparatuses (Notes towards an Investigation)." In *Lenin and Philosophy and Other Essays,* 127–86. London: Monthly Review Press.

Amin, Ash, ed. 1994. *Post-Fordism: A Reader.* Oxford: Blackwell.

Aminzade, Ronald. 1979. "The Transformation of Social Solidarities in Nineteenth-

Century Toulouse." In *Consciousness and Class Experience in Nineteenth-Century Europe*, ed. John M. Merriman, 85–105. New York: Holmes and Meier.

———. 1981. *Class, Politics, and Early Industrial Capitalism: A Study of Mid-Nineteenth-Century Toulouse, France*. Albany: State University of New York Press.

———. 1992."Historical Sociology and Time." *Sociological Methods and Research* 20: 456–80.

Anderson, Perry. 1980. *Arguments Within English Marxism*. London: Verso.

Anthropological Literature. 1984–94. Cambridge, Mass.: Tozzer Library, Harvard University.

Appadurai, Arjun. 1991."Global Ethnoscapes: Notes and Queries for a Transnational Anthropology." In *Recapturing Anthropology: Working in the Present*, ed. Richard G. Fox, 191–210. Santa Fe: School of American Research.

———. 1996. *Modernity at Large: Cultural Dimensions of Globalization*. Minneapolis: University of Minnesota Press.

Appleby, Joyce, Lynn Hunt, and Margaret Jacob. 1994. *Telling the Truth about History*. New York: W. W. Norton.

Arrighi, Giovanni. 1994. *The Long Twentieth Century: Money, Power, and the Origins of Our Times*. New York: Verso.

Arthur, W. Brian. 1988."Self-Reinforcing Mechanisms in Economics." In *The Economy as an Evolving Complex System*, ed. Philip W. Anderson, Kenneth J. Arrow, and David Pines, 9–31. Redwood City, Calif.: Addison-Wesley.

Asad, Talal. 1982."Anthropological Conceptions of Religion: Reflections on Geertz." *Man* 18: 237–59.

———. 1993. *Genealogies of Religion: Discipline and Reasons of Power in Christianity and Islam*. Baltimore: Johns Hopkins University Press.

Audiganne, Armand. 1860. *Les populations ouvrières et les industries de la France*. 2d ed. 2 vols. Paris: Capelle.

Aussel, Michel. 2002. *Nantes sous la monarchie de Juillet, 1830–1848: Du mouvement mutualiste aux doctrines utopiques*. Nantes: Ouest Éditions.

Austin, J. L. 1962. *How to Do Things With Words*. Cambridge, Mass.: Harvard University Press.

Austin-Broos, Diane J. 1987."Clifford Geertz: Culture, Sociology, and Historicism." In *Creating Culture: Profiles in the Study of Culture*, 141–59. Sidney: Allen and Unwin.

Baehrel, Réné. 1961. *Une croissance: La basse Provence rurale, fin XVIe siècle – 1789: Essai d'économie historique statistique*. Paris: S.E.V.P.E.N.

Baker. Keith M. 1964." The Early History of the Term 'Social Science.'" *Annals of Science* 20:211–26.

———. 1990. *Inventing the French Revolution*. Cambridge: Cambridge University Press.

———. 1994."Enlightenment and the Institution of Society: Notes for a Conceptual History." In *Main Trends in Cultural History: Ten Essays*, ed. Willem Melching and Wyger Velema, 95–120. Amsterdam and Atlanta: Rodopi.

Baker, Keith Michael, and Roger Chartier, 1994."Dialogue sur l'espace public." *Politix* 26:5–22.

Barthes, Roland. [1957] 1972. *Mythologies*. Translated by Annette Lavers. New York: Hill and Wang.

Barzman, John. 1999. "Les relations entre les pouvoirs publics et les dockers au Havre, XIXe-XXe siècles." *Dockers de la Méditerranée à la Mer du Nord: Des quais et des hommes dans l'histoire. Colloque international, 11 au 13 mars 1999*, 155–69. Aix-en-Provence: Edisud.

Bederman, Gail. 1995. *Manliness and Civilization: A Cultural History of Gender and Race in the United States, 1880–1917*. Chicago: University of Chicago Press.

Bell, Catherine. 1992. *Ritual Theory, Ritual Practice*. Oxford: Oxford University Press.

Bendix, Reinhard. 1956. *Work and Authority: Ideologies of Management in the Course of Industrialization*. New York: John Wiley.

———. 1964. *Nation-Building and Citizenship: Studies of Our Changing Social Order*. New York: John Wiley.

———. 1978. *Kings or People: Power and the Mandate to Rule*. Berkeley and Los Angeles: University of California Press.

Benedict, Ruth. 1934. *Patterns of Culture*. New York: Houghton Mifflin.

———. 1946. *The Chrysanthemum and the Sword*. New York: Meridian.

Berger, Peter, and Thomas Luckmann. 1966. *The Social Construction of Reality: A Treatise in the Sociology of Knowledge*. Garden City, N.Y.: Doubleday.

Bezucha, Robert J. 1974. *The Lyon Uprising of 1834: Social and Political Conflict in the Early July Monarchy*. Cambridge, Mass.: Harvard University Press.

Biernacki, Richard. 1995. *The Fabrication of Labor: Germany and Britain, 1640–1914*. Berkeley and Los Angeles: University of California Press.

Bloch, Marc. 1964. *Feudal Society*. 2 vols. Chicago: University of Chicago Press.

———. 1967. "A Contribution towards a Comparative History of European Societies." In *Land and Work in Medieval Europe*, trans. J. E. Anderson, 44–81. London: Routledge and Kegan Paul.

———. 1970. *French Rural History: An Essay on its Basic Characteristics*. Edited by Janet Sondheimer. Berkeley and Los Angeles: University of California Press.

Boas, Franz. 1966. *Kwakiutl Ethnography*. Edited by Helen Codere. Chicago: University of Chicago Press.

Bonnell, Victoria, and Lynn Hunt, eds. 1999. *Beyond the Cultural Turn: New Directions in the Study of Society and Culture*. Berkeley and Los Angeles: University of California Press.

Bois, Paul. 1960. *Les paysans de l'Ouest: Des structures économiques et sociales aux options politiques depuis l'époque révolutionnaire dans la Sarthe*. Le Mans: Vilaire.

Boltanski, Luc, and Laurent Thévenot. 1987. *De la justification: Les économies de la grandeur*. Paris: Presses Universitaires de France.

———. 1990. *L'amour et la justice comme competences: Trois essais de sociologie de l'action*. Paris: Métailié.

Bourdieu, Pierre. 1977. *Outline of a Theory of Practice*. Translated by Richard Nice. Cambridge: Cambridge University Press.

———. 1980. *Le sens pratique*. Paris: Editions du Minuit.

———. 1988. *Homo Academicus*. Translated by Peter Collier. Stanford, Calif.: Stanford University Press.

Bousquet, Casimir, and Tony Sapet. 1857. *Étude sur la navigation, le commerce et l'industrie de Marseille, pendant la période quinquennale de 1850 à 1854*. Marseille: Camoin et Dutertre.

Boyer, Robert. 1986. *La théorie de la régulation: Une analyse critique*. Paris: La Découverte.

Braudel, Fernand. 1958. "Histoire et sciences sociales: La longue durée." *Annales: Économies, Sociétés, Civilisations* 13:725–53.

———. 1966. *La Méditerranée et le monde méditerréen à l'époque de Philippe II*. 2 vols. Paris: Armand Colin.

Brenner, Robert. 1998. "The Economics of Global Turbulence." *New Left Review* 229:1–265.

———. 2002. *The Boom and the Bubble: The US in the World Economy*. London: Verso.

Briggs, Laura. 2002. *Reproducing Race: Race, Sex, Science and U.S. Imperialism in Puerto Rico*. Berkeley and Los Angeles: University of California Press.

Brightman, Robert. 1995. "Forget Culture: Replacement, Transcendence, Relexification." *Cultural Anthropology* 10:509–46.

Brubaker, Rogers. 1985. "Rethinking Classical Social Theory: The Sociological Vision of Pierre Bourdeiu." *Theory and Society* 14:745–75.

Bryant, Christopher G. A., and David Jary, eds. 1991. *Giddens' Theory of Structuration: A Critical Appreciation.* London: Routledge.

Burguière, André. 1983. "La notion de mentalités chez M. Bloch et L. Febvre: Deux conceptions, deux filiations." *Revue de Synthèse* 111/112: 333–48.

———. 1995. "Le changement social: Brève histoire d'un concept." In *Les formes de l'expérience: Une autre histoire sociale,* ed. Bernard Lepetit, 253–72. Paris: Albin Michel.

Burckhardt, Jacob. 1958. *The Civilization of the Renaissance in Italy.* New York: Harper.

Burawoy, Michael. 1989. "Two Methods in Search of Science: Skocpol versus Trotsky." *Theory and Society* 18:765–69.

Burke, Peter. 1987. "Les îles anthropologiques et le territoire de l'historien." In *Philosophie et histoire,* ed. Christian Descamps, 49–66. Paris: Centre Georges Pompidou.

———. 1990. *The French Historical Revolution: The Annales School, 1929–89.* Stanford: Stanford University Press.

———. 1992. "History of Events and the Revival of Narrative." In *New Perspectives on Historical Writing,* ed. Peter Burke, 232–48. University Park: Pennsylvania State University Press.

Burnham, Walter Dean. 1967. "Party Systems and the Political Process." In *The American Party Systems,* ed. William Nisbet Chambers and Walter Dean Burnham, 277–307. New York: Oxford University Press.

Burton, Antoinette. 2001. "Thinking Beyond Boundaries: Empire, Feminism and the Domains of History." *Social History* 26:60–71.

Cabrera, Miguel A. 1999. "Linguistic Approach or Return to Subjectivism? In Search of an Alternative to Social History." *Social History* 24:74–89.

———. 2004. *Postsocial History: An Introduction.* Translated by Marie McMahon. Foreword by Patrick Joyce. Lanham, Md.: Lexington Books.

Calhoun, Craig. 1996. "The Rise and Domestication of Historical Sociology." In *The Historic Turn in the Human Sciences,* ed. Terrence J. McDonald, 305–38. Ann Arbor: University of Michigan Press.

Calhoun, Craig, Edward LiPuma, and Moishe Postone, eds. 1993. *Bourdieu: Critical Perspectives.* Chicago: University of Chicago Press.

Carrière, Charles. 1973. *Négociants marseillais au XVIIIe siècle: Contribution à l'étude des économies maritimes.* 2 vols. Marseille: Institut Historique de Provence.

Certeau, Michel de. 1984. *The Practice of Everyday Life.* Translated by Steven Rendell. Berkeley and Los Angeles: University of California Press.

Chakrabarty, Dipesh. 1989. *Rethinking Working Class History: Bengal, 1890–1940* (Princeton: Princeton University Press.

———. 2000. *Provincializing Europe: Postcolonial Thought and Historical Difference.* Princeton: Princeton University Press.

Chartier, Roger. 1987. *Lecture et lecteurs dans la France d'Ancien Régime.* Paris: Seuil.

———. 1988. *Cultural History: Between Practices and Representations.* Translated by Lydia G. Cochrane. Ithaca: Cornell University Press.

———. 1995. *Forms and Meanings: Texts, Performances, and Audiences from the Codex to the Computer.* Philadelphia: University of Pennsylvania Press.

———. 1997. *On the Edge of the Cliff: History, Language, and Practice.* Baltimore: The Johns Hopkins University Press.

Chauncey, George. 1994. *Gay New York: Gender, Urban Culture, and the Making of the Gay Male World.* New York: Basic Books.

Chorley, Katherine. 1943. *Armies and the Art of Revolution.* London: Faber and Faber.

Clark, Terry Nichols. 1973. *Prophets and Patrons: The French University and the Emergence of the Social Sciences.* Cambridge, Mass.: Harvard University Press.

Claverie, Elisabeth. 1999. "De l'artisanat à l'age industriel sur les quais à Marseille: Du portefaix au docker (XIXe-XX siècles)." *Dockers de la Méditerranée à la Mer du Nord: Des quais et des hommes dans l'histoire. Colloque international, 11 au 13 mars 1999,* 75–83. Aix-en-Provence: Edisud.

Clifford, James. 1986. "On Ethnographic Allegory." In *Writing Culture: The Poetics and Politics of Ethnography,* ed. James Clifford and George Marcus, 98–121. Berkeley and Los Angeles: University of California Press.

———. 1988a. "Introduction: The Pure Products Go Crazy." In *The Predicament of Culture: Twentieth Century Ethnography, Literature, and Art,* 1–17. Cambridge, Mass.: Harvard University Press.

———. 1988b. "On Ethnographic Authority." In *The Predicament of Culture: Twentieth Century Ethnography, Literature, and Art,* 21–54. Cambridge: Harvard University Press.

Clifford, James, and George E. Marcus, eds. 1986. *Writing Culture: The Poetics and Politics of Ethnography.* Berkeley and Los Angeles: University of California Press.

Cohen, Jean. 1998. "Civil Society." In *Routledge Encyclopedia of Philosophy,* gen. ed. Edward Craig. 2 vols. London: Routledge.

Cohn, Bernard S. 1980. "History and Anthropology: The State of Play." *Comparative Studies in Society and History* 22:198–221.

———. 1981. "Anthropology and History in the 1980s: Towards a Rapprochement," *Journal of Interdisciplinary History* 12:227–52.

———. 1983. "Representing Authority in Victorian India." In *The Invention of Tradition,* ed. Eric Hobsbawm and Terence Ranger, 165–210. Cambridge: Cambridge University Press.

———. 1987. *An Anthropologist Among the Historians and Other Essays.* Introduction by Ranajit Guha. Delhi and New York: Oxford University Press.

———. 1996. *Colonialism and Its Forms of Knowledge: The British in India.* Princeton: Princeton University Press.

Coleman, James S. 1990. *Foundations of Sociological Theory.* Cambridge, Mass.: Harvard University Press.

Conze, Werner. 1967. "Social History." *The Journal of Social History* 1:7–16.

Corbin, Alain. 1975. *Archaisme et modernité en Limousin au 19e siècle.* 2 vols. Paris: M. Rivière.

———. 1982. *Le miasme et la jonquille: L'odorat et l'imaginaire social, 18e-19e siècles.* Paris: Aubier Montaigne.

———. 1994. *Les cloches de la terre: Paysage sonore et culture sensible dans les campagnes du XIXe siècle.* Paris: Albin Michel.

———. 1995. *Time, Desire, and Horror: Towards a History of the Senses.* Translated by Jean Birrell. Cambridge: Polity Press.

Cornu, Roger. 1974. "Les portefaix et la transformation du port de Marseille." *Annales du Midi* 86:181–202.

———. 1999. "Du portefaix au docker: Des mythes industructibles?" *Dockers de la Méditer-*

ranée à la Mer du Nord: Des quais et des hommes dans l'histoire. Colloque international, 11 au 13 mars 1999, 171–78. Aix-en-Provence: Edisud.

Coronil, Fernando, and Julie Skurski. 1991. "Dismembering and Remembering the Nation: The Semantics of Political Violence in Venezuela." *Comparative Studies in Society and History* 33:288–337.

Corvisier, André. 1983. *Histoire du Havre et de l'estuaire de la Seine.* Toulouse: Privat.

Cottereau, Alain. 1980. "Étude préalable: Vie quotidienne et résistance ouvrière à Paris en 1870." Introduction to Denis Poulot, *Question sociale: Le Sublime, ou le travailleur comme il est en 1870, et ce qu'il pent l'être,* 7–102. Paris: François Maspero.

Crapanzano, Vincent. 1986. "Hermes' Dilemma: The Masking of Subversion in Ethnographic Description." In *Writing Culture: The Poetics and Politics of Ethnography,* ed. James Clifford and George E. Marcus, 51–76. Berkeley and Los Angeles: University of California Press.

Darnton, Robert. 1971a. "In Search of the Enlightenment: Recent Attempts to Create a Social History of Ideas." *Journal of Modern History* 43:113–32.

———. 1971b. "Reading, Writing, and Publishing in Eighteenth Century France: A Case Study in the Sociology of Literature." *Daedalus* 100:214–56.

———. 1983. "Workers Revolt: The Great Cat Massacre of the Rue Saint-Saint Séverin." In *The Great Cat Massacre and Other Episodes in French Cultural History,* 75–106. New York: Basic Books.

Daumard, Adeline. 1963. *La bourgeoisie parisienne de 1815 à 1848.* Paris: S.E.V.P.E.N.

Davidoff, Lenore, and Catherine Hall. 1987. *Family Fortunes: Men and Women of the English Middle Class, 1780–1850.* Chicago: University of Chicago Press.

Davis, Natalie Zemon. 1975. *Society and Culture in Early Modern France.* Stanford: Stanford University Press.

———. 1983. *The Return of Martin Guerre.* Cambridge, Mass.: Harvard University Press.

———. 1988. "On the Lame." *American Historical Review* 93:572–603.

Derrida, Jacques. 1976. *Of Grammatology.* Translated by Gayatri Chakravorty Spivak. Baltimore: Johns Hopkins University Press.

Deyon, Pierre. 1967. *Amiens, capitale provinciale.* Paris: Mouton.

DiMaggio, Paul. 1979. "Review Essay: On Pierre Bourdeiu." *American Journal of Sociology* 84:1460–74.

Dirks, Nicholas B. 1996. "Is Vice Versa? Historical Anthropologies and Anthropological Histories." In *The Historic Turn in the Human Sciences,* ed. Terrence J. McDonald, 17–52. Ann Arbor: University of Michigan Press.

Dosse, François. 1987. *L'histoire en miettes: Des "Annales" à "la nouvelle histoire."* Paris: La Découverte.

———. 1994. *New History in France: The Triumph of the Annales.* Translated by Peter V. Conroy Jr. Urbana: University of Illinois Press.

———. 1997. *History of Structuralism.* 2 vols. Translated by Deborah Glassman. Minneapolis: University of Minnesota Press.

Downs, Laura Lee. 1993a. "If 'Woman' is Just an Empty Category, Then Why Am I Afraid to Walk Alone at Night? Identity Politics Meets the Postmodern Subject." *Comparative Studies in Society and History* 35:414–37.

———. 1993b. "Reply to Joan Scott." *Comparative Studies in Society and History* 35:444–51.

Duara, Prasenjit. 1995. *Rescuing History from the Nation: Questioning Narratives of Modern China.* Chicago: University of Chicago Press.

Dublin, Thomas. 1979. *Women at Work: The Transformation of Work and Community in Lowell, Massachusetts, 1826–60*. New York: Columbia University Press.

Dubosc, Prosper. 1848. *Quatre mois de République à Marseille, 24 fevrier–24 juin*. Marseille.

Duby, Georges. 1973. *Le dimanche de Bouvines*. Paris: Gallimard.

Durkheim, Emile. [1912] 1965. *The Elementary Forms of the Religious Life*. Translated by Joseph Ward Swain. New York: The Free Press.

Easthope, Anthony. 1993. "Romancing the Stone: History Writing and Rhetoric." *Social History* 18:235–49.

Egret, Jean. 1977. *The French Prerevolution 1787–1788*. Translated by Wesley D. Camp. Introduction by J. F. Bosher. Chicago: University of Chicago Press.

Eisenstadt, S. N. 1963. *The Political System of Empires*. Glencoe, Ill.: Free Press.

Eley, Geoff. 1996. "Is All the World a Text? From Social History to the History of Society Two Decades Later." In *The Historic Turn in the Human Sciences*, ed. Terrence McDonald, 193–243. Ann Arbor: University of Michigan Press.

Eley, Geoff, and Keith Nield. 1995. "Starting Over: The Present, the Post-modern and the Moment of Social History." *Social History* 20:355–64.

Epstein, James. 1999. "Spatial Practices/Democratic Vistas." *Social History* 24:294–310.

Ermakoff, Ivan. 2000. "Strukturelle Zwänge und Zufällige Geschehnisse: Die Selbstauflösung der französischen Republik in Vichy am 10. Juli 1940." In *Struktur und Ereignis*, ed. Andreas Suter and Manfred Hettling, 244–56. Sonderheft 19 of *Geschichte und Gesellschaft*. Göttingen: Vandenhoeck und Ruprecht.

Evans, Peter B., Dietrich Rueschemeyer, and Theda Skocpol. 1985. *Bringing the State Back In*. Cambridge: Cambridge University Press.

Farge, Arlette. 1986. *La vie fragile: Violences, pouvoirs, et solidarité à Paris au XVIIIe siècle*. Paris: Hachette.

Faure, Alain. 1977. "A propos de Perdiguier: Qu'est-ce que le compagonnage?" Introduction to Agricol Perdiguier, *Mémoires d'un compagnon*, 7–33. Paris: François Maspero.

Faure, Alain, and Jacques Rancière. 1976. *La parole ouvrière (1830–1840)*. Paris: Union Générale d'Éditions.

Febvre, Lucien. 1953. "Vive l'histoire: Propos d'initiation." In *Combats pour l'histoire*, 18–33. Paris: Armand Colin.

Finlay, Robert. 1988. "The Refashioning of Martin Guerre." *American Historical Review* 93:553–71.

Fink, Carole. 1989. *Marc Bloch: A Life in History*. Cambridge: Cambridge University Press.

Fitzsimmons, Michael P. 2003. *The Night the Old Regime Ended: August 4, 1789, and the French Revolution*. University Park: Pennsylvania State University Press.

Flandrin, Jean-Louis. 1976. *Familles: Parenté, maison, sexualité dans l'ancien société*. Paris: Hachette.

Foucault, Michel. 1971. *The Order of Things: An Archaeology of the Human Sciences*. New York: Pantheon Books.

———. 1977. *Discipline and Punish: The Birth of the Prison*. Translated by Alan Sherridan. New York: Vintage Books.

Furet, François. 1971. "Le catechisme révolutionnaire." *Annales: Économies, Sociétés, Civilisations* 26:255–89.

———. 1978. *Penser la Révolution français*. Paris: Gallimard.

———. 1981. *Interpreting the French Revolution*. Translated by Elborg Forster. Cambridge: Cambridge University Press.

———. 1988. *La Révolution: De Turgot à Jules Ferry, 1770–1880*. Paris: Hachette.

Furet, François, and Mona Ozouf, eds. 1988. *Dictionnaire critique de la Révolution française*. Paris: Flammarion.

Galison, Peter. 1997. *Image and Logic: A Material Culture of Micro-physics*. Chicago: University of Chicago Press.

Garden, Maurice. 1970. *Lyon et les lyonnais au 18e siècle*. Paris: Les Belles Lettres.

Gascon, Richard 1971. *Grand commerce et vie urbaine au 16e siècle: Lyons et ses marchands (environs 1520–1580)*. Paris: S.E.V.P.E.N.

Geertz, Clifford. 1960. *The Religion of Java*. Glencoe, Ill.: Free Press.

———. 1963a. *Agricultural Involution: The Process of Ecological Change in Indonesia*. Berkeley and Los Angeles: University of California Press.

———. 1963b. *Peddlers and Princes: Social Change and Modernization in Two Indonesian Towns*. Chicago: University of Chicago Press.

———. 1965. *The Social History of an Indonesian Town*. Cambridge, Mass.: Harvard University Press.

———. 1968. *Islam Observed: Religious Development in Morocco and Indonesia*. New Haven: Yale University Press.

———. 1973a. *The Interpretation of Cultures*. New York: Basic Books.

———. 1973b. "Deep Play: Notes on the Balinese Cockfight." In *The Interpretation of Cultures*, 412–53. New York: Basic Books.

———. 1973c. "Ethos, World View, and the Analysis of Sacred Symbols." In *The Interpretation of Cultures*, 126–41. New York: Basic Books.

———. 1973d. "The Growth of Culture and the Evolution of Mind." In *The Interpretation of Cultures*, 55–83. New York: Basic Books.

———. 1973e. "Ideology as a Cultural System." In *The Interpretation of Cultures*, 193–233. New York: Basic Books.

———. 1973f. "The Impact of the Concept of Culture on the Concept of Man." In *The Interpretation of Cultures*, 33–54. New York: Basic Books.

———. 1973g. "Person, Time, and Conduct in Bali," In *The Interpretation of Cultures*, 360–411. New York: Basic Books.

———. 1973h. "Religion as a Cultural System." In *The Interpretation of Cultures*, 87–125. New York: Basic Books.

———. 1973i. "Ritual and Social Change: A Javanese Example." In *The Interpretation of Cultures*, 142–69. New York: Basic Books.

———. 1973j. "Thick Description: Toward an Interpretive Theory of Culture." In *The Interpretation of Cultures*, 3–30. New York: Basic Books.

———. 1983a. *Local Knowledge: Further Essays in Interpretive Anthropology*. New York: Basic Books.

———. 1983b. "Art as a Cultural System." In *Local Knowledge: Further Essays in Interpretive Anthropology*, 94–120. New York: Basic Books.

———. 1983c. "Common Sense as a Cultural System." In *Local Knowledge: Further Essays in Interpretive Anthropology*, 73–93. New York: Basic Books.

———. 1983d. "Found in Translation: On the Social History of the Moral Imagination." In *Local Knowledge: Further Essays in Interpretive Anthropology*, 36–54. New York: Basic Books.

———. 1983e. "From the Native's Point of View: On the Nature of Anthropological Understanding." In *Local Knowledge: Further Essays in Interpretive Anthropology*, 55–70. New York: Basic Books.

————. 1983f. "The Way We Think Now: Toward an Ethnography of Modern Thought."
In *Local Knowledge: Further Essays in Interpretive Anthropology*, 147–63. New York: Basic
Books.

————. 1995. *After the Fact: Two Countries, Four Decades, One Anthropologist.* Cambridge,
Mass.: Harvard University Press.

Gelu, Victor. 1971. *Marseille au XIXe siècle.* Edited by Lucien Gaillard and Jorgi Reboul. Introduction by Pierre Guiral. Paris: Plon.

Genovese, Eugene. 1974. *Roll, Jordan, Roll: The World the Slaves Made.* New York: Pantheon.

Giddens, Anthony. 1976. *New Rules of Sociological Method: A Positive Critique of Interpretive
Sociologies.* London: Hutchinson.

————. 1979. *Central Problems in Social Theory: Action, Structure and Contradiction in Social
Analysis.* Berkeley and Los Angeles: University of California Press.

————. 1981. *A Contemporary Critique of Historical Materialism.* Volume 1: *Power, Property and
the State.* London: Macmillan.

————. 1984. *The Constitution of Society.* Berkeley and Los Angeles: University of California
Press.

Ginzburg, Carlo. [1976] 1980. *The Cheese and the Worms: The Cosmos of a Sixteenth-Century
Miller.* Translated by John and Anne C. Tedeschi. Baltimore: Johns Hopkins University
Press.

————. [1972] 1983. *The Night Battles: Witchcraft and Agrarian Cults in the Sixteenth and Seventeenth Centuries.* Translated by John and Anne C. Tedeschi. Baltimore: Johns Hopkins
University Press.

Girard, Louis. 1952. *La politique des travaux publics du Second Empire.* Paris: Armand Colin.

————. 1961. "La Politique des grands travaux à Marseille sous le Second Empire." In
Chambre de Commerce de Marseille, *Marseille sous le Second Empire: Exposition, confer-
ences, colloque organisés à l'occasion du centenaire du palais de Ia Bourse, 10–26 novembre 1960.*
Paris: Plon.

Girard, Réné. 1977. *Violence and the Sacred.* Translated by Patrick Gregory. Baltimore: Johns
Hopkins University Press.

Godechot, Jacques. 1970. *The Taking of the Bastille: July 14, 1789,* Translated by Jean Stewart.
Preface by Charles Tilly. New York: Scribners.

Goffman, Erving. 1959. *The Presentation of Self in Everyday Life.* New York: Doubleday.

————. 1967a. *Interaction Ritual: Essays on Face to Face Behavior.* New York: Pantheon.

————. 1967b. "On Face Work." In *Interaction Ritual: Essays on Face to Face Behavior,* 5–46.
New York, Pantheon Books.

Goldstein, Jan, ed. 1994. *Foucault and the Writing of History.* Oxford: Blackwell.

————. 2001. *Console and Classify: The French Psychiatric Profession in the Nineteenth Century.*
2d ed. Chicago: University of Chicago Press.

Goldstone, Jack A. 1990. *Revolution and Rebellion in the Early Modern World.* Berkeley and Los
Angeles: University of California Press.

————. 1994. "Is Revolution Individually Rational? Groups and Individuals in Revolutionary Collective Action." *Rationality and Society* 6:139–66.

Gontier, Claudie. 1988. *Docks en stock: La manutention portuaire marseillaise: hommes, territoires
et techniques, 19e-20e siècle.* Marseille: C.E.R.F.I.S.E.

Gordon, Daniel. 1994. *Citizens Without Sovereignty: Equality and Sociability in French Thought,
1670–1789.* Princeton: Princeton University Press.

Gordon, David M., Richard Edwards, and Michael Reich. 1982. *Segmented Work, Divided*

Workers: The Historical Transformations of Labor in the United States. Cambridge: Cambridge University Press.

Goubert, Pierre. 1960. *Beauvais et le Beauvaisis de 1600 à 1730: Contribution à l'histoire sociale de la France au XVIIe siècle.* 2 vols. Paris: S.E.V.P.E.N.

———. 1996. *Un parcours d'historien: Souvenirs 1915–1995.* Paris: Fayard.

Gould, Roger V. 1995. *Insurgent Identities: Class, Community, and Protest from 1848 to the Commune.* Chicago: University of Chicago Press.

Gould, Steven Jay. 1989. *Wonderful Life: The Burgess Shale and the Nature of History.* New York: W. W. Norton.

Gramsci, Antonio. 1971a. *Selections from the Prison Notebooks.* Edited and translated by Quintin Hoare and Geoffrey Nowell Smith. New York: International Publishers.

———. 1971b. "Americanism and Post-Fordism." In *Selections from the Prison Notebooks,* ed. and trans. Quentin Hoare and Geoffry Nowell Smith, 277–318. New York: International Publishers.

Grendi, Edoardo. 1996. "Repenser la microhistoire?" In *Jeux d'échelles: La micro-analyse à l'experience,* ed. Jacques Revel, 233–43. Paris: Seuil/Gallimard.

Griffin, Larry. 1992. "Temporality, Events, and Explanation in Historical Sociology: An Introduction." *Sociological Methods and Research* 20:403–27.

———. 1993. "Narrative, Event-Structure Analysis, and Causal Interpretation in Historical Sociology." *American Journal of Sociology* 98:1094–1133.

Guiral, Pierre. 1956. "Le cas d'un grand port de commerce: Marseille." In *Aspects de la crise et de la dépression de l'économie française au milieu du XIXe siècle, 1846–1851,* ed. C.-E. Labrousse, 200–225. Vol. 19 of *Bibliothèque de la révolution de 1848.* La Roche-sur-Yon: Imprimerie Centrale de l'Ouest.

———. 1957. "Quelque notes sur la politique des milieux d'affaires Marseillais de 1815 à 1870." *Provence historique* 7:155–74.

Habermas, Jürgen. 1973. *Theory and Practice.* Translated by John Viertel. Boston: Beacon Press.

———. 1984. *The Theory of Communicative Action.* Translated by Thomas McCarthy. 2 vols. Boston: Beacon Press.

Hall, John R. 1984. "Temporality, Social Action, and the Problem of Quantification in Historical Analysis." *Historical Methods* 17:206–18.

Hall, Stuart. 1988. *The Hard Road to Renewal: Thatcherism and the Crisis of the Left.* London: Verso.

Hanagan, Michael P. 1980. *Artisans and Industrial Workers in Three French Towns, 1871–1914.* Urbana: University of Illinois Press.

Handler, Richard. 2002. "Cultural Theory in History Today." *American Historical Review* 107:1512–20.

Harrison, Royden, ed. 1978. *Independent Collier: The Coal Miner as Archetypal Proletarian Reconsidered.* New York: Saint Martin's.

Harvey, David. 1982. *The Limits to Capital.* Oxford: Basil Blackwell.

———. 1985. *Consciousness and the Urban Experience: Studies in the History and Theory of Capitalist Urbanism.* Baltimore: Johns Hopkins University Press.

———. 1989. *The Condition of Postmodernity: An Enquiry into the Origins of Cultural Change.* Oxford: Basil Blackwell.

Hayden, Dolores. 1984. *Redesigning the American Dream: The Future of Housing, Work, and Family Life.* New York: W. W. Norton.

Hebb, D. O., and W. R. Thompson. 1954. "The Significance of Animal Studies." In *Handbook of Social Psychology*, ed. Gardner Linzsey, 532–61. Cambridge, Mass.: Addison-Wesley.

Held, David, and John B. Thompson, eds. 1989. *Social Theory of Modern Societies: Anthony Giddens and His Critics.* Cambridge: Cambridge University Press.

Higounet, Charles, ed. 1980. *Histoire de Bordeaux.* Toulouse: Privat.

Hill, Christopher. 1964a. *Puritanism and Revolution: Studies in Interpretation of the English Revolution.* London: Secker and Warburgh.

———. 1964b. *Society and Puritanism in Pre-Revolutionary England.* London: Secker and Warburgh.

———. 1972. *The World Turned Upside Down: Radical Ideas during the English Revolution.* New York: Viking.

Hilton, Rodney. 1973. *Bondmen Made Free: Medieval Peasant Movements and the English Rising of 1381.* London: Temple Smith.

Hindess, Barry. 1986. "Actors and Social Relations." In *Social Theory in Transition*, ed. Mark L. Wordell and Stephen P. Turner, 113–26. London: Allen and Unwin.

Hirsch, Joachim. 1983. "The Fordist Security State and New Social Movements." *Kapitalistate* 10:75–88.

Hobsbawm, E. J. 1959. *Primitive Rebels: Studies in Archaic forms of Social Movements in the 19th and 20th Centuries.* Manchester: Manchester University Press.

———. 1964. *Labouring Men: Studies in the History of Labour.* London: Weidenfeld and Nicholson.

———. 1971. "From Social History to the History of Society." *Daedalus* 100:20–45.

———. 1980. "The Revival of Narrative: Some Comments." *Past and Present*, no. 86:3–8.

———. 2002. *Interesting Times: A Twentieth-Century Life.* New York: Pantheon Books.

Hobsbawm, E. J., and George Rudé. 1968. *Captain Swing.* New York: Pantheon Books.

Hollander, Zander. 1973. *The Modern Encyclopedia of Basketball.* Rev. ed. New York: Four Winds.

Holt, Thomas C. 1995. "Marking: Race, Race-making, and the Writing of History." *American Historical Review* 100:1–20.

Huizinga, Johan. 1954. *The Waning of the Middle Ages: A Study of the Forms of Life, Thought, and Art in France and the Netherlands in the XIV and XV Centuries.* Garden City, N.Y.: Doubleday.

Hunt, Lynn. 1978. *Revolution and Urban Politics in Provincial France: Troyes and Reims, 1786–1790.* Stanford: Stanford University Press.

———. 1984. *Politics, Culture, and Class in the French Revolution.* Berkeley and Los Angeles: University of California Press.

———, ed. 1989. *The New Cultural History.* Berkeley and Los Angeles: University of California Press.

Ronald B. Inden. 1976. *Marriage and Rank in Bengali Culture: A History of Caste and Clan in Middle Period Bengal.* Berkeley and Los Angeles: University of California Press.

Jakobson, Roman. 1970. *Essais de linguistique générale.* 2 vols. Paris: Points-Seuil.

Jameson, Fredric. 1981. *The Political Unconscious: Narrative as a Socially Symbolic Act.* Ithaca: Cornell University Press.

———. 1984. "Postmodernism, Or, The Cultural Logic of Late Capitalism." *New Left Review* 146:59–92.

———. 1991. *Postmodernism, or, The Cultural Logic of Late Capitalism.* Durham, N.C.: Duke University Press.

———. 1998. *The Cultural Turn: Selected Writings on the Postmodern, 1983–1998.* London: Verso.

Jessop, Bob, et al. 1988. *Thatcherism: A Story of Two Nations* New York: Polity Press.

———. 1992. "Fordism and Post-Fordism: Critique and Reformulation." In *Pathways to Industrialism and Regional Development,* ed. Michael Storper and Allen J. Scott, 46–69. London: Routledge.

Johnson, Christopher H. 1971. "Communism and the Working Class before Marx: The Icarian Experience." *American Historical Review* 76:657–67.

———. 1974. *Utopian Communism in France: Cabet and the Icarians, 1839–1851.* Ithaca: Cornell University Press.

———. 1975. "Economic Change and Artisan Discontent: The Tailors' History, 1800–48." In *Revolution and Reaction: 1848 and the Second French Republic,* ed. Roger Price, 87–114. London: Croom Helm.

———. 1979. "Patterns of Proletarianization: Parisian Tailors and Lodève Weavers." In *Consciousness and Class Experience in Nineteenth-Century Europe,* ed. John M. Merriman. New York: Holmes and Meyer.

———. 1995. *The Life and Death of Industiral Languedoc, 1700–1920: The Politics of Deindustrialization.* New York: Oxford University Press.

Johnson, Richard. 1978. "Thompson, Genovese, and Socialist-Humanist History." *History Workshop Journal* 6:79–100.

Joyce, Patrick. 1993. "The Imaginary Discontents of Social History: A Note of Response to Mayfield and Thorne, and Lawrence and Taylor." *Social History* 18:81–85.

———. 1995. "The End of Social History." *Social History* 20:73–91.

———. 1996. "The End of Social History? A Brief Reply to Eley and Nield." *Social History* 21:96–98.

———, ed. 2002. *The Social in Question: New Bearings in History and the Social Sciences.* London: Routledge.

Judt, Tony. 1979. *Socialism in Provence, 1870–1917: A Study in the Origins of the Modern French Left.* Cambridge: Cambridge University Press.

Julliany, Jules. 1842. *Essai sur le commerce de Marseille.* 2d rev. ed. 3 vols. Marseille: J. Barile.

Kaye, Harvey J. 1984. *The British Marxist Historians: An Introductory Analysis.* Cambridge: Polity Press.

———, ed. 1988. *The Face of the Crowd: Studies in Revolution, Ideology, and Popular Politics: Selected Essays of George Rudé.* New York: Harvester/Wheatsheaf.

Kaye, Harvey J., and Keith McClelland, eds. 1990. *E. P. Thompson: Critical Perspectives.* Cambridge: Polity Press.

Kessel, Patrick. 1969. *La Nuit du 4 Août 1789.* Paris: Arthaud.

Keylor, William R. 1975. *Academy and Community: The Foundation of the French Historical Profession.* Cambridge, Mass.: Harvard University Press.

Kimeldorf, Howard. 1988. *Reds or Rackets? The Making of Radical and Conservative Unions on the Waterfront.* Berkeley and Los Angeles: University of California Press.

Kimbal, Roger. 1990. *Tenured Radicals: How Politics Has Corrupted Our Higher Education.* New York: Harper and Row.

Kirch, Patrick V., and Marshall Sahlins. 1992. *Anahulu: The Anthropology of History in the Kingdom of Hawaii.* Vol. 1, *Historical Ethnography,* by Marshall Sahlins. Chicago: University of Chicago Press.

Kirk, Neville. 1994. "History, Language, Ideas, and Postmodernism: A Materialist View." *Social History* 19:221–40.

Kleinman, Daniel Lee. 1995. *Politics on the Endless Frontier: Postwar Research Policy in the United States*. Durham, N. C.: Duke University Press.

Kristeva, Julia. 1980. *Desire in Language: A Semiotic Approach to Literature and Art*. Edited by Leon S. Roudiez. Translated by Thomas Gora, Alice Jardine, and Leon S. Roudiez. New York: Columbia University Press.

Kuhn, Thomas. 1962. *The Structure of Scientific Revolutions*. Chicago: University of Chicago Press.

Lacan, Jacques. 1977. *Ecrits*. Translated by Alan Sheridan. New York: Norton.

LaCapra, Dominick. 1972. *Emile Durkheim: Sociologist and Philosopher*. Ithaca: Cornell University Press.

———. 1982. *Madame Bovary on Trial*. Ithaca: Cornell University Press.

———. 1983. *Rethinking Intellectual History: Texts, Contexts, Language*. Ithaca: Cornell University Press.

———. 1985. *History and Criticism*. Ithaca: Cornell University Press.

———. 1989. *Soundings in Critical Theory*. Ithaca: Cornell University Press.

———. 2001. *Writing History, Writing Trauma*. Baltimore: Johns Hopkins University Press.

Laitin, David D. 1986. *Hegemony and Culture : Politics and Religious Change among the Yoruba*. Chicago: University of Chicago Press.

Lakatos, Imre. 1978. *The Methodology of Scientific Research Programmes*. Cambridge: Cambridge University Press.

Lamont, Michèle, and Annette Lareau. 1988. "Cultural Capital: Allusions, Gaps, and Glissandos in Recent Theoretical Development." *Sociological Theory* 6:153–68.

Lamont, Michèle, and Robert Wuthnow. 1990. "Betwixt and Between: Recent Cultural Sociology in Europe and the United States." In *Frontiers of Social Theory: The New Synthesis*, ed. George Ritzer, 287–315. New York: Columbia University Press.

Lash, Scott, and John Urry. 1987. *The End of Organized Capitalism*. Cambridge: Polity Press.

Laurent, Emile. 1865. *Le pauperisme et les associations de prévoyance: Nouvelles études sur les sociétés de secours mutuels, histoire-économie politique-administration*. 2d ed. 2 vols. Paris: Guillaumin.

Lawrence, Jon, and Miles Taylor. 1993. "The Poverty of Protest: Gareth Stedman Jones and the Politics of Language—A Reply." *Social History* 18:1–16.

Leach, Edmund R. 1968. "Ritual." In *International Encyclopedia of the Social Sciences*, ed. David L. Sills, vol. 13. New York: Macmillan.

Le Beuf, E. B. 1857. *Du commerce de Nantes: Son passé, son état actuel, son avenir*. Nantes: Imprimerie William Busseuil.

Lebrun, François. 1971. *Les hommes et la mort en Anjou au 17e et 18e siècles: Essai de démographie et de psychologie historiques*. Paris: Mouton.

Lefebvre, Georges. [1949] 1971. *The Coming of the French Revolution*. Translated by R. R. Palmer. Princeton: Princeton University Press.

———. [1932] 1973. *The Great Fear: Rural Panic in Revolutionary France*. Translated by Joan White. Introduction by George Rudé. New York: Vintage.

Lehning, James R. 1980. *The Peasants of Marlhes: Economic Development and Family Organization in Nineteenth Century France*. Chapel Hill: University of North Carolina Press.

Lepenies, Wolf. 1988. *Between Literature and Science: The Rise of Sociology*. Translated by R. J. Hollingdale. Cambridge: Cambridge University Press.

Lepetit, Bernard, ed. 1995a. *Les formes de l'experience: Une autre histoire sociale*. Paris: Albin Michel.

————. 1995b. "Histoire des pratiques, pratique de l'histoire." In *Les formes de l'experience: Une autre histoire sociale*, 9–22. Paris: Albin Michel.

Les Annales. 1989. "Tentons l'experience." *Annales: Économies, Sociétés, Civilisations* 44:1317–24.

Lequin, Yves. 1977. *Les ouvriers de la région lyonnaise*. Lyon: Presses Universitaires de Lyon.

Le Roy Ladurie, Emmanuel. 1966. *Les paysans de Languedoc*. 2 vols. Paris: S.E.V.P.E.N.

————. 1975. *Montaillou, village occitan de 1294 à 1324*. Paris: Gallimard.

————. 1978. *Montaillou: The Promised Land of Error*. Translated by Barbara Bray. New York: George Braziller.

————. 1979. *Carnival in Romans*. Translated by Mary Feeney. New York: George Braziller.

————. 1982. *Paris-Montpellier, P.C.-P.S.U., 1945–1963*. Paris: Gallimard.

Levi, Giovanni. 1988. *Inheriting Power: The Story of an Exorcist*. Translated by Lydia G. Cochrane. Chicago: University of Chicago Press.

————. 1991. "On Microhistory." In *New Perspectives in Historical Writing*, ed. by Peter Burke, 93–113. Cambridge: Polity Press.

Lévi-Strauss, Claude. 1949. *Les structures élémentaires de la parenté*. Paris: Presses Universitaires de France.

————. 1961. *Triste Tropiques*, Translated by John Russell. New York: Criterion Books.

————. 1963a. *Structural Anthropology*. New York: Basic Books.

————. 1963b. *Totemism*. Translated by Rodney Needham. Boston: Beacon Press.

————. 1966. *The Savage Mind*. Chicago: University of Chicago Press.

————. [1949] 1969. *The Elementary Structures of Kinship*. Translated by James Harle Bell, John Richard von Sturmer, and Rodney Needham. Boston: Beacon Press.

Lipietz, Alain. 1987. *Mirages and Miracles: The Crisis in Global Fordism*. Translated by David Macey. London: Verso.

Liu, Tessie P. 1994. *The Weaver's Knot: The Contradictions of Class Struggle and Family Solidarity in Western France, 1759–1914*. Ithaca: Cornell University Press.

Lomnitz-Adler, Claudio. 1991. "Concepts for the Study of Regional Culture." *American Ethnologist* 18:195–214.

Loyseau, Charles. 1666. *Traité des orders et simples dignitez*. In *Oeuvres de maistre Charles Loyseau*. Paris: Chez Jean Dupuis et G. Alliot.

————. 1994. *A Treatise of Orders and Plain Dignities*. Edited and translated by Howell A. Lloyd. Cambridge: Cambridge University Press.

Lucas, Colin. 1988. "The Crowd and Politics between Ancien Regime and Revolution in France." *Journal of Modern History* 60:421–57.

————. 1991. "Talking About Urban Popular Violence in 1789." In *Reshaping France: Town, Country and Region during the French Revolution*, ed. Alan Forrest and Peter Jones, 122–36. Manchester: Manchester University Press.

————. 1994. "Revolutionary Violence, the People, and the Terror." In *The French Revolution and the Creation of Modern Political Culture*, vol. 4, *The Terror*, ed. Keith Michael Baker, 57–79. Oxford: Pergamon.

Lüdtke, Alf. 1995. *The History of Everyday Life: Reconstructing Historical Experiences and Ways of Life*. Translated by William Templer. Princeton: Princeton University Press.

Lusebrink, H.-L., and R. Reichardt. 1983. "La 'Bastille' dans l'imaginaire social de la France à la fin du XVIIIe siècle (1774–1799)." *Revue d'histoire moderne et contemporaine* 30:196–234.

————. 1990. *Die Bastille: Zur Symbolgeschichte von Herrschaft und Freiheit*. Frankfurt: Fischer Taschenbuch Verlag.

Lyotard, Jean-François. [1979] 1984. *The Postmodern Condition: A Report on Knowledge*, Translated by Geoff Bennington and Brian Massumi. Minneapolis: University of Minnesota Press.

Mann, Michael. 1986. *The Sources of Social Power*. Vol. 1, *A History of Power from the Beginning to A.D. 1760*. Cambridge: Cambridge University Press.

———. 1993. *The Sources of Social Power*. Vol. 2, *The Rise of Classes and Nation States, 1760–1914*. Cambridge: Cambridge University Press.

Margadant, Ted W. 1979. *French Peasants in Revolt: The Insurrection of 1851*. Princeton: Princeton University Press.

Marin, Louis. 1988. *Portrait of the King*, Translated by Martha M. Houle. Introduction by Tom Conley. Minnesota: University of Minnesota Press.

———. 1993. *Des pouvoirs de l'image: Gloses*. Paris: Seuil.

Markoff, John. 1996. *The Abolition of Feudalism: Peasants, Lords, and Legislators in the French Revolution*. University Park: Penn State University Press.

Marcus, George E., and Michael Fischer. 1986. *Anthropology as Cultural Critique: An Experimental Moment in the Human Sciences*. Chicago: University of Chicago Press.

Marcuse, Herbert. 1964. *One-Dimensional Man: Studies in the Ideology of Advanced Industrial Society*. Boston: Beacon Press.

Martin, Emily. 1987. *The Woman in the Body: A Cultural Analysis of Reproduction*. Boston: Beacon Press.

Marx, Karl. 1977. *Capital: A Critique of Political Economy*. Translated by Ben Fowkes. Introduction by Ernst Mandel. New York: Vintage Books.

Marx, Karl, and Friedrich Engels. [1848] 1948. *The Communist Manifesto*. New York: International Publishers.

Massey, Douglas S., and Nancy Denton. 1993. *American Apartheid: Segregation and the Making of the Underclass*. Cambridge, Mass.: Harvard University Press.

Masson, Paul, ed. 1913. *Les Bouches-du-Rhône: Encyclopédie départementale*. Vol. 11, *Biographies*. Marseille: Archives Départementale des Bouches-du-Rhône.

———. 1922. *Les Bouches-du-Rhône: Encyclopédie départementale*. Vol. 9, *Le Mouvement économique*. Paris: Champion.

Mayer, Margit, and Roland Roth. 1995. "The New Social Movements and the Transformation to Post-Fordist Society." In *Cultural Politics and Social Movements*, ed. by Marcy Darnovsky, Barbara Epstein, and Richard Flacks, 299–319. Philadelphia: Temple University Press.

Mayfield, David. 1991. "Language and Social History," *Social History* 16:353–57.

Mayfield, David, and Susan Thorne. 1992. "Social History and Its Discontents: Gareth Stedman Jones and the Politics of Language." *Social History* 17:165–88.

———. 1993. "Reply to 'The Poverty of Protest' and 'The Imaginary Discontents.'" *Social History* 18:219–33.

Mazuy, François. 1853. *Essai historique sur les moeurs et coutumes de Marseille au XIXe siècle*. Marseille: Arnaud.

McDonald, Terence, ed. 1996. *The Historic Turn in the Human Sciences*. Ann Arbor: University of Michigan Press.

Megill, Allan. 1985. *Prophets of Extremity: Neitzche, Heidegger, Foucault, and Derrida*. Berkeley and Los Angeles: University of California Press.

Meyer, Jean. 1966. *La noblesse bretonne au XVIIIe siècle*. 2 vols. Paris, S.E.V.P.E.N.

Mills, C. Wright. 1959. *The Sociological Imagination*. Oxford: Oxford University Press.

Moch, Leslie Page. 1983. *Paths to the City: Regional Migration in Nineteenth Century France.* New York: Sage.

Molino, J. 1986. "L' événement de la logique à la sémiologie." In *L'événement: Actes du colloque organize à Aix-en-Provence par le centre Méridional d'Historie Sociale*, 251–70. Aix-en-Provence: Université de Provence.

Moore, Barrington, Jr. 1966. *Social Origins of Dictatorship and Democracy: Lord and Peasant in the Making of the Modern World.* Cambridge, Mass.: Harvard University Press.

Morrison, Ann M., Randall P. White, and Ellen Van Velsor. 1987. *Breaking the Glass Ceiling: Can Women Reach the Top of America's Largest Corporations?* Reading, Mass.: Addison-Wesley.

Moss, Bernard H. 1976. *The Origins of the French Labor Movement: The Socialism of Skilled Workers, 1830–1914.* Berkeley and Los Angeles: University of California Press.

Mousnier, Roland. 1972. "Les concepts d'ordres, d'états, de fidelité et de monarchie absolue en France de la fin du XVe siécle à la fin du XVIIIe siécle." *Revue historique* 502:289–312.

Namier, Sir Louis B. 1929. *The Structure of Politics at the Accession of George III.* 2 vols. London: Macmillan.

Nguyen, Victor. 1961. Crise et vie des portefaix marseillais, 1814–1914. Diplôme d'Études Superieure, Faculté des Lettres et des Sciences Humaines, Aix-en-Provence.

———. 1962. "Les Portefaix marseillais: Crise et déclin, survivances," *Provence historique* 12:363–97.

Novick, Peter. 1988. *That Noble Dream: The Objectivity Question and the American Historical Profession.* Cambridge: Cambridge University Press.

Nora, Pierre. 1974. "Le retour de l'événement." In *Faire de l'histoire*, vol. 1, *Nouveaux problèmes*, ed. J. Legoff and P. Nora, 285–308. Paris: Gallimard.

———, ed. 1984–92. *Les lieux de mémoire.* 3 vols. Paris: Gallimard.

———. 1996–98. *Realms of Memory: Rethinking the French Past.* Translated by Arthur Goldhammer. New York: Columbia University Press.

Obeyesekere, Gananath. 1992. *The Apotheosis of Captain Cook: European Mythmaking in the Pacific.* Princeton: Princeton University Press.

Olivesi, Antoine. 1950. *La commune de 1871 à Marseille et ses origines.* Paris: M. Riviere.

Ortner, Sherry B. 1984. "Theory in Anthropology since the Sixties." *Comparative Studies in Society and History* 26:126–66.

———. 1989. *High Religion: A Cultural and Political History of Sherpa Bhuddism.* Princeton: Princeton University Press.

———. 1995. "Resistance and the Problem of Ethnographic Refusal." *Comparative Studies in Society and History* 37:173–93.

———. 1996. *Making Gender: The Politics and Erotics of Culture.* Boston: Beacon Press.

Ozouf, Mona. 1976. *La fête révolutionnaire, 1789–1799.* Paris: Gallimard.

Paige, Jeffrey M. 1978. *Agrarian Revolution: Social Movements and Export Agriculture.* New York: Free Press.

Palmer, Bryan D. 1990. *Descent into Discourse: The Reification of Language and the Writing of Social History.* Philadelphia: Temple University Press.

———. 1987. "Response to Joan Scott." *International Labor and Working Class History* 31:14–23.

Parsons, Talcott. 1959. *The Social System.* Glencoe, Ill: Free Press.

Patterson, Thomas. 1989. "Post-structuralism, Post-modernism: Implications for Historians." *Social History* 14:83–88.

Perrot, Jean-Claude. 1975. *Genèse d'une ville moderne: Caen au XVIIIe siècle.* 2 vols. Paris: Mouton.

Perrot, Michelle. 1974. *Les ouvriers en grève: France 1871–1890.* Paris: Mouton.

———. 1987. "L'air du temps." In *Essais d'ego-histoire,* ed. Pierre Nora, 241–92. Paris: Gallimard.

Le Petit Robert. 1984. *Le Petit Robert: Dictionnaire alphabètique et analogique de la langue française.* Paris: Le Robert.

Pigenet, Michel. 2004. "Les travailleurs de la manutention portuaire ou les métamorphoses du modèle corporatif." In *La France malade du corporatisme? XVIIIe-XXe siècle,* ed. Steven L. Kaplan and Philippe Minard, 253-78. Paris: Editions BELIN.

Piore, Michael J., and Charles F. Sabel. 1984. *The Second Industrial Divide: Possibilities for Prosperity.* New York: Basic Books.

Pocock, J. G. A. 1975. *The Machiavellian Moment: Florentine Political Thought and the Atlantic Republican Tradition.* Princeton: Princeton University Press.

Poitrineau, Abel. 1965. *La vie rurale en basse Auvergne au XVIIIe siècle.* 2 vols. Paris: Presses Universitaires de France.

Postone, Moishe. 1993. *Time, Labour, and Social Domination: A Reinterpretation of Marx's Critical Theory.* Cambridge: Cambridge University Press.

Rabinbach, Anson. 1987. "Rationalism and Utopia as Languages of Nature: A Note." *International Labor and Working Class History* 31:30–36.

Ramsay, Clay. 1992. *The Ideology of the Great Fear: The Soissonnais in 1789.* Baltimore: Johns Hopkins University Press.

Ranger, Terence. 1983. "The Invention of Tradition in Colonial Africa." In *The Invention of Tradition,* ed. Eric Hobsbawm and Terence Ranger, 211–62. Cambridge: Cambridge University Press.

Rancière, Jacques. 1981. *La nuit des prolétaires.* Paris: Fayard.

Readings, Bill. 1996. *The University in Ruins.* Cambridge, Mass.: Harvard University Press.

Reddy, William M. 1984. *The Rise of Market Culture: The Textile Trade and French Society, 1750–1900.* Cambridge: Cambridge University Press.

———. 1997. *The Invisible Code: Honor and Sentiment in Postrevolutionary France, 1814–1848.* Berkeley and Los Angeles: University of California Press.

———. 2001. *The Navigation of Feeling: A Framework for the History of Emotions.* Cambridge: Cambridge University Press.

Réimpression de l'Ancien Moniteur. 1858. Vol. 1. Paris: Plon.

Revel, Jacques. 1995. "Introduction." In *Histories: French Constructions of the Past,* ed. Jacques Revel and Lynn Hunt, 1–63. New York: The New Press.

———, ed. 1996a. *Jeux d'échelles: La micro-analyse à l'experience.* Paris: Seuil/Gallimard.

———. 1996b. "Présentation." In *Jeux d'échelles: La micro-analyse à l'experience,* 7–14. Paris: Seuil/Gallimard.

———. 1996c. "Micro-analyse et construction du social." In *Jeux d'échelles: La micro-analyse à l'experience,* 15–36. Paris: Seuil/Gallimard.

Ricoeur, Paul. 1971. "The Model of the Text: Meaningful Action Considered as a Text." *Social Research* 38:529–62.

———. 1974. *The Conflict of Interpretations.* Edited by Don Ihde. Evanston: Northwestern University Press.

Riley, Denise. 1988. *"Am I That Name?" Feminism and the Category of "Women" in History.* Minneapolis: University of Minnesota Press.

Roche, Daniel. 1978. *Le siècle des lumières en province: Académies et académiciens provinciaux, 1690–1789.* Paris: Mouton.

Roediger, David R. 1991. *The Wages of Whiteness: Race in the Making of the American Working Class.* London: Verso.

Roemer, John E. 1982. "New Directions in the Marxist Theory of Exploitation and Class." *Politics and Society* 11:253–87.

Rosaldo, Renato I. 1980. *Ilongot Headhunting, 1883–1874: A Study in Society and History.* Stanford: Stanford University Press.

———. 1990. "Celebrating Thompson's Heroes: Social Analysis in History and Anthropology." In *E. P. Thompson: Critical Perspectives,* ed. Harvey J. Kaye and Keith McClelland, 103–24. Cambridge: Polity Press.

Roseberry, William. 1982. "Balinese Cockfights and the Seduction of Anthropology." *Social Research* 49:1013–28. Reprinted in *Anthropologies and Histories: Essays in Culture, History, and Political Economy,* 17–29. New Brunswick: Rutgers University Press, 1989.

Ross, Dorothy. 1991. *The Origins of American Social Science.* Cambridge: Cambridge University Press.

Rostow, W. W. 1960. *The Process of Economic Growth.* 2d ed. Oxford: Clarendon Press.

Rubin, Gayle. 1975. "The Traffic in Women: Notes on the 'Political Economy' of Sex." In *Toward an Anthropology of Women,* ed. Rayna R. Reiter, 157–210. New York: Monthly Review Press.

Rudé, George. 1959. *The Crowd in the French Revolution.* Oxford: Oxford University Press.

———. 1962. *Wilkes and Liberty: A Social Study of 1763 to 1774.* Oxford: Clarendon Press.

———. 1964. *The Crowd in History: A Study of Popular Disturbances in France and England.* New York: Wiley.

Sabean, David Warren. 1984. *Power in the Blood: Popular Culture and Village Discourse in Early Modern Germany.* Cambridge: Cambridge University Press.

———. 1990. *Property, Production, and Family in Neckarhausen, 1700–1870.* Cambridge: Cambridge University Press.

———. 1998. *Kinship in Neckarhausen, 1700–1870.* Cambridge: Cambridge University Press.

Sabel, Charles H. 1988. "Protoindustry and the Problem of Capitalism as a Concept: Response to Jean H. Quataert." *International Labor and Working-Class History* 33:30–37.

Sabel, Charles H., and Johnathan Zeitlin. 1985. "Historical Alternatives to Mass Production: Politics, Markets, and Technology in Nineteenth-Century Industrialization." *Past and Present,* no. 108:133–76.

Sahlins, Marshall. 1976. *Culture and Practical Reason.* Chicago: University of Chicago Press.

———. 1981. *Historical Metaphors and Mythical Realities: Early History of the Sandwich Islands Kingdom.* Ann Arbor: University of Michigan Press.

———. 1985. *Islands of History.* Chicago: University of Chicago Press.

———. 1989. "The Cosmology of Capitalism: The Trans-Pacific Sector of the World System." *Proceedings of the British Academy* 74:1–52. Oxford: Oxford University Press.

———. 1990. "The Political Economy of Grandeur in Hawaii from 1810 to 1830." In *Culture Through Time: Anthropological Approaches,* edited by Emiko Ohnuki-Tierney, 26–56. Stanford: Stanford University Press.

———. 1991. "The Return of the Event, Again: With Reflections on the Beginnings of the Great Fijian War of 1843 to 1855 between the Kingdoms of Bau and Rewa." In *Clio in Oceania: Toward a Historical Anthropology,* ed. Aletta Biersack, 37–100. Washington, D.C.: Smithsonian Institution Press.

———. 1994. "The Discovery of the True Savage." In *Dangerous Liaisons: Essays in Honor of Greg Denning*, edited by Donna Merwick, 41–94. Melbourne: University of Melbourne.

———. 1995. *How "Natives" Think, About Captain Cook, for Example*. Chicago: University of Chicago Press.

Salzinger, Leslie. 2003. "Market Subjects: Traders at Work in the Dollar/Peso Market." Presented at the American Sociological Association Meeting.

Samuel, Raphael. 1977. "The Workshop of the World: Steam Power and Hand Technology in Mid-Victorian Britain." *History Workshop Journal* 3:6–72.

———. 1991. "Reading the Signs." *History Workshop Journal* 32:88–109.

———. 1992. "Reading the Signs: II. Fact-Grubbers and Mind-Readers." *History Workshop Journal* 33:220–51.

Saussure, Ferdinand de. 1966. *Course in General Linguistics*. Edited by Charles Bally and Albert Sechehaye in collaboration with Albert Riedlinger. Translated by Wade Baskin. New York: McGraw-Hill.

Schneider, David M. 1968. *American Kinship: A Cultural Account*. Englewood Cliffs, N.J.: Prentice-Hall.

———. 1976. "Notes Toward a Theory of Culture." In *Meaning in Anthropology*, ed. Keith H. Basso and Henry A. Selby, 197–220. Albuquerque: University of New Mexico Press.

Scott, James. 1985. *Weapons of the Weak: Everyday Forms of Peasant Resistance*. New Haven: Yale University Press.

Scott, Joan W. 1974. *The Glassworkers of Carmaux; French Craftsmen and Political Action in a Nineteenth-Century City*. Cambridge, Mass.: Harvard University Press.

———. 1987a. "On Language, Gender, and Working Class History." *International Labor and Working Class History* 31:1–13.

———. 1987b. "A Reply to Criticism." *International Labor and Working Class History* 32:39–45.

———. 1988. *Gender and the Politics of History*. New York: Columbia University Press.

———. 1991. "Women's History." In *New Perspecives on Historical Writing*, ed. Peter Burke, 42–66. Cambridge: Polity Press.

———. 1992. "Experience." In *Feminists Theorize the Political*, ed. Joan W. Scott and Judith Butler, 22–40. New York: Routlege.

———. 1993. "The Tip of the Volcano." *Comparative Studies in Society and History* 35:438–43.

———. 1996. *Only Paradoxes to Offer: French Feminists and the Rights of Man*. Cambridge, Mass.: Harvard University Press.

Sewell, William H. 1988. "The Changing Institutional Structure of Sociology and My Career." In *Sociological Lives: Social Change and the Life Course*, vol. 2, ed. Matilda W. Riley, 119–43. Newbury Park, Calif.: Sage Publications.

Sewell, William H., Jr. 1967. "Marc Bloch and the Logic of Comparative History." *History and Theory* 6:208–18.

———. 1971. "The Structure of the Working Class of Marseille in the Middle of the Nineteenth Century." Ph.D. diss., University of California, Berkeley.

———. 1974a. "Etat, Corps and Ordre: Some Notes on the Social Vocabulary of the French Old Regime." In *Sozialgeschichte Heute: Festschrift für Hans Rosenberg zum 70 Geburtstag*, ed. H. U. Wehler, 49–68. Göttingen: Vandenhoek und Ruprecht.

———. 1974b. "Social Change and the Rise of Working-Class Politics in Nineteenth Century Marseille." *Past and Present*, no. 65:75–109.

———. 1974c. "The Working Class of Marseille under the Second Republic: Social Structure and Political Behavior." In *Workers in the Industrial Revolution*, ed. Peter Stearns and Daniel Walkowitz, 75–115. New Brunswick, N.J.: Transaction Books.

———. 1980. *Work and Revolution in France: The Language of Labor from the Old Regime to 1848.* Cambridge: Cambridge University Press.

———. 1981. "La Confraternité des prolétaires: Conscience de classe sous la monarchie de juillet." *Annales: Économies, Sociétés, Civilisations* 36:650–71.

———. 1985a. "Ideologies and Social Revolutions: Reflections on the French Case." *Journal of Modern History* 57:57–85.

———. 1985b. *Structure and Mobility: The Men and Women of Marseille, 1820–1870.* Cambridge: Cambridge University Press.

———. 1988. "Uneven Development, the Autonomy of Politics, and the Dockworkers of Nineteenth-Century Marseille." *American Historical Review* 93:604–37.

———. 1990a. "Collective Violence and Collective Loyalties in France: Why the French Revolution Made a Difference." *Politics and Society* 18:527–52.

———. 1990b. "How Classes Are Made: Critical Reflections on E. P. Thompson's Theory of Working-Class Formation." In *E. P. Thompson: Critical Perspectives*, ed. by Harvey J. Kaye and Keith McClelland, 50–77. Cambridge: Polity Press.

———. 1993. "Toward a Post-Materialist Rhetoric for Labor History." In *Rethinking Labor History: Essays on Discourse and Class Analysis*, ed. Lenard R. Berlanstein, 15–38. Urbana and Chicago: University of Illinois Press.

———. 1994. *A Rhetoric of Bourgeois Revolution: The Abbé Sieyes and What Is the Third Estate?* Durham, N.C.: Duke University Press.

———. 1996. "Historical Events as Structural Transformations: Inventing Revolution at the Bastille." *Theory and Society* 25:841–81.

———. 1998. "Language and Practice in Cultural History: Backing Away from the Edge of the Cliff." *French Historical Studies* 21:241–54.

Shankman, Paul. 1984. "The Thick and the Thin: On the Interpretive Theoretical Paradigm of Clifford Geertz." *Current Anthropology* 25:261–79.

Skinner, Quentin. 1978. *Foundations of Modern Political Thought.* Cambridge: Cambridge University Press.

Skocpol, Theda. 1979. *States and Social Revolutions: A Comparative Study of France, Russia, and China.* Cambridge: Cambridge University Press.

———, ed. 1984. *Vision and Method in Historical Sociology.* Cambridge: Cambridge University Press.

———. 1985. "Cultural Idioms and Political Ideologies in the Revolutionary Reconstructions of State Power: A Rejoinder to Sewell." *Journal of Modern History* 57: 86–96.

———. 1988–89. "An 'Uppity Generation' and the Revitalization of Macroscopic Sociology: Reflections at Mid-Career by a Woman from the Sixties." *Theory and Society* 17:627–44.

Skocpol, Theda, and Margaret Somers. 1980. "The Uses of Comparative History in Macrosocial Inquiry." *Comparative Studies in Society and History* 22:174–97.

Smelser, Neil J. 1959. *Social Change in the Industrial Revolution: An Application of Theory to the British Cotton Industry.* Chicago: Chicago University Press.

Smith, Bonnie G. 1980. *Ladies of the Leisure Class: The Bourgeoises of Northern France in the Nineteenth Century.* Princeton: Princeton University Press.

Social Sciences Citation Index, 1995 Annual. 1996. Philadelphia: Institute for Scientific Information.

Somers, Margaret Ramsay. 1986. "The People and the Law: The Place of the Public Sphere in the Formation of English Popular Identity." Ph.D. diss., Harvard University, Department of Sociology.

Spivak, Gayatri Chakravorty. 1988. "Can the Subaltern Speak?" In *Marxism and the Interpretation of Culture*, ed. Cary Nelson and Lawrence Grossberg, 271–313. Urbana: University of Illinois Press.

Stansell, Christine. 1987. "Response to Joan Scott." *International Labor and Working Class History* 31:24–29.

Stearns, Peter N. 1967. "Some Comments on Social History." *The Journal of Social History* 1:3–6.

Stedman Jones, Gareth. 1983. *Languages of Class: Studies in English Working Class History, 1832–1982*. Cambridge: Cambridge University Press.

———. 1996. "The Determinist Fix: Some Obstacles to the Further Development of the Linguistic Approach to History in the 1990s." *History Workshop Journal* 42:19–35.

———. 2002. "The New Social History in France." In *The Age of Cultural Revolutions: Britain and France, 1750–1820*, ed. Colin Jones and Dror Wahrman, 94–105. Berkeley and Los Angeles: University of California Press.

Steedman, Carolyn. 1986. *Landscape of a Good Woman: A Story of Two Lives*. London: Virago.

———. 1994. "Bimbos from Hell." *Social History* 19:57–67.

Steinmetz, George. Forthcoming. "Scientific Authority and the Transition to Post-Fordism: The Making and Unmaking of Modernity in American Sociology in the Second Half of the Twentieth Century." In *The Politics of Method in the Human Sciences: Positivism and Its Epistemological Others*, ed. George Steinmetz. Durham, N.C.: Duke University Press.

———. 2004. "American Sociology's Epistemological Unconscious and the Transition to Post-Fordism: The Case of Historical Sociology." In *Remaking Modernity: Politics, History, and Sociology*, ed. Julia Adams, Elisabeth Clemens, and Ann Orloff. Durham, N.C.: Duke University Press.

———. 1994. "Regulation Theory, Post-Marxism, and the New Social Movements." *Comparative Studies in Society and History* 36:176–212.

Steinmetz, George, and Ou-Byung Chae. 2002. "Sociology in an Era of Fragmentation: From the Sociology of Knowledge to the Philosophy of Science, and Back Again." *Sociological Quarterly* 43:111–37.

Stinchcombe, Arthur. 1978. *Theoretical Methods in Social History*. New York: Academic Press.

Stoler, Ann Laura. 1995. *Race and the Education of Desire: Foucault's History of Sexuality and the Colonial Order of Things*. Durham, N.C.: Duke University Press.

———. 2002. *Carnal Knowledge and Imperial Power: Race and the Intimate in Colonial Rule*. Berkeley and Los Angeles: University of California Press.

Stone, Lawrence. 1965. *The Crisis of the Aristocracy, 1559–1641*. Oxford: Clarendon.

———. 1979. "The Revival of Narrative: Reflections on a New Old History." *Past and Present*, no. 85:3–24.

Suny, Ronald Grigor. 2002. "Back and Beyond: Reversing the Cultural Turn?" *American Historical Review* 107:1476–99.

Suter, Andreas. 1997. "Histoire sociale et événements historiques: Pour une nouvelle approche." *Annales: Histoires, Sciences Sociales* 52: 543–69.

Swidler, Ann. 1984. "Culture in Action: Symbols and Strategies." *American Sociological Review* 51:273–86.

———. 2001. *Talk of Love: How Culture Matters*. Chicago: University of Chicago Press.

Taylor, Michael. 1988. "Rationality and Collective Revolutionary Action." In *Rationality and Revolution*, 63–97. Cambridge: Cambridge University Press.

Therborn, Goran. 1980. *The Ideology of Power and the Power of Ideology*. London: Verso.

Thernstrom, Stephan. 1964. *Poverty and Progress: Social Mobility in a Nineteenth Century City*. Cambridge, Mass.: Harvard University Press.

Thompson, E. P. 1963. *The Making of the English Working Class*. London: Victor Golancz.

———. 1978. *The Poverty of Theory and Other Essays*. London: Merlin Press.

Thompson, John B. 1989. "The Theory of Structuration." In *Social Theory of Modern Societies: Anthony Giddens and His Critics*, ed. D. Held and J. B. Thompson, 56–76. Cambridge: Cambridge University Press.

Tilly, Charles. 1964. *The Vendée*. Cambridge, Mass.: Harvard University Press.

———. 1969. "Collective Violence in European Perspective." In *Violence in America: Historical and Comparative Perspectives*, ed. Hugh Davis Graham and Ted Robert Gurr, 5–34. Washington, D.C.: U.S. Government Printing Office.

———. 1972a. "How Protest Modernized in France." In *The Dimensions of Quantitative Research in History*, ed. William Aydelotte, Allan Bogue, and Robert Fogel, 192–255. Princeton: Princeton University Press.

———. 1972b. "The Modernization of Political Conflict in France." In *Perspectives on Modernization: Essays in Memory of Ian Weinberg*, ed. Edward B. Harvey, 50–95. Toronto: University of Toronto Press.

———. 1977. "Getting it Together in Burgundy." *Theory and Society* 4:479–504.

———. 1981. "The Web of Contention in Eighteenth-Century Cities." In *Class Conflict and Collective Action*, ed. Louise Tilly and Charles Tilly, 27–52. Beverly Hills: Sage Publications.

———. 1984. *Big Structures, Large Processes, Huge Comparisons*. New York: Russell Sage Foundation.

———. 1986. *The Contentious French*. Cambridge, Mass.: Harvard University Press.

———. 1990. *Coercion, Capital, and European States: AD 990–1990*. Cambridge, Mass.: Blackwell.

———. 1993. *European Revolutions, 1492–1992*. Oxford: Blackwell.

———. 1995. *Popular Contention in Great Britain, 1758–1834*. Cambridge, Mass.: Harvard University Press.

Tilly, Charles, Louise Tilly, and Richard Tilly. 1975. *The Rebellious Century, 1830–1930*. Cambrige, Mass.: Harvard University Press.

Tilly, Louise A., and Joan W. Scott. 1978. *Women, Work, and Family*. New York: Holt, Rinehart and Winston.

Toews, John. 1987. "Intellectual History after the Linguistic Turn: The Autonomy of Meaning and the Irreducibility of Experience." *American Historical Review* 92:879–907.

Traugott, Mark. 1985. *Armies of the Poor: Determinants of Working-Class Participation in the Parisian Insurrection of June 1848*. Princeton: Princeton University Press.

Travaux de la société de statistique de Marseille. 1837–73. 36 vols.

Tristan, Flora. 2001. *Le tour de France: Journal 1843–44*. 2 vols. Paris: INDIGO et Côté-Femmes Editions.

Trotsky, Leon. 1932. *History of the Russian Revolution*. Translated by Max Eastman. New York: Simon and Schuster.

Turner, Steven Park, and Jonathan Turner. 1990. *The Impossible Science: An Institutional Analysis of American Sociology*. Newbury Park, Calif.: Sage.

Turner, Victor W. 1967. *The Forest of Symbols: Aspects of Ndembu Ritual.* Ithaca: Cornell University Press.

———. 1969. *The Ritual Process: Structure and Anti-Structure.* Chicago: Aldine.

Veeser, H. Aram, ed. 1989. *The New Historicism.* New York: Routledge.

Venturi, Robert, Denise Scott Brown, and Steven Izenour. 1977. *Learning from Las Vegas: The Forgotten Symbolism of Architectural Form.* Cambridge, Mass.: MIT Press.

Vernon, James. 1994. "Who's Afraid of the 'Linguistic Turn'? The Politics of Social History and Its Discontents." *Social History* 19:81–97.

Villar, Pierre. 1962. *La catalogne dans l'Espagne moderne: Recherches sur les fondements économiques des structures nationales.* 3 vols. Paris: S.E.V.P.E.N.

———. 1982. *Une histoire en construction: Approche marxiste et problématiques conjuncturelles.* Paris: Galimard, Seuil.

Vine, Barbara [Ruth Rendell]. *A Fatal Inversion.* New York: Bantam Books.

Vonnegut, Kurt. 1985. *Galapagos.* New York: Delacorte Press.

Vovelle, Michel. 1973. *Piété baroque et déchristianisation en Provence au XVIIIe siècle: Les attitudes devant la mort d'après les clauses des testaments.* Paris: Plon.

Wacquant, Loïc. 1989. "Towards a Reflexive Sociology: A Workshop with Pierre Bourdieu." *Sociological Theory* 7:26–63.

———. 1995. "The Pugilistic Point of View: How Boxers Think and Feel about Their Trade." *Theory and Society* 24:489–535.

———. 2004. *Body and Soul: Notebooks of an Apprentice Boxer.* New York: Oxford.

Wallace, Anthony F. C. 1978. *Rochdale: The Growth of an American Village in the Early Industrial Revolution.* New York: Knopf.

Wallerstein, Immanuel. 1974a. *The Modern World-System.* Vol. 1, *Capitalist Agriculture and the Origins of the Capitalist World Economy in the Sixteenth Century.* New York: Academic Press.

———. 1974b. "The Rise and Future Demise of the World Capitalist System: Concepts for Comparative Analysis." *Comparative Studies in Society and History* 16:387–415.

Walters, Ronald. 1980. "Signs of the Times: Clifford Geertz and the Historians." *Social Research* 47:537–53.

Watson, Graham. 1989. "Definitive Geertz." *Ethnos* 54:23–30.

———. 1991. "Rewriting Culture." In *Recapturing Anthropology: Working in the Present,* ed. Richard G. Fox, 73–92. Santa Fe: School of American Research.

Weber, Max. 1958. *The Protestant Ethic and the Spirit of Capitalism.* New York: Scribners.

———. 1978. *Economy and Society: An Outline of Interpretive Sociology.* 2 vols. Edited by Guenther Roth and Claus Wittich. Berkeley and Los Angeles: University of California Press.

Wedeen, Lisa. 1999. *Ambiguities of Domination: Politics, Rhetoric, and Symbols in Contemporary Syria.* Chicago: University of Chicago Press.

Weeks, Jeffrey. 1982. "Foucault for Historians." *History Workshop Journal* 14:106–19.

White, Hayden. 1973. *Metahistory: The Historical Imagination in the Nineteenth Century* Baltimore: Johns Hopkins University Press.

———. 1978. *Tropics of Discourse: Essays in Cultural Criticism.* Baltimore: Johns Hopkins University Press.

———. 1987. *The Content of the Form: Narrative Discourse and Historical Representation.* Baltimore: Johns Hopkins University Press.

———. 1999. *Figural Realism: Studies in the Mimesis Effect.* Baltimore: Johns Hopkins University Press.

Wiener, Annette. 1976. *Women of Value, Men of Renown: New Perspectives in Trobriand Exchange.* Austin: University of Texas Press.

Wilentz, Sean. 1984. *Chants Democratic: New York City and the Rise of the American Working Class, 1788–1850.* New York: Oxford University Press.

Williams, Raymond. 1958. *Culture and Society: 1780–1950.* New York: Columbia University Press.

———. 1973. *The Country and the City.* Oxford: Oxford University Press.

———. 1977. *Marxism and Literature.* Oxford: Oxford University Press.

———. 1983. *Keywords: A Vocabulary of Culture and Society.* Rev. ed. Oxford: Oxford University Press.

Willis, Paul. 1981. *Learning to Labor: How Working Class Kids Get Working Class Jobs.* New York: Columbia University Press.

Wilson, William J. 1987. *The Truly Disadvantaged: The Inner City, the Underclass, and Public Policy.* Chicago: University of Chicago Press.

———. 1996. *When Work Disappears: The World of the New Urban Poor.* New York: Knopf.

Wittgenstein, Ludwig. [1953] 1958. *Philosophical Investigations.* Translated by G. E. M. Anscombe. New York: Macmillan.

Young, Iris Marion. 1990a. "Breasted Existence: The Look and Feeling." In *Throwing Like a Girl and Other Essays in Feminist Philosophy and Social Theory,* 189–209. Bloomington: Indiana University Press.

———. 1990b. "Throwing Like a Girl: A Phenomenology of Feminine Body Comportment, Motility, and Spatiality." In *Throwing Like a Girl and Other Essays in Feminist Philosophy and Social Theory,* 141–59. Bloomington: Indiana University Press.

Zanzi, Josette. 1969. "Les Portefaix marseillais à la fin de l'ancien régime et sous la révolution française." Mémoire de Maîtrise, Faculté des Lettres d'Aix-en-Provence.

Zhao, Dingxin. 2001. *The Power of Tiananmen: State-Society Relations and the 1989 Bejing Student Movement.* Chicago: University of Chicago Press.

INDEX

Abbott, Andrew, 13n.5
abstracted empiricism, 40, 62
Abu-Lughod, Lila, 155
accords, 73
action: ambiguous, 213; meaningful as reference, 217; objective risk of, 203; scopes of,
260; subjective risk of, 203. *See also* agency
actors, as knowledgeable, 127, 138. *See also*
agency
After the Fact (Geertz), 190n
agency: as capacity to mobilize resources by
means of schemas, 142–43; as capacity to
transpose schemas to new contexts, 142; as
collective, 145; as constituent of structure,
143; as constituted by cultures and social
institutions, 128; definition of, 143, 145;
as empowered by structures, 143, 145; as
laden with power differentials, 145; microhistory as demonstration of, 74; and structure as presupposing each other, 127; as
transposition of schemas, 141; understood
as opposite of structure, 125; variations
in scope of, 145. *See also* action; actors;
subjects
Agulhon, Maurice, 69
Aiguillon, Emmanuel-Armand, duc d', 257
Albertas, Marquis de (prefect of Bouches-
du-Rhone), 285
Althusser, Louis, 189, 331
American Historical Review, 4n.1
American Journal of Political Science, 4n.1
American Journal of Sociology, 4n.1
American Revolution, 267

American Sociological Association, 82
anachronism, 183–84
Annales, 2, 25, 72–73, 74; founding of, 34;
special issue assessing state of history, 72
Annales school, 23, 34–37, 72–77; ascendancy
of after World War II, 25; attitude toward
events, 197; continued identity as social
historians, 76; early history of, 34; Dosse's
critique of, 72; implicit model of society,
35–36; redefinition of objects and methods, 76; relationship to Marxism, 36–37;
use of quantification, 36; *theses* of third
generation Annales historians, 35–36
anthropology, 6, 12, 13, 17; and colonialism, 17;
conception of structure in, 126; consensus
about culture in early 1970s, 152; critique
of culture concept, 155–56, 169; cultural,
130; debates about culture since 1980s,
152–56; disciplinary identity crisis of, 154;
emergence of, 2; feminism in, 193; impossibility of controlling culture concept, 155;
historical approaches in, 42–43; and history, 17; inability to give up culture concept, 155; influence of Geertz in 1970s, 153,
155; influence on cultural history, 41; language metaphor in, 332; and literary criticism, 17, 46–47; meaning of culture in, 319;
meaning of social in, 319; monopoly on
culture concept in 1960s and 1970s, 153;
reflexive, 193–94; the revelation of, 179;
seductiveness of, 179; structural, 198; and
study of culture, 130; synchronic approach
of, 17

397

Burguière, André, 39
Buzot, François, 241, 243

Cabrera, Miguel A., 49n.30
Capital, 348
capitalism, 49; abstract logic of, 150, 278; creation of privileged niches in, 279; deep structures of, 150; dynamics of, 149–51, 277–80; effects of on labor force, 279–80; effects of on Marseille's port, 300; importance of commodity form in, 348; as language game, 348; money and, 348; origins of (Wallerstein), 87; as quantitative semiotic practice, 348–49; responses of social sciences to transformations of, 59, 77; as semiotic practice, 343; structures of, 149–51; surface instability of, 150; temporality of, 274–80; transformations of since 1970s, 52, 55–59, 61; uneven development in, 149–50, 277–80. *See also* commodity form; flexible accumulation; money
Carnival in Romans (Le Roy Laudrie), 183
Central Problems in Social Theory (Giddens), 128, 129, 130, 132
Certeau, Michel de, 331, 335
charisma, 267
Chartier, Roger, 69, 334–35
Cheese and the Worms, The (Ginzburg), 73
China, ancient, 116, 117, 119
Chinese Revolution, 92, 93–94, 96, 99
Chirac, Jacques, 68
Chorley, Katherine, 104
Christianity, 119, 120
chronology, 10–11
Civilization of the Renaissance in Italy, The (Burckhardt), 179
civil society, 322
class, importance of in British historical scholarship, 67
Clifford, James, 155, 161, 163
Clinton, Bill, 62
Cloches de la terre, Les (Corbin), 70
code switch, 265–66
Cohn, Bernard, 42, 184n.11, 358
collective effervescence, 249, 254, 259, 267
combined development, 278
commodity form, 150, 348
Commune of 1871 in Marseille, 308
communism: Communist Party Historians' Group 32; in East and West Coast dockworkers' unions, 108; French Communist Party and historians, 67–69

Communist Manifesto (Marx and Engels), 275
Compagnie des Docks et Entrepôts de Marseille, 301–5
comparative method, 82, 103–4, 112, 120–21
Comte, Auguste, 16, 83
conjuncture, between spatially distinct power networks, 119. *See also* structure of the conjuncture
Constitution of Society, The (Giddens), 128, 130
contextualization, 10–11; 183
contingency, 101, 110, 273, 280: as central principle of history, 112–13, 219; global, 102; in Hawaiian history, 223; in Mann's macrohistory, 120; of social life, 179
Cook, Captain James, 200–204, 206, 214, 215, 217, 220, 222–23
Corbin, Alain, 70
creativity: explained by plural concept of structure, 213; in events, 212–13, 250; spurred by dislocation of structures, 250–51. *See also* agency; improvisation; subjects
Crisis of the Aristocracy, The (Stone), 32n.8
cultural construction. *See* social construction; society, as culturally constructed
cultural history, 40–53, 327: and anthropology, 41; claim of hegemony in late 1980s, 48–49; epistemological implications of anthropological approach for, 42; and feminism in Britain, 64; and feminism in U.S., 45, 48; French as pioneers of, 68; and history of identities, 48; implicit conception of culture in, 162; influence of humanities on, 46; language metaphor in, 332; and nostalgia in France, 70; ontological assumptions of, 333; retreat from macro causation in, 77; rise of in Britain, 64–65; seen as expansion of social history's program, 41; turn away from the socially marginal by, 52. *See also* history, as discipline, of mentalities
cultural studies, 153, 158–59
cultural system, 204; as distinguished from social system, 160; Geertz's conception of, 181
cultural turn, 3, affinity with flexible accumulation, 62; as conversion experience, 42; effects of capitalist transformations on, 60–61; epistemic assumptions of, 51; in history, 40–62; inadequacy of internalist explanations of, 53; in literary studies, 54; in popular discourse, 54; in social sciences, 54. *See also* linguistic turn

capacity of, 345; as signifier for ontological ground of human life, 328; as social mediation, 334; synchronic implications of language metaphor, 359; unique qualities of, 344–46; use in governing of semiotic practices, 345–46

language game(s): as articulations of language to other semiotic practices, 340, 344; capitalism as, 348–49; as game, 337–38; as implying that social life is entirely linguistic, 336; as implying that social life is not reducible to language, 336–38; as metaphor for social, 320–21, 334; as nodes of articulation between semiotic practices, 346; as part of a form of life, 336; relation to structure, 321, 341

langue: changes in, 331; contrasted to parole, 129, 331; as foundational concept in human sciences, 325; synchrony of, 359

Laslett, Peter, 34

Launay, Bernard Réné Jordan, Marquis de, 234, 237, 242, 250

Learning to Labor (Willis), 159

Lefebvre, Georges, 37, 99, 256

Lenin, Vladimir Illich, 277

Lepetit, Bernard, 73, 74

Le Roy Laudrie, Emmanuel, 69, 70, 179, 183

Lévi, Giovanni, 74

Lévi-Strauss, Claude, 129, 130, 157, 161, 189, 331, 359, 365; objectivism of, 371; synchronic nature of his analysis, 357–58

Lieux de mémoire, Les, (Nora), 70

linguistics, 129; privileging of synchrony in Saussurian paradigm, 359

linguistic structures, 147–48

linguistic turn, 3; as American, 335; historical turn within, 358–59; history of, 330–31; ontological claim of, 346. *See also* cultural turn

literary studies, 325; influence on historians, 44; focus on canonical texts, 153; transformation by French theory in 1970s, 153

Long-Term Capital Management, 354

Lono (Hawaiian god), 201, 220, 222–23

Louis XVI, 232, 234, 240

Lucas, Colin, 244n.8

Luckmann, Thomas, 356

Lyotard, Jean-François, 68

macrohistory, 113–15, 120

Making of the English Working Class, The (Thompson), 26, 33, 159, 179, 275

Malinowski, Bronislaw, 169

mana, 202, 214, 215; European goods as, 215; transformation of over time, 218

Mann, Michael, 114; caging of populations, 116–17; contingency of emergence of civilizations, 115–17; critique of equation of society with nation state, 117–20; differences from Wallerstein, 117; directionality of historical change, 122–23; Egypt as example of unitary society, 118; interconnections between conceptions of space and time, 121; interstitial ideologies, 119; spatial assumptions, 117; types of networks of social power, 118; use of comparison, 120–21

Marcus, George, 161

Marcuse, Herbert, 60

Marin, Louis, 335

Markoff, John, 53

Marseille: Chamber of Commerce of, 303–4; commerce of, 288; municipality of, 286–88; port of, 288, 299–306; rise of steam navigation in, 303

Marx, Karl, 2, 5, 83, 149, 189, 348

Marxism, 159; Althusserianism in Britain, 64; conception of capitalism, 277; French historians and, 36–37; paleomarxism, 274, 277, 279. *See also* British Marxist Historians

Massey, Douglas, 367

materialism, 176, 177–78, 185–86

Mazuy, François, 294n.27

Mead, Margaret, 169, 175

meaning: culture as, 158–64; as embodied in publicly available symbols, 180–81; Geertz's anthropology and, 180–82; importations of, 168; recalcitrance of world to predications of meaning, 168; relation to practice, 162–64, 167–68

mechanistic explanation: apparent incompatibility with semiotic conception of social life, 352; in language games of capitalism, 349; pragmatic use of, 355; in study of built environment, 369; use in natual science, 347; use in social science, 347; as way-station to interpretive account, 355

mediation: as fundamental in social process, 330; language as, 334; the social as, 329–30

Meiji Restoration, 93

merchants (Marseille): organization of business of, 296–97; relationship of with dockworkers, 296–99; support for dockworkers by during dispute with Compagnie des Docks, 303–4

political culture: as linguistic phenomenon, 333; transformation of in events, 245

political discourse: salience of "worker" in 1848, 312–13; theme of democratic and social republic in 1848, 313

political science, 6, 12–13, 325; emergence of, 2; empiricist narrowness in, 15; meaning of politics and rationality in, 319; meaning of social in, 319; rational choice theory in, 262

political structures, 148–49

politics: autonomy of, 311, 317; as linguistic phenomenon, 333; as ordering cultural difference, 172–73. See also state

Politics, Culture, and Class in the French Revolution (Hunt), 44

popular sovereignty: as articulated in ritual, 252–54; difficulty of distinguishing from mob violence, 240; implied in accounts of taking of Bastille, 237; its novel articulation with crowd violence, 236; use of concept before taking of Bastille, 233

Populations ouvrières et les industries de la France, Les (Audiganne), 310

positivism: association with quantitative methods, 369; author's earlier association with, 23; in critique of Geertz, 176; its dominance in American social science, 347; Scott's critique of, 50

postmodernism 59, 79, 176, 326, 327

post-structuralism, 208: in anthropology, 46, 155; death of subject, 206; effects on practice of history, 51; and history, 47; lack of influence on French historians, 69; in literary studies, 153; its obliteration of the social, 79

Poverty and Progress (Thernstrom), 26

Poverty of Theory, The (Thompson), 64

power: accumulation of social power over time, 122; forms of (Mann), 118; relation to culture, 173; and resources, 132; and scope of semiotic practices, 344

practice: as constituting structure, 127; discursive and nondiscursive, 334–35; language metaphor and, 331; not reducible to discourse, 338; relations of, 220; as semiotic, 338; theory of (Bourdieu), 138. See also semiotic practice

pragmatism, 199, 205, 206

Princeton University, 42

proletarianization, 276–78, 310, 316

Prussian Reform Movement, 93

Puget, Peter, 214

quantification 12, 13; abbreviating and summarizing function of, 350; author's dissatisfaction with, 40; batting average, 350; difference from interpretive methods exaggerated, 369–72; dominant role of in American social science, 347; epistemic continuity with interpretive method 371; fit with commodity form, 348; hermeneutical, 371–72; as ideology of social science, 349; importance of statistics in American sports, 349; made possible by historical spread of quantitative language games of capitalism, 349, 350; made possible by regularities of semiotic practice, 350; necessity of in interpretive study of capitalism, 348–49; new social historians' ambivalence about, 32; pragmatic utility of, 350; as proxy for semiotic practices, 351; relation to Fordism, 31; in social history, 27–28; in study of built environment, 369; use of in research on Marseille's dockworkers, 281; value in grasping dynamics of contemporary capitalism, 78

Ramsay, Clay, 256

Rancière, Jacques, 52

rational choice theory, 262–70; as applied to revolutions, 262–63, 268

Reagan, Ronald, 62–63

Reddy, William, 4, 5n.2, 42, 342

reductionism, 86, 198

reference: acts of, 202, as automatic, 212; as a marking of things as resources, 217; novelties of, 207; as risky, 212, 218; temporal extension of effects of, 217; in theory of event, 223. See also Sahlins, Marshall

reflexivity: and language, 345–46; left out of Sahlins's account of Hawaiian reception of Cook, 212–13

religion, 181; as enabling humans to live with threat of chaos, 188; replaced by society as ultimate ground of order, 325

repertoires of contention, 235

representation, 191

reproduction: in Bourdieu's habitus, 138–39; definition of, 272; as dependent on particular social ecologies, 273; in environment of change, 271–80, 317; as explained by inertia, 272–73; importance of in episodes of social change, 139; as opposite of events, 271; as taking place whether it is desired or not, 126; transformation as mode of, 200;

Shankman, Paul, 176n.4

Sieyès, Emmanuel-Joseph, Abbé, 52

Simiand, François, 36

Skinner, Quentin, 331

Skocpol, Theda, 91–100; analysis of Chinese Revolution, 93–94; on comparative method, 91, 93, 94; embrace of scientific methodology, 91; flaws in analysis, 93–97; narrative strategy of, 97–100; as structuralist, 126; theory of social revolution, 92–93; unconsciousness about event as theoretical category, 102

Smelser, Neil, 81n.1

Smith, Adam, 2, 353

Soboul, Albert, 37

social, the: as carrying a whiff of the divine, 326; common sense conceptions of, 329; as constituted by streams of mediated human action, 330; definition of, 369; as distinguished from the individual, 323; as distinguished from the societal, 323; as a fact of discourse, 326; feminine inflection of, 324; as historically constituted, 319; as intertextuality, 334; linguistic conception of, 332–34, 346; meaning of in social science disciplines, 318–19, 321–28; as name for really real, 326, 327; networks of semiotic practices, 346; not reducible to discourse, 335; obliteration of by radical poststructuralism, 79; as ontological concept, 318–19; as pertaining to companionship, 321, 329; as pertaining to reified totality, 323; as semiotic mediation, 346; as semiotic practice in built environments, 369; as signifying mediated forms of relationship, 329; as solidarity, 324; tautological definition of, 319; as the totality of interdependence in human relations, 328, 334, 346; as unmarked, 325; vagueness of, 318, 324–25

social boundaries: conceptualized as naturally existing, 329; difficulty of defining, 205–6; as historically constituted, 330; lack of correspondence to national boundaries, 171

social construction: affinity with interpretive method, 336; definition of, 357; diachronic temporality of, 358, 360; duration and, 360; emphasis on materiality of social life, 361; fit with built environment metaphor, 364; gender as, 364; history of uses of, 336; insufficiency of concept, 362; as naturaliza-

tion of cultural facts, 360; as necessary supplement to language metaphor, 359; race as, 364; timing of use corresponds with linguistic turn, 356

Social Construction of Reality, The (Berger and Luckmann), 356

social history, 25–40; abandonment of achievements of, 50; achievement of disciplinary hegemony in U.S., 29; assumed primacy of economic structures, 39; borrowings from social sciences, 28; in Britain, 32–34; capitalism as subject of, 39–40; consensus working model of, 38–39; decline from hegemony in 1980s, 48; embrace of by French historians, 73; embrace of by British historians, 67; as enlargement of scope of historical studies, 27; forms of evidence used in, 27; foundation of journals devoted to, 26; in France, 34–37; as history of society, 38; Hobsbawm on, 38–39; implications of term, 324; interest in cultural difference, 194; interest in ordinary people, 27; international rise of, 37; lack of explicit definition of, 38; lack of interest in events, 197; leftist affinities of, 37; mixture of interpretive and quantitative method in, 370; as mysterious, 326, 352; need for reinvention of, 79; use of quantification in, 27–28; relation to political commitments, 29–30; rise in 1960s and 1970s in U.S., 26, 180; theoretical and epistemological outlook of, 28; virtues of, 78; younger generation of British social historians, 34, 64. *See also* Annales School; British Marxist historians; cultural history; history: from the bottom up; new social history

Social History, 64, 66–67

socialism, 324

social laws, 16, 110, 114

social revolution. *See* Skocpol, Theda

social sciences: epistemological diversity of, 12–13; history of 2–3; as immature sciences 16; interpretive method in, 14; meaning of social in, 318–19; mechanical causation in, 355; natural science model and, 15; polysemy of leading concepts of, 324; positivism in, 12, 14; prestige of in 1950s and 1960s, 28; structural thinking in, 14; theory in, 3–4

social space: as manifold, 121; Mann's theory of, 117–18